STUDIES IN AMERICAN POLITICAL DEVELOPMENT

An Annual

Volume 2

Studies in American Political Development will publish theoretical and empirical research on political development and institutional change in the United States. A diversity of subject matters and methodologies is invited, including comparative or international studies that illuminate the American case. Manuscripts of up to 75 pages in length, excluding footnotes, will be considered. There is also a Notes and Exchanges section for shorter presentation of research perspectives and findings, comments on earlier articles, and review essays on bibliography of unusual interest.

Submissions will be accepted until July 1 for publication in the fall of the following year. Authors should send three copies of the manuscript (double-spaced), which will not be returned. After initial screening by the editors, selected manuscripts will be reviewed anonymously. Publication decisions will be made with regard to the total contents of each annual volume.

Please address all correspondence to: *Studies in American Political Development,* Department of Political Science, University of California, Los Angeles, California 90024.

The editing of *Studies in American Political Development* is assisted by funds from the College of Letters and Science, University of California, Los Angeles.

STUDIES IN
American
Political
Development

An Annual

VOLUME 2

Yale University Press
New Haven and London

Published with assistance from the Louis Stern Memorial Fund.

Designed by Nancy Ovedovitz
and set in Baskerville type with Avant Garde for display and
printed in the United States of America by
Vail-Ballou Press, Binghamton, N.Y.

Library of Congress catalog card number: 86-40192
International standard book number: 0-300-4055-5 (cloth)
0-300-4056-3 (paper)

The paper in this book meets the guidelines for permanence and durability of the Committee on Production Guidelines for Book Longevity of
the Council on Library Resources.

10 9 8 7 6 5 4 3 2 1

WITHDRAWN

Contents

From Fundamental Law to the Supreme Law of the Land: A
Reinterpretation of the Origin of Judicial Review   1
SYLVIA SNOWISS

Southern Leviathan: The Development of Central State
Authority in the Confederate States of America   68
RICHARD BENSEL

The Political Origins of Unemployment Insurance in Five
American States   137
EDWIN AMENTA, ELISABETH S. CLEMENS, JEFREN OLSEN,
SUNITA PARIKH, AND THEDA SKOCPOL

Choosing Sides: The Creation of an Agricultural Policy
Network in Congress, 1919–1932   183
JOHN MARK HANSEN

    "Choosing Sides": Comment   230
    LOUIS GALAMBOS

    Reply to Professor Galambos   234
    JOHN MARK HANSEN

Interests, Institutions, and Positive Theory: The Politics
of the NLRB   236
TERRY M. MOE

NOTES AND EXCHANGES

Right, Rage, and Remedy: Forms of Law in Political
Discourse   303
JOHN BRIGHAM

Organized Labor and the Invention of Modern Liberalism
in the United States   317
    KAREN ORREN

Letters to the Editors   337
    ERIC MONKKONEN
    SAMUEL KERNELL

STUDIES IN AMERICAN POLITICAL DEVELOPMENT

An Annual

Volume 2

SYLVIA SNOWISS
California State University, Northridge

From Fundamental Law to the Supreme Law of the Land: A Reinterpretation of the Origin of Judicial Review

For a long time the question of whether the framers of the U.S. Constitution intended to establish judicial review of legislation was the subject of extensive and repeated investigation. The issue, however, was never definitively resolved, a consequence, it is widely agreed, of ambiguities and internal contradictions in the early record.[1] More recently, interest in this basic question has declined, and it has simply been assumed that some form of judicial review was contemplated by the framers. At the same time support for the practice has deepened, and the debate, although still heated, has shifted to different grounds.

From the 1940s through the 1960s, the controversy over judicial review centered on the question of judicial activism versus judicial self-restraint. As argued by Justice Hugo Black and Justice Felix Frankfurter, the debate pitted a commitment to authoritative judicial application and interpretation of the

Research for this article was supported, in part, by a National Endowment for the Humanities Younger Humanist Fellowship, the Earhart Foundation, Ann Arbor, Michigan, and the California State University Foundation, Northridge. I am grateful to Mary Cornelia Porter, who was responsible for presentation of an earlier version of this work to the American Political Science Association, and who has continued to give this project indispensable support; and to the editors of this volume, whose contribution went beyond that involved in the customary responsibility. I would also like to thank my colleague Lonnie S. Turner for many fruitful conversations, and this volume's anonymous reviewer for a careful reading of an earlier draft.

1. See, for example, Jesse H. Choper, *Judicial Review and the National Political Process* (Chicago: University of Chicago Press, 1980), 62–63, and accompanying notes; Walter F. Murphy and C. Herman Pritchett, eds., *Courts, Judges, and Politics,* 3rd ed. (New York: Random House, 1979), 12; Gordon S. Wood, *The Creation of the American Republic, 1776–1787* (Chapel Hill: University of North Carolina Press, 1969; reprint ed., New York: W. W. Norton & Co., 1972), chap. 7, and particularly, pp. 291–305.

Constitution on the one hand against an insistence on systematic deference to legislative interpretation on the other. But by the 1970s the second position, urged by Frankfurter, had been largely rejected, and the issue was recast: interpretivism was opposed to noninterpretivism, or a "fundamental values" approach. The question as debated now concerns the proper way for judges to apply and interpret the Constitution; significant differences still separate the contending positions, but both sides accept the Court's role as the authoritative interpreter. This general acceptance of the practice, combined with the inconclusiveness of previous historical inquiry into the framers' intent, has shifted discussion from the legitimacy of judicial review per se to a preoccupation with its appropriate character and substantive content.

I will here, however, reopen the question of intent concerning the establishment of judicial review and present a new interpretation of its origin. My analysis removes the inconclusiveness of existing interpretations and resolves the purported inconsistencies and ambiguities in the pre-Marshall record. I do not offer it as an attack or a defense of the institution of judicial review, for I share the prevailing view that judicial authority over legislation has by now generated sufficient support to be unaffected by assessments of original intent. I have been motivated, rather, by the inadequacy of existing explanations and by the growing conviction, as I worked with material connected with the American founding, that the perceived ambiguities and inconsistencies in the pre-Marshall record mask an unrecognized underlying coherence.

At the same time, this investigation is of more than merely historical interest; it carries important implications for the current debate between a fundamental values approach and an interpretivist conception of constitutional law. According to the first view, the Constitution is best understood as a statement of first principles, or fundamental values, and judicial review as the defense of those values. In its most controversial aspect, this position supports judicial defense of fundamental values whether or not they are specifically identified in the constitutional text or shown to have been contemplated by the framers. This stance is reflected in the revival of substantive due process and in the Supreme Court's recognition of a constitutional right to privacy, including a right to abortion, in the general wording of the due process clause. Interpretivism, on the other hand, sees the Constitution in more conventional legal terms and would restrict the Court to defense of those values identified or implicit in the constitutional text and more or less contemplated by the framers.[2] The account of the origin of judicial review offered here does not, by

2. The seminal statement of the fundamental values approach is Alexander M. Bickel, *The Least Dangerous Branch* (Indianapolis: Bobbs-Merrill Co., 1962), 23–28. For subsequent development of the position, see Thomas C. Grey, "Do We Have an Unwritten Constitution?" *Stanford Law Review* 27, no. 3 (February 1975) : 703–18; and Ronald Dworkin, *Taking Rights Seriously* (Cambridge: Harvard University Press, 1977), chap. 5. On interpretivism, see Robert H. Bork, "Neutral Principles and Some First Amendment Problems," *Indiana Law Journal* 47, no. 1 (Fall 1971) : 4–20; Hans A. Linde, "Judges, Critics, and the Realist Tradition," *Yale Law Journal* 82, no. 2 (December 1972) : 253–56; and Hans A. Linde, "E Pluribus—Constitutional Theory and State Courts," *Georgia Law Review* 18, no. 2 (Winter 1984) : 193–96.

itself, resolve this debate, but if it holds up under scrutiny, it can redirect it significantly. First, it challenges assumptions about intent made explicitly by interpretivism and implicitly by proponents of the fundamental values approach. More important, in the process, it reopens and recasts what I take to be the most basic and perennial issue of American constitutional law—that of the relationship between its legal and political components. Although it supports fundamental values analysis more than interpretivism, it also argues for substantial modification of the program embraced by some of the first approach's most vocal proponents.

My reinterpretation of intent uses no new sources; rather, I present a re-reading of familiar ones. For example, I assign to Chief Justice John Marshall a degree of innovativeness far greater than have others. Although it has long been acknowledged that Marshall's active leadership was crucial for the development of American judicial review, neither the precise character nor the full extent of his leadership has ever been properly recognized. Marshall, it is generally thought, gave more forceful direction and implementation to ideas and practices that had previously been either tentatively or partially accepted. But Marshall's contribution was not simply the reinforcement or extension of ideas wholly or partially accepted; it was, rather, their radical transformation. Marshall effected this transformation, moreover, with no public acknowledgement of his purposes or methods. He disguised his actions in the clear understanding that the changes he was introducing went beyond anything supported by existing legal or political norms. The full magnitude of his innovations escaped notice because they were superficially minor and carefully disguised so as not to offend existing expectations. At the same time, the country's acceptance of his innovations, the rapid elimination of the circumstances that had given rise to the pre-Marshall practice, and his skillful manipulation and exploitation of the agreement underlying that practice have blinded succeeding generations to the precise terms of the original debate. Scholars have uniformly read back into eighteenth-century sources assumptions that did not develop until at least a half century later, and they have thereby made original intent inaccessible. Properly understood, the "statesmanlike deviousness" attributed to Marshall by Alexander Bickel was far more sweeping in its implications than anyone, including Bickel, has yet noted.[3]

OVERVIEW

The Historical Argument

I will argue that judicial review as we know it developed over three distinct periods: from independence to *Federalist 78; Federalist 78* to *Marbury;* and *Marbury* to the end of Marshall's tenure on the Court. During the first period a judicial check on unconstitutional legislation was often asserted, but just as often denied, and the status of judicial review remained highly controversial. Furthermore, the judicial power claimed, although it resembled modern judicial review, was nevertheless decisively different. Its most important differ-

---

3. *Least Dangerous Branch,* 14.

ence was that it understood a constitution, or fundamental law, to be a political instrument, distinguishable from ordinary law. That is, in its capacity as a restraint on sovereign power, the Constitution was not the kind of law ordinarily subject to judicial application, interpretation, or enforcement. The judicial authority to enforce the Constitution asserted in period 1 was, as a consequence, universally understood and exercised as a *political* responsibility, a judicial substitute for revolution, outside the conventional legal one. There existed, however, no coherent or uniform defense of this responsibility. In refusing to enforce particular laws, period 1 judges leaned on a variety of justifications, all of which were closer to outdated English precedent than to subsequent American doctrine.

Period 2 provided the coherent defense of judicial authority over unconstitutional legislation that had been absent in period 1. It was presented first by James Iredell in a North Carolina newspaper in 1786,[4] and was reformulated and popularized by Alexander Hamilton in *Federalist 78* and James Wilson in *Lectures on the Law.* This defense was the forerunner of *Marbury,* but was not then understood in terms conventionally ascribed to *Marbury.*

The judicial authority over unconstitutional acts claimed in period 2 was connected to the existence, in the American states, of a real state of nature, brought about by the revolutionary break from England and the emergence of real, explicit social contracts, or fundamental law, in the aftermath of that break. The distinctive characteristics of American as opposed to European fundamental law, which made the former enforceable in court, were the reality of American social contracts, in contrast to the fictional status of European ones, and the explicitness of their content, in contrast to the traditional, customary, and statutory content of European fundamental law. That American fundamental law also happened to be written down was, before Marshall, only of incidental importance, serving merely as the vehicle for its explicitness. Equally important, judicial enforcement of explicit fundamental law was still understood to be a political, not legal act. Period 2's achievement was to demonstrate that it was nevertheless one that judges were allowed and even required to perform. This authority was derived from an equality of the branches under explicit fundamental law and not from any uniquely judicial relationship to the written Constitution. Its exercise was also accompanied by political restraints appropriate for judicial defense of fundamental law.

Period 3 began with Marshall's assumption of the chief justiceship and consisted of his reworking of the period 2 position. Marshall's key innovations came not in *Marbury,* which was only a peculiarly worded restatement of the ground already won in period 2, but in the way he treated the Constitution in his great opinions of the 1810s and 1820s. First, Marshall ended seriatim opinion writing and with it the public airing of alternate approaches to fundamental law. Next, under this near monopoly of opinion writing, he introduced an unprecedented application to the Constitution of the rules for statutory interpretation, an application not to be found in period 2 cases, or in the concurring, dissenting, or Court opinions of his Supreme Court col-

4. "To the Public," in *Life and Correspondence of James Iredell,* ed. Griffeth J. McRee (New York: Peter Smith, 1949), 2 : 145–49.

leagues. Last, he achieved a seemingly slight, but portentous shift in the significance to be attributed to the Constitution as a written document. In Marshall's hands, the written Constitution lost its period 2 meaning as a vehicle of explicit fundamental law and acquired its character as supreme ordinary law. Through his use of the written Constitution, coupled with its subjection to the rules for statutory interpretation, Marshall transformed explicit fundamental law, different in kind from ordinary law, into supreme ordinary law, different only in degree. At the same time, judicial enforcement of the Constitution lost its character as a revolutionary defense of explicit fundamental law and became judicial application and interpretation of supreme written law. These changes also introduced the judicial supremacy that was absent from period 2 judicial review, but that remains the controversial core of the modern practice.

Legalization of the Constitution and of judicial review took about a half century to complete. Although there was some recognition at the time that Marshall's actions exceeded the terms of the period 2 agreement, there was no general awareness of the full scope or import of his innovations. Marshall was able to achieve this silent, unrecognized legalization of the Constitution and of judicial enforcement of it by maintaining period 2 language and form and by confining his results to those acceptable under period 2 terms. This careful exploitation of existing agreement, the seeming superficiality of the changes he introduced, and the strong public receptivity to judicial review as a legal enterprise eventually obscured both original intent and Marshall's transformation of it.

Contemporary Implications

From its inception, the legalized form of judicial review was accorded deep public acceptance. At the same time, the practice of constitutional law has always been accompanied by controversy over its proper operation. As the issues have changed with each generation, the terms of the debate have been reformulated. But the heart of the controversy remains the inability of constitutional law both to conform to all the requirements of law and to reconcile its legal and political components. On the one hand, Marshall's success has been so complete that constitutional law is now unintelligible outside a conventional legal framework. The Constitution is firmly established as a third branch or source of law, following common and statutory law, and judicial application and interpretation of it has become part of the ordinary legal responsibility. On the other hand, the practice of constitutional law contains an irrepressible political component beyond what is known and accepted in other branches of law. Judicial application and interpretation of the law of the Constitution as part of a legal check on unconstitutional legislation generates a policy-making that, unlike that of ordinary law, conflicts with the requirements of democracy and opens judicial review to the charge of invasion of the legislative sphere. This political component is what Bickel has called constitutional law's "counter-majoritarian difficulty."[5] Although other branches

5. *Least Dangerous Branch*, 16–23.

of law also necessitate judgments that blur the boundaries of separation of powers, only constitutional law has this particular problem.

Loss of access to the original understanding and to Marshall's silent, unrecognized transformation of it has made it impossible not only to resolve this central dilemma but, more generally, to understand the modern practice. Retrieval of this understanding and reactivation of the original distinction between fundamental law and ordinary law will not, by itself, resolve all controversy nor reestablish that distinction. It can, however, allow us to understand the modern practice and the contemporary debate more clearly than has been the case. For if this account of intent is accurate, it indicates, first, that legalization of fundamental law was, and remains, a relatively superficial phenomenon, achieved by application to it of ordinary law language and technique. Language and technique cannot, as they did not, eliminate the fundamental law attributes that originally made the Constitution different in kind from ordinary law and judicial review a political act. More specifically, they have not changed the fact that restraints on sovereign power must be different in kind from those on individual behavior, and this remains true despite the substantial legalization of fundamental law now achieved.

Recognition of the precise origin of modern judicial review suggests, further, that although, in the acceptance and institutionalization of Marshall's innovations, constitutional law became a new branch of law connected to common and statutory law, it also remained decisively different from them. In its evolution, it merged political components of fundamental law, as originally understood, with conventional legal attributes and technique, and became unable to conform strictly to the requirements of either. Yet so exclusive is the ordinary law framework within which constitutional law operates, so deep the assumption that the Constitution is and somehow always has been supreme ordinary law and that the framers contemplated something like the modern practice, that even when its unique attributes and political components are acknowledged by scholars, they are seen through the distorting lens of supreme ordinary law. This is reflected, for example, in the failure to identify properly the function performed by constitutional law. Even when it is recognized that courts cannot enforce the Constitution against sovereign power as routinely as they do ordinary law against individuals, there remains an inappropriate reliance on the manner in which ordinary law is enforced. I will return to this phenomenon in greater detail later in this article.

The dominance of ordinary law conceptions, with a concomitant failure to see constitutional law as a new field of law, is also visible in the repeated, but futile, attempts to remove the political, or policy, component from constitutional law. This attempt was a central part of James Bradley Thayer's and Justice Frankfurter's theory of self-restraint, and of Justice Black's and John Hart Ely's activism.[6] Thayer's and Frankfurter's self-restraint would remove

6. See James Bradley Thayer, "The Origin and Scope of the American Doctrine of Constitutional Law," *Harvard Law Review* 7, no. 3 (October 1893) : 129–56; Justice Frankfurter in *West Virginia Board of Education* v. *Barnette*, 319 U.S. 624, 646 (1943), dissenting opinion, and *Dennis* v. *United States*, 341 U.S. 494, 517 (1951), concurring opinion; Justice Black in

judicial review's policy component only by so restricting the occasions for judicial intervention as to keep the practice in name only; Black and Ely, on the other hand, succeeded more in disguising their own value commitments than in providing a persuasive, value-free judicial review.

The inability to eliminate constitutional law's policy component, coupled with the disinclination to accept Frankfurter's retreat from the practice, were critical parts of the reconceptualization, beginning in the 1960s, of constitutional law as the defense of fundamental values. As we shall see, in this reconceptualization, fundamental values analysis has retrieved some of the original and enduring elements of fundamental law, and that process has enabled it to explain what much of American constitutional law has in fact been. Fundamental values analysis also has acknowledged the inevitable policy component accompanying defense of first principles and has accepted it as an unavoidable part of the judicial responsibility to the law of the Constitution. Although the strength of this approach thus lies in a proper accounting of period 3 constitutional law, its difficulties have stemmed from failure to recognize that law's full novelty. Fundamental values analysis, especially in its more activist versions, has joined the ordinary law conception of law enforcement to the judicial defense of fundamental values and supported the latter with the same regularity and breadth with which judges enforce ordinary law. It has failed to recognize that if judicial review is in fact best understood as the defense of fundamental values, this function is sufficiently different from enforcement of ordinary law to require its own standards and limits. Without such limits, it easily leads to a judicial value choice insupportable under any sustainable conception of law. Yet, for the most part, the fundamental values approach has not addressed itself systematically to the question of the limits or restraints appropriate for the judicial defense of principle.

It was this breadth of judicial value choice, sanctioned by fundamental values analysis, that gave rise in the 1970s to contemporary interpretivism and its insistence that judges restrict themselves to the defense of values identified in the constitutional text and framers' intent. This analysis will suggest that interpretivism's call for some limits to the judicial defense of principle is sound, but that its location of those limits in constitutional text and intent is not. Interpretivism suffers, even more than the fundamental values approach, from an inappropriate reliance on ordinary law standards and conceptions. Text and intent are limits devised for ordinary law, where they serve to keep that law in credible conformity with the requirement that judges not make law. Because of the enduring differences between fundamental law and ordinary law, text and intent cannot achieve comparable results in constitutional law. If constitutional law is to achieve a credible conformity with the requirements of law, its differences from ordinary law must be acknowledged and restraints devised that are appropriate for its unique functioning.

Given the inapplicability of the institutional restraints of ordinary law, constitutional law must rely instead on some form of self-restraint. This cannot

---

Adamson v. *California,* 332 U.S. 46, 68 (1947), dissenting opinion; John Hart Ely, *Democracy and Distrust* (Cambridge: Harvard University Press, 1980).

be, however, the restrictive self-restraint of Thayer and Frankfurter, but rather that demonstrated in the original work of Marshall and, later, of John Marshall Harlan. Both Marshall and Harlan accepted, simultaneously, the political dimension of authoritative exposition of the Constitution and the need to confine that dimension. Marshall, as part of his silent, unacknowledged construction of modern judicial review, never addressed these issues openly. Nor did Harlan speak of constitutional law as a new field of law or engage in the kind of historical analysis to be presented here. Yet of all modern judges or commentators, his work best combined ordinary and fundamental law elements, and he provides an instructive model for the constitutional law that evolved in the acceptance of Marshall's innovations.

I will return to contemporary issues and Harlan's work at the end of this article. Before drawing any conclusions, however, it is necessary to make the case that the origin of judicial review does in fact rest in Marshall's unacknowledged legalization of fundamental law. Because presentation of the full historical argument and all supporting evidence is beyond the scope of this article, I will present here only the main components of the argument and the most important supporting evidence.[7]

FROM BLACKSTONE TO MARSHALL: THE DEVELOPMENT OF JUDICIAL REVIEW

Period 1

Discussion of judicial authority over unconstitutional legislation must start with Blackstone, the leading legal authority in the American states at the time of independence. Blackstone emphatically rejected judicial authority to enforce fundamental law against legislation that violated it, thereby closing off suggestions to the contrary that had existed in English jurisprudence until the triumph of parliamentary supremacy in the revolutionary settlement of 1688. Even in the face of the most unambiguous parliamentary violation of established principle, the judiciary could not uphold that principle but was obliged to enforce parliamentary will. In making his argument, Blackstone used the hypothetical example of legislation that concededly violated English fundamental law—an act that made a man judge of his own cause. Such a law was, in English terminology, unreasonable and contrary to the principles of common right. This point needed no argumentation, which was why the example was chosen. Blackstone was concerned not with how unreasonableness was to be determined but with the proper judicial attitude to a concededly unreasonable law.

Allowing a man to be judge in his own cause was so contrary to established principle that Blackstone granted that any general language in a statute that seemed to lead to such a result should be construed to avoid it. In such circumstances, the judges "are in decency to conclude that this consequence was not foreseen by the parliament, and therefore they are at liberty to expound the statute by equity, and only *quoad hoc* disregard it." However, "if we could

---

7. This article is a condensed version of a forthcoming book on the same subject.

conceive it possible for the parliament to enact that [a man] should try as well his own cause as those of other persons, there is no court that has power to defeat the intent of the legislature, when couched in such evident and express words, as leave no doubt whether it was the intent of the legislature or no."[8] To hold otherwise, Blackstone contended, would be to undermine political authority. Thus he defended not simply a legislative supremacy but a legislative omnipotence as well.

Although Blackstone's authority in the American states was strong, there also existed from the time of independence significant support for judicial power to refuse to enforce unconstitutional acts. The degree to which some judges and public officials supported this power was impressive testimony to a widespread repudiation of Blackstone. Yet no one, during period 1, confronted him directly, or attempted to refute his argument, or offered any coherent defense of the authority being exercised. Each period 1 case treated the problem somewhat differently, and in none was there any recognizable forerunner of arguments used today. Furthermore, in the act of repudiating Blackstone, period 1 judges still relied on a variety of English precedents and sources.

The two best known period 1 cases were *Rutgers* v. *Waddington* and *Trevett* v. *Weedon*. *Rutgers,* decided in New York in 1784, involved a trespass statute designed to provide compensation for citizens whose property had been confiscated and used by the English during the war.[9] The act was challenged on the ground that it was contrary to the Law of Nations, and that only the national government, not a state, could legislate contrary to that law.[10] Judge Duane, of the New York City Mayor's Court, was clearly sympathetic to this argument, but did not declare the law void.[11] Instead, he subjected it to an interpretation that barred recovery while avoiding conflict with the Law of Nations. In an obvious attempt to bring his actions into conformity with Blackstone, he paraphrased the passage from the *Commentaries* authorizing judicial construction of statutes to avoid conflict with common right and reason.[12] The legislature regarded Duane's construction as unwarranted and passed a resolution condemning this refusal to carry out its act. In so doing it also relied on Blackstone, invoking his main direct denial of judicial authority over legislation.[13]

Trevett v. *Weeden,* decided in Rhode Island in 1786, dealt with an act that made refusal to accept the state's paper money a criminal offense and that

8. William Blackstone, *Commentaries on the Laws of England,* 4 vols. Facsimile of the 1st ed. 1765–1769 (Chicago: University of Chicago Press, 1979), 1 : 91. Latin spelling is as in the original.

9. A full account of *Rutgers* v. *Waddington,* including the court opinion, is available in *The Law Practice of Alexander Hamilton,* ed. Julius Goebel, Jr. (New York: Columbia University Press, 1964) 1 : 282–315, 393–419.

10. It was also argued that the statute violated the peace treaty between England and the Americans, which contained an implied amnesty for the alleged trespass.

11. See *Law Practice of Hamilton,* ed. Goebel, 1 : 314–15.

12. Ibid., 416–17.

13. Ibid., 312. For Blackstone's formulation see *Commentaries,* 1 : 91.

denied a jury trial to those indicted under it. There is no recorded court opinion, and knowledge of the case comes from a pamphlet written by the defendant's lawyer, James Varnum.[14] The legislation was attacked for its denial of jury trial, and the Rhode Island court, although it did not declare the act unconstitutional, did refuse to enforce it, holding "that the information [was] not cognizable before [it]."[15]

Rhode Island at this time was governed by its colonial charter, as modified at independence, and the charter did not contain an explicit provision for jury trial. Varnum argued, nevertheless, that protection of jury trial was "a fundamental right, a part of our legal constitution."[16] He surveyed English history to demonstrate its centrality in English fundamental law and then argued that the colonial charter was "declaratory of, and fully confirmed to the people the Magna Carta, and other fundamental laws of England."[17] He insisted that an act that denied a right protected by fundamental law could not bind the judges and supported this proposition by appeal to English authorities, including Bacon, Coke, and Blackstone.[18] As had Judge Duane in *Rutgers,* Varnum drew on Blackstone's qualification of his own denial of judicial authority over legislation and ignored the main passages in which Blackstone rejected judicial review.

Reliance on English fundamental law is also visible in *Bowman* v. *Middleton,* a South Carolina case decided in 1792 at the beginning of period 2.[19] Here too a legislative denial of jury trial was successfully challenged, although in this case the law dated to 1712. The court declared the act void on the grounds that it was contrary to "common right, as well as against magna charta."[20] In another case four years later, after establishment of a distinctly American defense of judicial authority over legislation, this same court discussed its authority over legislation in terms of the South Carolina Constitution.[21]

In 1782 the Virginia court, in *Commonwealth* v. *Caton,* claimed authority over unconstitutional acts without overturning the legislation before it.[22] Judge George Wythe made the strongest statement and, in the process, offered another basis for it. After praising the modern "diffusion of knowledge" for its advancement of limited government and promotion of general liberty, he continued:

> But this beneficial result attains to higher perfection, when those, who hold the purse and the sword, differing as to the powers which each may exercise, the tribunals, who hold neither, are called upon to declare the law impartially

14. "The Case Trevett against Weeden" (1786). Available in microprint, American Antiquarian Society, Early American Imprints Series.
15. Ibid., 38–39.
16. Ibid., 11.
17. Ibid., 15.
18. Ibid., 30, 33.
19. 1 Bay (S.C.) 252 (1792).
20. Ibid., 254. Spelling in original.
21. *Lindsay* v. *Commissioners,* 2 Bay (S.C.) 38 (1796).
22. 4 Call (Va.) 5 (1782).

between them. For thus the pretensions of each party are fairly examined, their respective powers ascertained, and the boundaries of authority peaceably established. . . .

If the . . . legislature . . . should attempt to overleap the bounds prescribed to them by the people, I, in administering the public justice of the country, will meet [it] at my seat in this tribunal; and, pointing to the constitution, will say to [the legislature] here is the limit of your authority; and hither, shall you go, but no further.[23]

This defense of judicial power is reminiscent of Coke's attempt to make the common law courts the balance of power between king and Parliament. Although circumstances in seventeenth-century England and eighteenth-century Virginia were hardly comparable, Wythe's discussion is another example of period 1 groping for justification for judicial review and the absence of any forerunner of the modern argument.

Explicit Social Contracts. A second *Caton* opinion, that of Judge Edmund Pendleton, although it did not endorse judicial power over legislation, provided the only period 1 indication of differences between American and European circumstances that could justify American rejection of Blackstone. After asking whether the Constitution or legislation that violated it "shall prevail and be the rule of judgment" in court, Pendleton observed:

> The constitution of other governments in Europe or elsewhere, seem to throw little light upon this question, since we have a written record of that which the citizens of this State have adopted as their social compact; and beyond which we need not extend our researches. It has been very properly said, on all sides, that this act, declaring the rights of the citizens, and forming their government, divided it into three great branches, the legislative, executive, and judiciary, assigning to each its proper powers, and directing that each shall be kept separate and distinct, must be considered as a rule obligatory upon every department, not to be departed from on any occasion. But how far this court, in whom the judiciary powers may in some sort be said to be concentrated, shall have power to declare the nullity of a law, passed in its forms by the legislative power, without exercising the power of that branch, contrary to the plain terms of that constitution, is indeed a deep, important, and I will add, a tremendous question, the decision of which might involve consequences to which gentlemen may not have extended their ideas.[24]

This brief, unelaborated passage states the shared assumptions of period 1. The starting point is the perception that American circumstances were different from those of Europe. Pendleton located that difference in the existence of "a written record of [our] social compact." Written social contracts, or constitutions, were in fact instrumental in the widespread period 1 willingness to reject Blackstone. But, as evidenced by the absence of significant reliance on

23. Ibid., 7–8.
24. Ibid., 17.

them in the cases, or of any attempt to refute Blackstone's argument or even to present a coherent defense of judicial authority over legislation, no systematic connection had yet been made between written constitutions and this judicial authority. Pendleton's is the only period 1 source even to allude to such a connection, and in order to understand its meaning, it will be necessary to draw on fuller, but still relatively sparse, period 2 sources.

During both periods 1 and 2, the American constitutions' commitment to writing meant that fundamental law had an explicit, fixed, and publicly verifiable content, in contrast to the traditional, customary, and hence uncertain content of European fundamental law. As explicit social contracts, these constitutions were also of superior status to ordinary law and thus bound subsequent legislation in a way that European fundamental law, of entirely statutory content, could not. Written constitutions did not, initially, carry the meaning that was to be accorded them after *Marbury*. Specifically, commitment to writing in no way made fundamental law the kind of law rightly amenable to judicial application, interpretation, and enforcement.

The precise relationship between the explicitness of American fundamental law and periods 1 and 2 judicial review will be spelled out shortly. But first it is necessary to emphasize that the significance of a written constitution lay in its explicitness, not in its having the character of law enforceable in court. The latter widely held but unjustified modern reading is reflected in Thayer's 1893 account of the period 2 understanding. According to Thayer, the courts "began by resting [judicial review] upon the very simple ground that the legislature had only a delegated and limited authority under the constitutions; that these restraints, in order to be operative, must be regarded as so much law; and, as being law, that they must be interpreted and applied by the court."[25] Only the first of these propositions can, in fact, be found in periods 1 and 2 sources. The notion that American constitutions were "so much law" and, as such, were to be interpreted and applied in court, is typical of the unfounded modern practice of reading Marshall's legalization of fundamental law into eighteenth-century statements.

That the uniqueness of American fundamental law inhered in the explicitness and certitude of its content is reflected in Pendleton's comment that the existence of written social contracts precluded the need to "extend our researches" beyond it. Period 2 sources would make the same point more fully. The most complete statement is that of Judge St. George Tucker in *Kamper* v. *Hawkins*, the leading period 2 exercise of judicial review in Virginia. After noting that written constitutions were unknown before the American Revolution, Tucker continued:

> What the *constitution* of any country *was* or rather *was supposed to be*, could only be collected from what the *government had at any time done;* what had been *acquiesced* in by the people, or other component parts of the government; or what had been *resisted* by either of them. Whatever the government, or any branch of it had *once done*, it was inferred they had a *right* to do *again*. . . . But,

25. "Doctrine of Constitutional Law," 138.

with us, the constitution is not an "ideal thing, but a real existence: it can be produced in a visible form": its principles can be ascertained from the living letter, not from obscure reasoning or deductions only.[26]

James Iredell made the same point in a letter to Richard Spaight: "The Constitution [is] not . . . a mere imaginary thing, about which ten thousand different opinions may be formed, but a written document to which all may have recourse.[27] In *VanHorne's Lessee* v. *Dorrance,* Justice William Paterson formulated the issue as follows:

> It is difficult to say what the constitution of England is; because, not being reduced to written certainty and precision, it lies entirely at the mercy of the parliament. . . . In England there is no written constitution, no fundamental law, nothing visible, nothing real, nothing certain, by which a statute can be tested. In America the case is widely different: Every state in the union has its constitution reduced to written exactitude and precision.[28]

Although explicit written constitutions were thus identified as the chief distinguishing characteristic of American fundamental law, they could not, in fact, carry all the weight ascribed to them nor account, by themselves, for the willingness to reject Blackstone evident at the time of independence. For one thing, all the states did not immediately produce written constitutions. Rhode Island, as we have seen, continued to function under a modified version of its colonial charter, yet it produced one of the major period 1 exercises of judicial review. And among those states that did have new written constitutions, not all were the products of drafting and ratification procedures that could distinguish the constitutions from statutes, and thus from European fundamental law. Virginia is a leading example.

The convention that produced the Virginia Constitution had no specific mandate to do so. It also sat as the newly independent state's first legislature and enacted ordinary legislation at the same time that it framed the constitution. This posed no particular difficulty until the consolidation of period 2 judicial review. At that point, doubt about the constitution's superior status, generated by the absence of extraordinary authorization, threatened to undermine judicial claims to enforce it against legislation that was said to have violated it. In *Kamper* v. *Hawkins,* all five participating judges addressed the question of the constitution's status before defending their decision not to execute the legislation before it. All of them argued that despite the absence of clarity about the convention's status, the constitution was binding fundamental law. This was achieved, they claimed, by the constitution's function in bringing Virginia out of a state of nature, by its subject matter, and by its subsequent popular acceptance.[29]

26. 1 Va. Cases 20, 78 (1793). Emphasis in original.
27. *Correspondence of Iredell,* ed. McRee, 2 : 174.
28. 2 U.S. (2 Dall.) 304, 308 (1795).
29. See 1 Va. Cases 20, 27–28, 36–38, 46–48, 57–58, 69–74 (1793) for the discussions of Judges William Nelson, Spencer Roane, James Henry, John Tyler, and St. George Tucker, respectively.

The most important factor in establishing the constitution's superior status was that the convention that framed it was convened in the absence of civil government, and with no connection whatever to any previous government. In Judge John Tyler's words:

> To investigate this subject rightly, we need but go back to that awful period of our country when we were declared out of the protection of the then mother country—and take a retrospective view of our situation, and behold the bands of civil government cut asunder, and destroyed:—no social compact, no system of protection and common defence against an invading tyrant—in a state of nature, without friends, allies, or resources:—In such a case what was to be done?
>
> Those eminent characters to whom so much gratitude is . . . due . . . recommended a convention of delegates to be chosen . . . who were to meet together for the express design of completely protecting and defending the rights, both civil and religious, of our common country. . . . What power had the people therefore that was not confided to their representatives?
>
> . . . And shall [the convention's] validity be now questioned? for what purpose? To revert back to our former insignificancy? It cannot be.[30]

Judge Spencer Roane made the same argument:

> This convention was not chosen under the sanction of the former government; it was not limited in its powers by it, if indeed it existed, but may be considered as a spontaneous assemblage of the people of Virginia, under a recommendation of a former convention, to consult for the good of themselves, and their posterity. . . . This constitution is sanctioned by the consent and acquiescence of the people for seventeen years; and it is admitted by the almost universal opinion of the people, by the repeated adjudications of the courts of this commonwealth, and by very many declarations of the legislature itself, to be of superior authority to any opposing act of the legislature.[31]

In addition to making these same points, Judge Tucker's opinion drew the sharpest contrast between American and European circumstances:

> Our case was much stronger than either [the English in 1688 or the French in 1789]. There was at least the shadow of legal, constitutional authority in the convention parliament of England in 1688, as the ordinary legislature; and the national assembly of France was constitutionally assembled under the authority of the government it subverted. The convention of Virginia had not the shadow of a legal, or constitutional form about it. It derived its existence and authority from a higher source; a power which can supercede all law, and annul the constitution itself—namely, the *people,* in their *sovereign, unlimited,* and *unlimitable* authority and capacity.[32]

---

30. Ibid., 57–58.
31. Ibid., 37.
32. Ibid., 74. Emphasis in original.

What distinguished American from European fundamental law, thus, was not its technically correct existence as a written social contract, but its role in bringing the American states out of a real state of nature. The experience of having passed through a literal, if brief, state of nature and having emerged with a totally new set of institutions imparted an unprecedented concreteness and reality to American fundamental law. Participation in this experience made all the states, whether or not they had technically correct social contracts, more like each other than like England. It helps explain how Rhode Island, which did not have a written constitution at all, nevertheless produced one of the major period 1 exercises of judicial review. Virginia's and Rhode Island's social contracts, although technically deficient, nevertheless had a reality that, to eighteenth-century Americans, stood in decisive contrast to the fictional and imaginary ones of European analysis. This concrete reality of American social contracts was the deepest component in the widely held perception that the uniqueness of American fundamental law lay in its explicitness. Commitment to writing was clearly important, but it reinforced, rather than created, this explicitness.

In period 1, the most important consequence of the reality and explicitness of American social contracts was that it overturned the doctrine of legislative omnipotence. Despite the strength of European fundamental law and social contract traditions, and the emergence of meaningfully limited government in England, legislative omnipotence was still the rule. In the absence of anything comparable to the American social contracts, the English had nothing tangible to hold up against the latest expression of parliamentary will, the sole embodiment of sovereignty. As Blackstone underscored, even a legislative act that concededly violated fundamental law was valid.

The real and explicit American social contracts, in contrast, provided precise, publicly stated boundaries for each of the branches, and thus, for the first time, for literally limited government. In Pendleton's words, the Virginia Constitution, which "assign[ed] to each [branch] its proper powers, and direct[ed] that each shall be kept separate and distinct, must be considered as a rule obligatory upon every department, not to be departed from on any occasion."[33] This unremarkable statement, easily overlooked today, initially carried with it enormous significance. The existence of explicit, publicly verifiable limits on each of the branches introduced the powerful idea that it was now, for the first time, possible to identify with certitude a legislative act that, in its violation of fundamental law, was on its face void, or not law. American legislatures could not violate fundamental law as it was conceded Parliament could violate English fundamental law. Statements comparable to Pendleton's are an integral part of periods 1 and 2 discussions of judicial review. Among the clearest is Justice Paterson's in *VanHorne's Lessee* v. *Dorrance:*

> The constitution is the work or will of the people themselves, in their original, sovereign, and unlimited capacity. . . . The constitution fixes limits to the ex-

33. *Commonwealth* v. *Caton,* 4 Call (Va.) 5, 17 (1782). Quoted above at n. 24.

ercise of legislative authority, and prescribes the orbit within which it must move. . . . Whatever may be the case in other countries, yet in this, there can be no doubt, that every act of the legislature, repugnant to the constitution, is absolutely void.[34]

That written, explicit social contracts bound government in an unprecedented way was, furthermore, not disputed. As Pendleton indicated, it was agreed to "on all sides."[35] The end of legislative omnipotence was novel and of major importance, but, by virtue of widespread agreement, also uncontroversial. The absence of contemporary controversy and the utter triviality since associated with the ideas that an unconstitutional act is void and that American legislators are literally bound by American fundamental law, combined with Marshall's skillful manipulation of this agreement, have made it impossible for subsequent generations to appreciate how revolutionary this development was.

The pervasiveness of period 1 support for a judicial check on legislation, coupled with the absence of any uniform or coherent defense, indicates that supporters moved directly from the agreed-upon end of legislative omnipotence and the invalidity of an act that violated the Constitution to support for judicial refusal to execute such an act. The conclusion that the end of legislative omnipotence authorized judicial invalidation of unconstitutional legislation was not, however, universally shared. Opponents of a judicial check accepted without reservation the propositions that the legislature must not violate the Constitution and that an unconstitutional act was void. Nevertheless, they denied that these innovations conveyed to the judiciary authority to refuse to enforce a properly enacted piece of legislation. The key proposition of period 1 opposition to judicial review maintained that, although legislative omnipotence no longer obtained, legislative supremacy did.

The concrete expression of legislative supremacy was that the Constitution was "a rule to the *legislature only*"[36] and could not be invoked by the judiciary to overturn a legislative determination. Although American legislatures, unlike the English Parliament, were bound by the explicit content of a concrete fundamental law, and an act that violated fundamental law was void, judges

---

34. 2 U.S. (2 Dall.) 304, 308 (1795). For other formulations of the same point, see *Kamper* v. *Hawkins*, 1 Va. Cases 20, 25–30, 36–38, 59, (1793), Judges Nelson, Roane, and Tyler, respectively; James Iredell, "To the Public," in *Correspondence of Iredell*, ed. McRee, 2 : 145–46, quoted and discussed below, 20–21; Alexander Hamilton, *The Federalist, No. 78*, Modern Library (New York: Random House, n.d.), 505–06, quoted and discussed below, 32–35.

35. *Commonwealth* v. *Caton*, 4 Call (Va.) 5, 17 (1782), quoted in full above at n. 24.

36. This is part of Tucker's formulation of the period 1 opposition to judicial review, which he summarized before rebutting in his *Kamper* opinion. His full statement of the period 1 position is as follows: "But here an objection [to judicial authority over legislation] will no doubt be drawn from the authority of those writers who affirm, that the constitution of a state is a rule to the *legislature only*, and not to the *judiciary*, or the *executive:* the legislature being bound not to transgress it; but that neither the executive nor judiciary can resort to it to enquire whether they do transgress it, or not" (*Kamper* v. *Hawkins*, 1 Va. Cases 20, 77 [1793]; emphasis in original).

still could not refuse to enforce a duly enacted piece of legislation. As Pendleton suggested in *Commonwealth* v. *Caton,* such action went beyond any known boundary of legitimate judicial power and compounded the wrong done by the legislature.[37] Others denounced judicial review in stronger terms. No matter "what law they have declared void," judicial refusal to enforce a properly enacted law was a "usurpation" of power, "an absolute negative on the proceedings of the legislature, which no judiciary ought ever to possess."[38] The remedy for legislative violation of fundamental law—even under a real social contract of explicit content—remained what it had always been, popular action and, ultimately, revolution.[39]

The Concededly Unconstitutional Act. The extent of judicial authority should the legislature *"in fact"* violate the constitution was the central controversy of period 1 and the issue that was resolved in period 2.[40] It must be stressed that the judicial power over legislation contemplated by both sides in the periods 1 and 2 controversy was confined to power over *concededly* unconstitutional acts. Despite substantial evidence that periods 1 and 2 judicial review was, in fact, so confined, and because authority over concededly unconstitutional acts has not been the subject of judicial review since Marshall, modern scholarship has not taken the proposition seriously, regarding it as a trivial and irrelevant issue.[41] At the time, however, it was at the center of theoretical and practical interest. Theoretically, it touched the debate about legislative omnipotence and supremacy as defended by Blackstone, who had deliberately couched his argument in terms of a concededly unconstitutional act—one that made a man judge of his own cause. Judicial refusal to enforce parliamentary will, he

37. 4 Call (Va.) 5, 17 (1782). Quoted above at n. 24.

38. Richard Spaight to James Iredell, August 12, 1787, *Correspondence of Iredell,* ed. McRee, 2 : 169.

39. Ibid., 169–70.

40. See Iredell's formulation of the period 1 opposition to judicial review, which he summarized before rebutting in "To the Public": "The great argument is, that though the Assembly have not a *right* to violate the constitution, yet if they *in fact* do so, the only remedy is, either by a humble petition that the law may be repealed, or a universal resistance of the people. But that in the mean time, their act, whatever it is, is to be obeyed as a law; for the judicial power is not to presume to question the power of an act of assembly" (*Correspondence of Iredell,* ed. McRee, 2 : 147; emphasis in original). This is the most succinct statement of the two components of the period 1 debate: the agreement that the legislature could not violate the Constitution, and the disagreement over judicial authority should the legislature nevertheless violate it.

41. Thayer had argued in 1893 that period 2 judicial review was limited to the concededly unconstitutional act and suppported his argument with numerous references to eighteenth- and early nineteenth-century defenses of judiciary review which insisted that the judiciary could refuse to enforce an act only where there was no doubt about the legislation's unconstitutionality ("Doctrine of Constitutional Law," 139–42). Although no one has ever challenged Thayer's evidence, his general analysis remains unpersuasive. I am not attempting here to revive Thayer's position, but rather to show that it was only partially correct. That the doubtful case rule was an operative part of 1790s judicial review is clearly the case. What Thayer missed was that it was part of a practice different from that which he and we know.

argued, would undermine political authority. Those Americans who followed Blackstone had applied this position to American circumstances and denied that judges had any authority whatever over duly enacted legislation. Refutation of Blackstone's position and establishment of the proposition that the courts could refuse to execute a concededly unconstitutional act was not, in the years following independence, a trivial undertaking.

Furthermore, judicial review, limited to the concededly. unconstitutional act, was initially as important practically as it was theoretically. Period 1 judicial review developed in contemplation of a legislative record in many of the states that included enough clearly unconstitutional measures to make debate in these terms meaningful. The leading source of concededly unconstitutional legislation of the 1780s was "revolutionary justice," which, in the context of the American Revolution, consisted mainly of confiscation of Loyalist property in violation of established principle, notably without protection of trial by jury. Also of concern was the debtor relief legislation and what Madison called the "mutability and multiplicity of laws." in many of the states under the Articles of Confederation.[42] Although the latter was often distinguished from denial of trial by jury as legislation that was "unjust . . . unwise . . . [but] not . . . unconstitutional"[43] and was on this ground excluded from judicial cognizance, the legislative record under the Articles generated substantial fear of an unchecked legislative supremacy capable of willful violation of long-standing principle. The major response to this aggressive legislative supremacy of the 1780s was the movement for a stronger national government that would assume much of the legislative authority then lodged in the states. Period 2 judicial review was another response, and in the context of the revolutionary instability and untested republicanism of the decades following independence, it was wholly intelligible as a judicial power over concededly unconstitutional acts.

The actual practice of judicial review during periods 1 and 2 confirms that it was in fact reserved for clear violation of fundamental law. There were eight cases for which records indicate judges actually refused to enforce legislation. Six of them involved legislative interferences with trial by jury.[44] The

42. James Madison, "Vices of the Political System of the United States," in *The Writings of James Madison*, ed. Gaillard Hunt (New York: G. P. Putnam's Sons, 1900–1910), 2 : 365–67.

43. James Wilson at the Constitutional Convention, *The Records of the Federal Convention of 1787*, ed. Max Farrand, 4 vols. (New Haven: Yale University Press, 1937), 2 : 73. See also Alexander Hamilton in *Federalist 78*, 509, where unjust legislation is distinguished from unconstitutional legislation and is excluded from the judicial authority being claimed. Hamilton's position is discussed below at n. 100 and accompanying text.

44. The jury trial cases were *Holmes* v. *Walton* (New Jersey, 1780); *Trevett* v. *Weeden* (Rhode Island, 1786); *Bayard* v. *Singleton*, 1 N.C. 5 (1787); *Bowman* v. *Middleton*, 1 Bay (S.C.) 252 (1792); *VanHorne's Lessee* v. *Dorrance*, 2 U.S. (2 Dall.) 304 (1795); and *Stidger* v. *Rogers*, 2 Ky. Decisions 52 (1801). There were altogether about a dozen cases in which the issue of judicial review was raised. In some, judges claimed authority over unconstitutional acts without exercising it in the particular case. See, for example, *Commonwealth* v. *Caton*, 4 Call (Va.) 5 (1782). In others, judges avoided implementing legislation through statutory construction. See, for example, *Rutgers* v. *Waddington* (New York, 1784), reprinted in *Law Practice of Ham-*

other two involved legislation dealing with the organization and exercise of judicial power, an area touching the doctrine of concurrent review.[45] By this doctrine, it was agreed that each branch could determine the constitutionality of legislation dealing with its own operation.

That periods 1 and 2 judicial review centered on the dual questions of, first, whether the legislature could violate the Constitution, and second, whether judges were obliged to enforce an act that did, and that it was limited to the concededly unconstitutional act are most clearly revealed in the structure of the *Marbury* argument. But because we have been so misled by Marshall's diversion of the original issues, we have been unable to recognize this or understand its significance. Marshall, in *Marbury,* phrased the first question as "whether an act, repugnant to the constitution, can become the law of the land."[46] The second was "if an act of the legislature, repugnant to the constitution, is void, does it, notwithstanding its invalidity, bind the courts, and oblige them to give it effect?"[47] Bickel is surely correct in pointing out that *Marbury* begs the real question of the judicial review we know—namely, who is to decide in the first place whether an act is repugnant to the Constitution.[48] But *Marbury* only begs the real question of the judicial review Marshall had yet to put into place. In 1803 the issue was precisely as Marshall stated it. He posed the two questions as they had been posed repeatedly during the preceding decades and gave the answers that had been given successfully during the 1790s. The clear-cut cases, which Marshall invoked in *Marbury* and which are dismissed today as trivial and irrelevant, were then at the center of controversy. They were the kinds of examples uniformly given whenever examples were used in 1790s' defenses of judicial review.[49] Unless we are to conclude that leading judges and public figures carried on a trivial and irrelevant debate for over twenty years, we have to understand that it was initially directed at a different order of question from that which developed later.

Period 2

Period 2 provided the convincing answer to the second question of the period 1 controversy. Judges, it was successfully argued, were not obliged to enforce an unconstitutional act. This period 2 conclusion was reached and supported by drawing more implications from the existence of real and explicit fundamental law than had been the case in period 1.

ilton, ed. Goebel, 1 : 393–419. For a review of the most significant cases, see Charles Grove Haines, *The American Doctrine of Judicial Supremacy* (New York: Macmillan Co., 1914), chaps. 4, 5, and 7.

45. *Hayburn's Case,* 2 U.S. (2 Dall.) 409 (1792), and *Kamper* v. *Hawkins,* 1 Va. Cases 20 (1793).

46. *Marbury* v. *Madison,* 5 U.S. (1 Cr.) 137, 176 (1803).

47. Ibid., 177.

48. *Least Dangerous Branch,* 2 and 3.

49. See Iredell to Spaight, August 26, 1787, *Correspondence of Iredell,* ed. McRee, 2 : 174; Judge Tucker in *Kamper* v. *Hawkins,* 1 Va. Cases 20, 79–81 (1793); Justice Paterson in *VanHorne's Lessee* v. *Dorrance,* 2 U.S. (2 Dall.) 304, 309 (1795).

Period 2 began in 1786 with publication of James Iredell's "To the Public" in a North Carolina newspaper.[50] Iredell was then representing a client whose property had been confiscated during the Revolution. A state statute provided that subsequent claims on behalf of such property were to be dismissed upon presentation of an affidavit that the property had been purchased from the commissioner of forfeited estates. The right to trial by jury, specifically mentioned in the North Carolina Constitution, had been denied. As its name indicates, "To the Public" was a public appeal for support of Iredell's argument that judges, rightly, could refuse to enforce the act.[51]

Iredell repeated and reformulated this defense of judicial refusal to enforce an unconstitutional act in a letter to Richard Spaight, one of the North Carolina delegates to the Constitutional Convention. This letter was dated August 26, 1787, while the convention was still sitting.[52] I do not know when, or even if, this letter arrived in Philadelphia, but judging from the overall evidence I have concluded that both Hamilton and Wilson became familiar with Iredell's defense of judicial review at this time. Each proceeded to make major restatements of Iredell's argument within the next few years, Hamilton in *Federalist 78* and Wilson in *Lectures on the Law,* delivered in 1790–91. Iredell's argument, which tied judicial review to the existence of an "express" constitution, had not appeared before this time, either in court or out. *Federalist 78,* although varying the emphasis given to specific points, repeated in striking detail most of those made by Iredell and added no new ones. Wilson's earlier discussion of enforcement of specific constitutional prohibitions had betrayed no expectation of a judicial role, yet *Lectures on the Law* made the standard period 2 defense of judicial review.[53]

"To the Public" opened with a statement of the end of legislative omnipotence brought about by the social contracts following the break from England:

> We were not ignorant of the theory *of the necessity of the legislature being absolute in all cases,* because it was the great ground of the British pretensions. . . . When we were at liberty to form a government as we thought best, . . . we decisively gave our sentiments against it, being willing to run all the risks of a government to be conducted on the principles then laid as the basis of it. The

50. *Correspondence of Iredell,* ed. McRee, 2 : 145–49.

51. The North Carolina court did refuse to enforce the act in *Bayard* v. *Singleton,* 1 N.C. 5 (1787).

52. *Correspondence of Iredell,* ed. McRee, 2 : 172–76.

53. Wilson opposed a prohibition on ex post facto laws, at the Constitutional Convention, agreeing with Oliver Ellsworth that such laws were "void of themselves" and thus not in need of prohibition. Wilson added that a prohibition "will bring reflections on the constitution—and proclaim that we are ignorant of the first principles of Legislation." He went on to observe that similar provisions in the state constitutions had proven useless, as their violations went unchecked (*Records of the Federal Convention,* ed. Farrand, 2 : 376). Edward S. Corwin noted a change in Wilson's attitude toward judicial review between the convention, which ended in September 1787, and the Pennsylvania Ratifying Convention, which convened in November 1787. He did not offer any explanation for this change ("The Supreme Court and Unconstitutional Acts of Congress," *Michigan Law Review* 4, no. 8 [June 1906] : 620).

instance was new in the annals of mankind. No people had ever before deliberately met for so great a purpose. Other governments have been established
by chance, caprice, or mere brutal force. Ours . . . sprang from the deliberate
voice of the people. . . .

I have therefore no doubt, but that the power of the Assembly is limited
and defined by the constitution. It is a *creature* of the constitution. (I hope this
is an expression not prosecutable.) The people have chosen to be governed
under such and such principles. They have not chosen to be governed, or
promised to submit upon any other; and the Assembly have no more right to
obedience on other terms, than any different power on earth has a right to
govern us; for we have as much agreed to be governed by the Turkish Divan
as by our own General Assembly, otherwise than on the express terms prescribed.[54]

That it was explicit fundamental law and real social contracts that ended legislative omnipotence is more concisely stated in Iredell's letter to Spaight:

Without an express Constitution the powers of the Legislature would undoubtedly have been absolute (as the Parliament in Great Britain is held to
be), and any act passed, *not inconsistent with natural justice* (for that curb is
avowed by the judges even in England), would have been binding on the
people. The experience of the evils which the American war fully disclosed,
attending an absolute power in a legislative body, suggested the propriety of
a real, original contract between the people and their future Government,
such, perhaps, as there has been no instance of in the world but in America.[55]

As already noted in our examination of period 1 material, the end of legislative omnipotence has never been considered an event of particular importance in American historical analysis. But it obviously was to Iredell. He drew
specific attention to its novelty and even betrayed a mild apprehension that it
entailed some risk. At the same time Iredell recognized that despite its novelty
and importance, it was universally accepted and not the subject of controversy. Immediately following his statement on the American disavowal of legislative omnipotence in "To the Public," Iredell went on to say, "These are
consequences that seem so natural, and indeed so irresistible, that I do not
observe they have been much contested."[56] This echoes Pendleton's remark
that it was said "on all sides" that written social contracts established literally
binding limits on all the branches. Having thus stated the uncontroversial first
component of the period 1 debate, that the legislature could not violate the
constitution, Iredell moved to its second, contentious part: "The great argument is, that though the Assembly have not a *right* to violate the constitution,
yet if they *in fact* do so, the only remedy is, either . . . petition . . . or universal
resistance."[57] He proceeded to reject petition as demeaning to a self-govern-

---

54. *Correspondence of Iredell,* ed. McRee, 2 : 146. Emphasis in original.
55. Ibid., 172–73. Emphasis in original.
56. Ibid., 147.
57. Ibid. Emphasis in original. The full quotation is given above, n. 40.

ing people and revolution as too extreme to be useful. He then inquired "whether the judicial power hath any authority to interfere in such a case" and answered with what was to be the successful period 2 defense of judicial authority to refuse to enforce an unconstitutional act:

> The [judicial] duty . . . I conceive, in all cases, is to decide according to the *laws of the State*. It will not be denied, I suppose, that the constitution is *a law of the State*, as well as an act of Assembly, with this difference only, that it is the *fundamental* law, and unalterable by the legislature, which derives all its power from it. One act of Assembly may repeal another act of Assembly. For this reason, the latter act is to be obeyed, and not the former. An act of Assembly cannot repeal the constitution, or any part of it. For that reason, an act of Assembly, inconsistent with the constitution is *void*, and cannot be obeyed, without disobeying the superior law to which we were previously and irrevocably bound. The judges, therefore, must take care at their peril, that every act of Assembly they presume to enforce is warranted by the constitution, since if it is not, they act without lawful authority. This is not a usurped or a discretionary power, but one inevitably resulting from the constitution of their office, they being judges *for the benefit of the whole people*, not *mere servants of the Assembly*.[58]

This is the core of Iredell's defense of judicial authority over legislation. On first reading it could easily be taken as part of a single line of reasoning leading to *Marbury* and the doctrine we accept today. As represented in Thayer's formulation,[59] under this modern doctrine, judicial authority over legislation is said to flow from the fact that the Constitution, as supreme law, is subject, like other law, to judicial application and enforcement. The *Marbury* doctrine assumes no difference in kind between the two that would preclude authoritative judicial application and interpretation of fundamental law.

Iredell, in this passage, held no such assumption and made no such argument, implicitly or explicitly. He did assert that the judicial obligation was to decide according to the laws of the state and included the Constitution as a law of the state, cognizable in court. In so doing, he introduced a major period 2 innovation, but he was neither contemplating nor implying that the Constitution and ordinary law were cognizable in the same way or that the judicial responsibility to them was comparable. In arguing that fundamental law was cognizable in court he was rejecting only the proposition that the Constitution was a rule to the legislature only. In its explicitness, the Constitution was a rule for each branch equally, and the judiciary, as well as the legislature, was bound by and answerable directly to it. The judicial duty to decide according to the laws of the state meant that the judiciary was precluded from enforcing legislation that, in its violation of the Constitution, was void, or not law. This preclusion followed the judiciary's unique responsibility

---

58. Ibid., 148. Emphasis in original.
59. "Doctrine of Constitutional Law," 138, quoted above at n. 25.

to ordinary law and its common responsibility, along with the other branches, to fundamental law.[60]

Iredell, in this passage, was rejecting Blackstone's contention that the judiciary could not take cognizance of the Constitution at all, even when confronting a concededly unconstitutional act. It followed his reaffirmation of the uniquely American phenomenon of the end of legislative omnipotence, and the absence of any legislative authority to violate the Constitution. It was made in contemplation of an unambiguously unconstitutional act, one that denied trial by jury to those whose property had been confiscated during the war. This was an act comparable to Blackstone's hypothetical example of legislation that made a man judge of his own cause.

The judicial responsibility over unconstitutional legislation, defended in "To the Public," derived, furthermore, from the judiciary's responsibility to "the whole people," and not from any uniquely judicial relationship to fundamental law, as hinted at in *Marbury*.[61] Enforcement of fundamental law was a political act, a peaceful substitute for revolution, presented as a superior alternative to petition or universal resistance.[62] By the same token, the act of determining a law's unconstitutionality was also a public, or political act, not a legal one. This remained the case even when the act was performed by the judiciary. Since it grew out of the existence of real social contracts and publicly verifiable limits on legislative power, it could therefore be made by any of the branches, the executive as well as the judiciary.

The most important implication of Iredell's argument was that judicial enforcement of fundamental law, unlike enforcement of ordinary law, carried with it no assumption of, or sanction for, judicial interpretation or exposition of fundamental law. The judiciary's common law responsibility to ordinary law necessitated authoritative determination of whether or not that law was violated in particular cases. This, in turn, necessitated exposition of ordinary law. Enforcement of fundamental law, in contrast, was limited to the publicly verifiable, concededly unconstitutional act. As such, it required neither authoritative determination of whether or not fundamental law was in fact violated in particular cases nor authoritative exposition of that law. On the contrary, uncertainty over whether an act violated fundamental law marked the limit of judicial power over legislation.

Assumption of judicial authority to expound or interpret the law of the Constitution was to be the distinguishing characteristic of period 3 judicial review. Because interpretation is the vehicle through which policy considerations enter the act of judging, this is the source of period 3's controversial assertion of judicial supremacy. Period 2 judicial review, in contrast, was an expression of the equality of the branches under explicit fundamental law,

<hr/>

60. For another statement of the period 2 position that articulates more clearly this reading of Iredell, see Judge Tucker in *Kamper* v. *Hawkins*, 1 Va. Cases 20, 78–31 (1793), quoted and discussed below at n. 70 and accompanying text.

61. See the discussion of *Marbury* below at n. 104 and accompanying text.

62. See the discussion above at n. 57 and accompanying text.

made in reply to the legislative supremacy of period 1. It neither needed nor contemplated authority to expound or interpret the Constitution. It was, simply but significantly, legitimation and regularization of the judicial refusal to execute a concededly unconstitutional act, one made so by the force of a real, explicit social contract. It was rejection of the view that judicial refusal to enforce a concededly unconstitutional act was a "usurped or a discretionary power."[63] Far from that, Iredell demonstrated that it was an inescapable obligation under a constitution of fixed and explicit limits. This sense of judicial obligation growing out of a real social contract was more forcefully expressed in Iredell's letter to Spaight: "It really appears to me, the exercise of the power is unavoidable, the Constitution not being a mere imaginery thing, about which ten thousand different opinions may be formed, but a written document to which all may have recourse, and to which, therefore, the judges cannot willfully blind themselves."[64]

The Significance of the Doubtful Case Rule. Modern scholarship, for reasons we have already examined, has difficulty taking seriously period 2 judicial review's confinement to the concededly unconstitutional act and to its accompanying doubtful case rule. Under this rule if there was any doubt whatsoever whether the legislation violated fundamental law, judges must enforce it. At the root of the difficulty is our failure to recognize the discontinuity between periods 2 and 3 judicial review and the fact that, before Marshall, judicial review was a political, not legal undertaking, different in kind from judicial enforcement of ordinary law. As part of the enforcement of fundamental law—a political responsibility to "the whole people" devised in a period of revolutionary instability—the doubtful case rule marked an intelligible and practical limit on judicial power. As part of supreme ordinary law, under conditions of basic political stability as became the case during period 3, it is unworkable.

This problem is highlighted in the contrasting assessments of the doubtful case rule made by Judge John Gibson in 1825,[65] and by Thayer in 1893.[66] Gibson, in the first decades of the nineteenth century, was still in touch with the original political understanding of fundamental law at the same time that he was observing its legalization. He regarded both Marshall's judicial review and its legalization as unwarranted, and he rejected all judicial authority over legislation, including that limited to "cases that are free from doubt or difficulty."[67] If power over legislation were, in fact, a necessary part of judicial responsibility, he argued, then refusal to determine constitutionality in cases of doubt would constitute an evasion of that responsibility. No judge, he pointed

---

63. "To the Public," *Correspondence of Iredell,* ed. McRee, 2 : 148, quoted above at n. 58.
64. Ibid., 174.
65. *Eakin* v. *Raub,* 12 Sergeant & Rawles (Pa.) 330, 343 (1825), dissenting opinion.
66. "Doctrine of Constitutional Law," 138–56.
67. *Eakin* v. *Raub,* 12 Sergeant & Rawles (Pa.) 330, 352 (1825).

out, would refuse to give authoritative interpretation of ordinary law because of the difficulty or doubt entailed.[68]

By the time Thayer wrote, legalization of fundamental law was complete. Thayer had no other conception of the Constitution except as "so much law," and he accepted its inclusion as part of that law rightly amenable to judicial application and interpretation. As part of such a conception, the doubtful case rule, which Thayer attempted to revive, did, as Gibson had recognized, partake of an evasion of legal responsibility. It was, among other reasons, because it was so perceived that Thayer's and Frankfurter's attempt to implement it failed. In period 2, however, the doubtful case rule was not an evasion of legal responsibility because constitutional enforcement was no part of that responsibility to begin with. As a new political responsibility, it had its own properties and limits. Precisely because it was understood to be beyond the boundary of the judiciary's common law responsibility, it needed the doubtful case rule, or some equivalent, to confine it within acceptable limits.

The Development of Iredell's Argument. The most influential and instructive period 2 restatement of Iredell's argument, aside from those of Hamilton and Wilson,[69] was Judge Tucker's in *Kamper* v. *Hawkins*. It was also the obvious immediate source of crucial passages in *Marbury:*

> [The constitution is] the first law of the land, and as such must be resorted to on every occasion, where it becomes necessary to expound *what the law is.* This exposition it is the duty and office of the judiciary to make; our constitution expressly declaring that the legislative, executive, and judiciary, shall be separate and distinct, so that neither exercise the powers properly belong *[sic]* to the other. Now since it is the province of the legislature to make, and of the executive to enforce obedience to the laws, the duty of expounding must be exclusively vested in the judiciary. But how can any just exposition be made, *if that which is the supreme law of the land be withheld from their view?* . . .
>
> But that the constitution is a rule to all the departments of the government, to the judiciary as well as to the legislature, may, I think, be proved by reference to a few parts of it. [Tucker then examined several provisions of the constitution, including those protecting trial by jury and the free exercise of religion. He conjured up hypothetical examples of umambiguous violation of these provisions and argued that the judiciary was not obliged to enforce such violations.]

68. A full discussion of Gibson's position is beyond the scope of this article. Here I can only note that Gibson's criticism of *Marbury* maintained the period 2 perception of fundamental law as different in kind from ordinary law. Gibson had, however, lost touch with the practical dimensions of periods 1 and 2 judicial review, particularly with the urgency of checking concededly unconstitutional acts. See Gibson's comments on Paterson's period 2 defense of judicial review, ibid., 356, and quoted below at n. 88. Gibson's criticism of emerging period 3 judicial review, thus, came from a unique perspective, reflecting fully neither periods 2 nor 3 assumptions.

69. See below at nn. 90–100 and 84–86.

> From all these instances it appears to me that this deduction clearly follows, viz. that the *judiciary* are *bound* to take notice of the constitution, *as the first law of the land;* and that whatsoever is contradictory thereto, is *not* the law of the land.[70]

This formulation, even more so than Iredell's, appears on first reading to be a simple precursor of *Marbury*. But as with "To the Public," it was decisively different from it. Most important, Tucker did not, in this passage, make any claim to judicial authority to expound the constitution or to say what the law of the constitution is. For Tucker, the judicial authority was to expound ordinary law, and following Iredell, he insisted that to make a "just exposition" of the ordinary law judges had to "resort to" and "take notice of the constitution." The constitution could not be "withheld from [judicial] view." Tucker's argument, like Iredell's, was in reply to the assertion of Blackstone and his period 1 followers that the constitution was "a rule to the legislature only." It was a direct repudiation of Blackstone's contention that judges must not consider fundamental law at all, even when confronted with a conceded violation of it, but that they were obliged, in fact, to close their eyes to the constitution and see only the statute. Tucker's reply insisted that it was necessary for judges to take notice of or to regard the constitution if they were to fulfill properly their common law responsibility to expound (ordinary) law. To fail to resort to the constitution was to risk putting into effect that which in its violation of the constitution was void, or "not the law of the land."

The judiciary, for Tucker as for Iredell, could legitimately take notice of the constitution because it was "a rule to all . . . departments, to the judiciary as well as to the legislature." Unlike the *Marbury* doctrine, Tucker made no claim to a uniquely judicial relationship to fundamental law. The only exclusively judicial responsibility was to expound ordinary law.

Tucker's language was not accidental. During the 1790s no claim was ever made to any judicial authority to apply, interpret, or expound the Constitution.[71] The only claim made was to a judicial authority to "resort to" or "take notice" of the Constitution. The North Carolina court, in *Bayard* v. *Singleton*, used the same language: "Consequently, the Constitution (which the judicial power was bound *to take notice of* as much as of any other law whatever), standing in full force as the fundamental law of the land, notwithstanding the act on which the present motion was grounded, the same act must of course . . . stand as abrogated and without any effect."[72] So did Spencer Roane in his *Kamper* opinion: "In *expounding laws,* the judiciary *considers* every law which relates to the subject: would you have them *to shut their eyes against* that law which is the highest authority of any."[73] And Iredell stated in his letter to Spaight: "The Constitution, therefore, being a fundamental law, and a law in writing of the solemn nature I have mentioned . . . the judicial power, in the

70. 1 Va. Cases 20, 78–81 (1793). Emphasis in original.

71. The only exception, and it is a partial and indirect one, is Hamilton's argument in *Federalist 78*. See the discussion below at nn. 92–97.

72. 1 N.C. 5, 7 (1787). Emphasis added.

73. 1 Va. Cases 20, 38 (1793). Emphasis added.

exercise of their authority, must *take notice of it* as the groundwork of that as well as of all other authority."[74]

The uniformity of this language, as well as the absence of any attempt to call attention to the distinction between expounding ordinary law and considering, regarding, or taking notice of the Constitution, is testimony to the strength and pervasiveness of the periods 1 and 2 recognition of a difference in kind between fundamental law and ordinary law, and thus of the utter inappropriateness of judicial exposition of fundamental law.

Natural Law and Positive Law. The period 2 judicial review initiated by Iredell contained positive law and natural law elements, but was not a direct manifestation of either tradition. The uniqueness of explicit fundamental law brought with it a new judicial responsibility that combined natural and positive law elements in a novel way. The preeminent positive law feature of period 2 judicial review was its connection to a written constitution. Its positive law side was bolstered by the insistence that judicial enforcement of the Constitution was a necessary part of the judiciary's common law responsibility to ordinary law. Nevertheless, period 2 judicial review drew its main ideas from the natural law tradition. Despite the fairly widespread invocation of written constitutions, their status as concrete social contracts was more important than their commitment to writing per se. It was this status that ended legislative omnipotence, established the invalidity of laws that violated it, and authorized judicial refusal to enforce such acts. The notion of a social contract establishing and limiting government was, furthermore, unintelligible outside the natural law tradition. Judicial enforcement of them was a political act, a peaceful substitute for revolution, and the legitimacy of revolution, whether carried out popularly or judicially, was established by governmental invasion of natural rights.

The relative unimportance of a written constitution was reflected in the absence of any mention of, or reliance on it, in the three leading period 2 defenses of judicial review: Iredell's "To the Public," Hamilton's *Federalist 78,* and Wilson's *Lectures on the Law.* More significant than this eloquent silence, however, was the fact that despite period 2 reliance on an explicit text, the precise content of fundamental law restraints in particular cases was not established through textual interpretation or exposition. That content, as we shall see in examining periods 2 and 3 cases, inhered, rather, in first principles of government identified by the existence of explicit fundamental law. Reflecting the English legacy, it was a mixture of a few natural law principles and common law precedents, constituting a consensus on the meaning of fundamental law, and included in the American state and federal constitutions. The Constitution was the supreme law of the land, but judicial enforcement of it was not in the application and interpretation of that law. It was, rather, in the defense of first principle committed to writing.

This peculiar merger of natural and positive law elements is visible in the judicial attitude toward the constitutional text in period 2 cases. Although

74. *Correspondence of Iredell,* ed. McRee, 2 : 173. Emphasis added.

judges drew on relevant text, they did so in an offhand way. Often they did not cite or quote the particular provisions of the state constitutions upon which they were relying, and in no case was there the kind of textual exposition familiar then and now in ordinary law and in constitutional law today.[75] In *Bayard* v. *Singleton*, for example, the North Carolina court declared void a law that dispensed with trial by jury in certain civil cases. Although jury trial was explicitly protected in the North Carolina Constitution, the opinion did not quote or cite this provision directly. The relevant part of the opinion read: "That by the Constitution every citizen had undoubtedly a right to a decision of his property by a trial by jury."[76] The court went on to discuss limited government in general.[77]

In *VanHorne's Lessee* v. *Dorrance*, Justice Paterson, riding circuit in Pennsylvania, rejected the state's attempt to settle disputed property claims without provision for either trial by jury or mutual choice of referee.[78] Paterson held that in the absence of agreement by the parties, only one of these alternate methods was allowable. In defending his decision Paterson drew heavily on existing natural law principles concerning property rights to the virtual exclusion of any reliance on the constitutional text. His entire discussion of the text consisted of a reference to "certain parts of the late bill of rights and constitution of Pennsylvania, which I shall now read."[79] The reports then indicated, in parentheses, that Paterson read three articles of the Declaration of Rights and two sections of the Constitution of Pennsylvania, and referred the reader to a source for the precise text. The provisions referred to were not reproduced in the reports.[80]

Lindsay v. *Commissioners*, decided in South Carolina in 1796, raised the issue of whether the city of Charleston had to compensate property holders in taking private property to put in a street.[81] The state constitution provided "that

75. The only textual exegesis anticipating modern practice in a period 1 or 2 case is to be found in *Kamper* v. *Hawkins*. Even here it was scanty by modern standards. See 1 Va. Cases 20, 34–35, 52–53, 63–64, 88–91 (1793) for the textual exegesis of Judges Nelson, Henry, Tyler, and Tucker, respectively. *Kamper*, as did *Marbury*, overturned an act dealing with judicial organization. It did not, as did most other periods 1 and 2 cases, involve a preexisting natural or common law principle.

76. 1 N.C. 5, 7 (1787).

77. "For that if the Legislature could take away this right, and require him to stand condemned in his property without a trial, it might with as much authority require his life to be taken away without a trial by jury, and that he should stand condemned to die, without the formality of any trial at all: that if the members of the General Assembly could do this, they might with equal authority, not only render themselves the Legislators of the State for life, without any further election of the people, from thence transmit the dignity and authority of legislation down to their heirs male forever" (Ibid.).

78. 2 U.S. (2 Dall.) 304 (1795).

79. Ibid. Paterson's discussion in *VanHorne's Lessee* was a jury charge.

80. The references were to a statement of the inherent and inalienable right to property; a provision protecting trial by jury; a statement that the Declaration of Rights was part of the Constitution; and a prohibition against legislative interference with any part of the Constitution.

81. 2 Bay (S.C.) 38 (1796).

no freeman shall be divested of his property, but by the judgment of his peers, or the law of the land." Members of the court were unanimous in recognizing a right of eminent domain that was bound by "the law of the land." They were evenly divided on what the law of the land demanded in this case. In discussing the issue, Judge John Grimke remarked:

> The 2d section of the 9th article of our state constitution, confirms all the before mentioned principles. It was not declaratory of any new law, but confirmed all the ancient rights and principles, which had been in use in the state, with the additional security, that no bills of attainder, nor ex post facto laws, or laws impairing the obligation of contracts, should ever be passed in the state.[82]

In indicating that the constitution "was not declaratory of any new law, but confirmed all the ancient rights and principles, which had been in use in the state," Grimke captured the merger of text and principle that characterized period 2 judicial review and, as we shall see, remained in the judicial review of Marshall's Supreme Court colleagues. The constitutional text was important as indisputable evidence of limited government and, generally, for identification of those principles that bound governmental power. The meaning of those principles for the purposes of judicial review, however, was to be found not by textual exegesis but by invocation of a preexisting, commonly agreed-upon content.

The mixture of natural and positive law elements that underlay Iredell's initial defense of judicial review remained in evidence throughout period 2. It was not Iredell's formulation, however, but those of Hamilton and Wilson that were most influential in the widespread acceptance of judicial control over legislation during the 1790s. The major court cases of that decade quoted, paraphrased, or closely followed the reasoning of one or another of these two leading sources.[83] Of the two, Wilson's was closer to Iredell's in that it displayed both the natural and positive law components of the source. Hamilton, on the other hand, ignored the natural law elements in and underlying Iredell's analysis and expanded the positive law ones. Marshall leaned totally on the positive law component, and the *Marbury* text drew heavily and freely from *Federalist 78* and *Kamper* v. *Hawkins,* the leading period 2 case drawing on Hamilton's version of Iredell. Marshall also extended and transformed the positive law side beyond that displayed in *Federalist 78* and, in the process, gave the institution its modern form.

Before looking at Hamilton's and Marshall's development of the positive law components of period 2 judicial review, it is instructive to examine Wilson's version. *Lectures on the Law* not only provides more evidence of the original understanding but illuminates Marshall's purposes in turning judicial review away from its natural law components.

---

82. Ibid., 57.
83. *Kamper* v. *Hawkins,* 1 Va. Cases 20 (1793) and *Lindsay* v. *Commissioners,* 2 Bay (S.C.) 38 (1796) followed Hamilton; *VanHorne's Lessee* v. *Dorrance,* 2 U.S. (2 Dall.) 304 (1795) followed Wilson.

Wilson opened his chapter on the differences between the American and English constitutions as follows:

> You will be surprised on being told that . . . no such thing as a constitution, properly so called, is known in Great Britain. What is known, in that kingdom, under that name, instead of being the controller and the guide, is the creature and the dependent of the legislative power. The ₒupreme power of the people is a doctrine unknown and unacknowledged in the British system of government. The omnipotent authority of parliament is the dernier resort, to which recourse is had in times and in doctrines of uncommon difficulty and importance. The natural, the inherent, and the predominating rights of the citizens are considered as so dangerous and so desperate a resource, as to be inconsistent with the arrangements of any government, which does or can exist.[84]

Wilson did not identify the written constitution as the chief distinguishing characteristic of American constitutionalism, nor did he invoke the written constitution in his specific defense of judicial review later in this chapter.[85] For Wilson, the Constitution was the supreme law of the land,[86] but it remained fundamental law and as such consisted of extraordinary political attributes and restraints, not conventional legal ones. The Constitution was the supreme power of the people, and in eighteenth-century America this meant "the natural, the inherent, and the predominating rights of the citizens." It was of course through commitment to writing that the supremacy of popular power and rights was unequivocally acknowledged in America. But this commitment to writing was not seen as working any major transformation in the nature of fundamental law. It was certainly not powerful enough to bring its enforcement within the confines of ordinary law enforcement. Constitutional enforcement remained an assertion of popular rights; it entailed revolution, or the threat of revolution, a desperate and dangerous resource. Commitment of fundamental law to writing did, however, provide an avenue for judicial participation in its defense, and if successful, judges might be able to forestall more drastic action. But in the enforcement of fundamental law, judicial action remained separate from that involved in enforcement of ordinary law and took on some of the desperate and dangerous quality that necessarily adheres to the enforcement of fundamental law.

Iredell expressed himself in comparable terms when, in *Calder* v. *Bull*, he referred to the judicial refusal to enforce a law as a "delicate and awful" power.[87]

---

84. *The Works of James Wilson*, ed. Robert Green McCloskey (Cambridge: Harvard University Press, Belknap Press, 1967), 1 : 309.

85. Ibid., 329–30.

86. Wilson used this formulation (ibid., 330) outside the federalism context of the supremacy clause, where it appears in the U.S. Constitution.

87. 3 U.S. (3 Dall.) 386, 399 (1796). It is also worth noting that Iredell's famous debate with Justice Samuel Chase, in this same case, was not, as is generally thought, one between a positive and natural law understanding of judicial review. Rather, each justice was stressing one of the two elements in period 2's merger of positive and natural law.

Today we still refer to judicial review as a delicate power, but we no longer consider it awful. It has become a special part of routine law enforcement, but a part nevertheless. Perhaps the most graphic statement of the extent to which 1790s judicial review, as a substitute for revolution, was understood to be an extraordinary political act is to be found in Judge Gibson's characterization of Paterson's argument in *VanHorne's Lessee* v. *Dorrance,* the leading period 2 case following Wilson's formulation. Recognizing the difference between Paterson's and Marshall's defenses of judicial review and explicitly reserving this particular criticism for Paterson's, Gibson remarked:

> In *VanHorne v. Dorrance* . . . the right is peremptorily asserted, and examples of monstrous violations of the constitution are put in a strong light, by way of example; such as taking away the trial by the jury, the elective franchise, or subverting religious liberty. But any of these would be such a usurpation of the political rights of the citizens, as would work a change in the very structure of the government; or, to speak more properly, it would be a revolution, which, to counteract, would justify even insurrection; consequently, a judge might lawfully employ every instrument of official resistance within his reach. By this, I mean, that while the citizen should resist with pike and gun, the judge might co-operate with *habeas corpus* and *mandamus.* It would be his duty, as a citizen, to throw himself into the breach, and if it should be necessary, perish there; but this is far from proving the judiciary to be a *peculiar organ,* under the constitution, to prevent legislative encroachment on the powers reserved by the people; and this is all I contend it is not.[88]

It was, among other reasons, to strip judicial review of its "awful" quality as part of a "dangerous and . . . desperate resource" that Marshall set out to transform it from enforcement of explicit fundamental law into application and enforcement of supreme written law.[89] In so doing, he removed the revolutionary potential that inhered in a restraint of first principle by turning that restraint into one of supreme ordinary law. This was, and is, a more problematic undertaking than has yet been appreciated, and I shall return to it after presentation of the historical material. Before that, it is necessary to examine the positive law strand of period 2 judicial review as developed in *Federalist 78.*

Federalist 78 differed from "To the Public," first, in tone and emphasis. Hamilton dropped the argumentativeness to be found in Iredell and others, an argumentativeness that in itself acknowledged that fundamental law had not previously been considered the kind of law enforceable in court. *Federalist 78* in general conveyed the impression that the power being defended was a routine and unexceptional one and that there existed greater agreement on this point than was in fact the case at the beginning of the 1790s.

Federalist 78 also devoted a good deal of attention to the analogy between judicial enforcement of the Constitution and judicial responsibility in ordi-

88. *Eakin* v. *Raub,* 12 Sergeant & Rawles (Pa.) 330, 356 (1825). Emphasis in original.
89. The closest Marshall came to an explicit discussion of this aim was in the first paragraph of the defense of judicial review in *Marbury* v. *Madison,* 5 U.S. (1 Cr.) 137, 176 (1803).

nary conflict-of-laws situations. This analogy was first made by Iredell, a fact adding, incidentally, additional evidence that he was the source for *Federalist 78*.[90] Hamilton expanded this part of Iredell's discussion and emphasized the positive law aspects of judicial review while omitting all parts of the argument that revealed its extraordinary character and political nature. Hamilton did not speak of the Constitution as a social contract, of the natural law basis of limited government, or of judicial enforcement as a substitute for revolution. There is no hint in *Federalist 78* that the American Constitution constituted public acknowledgment of any "dangerous and desperate" resource or that judicial enforcement of it was the exercise of an "awful" authority.

Beyond this, Hamilton's presentation, although following the familiar period 2 form, made a major advance in the positive law conception of judicial review. *Federalist 78* argued, first, that an act that violated the Constitution was void:

> There is no position which depends on clearer principles, than that every act of a delegated authority, contrary to the tenor of the commission under which it is exercised, is void. No legislative act, therefore, contrary to the Constitution, can be valid. To deny this, would be to affirm, that the deputy is greater than his principal; that the servant is above his master; that the representatives of the people are superior to the people themselves: that men acting by virtue of power, may do not only what their powers do not authorize, but what they forbid.[91]

In dealing with the contentious second question of the period 1 debate— whether judges could refuse to enforce an unconstitutional act—Hamilton alluded, as had no one else, to the issue of constitutional exposition:

> If it be said that the legislative body are themselves the constitutional judges of their own powers, and that the construction they put upon them is conclusive upon the other departments, it may be answered, that this cannot be the natural presumption, where it is not to be collected from any particular provisions in the Constitution. It is not otherwise to be supposed, that the Constitution could intend to enable the representatives of the people to substitute their *will* to that of their constituents. It is far more rational to suppose, that the courts were designed to be an intermediate body between the people and

90. Iredell's formulation of the conflict of laws analogy was as follows: "It is not that the judges are appointed arbiters, and to determine as it were upon any application, whether the Assembly have or have not violated the Constitution; but when an act is necessarily brought in judgment before them, they must, unavoidably, determine one way or another. If it is doubted whether a subsequent law repeals a former one, in a case judicially in question, the judges must decide this; and yet it might be said, if the Legislature meant it a repeal, and the judges determined it otherwise, they exercised a *negative* on the Legislature in resolving to keep a law in force which the Assembly had annihilated. This kind of objection, if applicable at all, will reach all judicial power whatever, since upon every abuse of it (and there is no power but what is liable to abuse) a similar inference may be drawn" (Iredell to Spaight, *Correspondence of Iredell*, ed. McRee, 2 : 173; emphasis in original).

91. *The Federalist*, 505–06.

the legislature, in order, among other things, to keep the latter within the limits assigned to their authority. The interpretation of the laws is the proper and peculiar province of the courts. A constitution is, in fact, and must be regarded by the judges, as a fundamental law. It therefore belongs to them to ascertain its meaning, as well as the meaning of any particular act proceeding from the legislative body. If there should happen to be an irreconcilable variance between the two, that which has the superior obligation and validity ought, of course, to be preferred; or, in other words, the Constitution ought to be preferred to the statute, the intention of the people to the intention of their agents.[92]

This paragraph includes the most sweeping claim of period 2 judicial review. Not only was fundamental law cognizable in court, but, as a consequence of its attribute as law, it belonged to the judges "to ascertain its meaning." It is likely that Marshall's assimilation of fundamental law to ordinary law owed much to this passage. The conclusion that Hamilton was here anticipating or contemplating modern judicial review or that he was claiming authority for authoritative judicial exposition of the Constitution would, however, be premature. When read from within the period 2 context, Hamilton's claim is no more than a stronger version of the period 2 contention that judges could refuse to enforce a concededly unconstitutional act. In following the standard format, the paragraph defending judicial review assumed the existence of an unconstitutional act—that "no legislative act . . . contrary to the Constitution, can be valid."[93] It addressed the period 1 contention that the legislators were nevertheless "the constitutional judges of their own powers." Hamilton repeated and reinforced Iredell's insistence that the Constitution was cognizable in court and subject, rightly, to judicial enforcement.

In evaluating Hamilton's position it is important to note that none of the period 2 statements that relied heavily on it interpreted *Federalist 78* as a sanction for judicial exposition of the Constitution. All defended judicial authority to "take notice of" the Constitution in the course of expounding ordinary law.[94] Supreme Court justices before Marshall who sanctioned judicial authority over legislation routinely coupled this sanction with enunciation of the doubtful case rule, a rule that is a denial of judicial authority to expound the Constitution.[95] Marshall himself, while developing this idea suggested by Hamilton in *Federalist 78*, refrained from making a claim to judicial application and interpretation of the Constitution in language even as direct as that of *Federalist 78*.[96] Nor was there any acknowledgment of judicial authority to

92. Ibid., 506. Emphasis in original.

93. Quoted above at n. 91. This is Hamilton's formulation of the first proposition of period 1 judicial review—that the legislature cannot violate the Constitution.

94. See above at nn. 70–74.

95. See *Hylton* v. *United States*, 3 U.S. (3 Dall.) 171, 173, 175 (1796); *Calder* v. *Bull*, 3 U.S. (3 Dall.) 386, 395, 399 (1798); *Cooper* v. *Telfair*, 4 U.S. (4 Dall.) 14, 18, 19 (1800); *Ogden* v. *Saunders*, 25 U.S. (12 Wheat.) 213, 270, 294 (1827); *Craig* v. *Missouri*, 29 U.S. (4 Pet.) 410, 444, 446, 458–59 (1830).

96. See the discussion below at nn. 101–14.

expound the Constitution, as judges routinely expound ordinary law, by any of Marshall's Supreme Court colleagues.[97] Every source save *Federalist 78* reflected, unambiguously, the period 2 understanding whereby the judicial refusal to execute an unconstitutional act was the defense of first principle stated in fundamental law, not the exposition of supreme ordinary law. Even if Hamilton intended something more, this statement in *Federalist 78*, by itself, did not achieve it.

Additional differences between *Federalist 78* and Marshall's judicial review have convinced me that whatever the precise scope of Hamilton's intent (and I am not confident that this can be identified as surely as can the intent of others) he did not anticipate modern judicial review. The first and most important difference is the absence of any mention of, or reliance on, the written constitution in *Federalist 78*. Hamilton's argument rested entirely on the need for judicial power to enforce the explicit limits contained in the Constitution. His defense of judicial review opened with the following statement:

> The complete independence of the courts of justice is peculiarly essential in a limited Constitution. By a limited Constitution, I understand one which contains certain specified exceptions to the legislative authority; such, for instance, as that it shall pass no bills of attainder, no *ex-post-facto* laws, and the like. Limitations of this kind can be preserved in practice no other way than through the medium of courts of justice, whose duty it must be to declare all acts contrary to the manifest tenor of the Constitution void. Without this, all the reservations of particular rights or privileges would amount to nothing.[98]

In a summary statement toward the end of the central part of *Federalist 78* he used the same language: "If, then, the courts of justice are to be considered as the bulwarks of a limited Constitution against legislative encroachments, this consideration will afford a strong argument for the permanent tenure of judicial offices."[99]

Next, in the concluding part of *Federalist 78,* Hamilton accepted the distinction between the injustice and the unconstitutionality of legislation and restricted judicial authority over legislation to the latter. In contemplation, likely, of the debtor relief legislation of the 1780s, Hamilton wrote:

> But it is not with a view to infractions of the Constitution only, that the independence of the judges may be an essential safeguard against the effects of occasional ill humors in the society. These sometimes extend no farther than to the injury of the private rights of particular classes of citizens, by unjust and partial laws. Here also the firmness of the judicial magistracy is of vast importance in mitigating the severity and confining the operation of such laws.[100]

97. See the discussion below, at nn. 118–59.
98. *The Federalist,* 505.
99. Ibid., 508.
100. Ibid., 509.

The distinction between unjust and unconstitutional laws was blurred irrevocably in Marshall's treatment of the Constitution and has remained problematic since. It was, however, an essential and totally intelligible part of periods 1 and 2 judicial review, and Hamilton treated it in these terms. He confined judicial authority over legislation to "infractions of the Constitution"; for unjust and partial laws the judges can only "mitigat[e their] severity and confin[e their] operation." This easy acceptance of the distinction between unjust and unconstitutional laws and the absence of any mention of or reliance on the written constitution indicate that whatever the precise scope of the judicial review Hamilton was contemplating, it lacked the crucial elements of Marshall's.

Hamilton's assertion that the courts' proper and peculiar province to interpret the laws included ascertaining the meaning of fundamental law was, nevertheless, of great significance. It was the second major step in transformation of fundamental law into supreme ordinary law, after the assertion of its cognizability in court, and obviously of great significance for Marshall. But in 1788 no conception of the Constitution as supreme ordinary law existed, and none was likely intended here. Clearly, none of Hamilton's contemporaries so interpreted *Federalist 78,* and Marshall did not effectuate transformation of fundamental law into supreme ordinary law by simple repetition of this contention. The full assimilation of fundamental law into ordinary law and the development of the judicial authority to expound the Constitution were forged in the doing—in the great opinions Marshall wrote after *Marbury.*

Period 3

Marbury opened period 3 in the evolution of judicial review, but, as we have already seen, it did so with a restatement of the period 2 argument. Marshall divided the issue into its two established parts. The first was "whether an act, repugnant to the constitution, can become the law of the land."[101] By 1803 the argument against legislative omnipotence hardly had to be made, but Marshall made it nevertheless. The first several paragraphs of the defense of judicial review in *Marbury* repeat the period 1 agreement that explicit fundamental law ended legislative omnipotence, that an unconstitutional act was indeed void. Marshall's only innovation was to stress the written character of American "superior," "paramount," and "fundamental" law.

The periods 1 and 2 rejection of legislative omnipotence had always been asserted in contemplation of a concededly unconstitutional act, as was the *Marbury* formulation. Marshall did not inquire whether an unconstitutional act could be valid law until after he declared void a section of the Judiciary Act of 1789. This latter action was acceptable within the boundaries of concurrent review. In any event, Marshall was under no more obligation to discuss who should determine the constitutionality of legislation than was any period 2 source.[102]

101. 5 U.S. (1 Cr.) 137, 176 (1803).
102. Failure to discuss this issue is the classic modern criticism of *Marbury.* See Bickel, *Least Dangerous Branch,* 3.

The second inquiry as stated in *Marbury* was "does [an act which is void] notwithstanding its invalidity, bind the courts, and oblige them to give it effect?"[103] This was the standard second question of the periods 1 and 2 debate. In responding, Marshall drew on the period 2 answers, particularly on Hamilton's and Tucker's formulations. The key paragraph of *Marbury* reads as follows:

> It is, emphatically, the province and duty of the judicial department, to say what the law is. Those who apply the rule to particular cases, must of necessity expound and interpret that rule. If two laws conflict with each other, the courts must decide on the operation of each. So, if a law be in opposition to the constitution; if both the law and the constitution apply to a particular case, so that the court must either decide that case, conformable to the law, disregarding the constitution; or conformable to the constitution, disregarding the law; the court must determine which of these conflicting rules governs the case: this is of the very essence of judicial duty. If then, the courts are to regard the constitution, and the constitution is superior to any ordinary act of the legislature, the constitution, and not such ordinary act, must govern the case to which they both apply.[104]

The first sentence combined key phrases from *Federalist 78* and Tucker's *Kamper* opinion.[105] In Tucker's opinion the word *law* referred to ordinary law, not the Constitution. Since Marshall's time the *law* mentioned in this first sentence has been universally read to include the Constitution. It is unlikely that any of Marshall's contemporaries read it that way. In the second sentence Marshall used the word *rule* rather than *law* or *Constitution*. In period 2 usage, *rule* was widely used to refer to the Constitution,[106] but Wilson had also used it to refer to legislative acts.[107] In this same second sentence Marshall described the judicial function as it applied to ordinary law. Later in the paragraph Marshall included both the Constitution and ordinary legislation within the term *rule*, and in the last sentence he spoke of the Constitution and ordinary law as "applying" to the same case. This ambiguous use of the term *rule* is as close as Marshall ever came to a direct statement of the modern *Marbury* doctrine that applying, expounding, and interpreting the law of the Constitution is part of the province and duty of the judicial department.[108] There is, actually, only the barest support for such a reading, and that only because of subsequent events. This key paragraph, aside from the enigmatic second sentence, is pure period 2 judicial review. The concluding sentence reaf-

103. 5 U.S. (1 Cr.) 177 (1803).
104. Ibid., 177–78.
105. Quoted above at nn. 92 and 70, respectively.
106. See Judge Pendleton in *Commonwealth* v. *Caton*, 4 Call (Va.) 5, 17 (1782); James Wilson, *Lectures on the Law, Works of Wilson*, ed. McCloskey, 1 : 330; Judge Tucker in *Kamper* v. *Hawkins*, 1 Va. Cases 20, 77 (1793); Justice Paterson in *VanHorne's Lessee* v. *Dorrance*, 2 U.S. (2 Dall.) 304, 309 (1795).
107. *Lectures on the Law, Works of Wilson*, ed. McCloskey, 1 : 330.
108. For statements of the modern *Marbury* doctrine, see *Cooper* v. *Aaron*, 358 U.S. 1, 18 (1955) and *United States* v. *Nixon*, 418 U.S. 683, 703 (1974).

firmed Court authority "to regard" the Constitution and thereby the key period 2 innovation, the rejection of Blackstone.

The rest of *Marbury* also maintained period 2 analysis and language. Marshall asserted the right of courts "to regard," "to [look] into," and "to examin[e]" the Constitution; he denied that courts "must close their eyes on the constitution."[109] In asserting that "the constitution is to be considered, in court, as a paramount law,"[110] Marshall was only denying that the Constitution was a rule to the legislature only. His examples of clear constitutional violations practically duplicated a section of Tucker's *Kamper* opinion.[111] Marshall's argument on the judicial oath was intended to demonstrate "that the framers of the constitution contemplated that instrument as a rule for the government of courts, as well as of the legislature."[112] The inability of the judicial oath to sustain the judicial supremacy of period 3 is a staple of the modern criticism of *Marbury*. But in context it merely repeated the period 2 claim of the equality of the branches in rejection of the legislative supremacy of period 1. The concluding paragraph made the same point: "Thus, the particular phraseology of the constitution of the United States confirms and strengthens the principle, supposed to be essential to all written constitutions, that a law repugnant to the constitution is void; and that *courts, as well as other departments*, are bound by that instrument."[113]

Marbury departed from the period 2 defense of judicial power over unconstitutional legislation in only two ways, neither of them recognizable at the time. The first was the hidden suggestion that the province and duty of the judicial department included saying what the law of the Constitution is; the second departure was his liberal references to the "written constitution." There were almost as many references to the "written constitution" in *Marbury* as in all period 2 discussions combined.[114] As they appeared in *Marbury*, however, these references to the "written constitution" were bland. They carried neither the period 2 meaning of explicit fundamental law nor the period 3 meaning of supreme ordinary law. They served more than anything else to associate the judicial refusal to execute an unconstitutional act with a written constitution and to prepare the ground for judicial exposition of the text of a written constitution that was to begin at some opportune time in the future.

The Rules for Statutory Interpretation. *Marbury* accommodated modern judicial review but by itself did not lay claim to or establish it. Modern judicial review was forged in the character of Marshall's opinions in the contract clause and

109. 5 U.S. (1 Cr.) 137, 178–79 (1803).
110. Ibid., 178.
111. Compare ibid., 179, and 1 Va. Cases 20, 79–81 (1793).
112. 5 U.S. (1 Cr.) 137, 179–80 (1803).
113. Ibid., 180. Emphasis added.
114. The word is used nine times in *Marbury*. I have found it ten times in period 2 discussions: twice in Iredell to Spaight, *Correspondence of Iredell*, ed. McRee, 2 : 173, 174; twice in Tucker's *Kamper* opinion, 1 Va. Cases 20, 77, 78 (1793); once in Nelson's *Kamper* opinion, ibid., 23; five times in Paterson's *VanHorne's Lessee* opinion, 2 U.S. (2 Dall.) 304, 308, 314 (1795).

federalism cases of the 1810s and 1820s. The centerpiece of Marshall's constitutional adjudication was an unprecedented application of the rules for statutory interpretation to the Constitution for the purpose of determining the constitutionality of legislation. According to the rules for statutory interpretation, judges determine the meaning of a statute by first seeking the meaning of its words and of its words in context and then moving to the statute's intent or spirit if analysis of the words proves inadequate. The end point of statutory interpretation is the authoritative pronouncement of the meaning of the statute, or "what the law is." Through this interpretation, policy considerations of the sort central to legislation enter adjudication. But law enforcement requires law's authoritative exposition, and under the separation of powers, responsibility for that exposition is assigned to the judiciary. The policy component in judicial application of ordinary law is thus an inescapable part of the rule of law.

In a reflection of its status as fundamental law, different in kind from ordinary law, period 2 judges and Marshall's Supreme Court colleagues approached the Constitution in precisely the opposite order from that followed in statutory interpretation. The meaning of the Constitution, for the purpose of refusing to execute an unconstitutional act, was determined from its spirit or intent, and its words were examined to support an otherwise determined intent. The written constitutional text, during period 2 and into period 3, served to identify which preexisting first political principles were part of American fundamental law and thus to be enforced against the legislature. The precise meaning of these preexisting principles was to be found in common consent or applicable English precedent. If these sources were insufficient to fix the meaning in a particular case, the doubtful case rule came into operation and judges were to respect the legislative exposition of the Constitution embodied in the statute. This respect reflected the view that, short of the concededly unconstitutional act, the specific interpretation of fundamental law was a policy issue and properly subject for determination by democratic process. Unlike the case in ordinary law, authoritative exposition of fundamental law was unnecessary for its integrity. Its principles retained all their vitality, while contending, legitimate interpretations vied for acceptance.

Marshall himself, however, not only applied the rules for statutory interpretation to the Constitution, but did so with no acknowledgment of its novelty or justification for departing from existing practice. In this innovative and successful application of ordinary law technique, he took for the Court a special authority to expound the Constitution, to say what the law of the Constitution is. This was the significant step—obliquely hinted at in *Marbury* and put into practice at the outer limits of the doubtful case rule under conditions of basic political stability—that transformed the Constitution from politically binding fundamental law into legally binding supreme ordinary law, and judicial review from an extraordinary political act into a routine legal one. In the process, the Constitution's restraints on majority will came to be those of supreme ordinary law, subject in all cases to adjudication in court. With this came the judicial policy-making and judicial supremacy that remain the controversial core of modern judicial review.

A variety of factors have helped obscure from subsequent generations the very existence and thereby the significance of Marshall's innovations. We have already examined the first—the conformity of *Marbury* to period 2 judicial review and it simultaneous accommodation of period 3 practice. The second is the relative paucity of opinions by Marshall's Supreme Court colleagues. This is not, however, an accident of history but additional evidence of Marshall's unacknowledged single-handed transformation of judicial review from enforcement of fundamental law into exposition of supreme written law. There is no question that Marshall alone was responsible for ending the practice of seriatim opinion writing on the Supreme Court. According to Justice William Johnson's testimony even acceptance of concurring and dissenting opinions was a compromise on Marshall's part.[115] In eliminating other opinions Marshall eliminated the display of alternate approaches to constitutional adjudication, focused maximum attention on his own approach, and generated additional pressure on members of the Court for agreement with his own positions. His masterful style is so dominating that hardly anyone reads the few other opinions that do exist, and they are certainly not read carefully. When they are, they display a consistently different approach to the process of constitutional adjudication, regardless of whether or not the justices writing them agreed with the result in particular cases.

Finally, Marshall's innovation in constitutional method was masked under a conformity to period 2 results. With one trivial exception,[116] the laws invalidated by the Marshall Court were found either to have violated the contract clause or to be barred by the principles of federalism. For Marshall's colleagues, the contract clause cases were understood as vested rights cases in period 2 terms; thus, the contract clause was the explicit constitutional provision that declared publicly that the principle of vested rights was part of fundamental law. American judges consequently could "take notice of" this principle and, as part of their political responsibility to the people, enforce it against legislation to the contrary. For them, the outcome of particular contract clause cases depended not on judicial exposition of the clause but on some combination of natural law and common law precedent that delineated the scope of vested rights. In most cases, Marshall's exposition of the contract clause text and his colleagues' application of natural and common law precedent led to the same conclusion, and there was no disagreement on holdings.[117] The federalism cases did not pose the issue of judicial power as sharply as did the contract clause cases because the Constitution explicitly gave the Court authority to resolve conflicts over federalism. Nevertheless, as we shall see below, differences in approach to fulfilling this constitutionally sanctioned power still

115. See William Johnson to Thomas Jefferson, December 10, 1822, quoted in Donald G. Morgan, *Justice William Johnson: The First Dissenter* (Columbia: University of South Carolina Press, 1954), 181–82.

116. See *Craig v. Missouri*, 29 U.S. (4 Pet.) 410 (1830), in which certificates issued by Missouri were stuck down as bills of credit prohibited by the Constitution.

117. The most notable exception was *Ogden v. Saunders*, 25 U.S. (12 Wheat.) 213 (1827). *Craig v. Missouri*, 29 U.S. (4 Pet.) 410 (1830), was decided by a 4–3 vote, with Justices Johnson, Thompson, and McLean dissenting.

remained, and these differences paralleled those that are more striking in the contract clause cases. The agreement on holdings in the contract clause and federalism cases, the fact that few laws were struck down on other grounds, the elimination of seriatim opinions, the forcefulness of Marshall's opinions, and our neglect of the few opinions written by other justices have all combined to obscure the degree to which Marshall deviated from existing practice.

In focusing on Marshall's application to the Constitution of the rules for statutory interpretation, I am not suggesting that no judicial construction of the Constitution had ever taken place before Marshall. On the contrary, it was done all the time by members of all branches of government in circumstances where constitutional words were not self-executing and their intent was unclear. Had this not been the case, Marshall's actions would have been too great a departure from existing practice to be sustained. *It had never, however, been done or claimed by the judiciary as part of the authority to refuse to execute an unconstitutional act, and as a way of fixing authoritatively the meaning of the Constitution over a credible legislative exposition to the contrary.* Nor had it ever been linked, however ambiguously, to the exclusively judicial responsibility to say what the law is.

The Period 3 Cases. The contrast between Marshall's and his colleagues' opinions begins with *Fletcher* v. *Peck,* the first of the contract clause cases.[118] In *Fletcher,* Marshall held that the state lacked power to pass the challenged statute "either by general principles which are common to our free institutions, or by the particular provisions of the Constitution of the United States."[119] As a prelude to this conclusion he had engaged in extensive discussion of the principle of vested rights and detailed exposition of the contract clause text. *Fletcher* was, thereby, the link between periods 2 and 3 judicial review, its textual exposition masked by a parallel inquiry into first principles. Marshall wrote for a unanimous Court in *Fletcher,* but Justice Johnson's concurrence disavowed the conclusions reached through Marshall's textual exposition of the contract clause. Johnson's decision rested on "a general principle, on the reason and nature of things: a principle which will impose laws even on the Deity."[120] In subsequent cases Marshall determined the meaning of the Constitution exclusively through textual exposition,[121] while his colleagues maintained their reliance on the principle of vested rights,[122] common law precedent,[123]

118. 10 U.S. (6 Cr.) 87 (1810).

119. Ibid., 139.

120. Ibid., 143.

121. Marshall invoked natural law only one other time, in dissent in *Ogden* v. *Saunders,* 25 U.S. (12 Wheat.) 213, 344–47 (1827). It is unlikely he would have done so if he were writing for a majority.

122. *Terrett* v. *Taylor,* 13 U.S. (9 Cr.) 43, 52 (1815). Court opinion by Justice Joseph Story. Discussed below at n. 126 and accompanying text.

123. *Dartmouth College* v. *Woodward,* 17 U.S. (4 Wheat.) 518, 654, 666 (1819). Concurring opinions by Justices Bushrod Washington and Story. Discussed below at nn. 129–31 and accompanying text.

or the spirit of the Constitution.[124] In its dual reliance on first principle and textual exposition *Fletcher* was a microcosm of period 3 judicial review. Marshall used textual exposition to reach results identical or comparable to those arrived at by others through period 2 means.

The next contract clause case with an opinion by a judge other than Marshall was *Terrett* v. *Taylor*.[125] In this case the Court invalidated a Virginia statute that had attempted to take state control of church property. Joseph Story wrote the Court opinion, invalidating the legislation and relying on "the principles of natural justice, upon the fundamental laws of every free government, upon the spirit and the letter of the constitution of the United States, and upon the decisions of most respectable judicial tribunals."[126] This order reflects the period 2 understanding and the primacy of first principles and the spirit or intent of the Constitution over its letter. There is not only no textual analysis in the entire opinion; there is no mention of the specific clause or "letter" of the Constitution that was violated.

Dartmouth College v. *Woodward,* decided in 1819, was the next major contract clause case.[127] Dartmouth College had been chartered by the English king in 1769. In 1816 the New Hampshire legislature changed the terms of the charter and attempted to bring the college under public control. The issue argued in Court was whether the U.S. Constitution imposed a bar to this assumption of state control, and an almost unanimous Court agreed that the contract clause constituted such a bar. Marshall wrote the Court opinion, holding that the charter was a contract and that it was a contract within the meaning of the constitutional prohibition.

Whether or not the charter was a contract within the protection of the Constitution hinged on the answers to a variety of questions relating to the law of contracts. Marshall examined these issues at great length, but without citing any precedents aside from a few references to Blackstone. His opinion leaves the impression that the issues were being thought through for the first time. He then linked the conclusions he had reached to the Constitution in a protracted discussion downplaying original intent and defending a determination of constitutional meaning through exposition of its text:

> This is plainly a contract to which the donors, the trustees, and the crown
> . . . were the original parties. It is a contract made on a valuable consideration.
> It is a contract for the security and disposition of property. It is a contract, on
> the faith of which real and personal estate has been conveyed to the corpo-
> ration. It is then a contract within the letter of the constitution, and within its
> spirit also, unless . . . [its peculiar attributes] . . . shall create a particular ex-
> ception, taking this case out of the prohibition contained in the constitution.
>
> It is more than possible, that the preservation of rights of this description
> was not particularly in the view of the framers . . . when [this] clause . . . was

124. See Justice Johnson's characterization of the *Sturges* opinion in *Ogden* v. *Saunders,* 25 U.S. (12 Wheat.) 213, 272–73 (1827).

125. 13 U.S. (9 Cr.) 43 (1815).

126. Ibid., 52.

127. 17 U.S. (4 Wheat.) 518 (1819).

introduced. . . . But although a particular and a rare case may not, in itself, be of sufficient magnitude to induce a rule, yet it must be governed by the rule, when established, unless some plain and strong reason for excluding it can be given. It is not enough to say, that this particular case was not in the mind of the Convention, when the article was framed, nor of the American people, when it was adopted. It is necessary to go farther, and to say that, had this particular case been suggested, the language would have been so varied, as to exclude it, or it would have been made a special exception. The case being within the words of the rule, must be within its operation likewise, unless there be something in the literal construction so obviously absurd, or mischievous, or repugnant to the general spirit of the instrument, as to justify those who expound the constitution in making it an exception.

On what safe and intelligible ground can this exception stand? There is no expression in the constitution, no sentiment delivered by its contemporaneous expounders, which would justify us in making it. In the absence of all authority of this kind, is there, in the nature and reason of the case itself, that which would sustain a construction of the constitution, not warranted by its words?[128]

This kind of analysis has become so commonplace that it does not immediately appear noteworthy. But in 1819 it was by no means routine. The meaning of the Constitution, for the purposes of judicial review, was thought to be established by its spirit, by the intent of the framers who framed it and the people who adopted it, and by the sentiments of its contemporaneous expounders. Marshall, in this passage, acknowledged these key components of his contemporaries' conception of constitutional law. But in the act of making this acknowledgment, he subordinated intent to constitutional words, pursued a literal interpretation of those words separate from intent, and in passing, laid claim to a judicial authority to expound the constitutional words.

Marshall's procedure takes on more significance when the Court opinion is contrasted with the concurring opinions of Justices Story and Bushrod Washington. There were no substantive differences to speak of in the three *Dartmouth College* opinions, only one of approach. There was, first, nothing comparable in Story's and Washington's opinions to Marshall's emphasis on the words of the Constitution and their literal construction. For Story and Washington the nature of the Dartmouth College charter, the substantive law of the Constitution, and the unconstitutionality of the New Hampshire statute were established from sources outside the Constitution—from English common law precedent and the doctrine of vested rights.

Story began his opinion with a discussion of the status of the original charter. Unlike Marshall's it involved discussion and citation of over a dozen English cases. Story then turned to the question of whether the college charter was protected by the Constitution and opened this inquiry by remarking that "the constitution certainly did not mean to create any new obligations. . . . On the other hand . . . the constitution did intend to preserve all the obligatory

128. Ibid., 643–45.

force of contracts, which they have by the general principles of law.[129] These general principles of law were, again, those in the existing law of contracts. Story proceeded to cover the same ground covered by Marshall and to reach the same conclusions. Only he did so through examination of English precedent, paying no particular attention to the text of the contract clause. To have established the substance of the general principles of the law of contracts was to have brought the charter within constitutional protection.

Washington's opinion, although not containing as exhaustive an examination of English precedents as did Story's, placed heavy reliance on them, particularly on the leading case, *Philips* v. *Bury:*

> It has been insisted in the argument at the bar, that Dartmouth College was a mere civil corporation, created for a public purpose, the public being deeply interested in the education of its youth; and that, consequently, the charter was as much under the control of the government of New-Hampshire, as if the corporation had concerned the government of a town or city. But it has been shown, that the authorities are all the other way. There is not a case to be found which contradicts the doctrine laid down in the case of Philips *v.* Bury, viz. that a college founded by an individual, or individuals, is a private charity, subject to the government and visitation of the founder, and not to the unlimited control of the government.[130]

Washington also gave considerable attention to *Terrett* v. *Taylor* and, in the process, focused on the vested rights components of *Dartmouth* more than did the other opinions:

> The case Terrett v. Taylor . . . fully supports the distinction above stated, between civil and private corporations, and is entirely in point. . . . It is denied, that [the legislature] has power to repeal statutes creating private corporations, or confirming to them property already acquired under the faith of previous laws; and that it can, by such repeal, vest the property of such corporations in the state, or dispose of the same to such purposes as it may please, without the consent or default of the corporators. Such a law, it is declared, would be repugnant both to the spirit and the letter of the constitution of the United States.[131]

Story, too, it should be noted, cited *Terrett* v. *Taylor* as well as *Fletcher* v. *Peck.* Marshall, on the other hand, ignored not only English precedents but the American ones as well. He summarized his own *Dartmouth* argument with the remark: "This opinion appears to us to be equally supported by reason, and by the former decisions of this Court."[132]

The two insolvency law cases, *Sturges* v. *Crowninshield*[133] and *Ogden* v. *Saunders*,[134] were also understood by Marshall's colleagues to be vested rights cases,

129. Ibid., 683.
130. Ibid., 665.
131. Ibid., 663–64.
132. Ibid., 650.
133. 17 U.S. (4 Wheat.) 122 (1819).
134. 25 U.S. (12 Wheat.) 213 (1827).

only here there was not the same agreement that vested rights had in fact been invaded. In *Sturges* the Court invalidated an insolvency law applied to a contract entered into before passage of the law. Although Marshall wrote for a unanimous Court this unanimity masked substantial disagreement. Nine years after *Sturges*, Justice Johnson, in *Ogden* v. *Saunders*, commented that the decision in *Sturges* partook "as much of a compromise as of a legal adjudication."[135] In *Ogden,* when a similar bankruptcy act was applied to a contract entered into after the passage of the law, a Court majority upheld the law over Marshall's dissent. This latter decision contains four separate opinions from the majority justices.

The defense of the constitutionality of insolvency laws rested, in standard period 2 fashion, on invocation of constitutional intent. The contract clause, it was argued, was intended to prohibit the widely condemned debtor legislation prevalent under the Articles of Confederation. This included paper money legislation, legislation making worthless property valid as payment of debts, and legislation extending the time schedule for payment of debts. Bankruptcy laws, on the other hand, had a long and unchallenged history as necessary and beneficial legislation. They were so widespread and uncontroversial that it was unimaginable that an intent to prohibit them would have been manifested by anything less than an explicit constitutional prohibition.[136]

Marshall's *Sturges* opinion recapitulated and eventually rejected this argument. Before doing so, however, he attempted to dispose of the constitutionality of bankruptcy laws by a straightforward textual analysis: "In discussing the question whether a state is prohibited from passing such a law as this, our first inquiry is into the meaning of words [of the Constitution] in common use. What is the obligation of a contract? and what will impair it?"[137] He then proceeded to define the words *contract, obligation of contract,* and *impair.* His definitions led him to conclude that the law violated the Constitution: "The words of the constitution, then, are express and incapable of being misunderstood. They admit of no variety of construction, and are acknowledged to apply to that species of contract, an engagement between man and man for the payment of money, which has been entered into by these parties."[138] After acknowledging that despite this clarity in the meaning of the words, dispute remained, he turned to the opposition arguments. The one

> which has been pressed most earnestly at the bar, is, that although all legislative acts which discharge the obligation of a contract without performance are within the very words of the constitution, yet an insolvent act, containing this principle, is not within its spirit, because such acts have been passed by colonial and state legislatures from the first settlement of the country, and because we know from the history of the times that the mind of the conven-

135. Ibid., 272.
136. See *Sturges* v. *Crowinshield,* 17 U.S. (4 Wheat.) 122, 202 (1819), and *Ogden* v. *Saunders,* 25 U.S. (12 Wheat.) 213, 265–69, 286–90, 303–07, 328–31 (1827).
137. 17 U.S. (4 Wheat.) 122, 197 (1819).
138. Ibid., 198.

tion was directed to other laws . . . not to this, which is beneficial in its operation.[139]

Marshall prefaced his reply to this argument by observing: "Before discussing this argument, it may not be improper to premise that, although the spirit of an instrument, especially of a constitution, is to be respected not less than its letter, yet the spirit is to be collected chiefly from its words."[140] This statement, almost hidden in the middle of a long opinion, is the heart of Marshall's innovation in constitutional interpretation. For the most part he simply followed this procedure, establishing the meaning of the Constitution from its words and subordinating spirit to text. He called attention to it openly only three times, in cases where there was disagreement on the meaning of the Constitution.[141]

Marshall continued, in *Sturges,* to defend the primacy of constitutional words over intent, arguing, in part:

It would be dangerous in the extreme to infer from extrinsic circumstances, that a case for which the words of an instrument expressly provide, shall be exempted from its operation. . . . If, in any case, the plain meaning of a provision, not contradicted by any other provision in the same instrument, is to be disregarded, because we believe that the framers of that instrument could not intend what they say, it must be one in which the absurdity and injustice of applying the provision to the case would be so monstrous that all mankind would, without hesitation, unite in rejecting the application.[142]

The rest of Marshall's *Sturges* opinion attempts to demonstrate through textual analysis of the Constitution the unsoundness of propositions about intent drawn from claims about common understanding at the time of the framing. It is a masterpiece of constitutional exposition that not only shows why a literal application of the words of the contract clause would not be absurd and unjust but, by its existence, constitutes a forceful precedent for such exposition.

None of the justices in the four majority opinions in *Ogden* v. *Saunders* disavowed the holding of *Sturges.* On the contrary, several, in defending bankruptcy laws applied to contracts entered into after passage of the act, reaffirmed their agreement that the Constitution did prohibit retrospectively operating bankruptcy laws. According to Justice Johnson, invalidation of

---

139. Ibid., 202.

140. Ibid.

141. The three cases are *Sturges* v. *Crowninshield,* ibid.; *Ogden* v. *Saunders,* 25 U.S. (12 Wheat.) 213, 332 (1827); and *Brown* v. *Maryland,* 25 U.S. (12 Wheat.) 419, 437 (1827). *Brown* was a federalism case, and in this opinion Marshall made the fullest statement of the applicability of the rules of statutory interpretation: "In performing the delicate and important duty of construing clauses in the constitution of our country, which involve conflicting powers of the government of the Union, and of the respective States, it is proper to take a view of the literal meaning of the words to be expounded, of their connection with other words, and of the general objects to be accomplished by the prohibitory clause, or by the grant of power."

142. 17 U.S. (4 Wheat.) 122, 202–03 (1819).

bankruptcy laws limited to anterior contracts could "do no harm, but, in fact, imposed a restriction conceived in the true spirit of the constitution."[143] This is as good a description of the Marshall Court's entire contract clause litigation as it is of the *Sturges* opinion. As long as Marshall's exposition of the words of the contract clause coincided with his colleagues' conception of the true spirit of the Constitution, he could hold the Court together. While his colleagues were defending vested rights protected in the fundamental law, he was applying and interpreting the text of the supreme law of the land.

For the majority justices in *Ogden* v. *Saunders* a bankruptcy law passed before a contract was made did not impair the obligation of that contract or affect rights vested by that contract. Their central argument was that the municipal law of the state constituted the obligation of contracts safeguarded in the Constitution. This municipal law could "affect and control the validity, construction, evidence, remedy, performance and discharge of the contract."[144] A bankruptcy law passed before a contract was made formed part of that contract and could not be said to impair its obligation.

In defending their interpretation of the Constitution, the majority justices invoked original intent and common usage. Justice Washington prefaced his analysis by declaring, "I have examined both sides of this great question with the most sedulous care, and the most anxious desire to discover which of them, when adopted, would be most likely to fulfill the intentions of those who framed the constitution of the United States."[145] He then defended his understanding of the obligation of contract by appealing to common understanding:

> It is so regarded by all the civilized nations of the world, and is enforced by the tribunals of those nations according to its own forms. . . . This law, which accompanies the contract, as forming a part of it, is regarded and enforced everywhere, whether it affect the validity, construction, or discharge of the contract. It is upon this principle of universal law, that the discharge of the contract, or one of the parties to it, by the bankrupt laws of the country where it was made, operates as a discharge everywhere.[146]

Neither Washington nor any of his colleagues in the majority followed Marshall's stipulations in *Dartmouth* and *Sturges* and subordinated intent to constitutional words or asked first whether the particular case fell within the reach of those words. All relied on the existing law of contracts, and two of the four justices invoked the doubtful case rule,[147] Justice Smith Thompson, in a second majority opinion, repeated Justice Washington's argument on the meaning of the obligation of contract and concluded that "this doctrine is universally recognized, both in the English and American courts."[148] Justice Johnson,

143. 25 U.S. (12 Wheat.) 213, 273 (1827).
144. Justice Washington, ibid., 259.
145. Ibid., 256.
146. Ibid., 259–60.
147. Justice Washington, ibid., 270; Justice Thompson, ibid., 294.
148. Ibid., 299.

as was often the case, provided the most direct contrast to Marshall's analysis. He not only appealed to history and common understanding to determine the meaning of the Constitution but explicitly criticized Marshall's literal analysis. After giving his own formulation of the majority argument, he suggested, "It appears to me, that a great part of the difficulties of the cause, arise from not giving sufficient weight to the general intent of this clause in the constitution, and subjecting it to a severe literal construction, which would be better adapted to special pleadings." [149]

Later in his opinion he criticized Marshall's approach even more sharply. After stating his reliance on the "whole history of the times" and "contemporaneous exposition" of the Constitution by the founding generation to sustain the constitutionality of the bankruptcy law, he continued: "If it be objected to the views which I have taken of this subject, that they imply a departure from the direct and literal meaning of terms, in order to substitute an artificial or complicated exposition; my reply is, that the error is on the other side." [150]

Although the *Ogden* majority relied primarily on original intent to determine the meaning of the Constitution, they did not disavow all textual analysis. But they used the text to bolster a previously determined intent rather than as a guide to that intent. The majority reliance on the constitutional text was not an inquiry into the meaning of particular words but an analysis of the relationship of whole clauses. Greatest reliance was placed on the fact that the contract clause was placed together with the prohibitions on bills of attainder and ex post facto laws. These provisions, it was argued, were linked by their common subject matter of retrospective laws, thereby providing additional evidence that the framers intended the contract clause to be applied only to retrospectively operating bankruptcy laws. [151]

Aside from laws invalidated as violations of the contract clause, the laws struck down most often by the Marshall Court were state laws adjudged to invade national authority. This kind of judicial review was authorized by the supremacy clause, and it was here, in connection with federalism and this explicit grant of power, that the Constitution was referred to as the supreme law of the land. [152] This authorization made the federalism litigation significantly different from all other constitutional adjudication. As the authorized arbiter of conflicts over federalism, the Court was obliged to make final determinations of law, including the law of the Constitution, in all cases. The Court was thereby obliged to give authoritative exposition to the meaning of the constitutional text, and the doubtful case rule was never invoked in this context.

Furthermore, unlike the judicial review exercised outside the federalism context, there was no preexisting content attached to the key constitutional

149. Ibid., 286.

150. Ibid., 290.

151. Justice Washington, ibid., 265–67; Justice Johnson, ibid., 286; Justice Thompson, ibid., 303–04.

152. For a chronology of changes in the wording of the supremacy clause made at the Constitutional Convention see *Records of the Convention*, ed. Farrand, 2 : 28–29, 389, 603.

provisions invoked in these cases. Non-federalism-related judicial review, in both the state and federal courts, had dealt almost exclusively with either denials of trial by jury or invasions of vested rights. The supremacy clause, the necessary and proper clause, and the commerce clause had no comparable history but were devised for the newly constructed American regime. In resolving conflict under these constitutional provisions, judges both were authorized to fix the meaning of the text and were of necessity thrown more on their own resources than was otherwise the case.

Although these attributes of the federalism cases might be thought to eliminate the differences between Marshall's and his colleagues' approaches to the Constitution, this is not the case. Differences parallel to those evident in the contract clause cases also appear in the federalism cases, where Marshall continued to approach the Constitution the way judges approach statutes. He stressed the meaning of words and moved from words to words in context and only then to intent. There are fewer contrasting concurring and dissenting opinions in these cases, but in the main one, Johnson's concurrence in *Gibbons* v. *Ogden,* we find the same concentration on intent as the key to the meaning of the Constitution and an even sharper denigration of the words.

Marshall started his analysis of the commerce clause in *Gibbons* by suggesting that "to ascertain the extent of the power it becomes necessary to settle the meaning of the word." [153] He followed this with several pages devoted to the meaning of *commerce* and followed that by an analysis of the meaning of *among.* This is, perhaps, the high point of Marshall's textual exegesis of the Constitution:

> The subject to which the power is next applied, is to commerce "among the several States." The word "among" means intermingled with. A thing which is among others, is intermingled with them. Commerce among the States, cannot stop at the external boundary line of each State, but may be introduced into the interior.
>
> It is not intended to say that these words comprehend that commerce which is completely internal, which is carried on between man and man in a State, or between different parts of the same State, and which does not extend to or affect other states. . . .
>
> Comprehensive as the word "among" is, it may very properly be restricted to that commerce which concerns more States than one. . . . The genius and character of the whole government seem to be, that its action is to be applied to all the external concerns of the nation, and to those internal concerns which affect the States generally; but not to those which are completely within a particular State, which do not affect other States, and with which it is not necessary to interfere, for the purpose of executing some of the general powers of the government. [154]

Johnson's concurrence, in contrast, opened with a disavowal of the need for extensive constitutional construction:

153. *Gibbons* v. *Ogden,* 22 U.S. (9 Wheat.) 1, 189 (1824).
154. Ibid., 194–95.

In attempts to construe the constitution, I have never found much benefit resulting from the inquiry, whether the whole, or any part of it, is to be construed strictly, or literally. The simple, classical, precise, yet comprehensive language, in which it is couched, leaves, at most, but very little latitude for construction; and when its intent and meaning is discovered, nothing remains but to execute the will of those who made it, in the best manner to effect the purpose intended.[155]

From here he moved to a statement of constitutional purpose couched in exceedingly broad terms:

The great and paramount purpose, was to unite this mass of wealth and power, for the protection of the humblest individual; his rights, civil and political, his interests and prosperity, are the sole *end*; the rest are nothing but the *means*. But the principal of those means, one so essential as to approach nearer the characteristics of an end, was the independence and harmony of the States, that they may the better subserve the purposes of cherishing and protecting the respective families of this great republic.[156]

To make this general statement more specific he turned to the history of the Confederation and the movement to replace the Articles of Confederation. In Johnson's view dissatisfaction with the condition of commercial life was the chief source of unhappiness under the Articles, and, by universal agreement, was to be remedied by giving the national government exclusive power over commerce:

The history of the times will, therefore, sustain the opinion, that the grant of power over commerce, if intended to be commensurate with the evils existing, and the purpose of remedying those evils, could be only commensurate with the power of the States over the subject. And this opinion is supported by a very remarkable evidence of the general understanding of the whole American people, when the grant was made.

There was not a State in the Union, in which there did not, at that time, exist a variety of commercial regulations, concerning which it is too much to suppose, that the whole ground covered by those regulations was immediately assumed by actual legislation, under the authority of the Union. But where was the existing statute on this subject, that a State attempted to execute? or by what State was it ever thought necessary to repeal those statutes? By common consent, those laws dropped lifeless from their statute books, for want of the sustaining power, that had been relinquished to Congress.[157]

Johnson's reliance on "common consent," "the history of the times," and "contemporaneous and continued assent"[158] continued the thrust of his constitutional analysis established in the contract clause cases. It was only after he

155. Ibid., 223.
156. Ibid. Emphasis in original.
157. Ibid., 225–26.
158. Ibid., 229.

established the meaning of the commerce clause by inquiry into intent that he turned to the text:

> And the plain and direct import of the words of the grant, is consistent with this general understanding.
>
> The words of the constitution are: "Congress shall have power to regulate commerce with foreign nations, and among the several states, and with the Indian tribes."
>
> It is not material, in my view of the subject, to inquire whether the article *a* or *the* should be prefixed to the word "power." Either, or neither, will produce the same result: if either, it is clear that the article *the* would be the proper one, since the next preceding grant of power is certainly exclusive, to wit: "to borrow money on the credit of the United States." But mere verbal criticism I reject.
>
> My opinion is founded on the application of the words of the grant to the subject of it.[159]

Johnson not only reversed Marshall's order, subordinating constitutional words to constitutional intent or general understanding, but ridiculed what he obviously regarded as an inappropriate literalism.

THE SUPREME LAW OF THE LAND

The differences in approach to the determination of constitutionality, for the purposes of judicial review, between Marshall and his colleagues were not random, but followed from his colleagues' adherence to the original distinction between fundamental law and ordinary law and from Marshall's attempt to obliterate that distinction. The search for the meaning of the Constitution in the original intent and a few great principles reflected the position that beyond identification of a realistically discoverable intent and of those few principles, constitutional exposition was not a judicial responsibility. The application of fundamental law to particular circumstances was considered to be a subject for general discussion and political determination. When judges took it upon themselves to refuse to execute an unconstitutional act, they were bound by the strict meaning of constitutionality and the doubtful case rule conscientiously applied. When they were expressly obliged to ascertain the meaning of the Constitution in federalism cases, they turned directly to evidence of intent.

Marshall succeeded in his attempt by taking existing doctrinal raw materials and, with consummate skill, redirecting them to other purposes. By the time he came to the Court, the judicial refusal to enforce an unconstitutional act was well established and beyond controversy. Nor was judicial exposition of the constitutional text Marshall's innovation, foisted on a compliant Court.

159. Ibid., 226–27. Emphasis in original.

Precedents for both existed, but what was unprecedented was the *simultaneous* exposition of the constitutional text *and* invalidation of legislation supported by a plausible legislative construction to the contrary. In linking the two, Marshall asserted, in the doing, a judicial claim to be the authoritative expounder of the Constitution, analogous to its function with respect to ordinary law. It was the first assertion of such a claim, and it was made with no overt acknowledgment or defense of its propriety.

Marshall applied not only the rules of statutory interpretation to the Constitution but also the logic of the lawyer and the form of the legal argument. He insisted on the primacy of the meaning of words and relied for the determination of constitutionality on a process of analytic reasoning. Furthermore, in addition to changing the quality of the judicial refusal to execute an unconstitutional act, Marshall also provided more occasions for the exercise of judicial review. Before Marshall, this was a "delicate and awful" act, reserved for the clearest violation of principle. By invalidating legislation that could be plausibly defended, as in *Dartmouth* and *Sturges,* and in arriving at this determination through legal rather than political rhetoric, Marshall made judicial enforcement of the Constitution increasingly ordinary and unexceptional. Also of importance here was the constitutional grant of power to the judiciary in federalism cases. This increased the occasions for judicial consideration of the Constitution and for Marshall's application to it of the rules for statutory interpretation.

Marshall's audacity was a gamble that could easily have backfired. But he was able to maintain his position for over thirty years, during which time he exercised a near monopoly on opinion writing. In long, detailed, masterful, and meticulous opinions, he treated the Constitution, in fact, as I have shown, as though it were supreme ordinary law. Shielded by the overlap between the principle of vested rights and his reading of the contract clause, and by the judicial responsibility as arbiter of federalism, Marshall habituated the bench, the bar, and the public to the judicial application and interpretation of the constitutional text. The more Marshall framed his discussion in these terms, the more he invited litigants to do so, forcing other judges to meet him on this ground.

It is interesting to speculate on what may have happened, absent Marshall, since it is undoubtedly the case that factors other than his daring and skill were responsible for his success. The most important were the country's commitment to limited government, as inherited from England, and the strength of the literal American version of it, as reflected in the universal agreement, dating to independence, that an unconstitutional act was void. As receptive as this atmosphere was, however, it is unlikely that modern judicial review could have developed without the specific steps that were taken. If seriatim opinion writing had prevailed, and if the only precedents for the judicial refusal to execute an unconstitutional act were those of *Bayard* v. *Singleton, VanHorne's Lessee* v. *Dorrance,* Johnson's opinion in *Fletcher* v. *Peck,* and Story's in *Terrett* v. *Taylor* and *Dartmouth College,* it is hard to see how modern judicial review could ever have come into being. Without Marshall, the doubtful case rule would likely have been adhered to rigorously and *Cooper* v. *Telfair*[160] might have held the place *Marbury* holds today. In *Cooper* judges acknowledged the existence of judicial authority to refuse to enforce an unconstitutional act, but declined to exercise the power in that case. It is likely that as time passed and the gross legislative irresponsibility of the revolutionary era declined and the doctrine of vested rights lost its preeminence, judges would have found little occasion to use the "awful" power they all agreed they had. But, most of all, the modern, routine, legalized judicial review with which we are familiar depended on Marshall's insistence on gathering constitutional intent from its words and on his long, detailed, skillful expositions of the constitutional text, maintained in the face of controversy over its meaning. It depended on a subordination of constitutional spirit and first principle to constitutional text, and that is nowhere to be found except in Marshall's opinions. Without them, even with *Marbury*, it is impossible to imagine how the Constitution could ever have come to be included within that law for which it is the province and duty of the judicial department to say what the law is.

Constitutional Law as a New Form of Law

Judicial review, then, as practiced today, may fairly be said to be Marshall's judicial review, introduced in the contract and supremacy clause cases, and not that of Iredell, Hamilton, or Wilson, or even *Marbury*. It developed with public acceptance of Marshall's treatment of the Constitution as supreme ordinary law and is an essentially new creation, unanticipated by the framers. It emerged slowly, not reaching its current form until sometime in the nineteenth century. Professor Edward Corwin has noted that before the Civil War constitutional law was predominantly a natural law phenomenon.[161] What Corwin identified as the dominance of natural law was a reflection of the period 2 self-understanding: the pervasive, unarticulated acceptance of fundamental law as different in kind from ordinary law, and of judicial review as the declaration and enforcement of fundamental law, not application and interpretation of supreme written law. The content of fundamental law in particular cases, accordingly, was not found through textual exposition but in a consensus on the content of first principle. In the first part of the nineteenth century, this meant natural law and, particularly, vested rights. The prevalence of period 2 conceptions is also visible in the widespread expectation of congressional, rather than judicial, implementation of the Civil War amendments. This was another reflection of an unarticulated difference in kind between fundamental law and ordinary law, under which the former was not thought to be implemented, routinely, in court.

Over time, however, Marshall's judicial review continued to spread, eventually blotting out all access to the original distinctions. Whereas first principle

160. 4 U.S. (4 Dall.) 14 (1800).
161. Edward S. Corwin, "The Basic Doctrine of American Constitutional Law." *Michigan Law Review* 12, no. 4 (February 1914) : 247–76, and particularly, 247–55.

and constitutional text had coexisted actively during Marshall's tenure, in succeeding decades the text became the effective restraint, subordinating the principle enunciated in the text. Judicial application and interpretation of this text succeeded in gaining deep and likely irreversible public acceptance. Certainly by Thayer's time at the turn of the century, and undoubtedly sometime before, the Constitution had become a routine form of law, an extension of common and statutory law. It lost its identity as first principles committed to writing to become supreme written law; fundamental law became the supreme law of the land.

As the perpetual controversy over constitutional law indicates, however, this transformation has not been an easy one. Differences in kind between restraints on sovereign power and those on individual behavior are too deep to have been removed by fundamental law's adoption of ordinary law technique and by public acceptance of judicial application and interpretation of the Constitution. The origin of judicial review in the silent, unrecognized assimilation of fundamental law into ordinary law and the strength of our acceptance of the Constitution as an ordinary law restraint on the majority will have obscured the extent of these differences. In their enduring vitality, however, they are the source of the inescapable political component of constitutional law and of its unresolved controversy.

Mature period 3 judicial review is, as was suggested at the beginning of this article, best understood as a new form of law, connected to common and statutory law and to the ordinary law tradition, but also decisively different from it. The Constitution is not "so much law,"[162] as Thayer and all who have followed him assume it to be. It has become, by now, a unique and inextricable blend of fundamental law and ordinary law. On the one hand, it cannot be understood properly apart from the predominantly ordinary law framework within which it has been viewed for at least the last century. It has developed enough internal consistency to sustain itself as a form of law, and it is now literally impossible to think about the Constitution except as supreme ordinary law. The legitimacy of judicial application and interpretation of the Constitution rests in public and professional acceptance of the practice, and this acceptance follows from the Constitution's established identity as a form of law. Constitutional law has also produced a sizable body of substantive law and, most impressively, has shown itself transplantable, as law, to other political systems.[163]

Nevertheless, constitutional law continues to lack certain attributes typically associated with law. The judiciary is unable, in constitutional law, to fulfill its most basic responsibility to law, that of enforcement against violation. No matter how close we come to recognizing this difficulty, we do not confront it adequately, but fall back, repeatedly and inappropriately, on ordinary law's enforcement model to explain the functioning of constitutional law. Author-

162. See above at n. 25.
163. See Walter F. Murphy and Joseph Tanenhaus, eds., *Comparative Constitutional Law: Cases and Commentaries* (New York: St. Martin's Press, 1977).

itative judicial exposition of the Constitution also necessitates a policy choice qualitatively different from that in ordinary law. This policy component can neither be simply accepted, as is that of ordinary law, as an unavoidable part of judicial responsibility to law, nor eliminated by the proper practice of judicial review. On the contrary, it needs justification in terms of the function constitutional law does fulfill and, given that framework, development of appropriate limits.

The Inappropriateness of an Enforcement Model. The starting point in any inquiry into constitutional law's function, then, is full recognition of the inapplicability of ordinary law's enforcement model. Statutes, and ordinary law generally, regulate individual behavior. When ordinary law is enacted, there is an expectation of a certain amount of violation and an enforcement process that includes definitive determination of the meaning of the law in each case where it is officially invoked. Under conventional separation of powers, this determination is assigned to the judiciary. Judicial finality over ordinary law is a necessary part of the rule of law in the most rudimentary sense, and every society has some mechanism for authoritative exposition of its commands, whether or not it has a separate or independent judiciary. The judicial authority to fix the meaning of ordinary law is not only an unexceptional part of law enforcement; law enforcement itself is a wholly unproblematic undertaking. In enforcing ordinary law the judge acts as agent for the entire community, enforcing the collective will against individual violators. As he speaks for the entire society he is able to enforce the law against even the strongest individual violator, including, for example, a modern corporation.

A constitution, in contrast, is directed at sovereign power. It provides for the distribution and organization of political authority and stipulates a few general principles guiding its exercise. Unlike a statute, a constitution contemplates compliance, not violation. A constitution, and the regime it establishes, could never maintain itself if it were to encounter the extent of violation contemplated by a statute. As was clearly understood before the confounding of fundamental law and ordinary law, the genuine constitutional violation is, by definition, a revolutionary activity, wholly unlike the routine, if unwelcome, violation of ordinary law. Frequent violation is incompatible with maintainence of the regime.

Furthermore, assuming for the moment that a regime could tolerate repeated constitutional violations, no judiciary would be able to enforce the constitution against these violations as routinely as it does ordinary law. Genuine constitutional violation, in a republican regime, entails either large-scale popular disaffection or a minority coup strong enough to succeed. By definition, such violations, if they are to prevail, must be backed by the predominant amount of force in the community. Attempted violations not so backed can be repelled by that same force. But whenever the dominant force, for whatever reason, withdraws support from the basic principles of the system, a judge attempting to enforce those principles would stand alone or, with a minority of the community, confront the superior numbers and power of those not abiding by the original agreement. The judge would no longer be society's agent, as in ordinary law, but now must attempt to uphold a principle against a majority unwilling to honor it.

Over a century of experience with Marshall's judicial review has forced some awareness of these problems of constitutional enforcement. That the judiciary lacks the force to uphold the Constitution against genuine violation has been publicly acknowledged at least since Thayer.[164] The classic formulation is that of Learned Hand: "A society so riven that the spirit of moderation is gone, no court *can* save; . . . a society where that spirit flourishes, no court *need* save."[165] Nevertheless, the dominance of ordinary law conceptions has hindered us from grasping the full implications of this awareness. Having accepted the Constitution as supreme ordinary law and with it, its enforcement model, we focus on great constitutional decisions and major Court achievements, and regard these as "enforcement" of the Constitution. In the process, we have ignored the genuine constitutional violations in American political life and the Court's utter incapacity to deal with them. We think of constitutional enforcement in terms of *Brown* v. *Board of Education* and its condemnation of racial segregation in public schools rather than the more serious violations of black rights over the preceding century. These included denial of basic physical protection, of meaningful due process, and of voting rights. This racial injustice is, without doubt, this country's most massive and sustained constitutional violation, and it was never rectified in court. By the same token, we think about enforcement of the First Amendment in terms of Court decisions upholding rights of demonstrators in the 1960s or narrowing the definition of libel, while we ignore the legal system's incapacity to end the unambiguous First Amendment violation constituted by the suppression of black protest until the 1960s. Other serious constitutional violations, I suggest, were the Japanese relocation of World War II and the excesses of McCarthyism of the 1950s, as well as its earlier manifestations. These too were never checked in court. Thus it may be said that one major consequence of the legalization of fundamental law has been a literal forgetting of the areas and time periods within which the Constitution has simply gone unenforced. What we call constitutional enforcement has been instead, for the most part, judicial resolution of conflict over contending valid interpretations of the Constitution, an essentially political and popular responsibility in a self-governing regime. Although some of these interpretations are less defensible than others, nevertheless, clear, genuine violations have remained out of Court reach and still remain so by their command of active or tacit societal support.

Strictly speaking, although the judiciary routinely enforces ordinary law, it can never enforce constitutions. If it could, the universal problem of abuse of political power would have been solved long ago. It was the clear recognition of these relationships that initially made, and kept, fundamental law different

164. "Doctrine of Constitutional Law," 56.

165. "The Contribution of an Independent Judiciary to Civilization," in *The Spirit of Liberty*, ed. Irving Dilliard (New York: Alfred A. Knopf, 1952), 181. Emphasis in original. See also Robert A. Dahl, "Decision-Making in a Democracy: The Supreme Court as a National Policy-Maker," *Journal of Public Law* 6, no. 2 (Fall, 1957) : 279–95.

in kind from ordinary law and explains why periods 1 and 2 interpreted judicial review as an extraordinary political act, not a conventional legal one. Judicial defense of constitutional principle was only one political force among other stronger ones accompanying the passing of the revolutionary era and the consolidation of national power, which ended the constitutional violations to which it was addressed. Period 2 judicial review represented the attempt to rally seemingly forsaken principles in a context of revolutionary instability and untested republicanism. With the coming of political stability in the 1790s, confidence in legislative commitment to first principles increased. Although judges continued to insist on their right to refuse to execute unconstitutional acts, they found fewer and fewer occasions to use this power, and on the Supreme Court, it was not used at all. Had Marshall not reinvigorated and redirected the practice, applying it outside the unambiguous violation of principle in cases like *Dartmouth College* and *Sturgis* v. *Crowninshield,* it is likely it would have died out completely. Separation of judicial exposition of the Constitution from a true enforcement function and from an assigned arbiter role created the novel legal-political institution that is modern constitutional law. It conveyed to constitutional law, simultaneously, the legal attribute of regularity and its ineradicable, extralegal policy component.

Before considering what function period 3 constitutional law does fulfill if not that of enforcing the Constitution, it is worth emphasizing the tenacity of the enforcement model, despite widespread sensitivity to its inapplicability. It has been acknowledged, for example, that the Court can act only within a receptive public environment. It is in no way shocking to assert that *Brown* v. *Board of Education* did not come until there was sufficient national support for such a decision. Nor is it surprising to recognize that sustained judicial application of individual rights guarantees against state and local authority did not begin until the 1940s when the New Deal coalition of the locally powerless had achieved power at the national level. Yet, it does not strike us an inappropriate or inconsistent to hear the Court's function described as the "protect[ion of] minorities from the unchecked exercise of the majority's will."[166] Similarly, despite acknowledgment of the problems of constitutional enforcement, it is still often assumed that these are not intrinsically different from the selective enforcement of ordinary law. There is, however, a basic unbridgeable difference between the two. Selective enforcement of ordinary law can be remedied with a change of executive policy or administrations. Enforcement of fundamental law, on the other hand, requires the voluntary cooperation of the potential violator.

The Function of Constitutional Law. The inapplicability of ordinary law's enforcement model is a consequence of the inability to restrain sovereign power as routinely as society restrains individual behavior. Nevertheless modern judicial review does function as a legal restraint on majority will. It is, however, a new kind of restraint, in the sense both that it was unanticipated by the framers and that it restrains in a way different from that of ordinary law.

---

166. This is Ely's formulation in *Democracy and Distrust,* 69.

Despite Marshall's real success in legalizing fundamental law, the law of the Constitution remains a unique mixture of moral and legal restraint. To reach a satisfactory account of the function of constitutional law, it is necessary to get a proper understanding of this mixture.

The first fundamental law property that remains in contemporary constitutional law is the Constitution's basic identity as first principle rather than legal text. The framers understood the text to be the enunciation of basic principles. Designed for future adaptation in unforeseeable circumstances, it was, in key provisions, necessarily general. It was not, like ordinary law, an endless succession of new expressions of legislative will, accessible primarily through its words. Its specific content, on the contrary, had to be found outside the text. For purposes of judicial enforcement that content was found in common consent. Beyond the clear violation, the Constitution was to be implemented by the political branches in the course of political life, as future generations responded to changing needs.

It was also the case that initially the specific limits on governmental power included in the constitutional text, such as protection for freedom of speech or against unreasonable searches and seizures, were not thought to exhaust the legitimate boundaries of governmental power. Limited government meant, in Wilson's words, the "natural, the inherent, and the predominating rights of the citizens." [167] It was established by the existence of explicit fundamental law, not by the specific provisions of the written constitution. Commitment to limited government beyond that embodied in specific prohibitions also found expression in the so-called open-textured clauses of the Constitution such as the Ninth Amendment [168] and the due process and privilege and immunities clauses. These open-textured provisions are today the center of controversy over the exercise of judicial review. They are particularly troublesome because their judicial exposition invites a policy-making even beyond that connected with the more specific provisions and hard, if not impossible, to reconcile with ordinary law requirements. Initially the open-textured clauses were not troublesome because it was never contemplated that the judiciary would interpret or expound any constitutional limit, for the purposes of judicial review, whose specific content could not be found in common consent.

Acceptance of the Constitution as legal restraint on sovereign power cannot change the nature of its text or impart to it a capacity comparable to that of ordinary law text. As the grants and limits of political power whose implementation cannot in the nature of things be contemplated in its text or intent, it remains, unlike any other legal text, a statement of general principle. To treat the Constitution otherwise deprives it of its essential character as the charter of government and expression of the principled limits on the use of political power.

We have already examined the second fundamental law property that remains in modern constitutional law. Fundamental law cannot be enforced

167. See above at n. 84.
168. The Ninth Amendment reads: "The enumeration in the Constitution, of certain rights, shall not be construed to deny or disparage others retained by the people."

against genuine violation. In the absence of sufficient societal force to check majority violation of established principle, the Constitution retains some of its original character as moral exhortation rather than enforceable law. Having said this, modern constitutional law is more than simply the majority's acceptance of the legitimacy of restraint on its own power. Although it is not, and cannot be, enforcement of constitutional principle against majority violation, it can and does function to augment or enhance the role of principle in public life.[169] In so functioning, it operates, first, in the only way that a restraint on sovereign power can operate—where there already exists political receptivity to the principles defended in court. Having lost the revolutionary potential inherent in direct challenges of principle, modern legalized judicial review is, in addition, one of comparatively low stakes couched in legalisms. In its regularization and institutionalization as a form of law, it provides systematic opportunity to test governmental power against the demands of principle and to challenge particular exercises of power without challenging political authority itself. This regularized and institutionalized consideration of principle through the forms of law has become, perhaps, a more pervasive phenomenon than even Marshall contemplated. At its best, it elevates the quality of public life. It is, of course, also capable of reinforcing harmful principle. *Brown* v. *Board of Education* is the least controversial example of the former, *Dred Scott* of the latter.

Third, constitutional law remains open to the charge that it is, in reality, the restraint of judges rather than law. In the enduring differences in kind between fundamental law and ordinary law, this charge will always retain substantial truth. The challenge for constitutional law is not to deny or eliminate but to justify its policy component. This can be done in terms of the ends constitutional law serves. Just as the incidental policy-making of ordinary law is accepted as an unavoidable part of the rule of law, so the more significant policy-making of constitutional law can be accepted as part of the internalization of popular and legislative self-restraint, and the systematic consideration of the demands of principle. This still leaves ample room for confining that policy component, but it does close off futile attempts to deny its existence or to make it conform to that acceptable in ordinary law.

Despite these problems, the practice Marshall built contains enough legal identity to have enabled it to maintain itself as an acceptable democratic restraint. This comes from its retention of certain legal attributes as known in ordinary law. For one thing, there is its reliance on reason as its highest authority. Reason in ordinary law, as in constitutional law, does not yield particular substantive results. It is, as Ely has observed, empty of content.[170] Reli-

169. Both Bickel and Dworkin have made comparable arguments. See Bickel, *Least Dangerous Branch*, 23–28, and Ronald Dworkin, "The Forum of Principle," *New York University Law Review* 56, nos. 2–3 (May-June 1981) : 469–518, particularly 517–18. Neither, however, sees Court fulfillment of such a function as part of a new field of law, and neither has separated it sufficiently from enforcement conceptions of ordinary law. These points are discussed more fully below at nn. 173–79.

170. *Democracy and Distrust*, 56–58.

ance on reason serves, rather, to reduce the forces of interest, will, and arbitrariness and to augment that of principle in the resolution of human conflict. Constitutional law, as the reasoned consideration of the requirements of political principle, is an extension of the legal regulation of individual behavior and represents the human capacity, however incomplete, for principled consideration of the limits on power. With reason as its ultimate authority, it does not introduce essentially undemocratic restraint.

Constitutional law also retains the legal process's openness to the ideas and values prevalent in society.[171] Law does not systematically represent a partial interest or one alien from society as a whole, nor do judges and lawyers constitute a distinct or permanent class or group. This remains the case despite the ease with which individual lawyers and judges have adopted the outlook and ideology of partial interests. The fallibility of human reasoning and the strength of partial interests makes this partiality an ongoing problem. At times it has threatened the viability of constitutional law and could yet be its undoing. Yet it remains the case that the substance of constitutional law is tied to the contending interests and values alive in society, which work their way into court in contending briefs. This built-in openness is another crucial part of constitutional law's capacity to function as a viable democratic restraint.

THE CONTEMPORARY DEBATE: FUNDAMENTAL VALUES AND INTERPRETIVISM

Constitutional law's staying power over nearly two centuries is itself testimony to the attractiveness of law as a check on majority power. So entrenched has this restraint become that no one since Gibson has rejected all judicial control of legislation.[172] To do so would be to declare publicly that there are no legitimate limits on the exercise of popular power. Judicial review is stronger than ever in the second half of the twentieth century amid widespread recognition that unprincipled use of power is a permanent political problem, and not just a feature of insufficiently popular regimes. One of the most striking aspects of the continuing debate over judicial review is that as constitutional law's inability to conform to all the requirements of law is underscored anew each generation, critics most troubled by this nonconformity—Thayer, Wechsler, Ely, for example—have sought to bring about that conformity rather than to dismantle the institution itself.

The intensity of these efforts reflects both constitutional law's integrity as a form of law and the depth of law's attractiveness as a restraint on popular majority power. The point is this is the integrity of a *new* form of law. As a restraint on sovereign power, it functions to augment, not enforce constitutional principle. In implementing general political principle, it necessitates political judgments neither contemplated in ordinary law nor amenable to its restraints. Maintenance of constitutional law in credible conformity with the

171. See Edward H. Levi, *An Introduction to Legal Reasoning* (Chicago: University of Chicago Press, 1948), 1–8.

172. See *Eakin* v. *Raub*, 12 Sergeant & Rawles (Pa.) 330, 352 (1825).

requirements of law requires acceptance of its policy component and development of appropriate restraint—one that respects its function and compensates for the inapplicability of ordinary law restraints.

These issues are central to the contemporary debate between fundamental values analysis and interpretivism. Of the two, fundamental values analysis is clearly closer to the conception of constitutional law presented here. But it shares the general failure to see constitutional law as a new form of law. It relies, at crucial points, on inappropriate ordinary law conceptions and fails to address adequately the issue of restraint.

Judicial Review as the Defense of Fundamental Values

The understanding that judicial review is the defense of first principles, or fundamental values, dates to the early 1960s and Alexander Bickel's *The Least Dangerous Branch*.[173] It was initially a product of two converging forces: the widespread disinclination to retreat from authoritative judicial application and interpretation of the Constitution, as counseled by Frankfurter's rule of self-restraint, and the growing inability to explain constitutional law's operation from within a conventional legal framework. This was particularly evident in the response to *Brown* v. *Board of Education* and the dismantling of racial segregation. Many of those charged with its implementation routinely denounced it as extralegal judicial policy-making, and this charge was echoed even among those who enthusiastically welcomed its results.[174] In the 1960s, after decades of experience with the mature modern practice, it was also impossible to defend *Brown* in traditional legal terms, as policy-neutral application and interpretation of equal protection text and intent. Indeed, whatever evidence on intent existed argued as much against as for the decision.

Bickel acknowledged these problems by opening *The Least Dangerous Branch* with an exhaustive critique of the modern *Marbury* doctrine, with its suggestion that judicial control over legislation followed from the Constitution's status as supreme written law.[175] It was precisely the defect of the legal conception of judicial review, coupled with its demonstrated staying power, that demanded more adequate justification. Bickel found this justification in the idea that judicial review was best understood as the defense of fundamental values and long-term principle.[176] In supporting this proposition Bickel leaned implicitly, but heavily, on *Brown*. If *Brown* was not credible as application of Fourteenth Amendment text and intent, it was totally intelligible as defense of the principle of racial equality.

Bickel's criticism of *Marbury* and his reformulation of judicial review as the defense of fundamental values was drawn from observation of constitutional law's functioning, not from any reinterpretation of the original understanding. Yet, in so reformulating judicial review's function, Bickel touched upon

173. (Indianapolis: Bobbs-Merrill, 1962).
174. Herbert Wechsler, "Toward Neutral Principles of Constitutional Law," *Harvard Law Review* 73, no. 1 (November 1959) : 1–35.
175. *Least Dangerous Branch*, chap. 1.
176. Ibid., 23–28.

and retrieved the original and enduring fundamental law elements that remain in the modern practice. *The Least Dangerous Branch* thus stands as a watershed in the understanding of judicial review. Nevertheless, despite this sensitivity, Bickel, too, failed to free himself sufficiently from ordinary law perceptions, particularly from its enforcement model. In Bickel's hands, the judicial defense of fundamental values was, at bottom, enforcement of first principle only against unambiguous violation. This is as incomplete an account of the modern practice as was period 2 judicial review.

As students of constitutional law are aware, over the years Bickel found it increasingly more difficult to support particular instances of judicial review as he had supported *Brown* in 1962.[177] The enormity of American racial injustice had made *Brown* a literal enforcement of Fourteenth Amendment principle against unambiguous violation, the judicial implementation of clear moral requirements. But no other constitutional principle has been so openly, willfully, and protractedly violated as has the commitment to racial equality. If judicial review, as the defense of principle, is to be confined to violations of the magnitude, as it was in fact for Bickel, we confront here again the untenability of an enforcement model. If, on the one hand, the American regime were to face, with any frequency, departures from constitutional principle comparable to the country's flouting of the requirement of racial equality, it could not continue in recognizable form; if, on the other hand the judiciary were to confine itself to such mammoth violations of principle, its actions would be too infrequent and too irregular to be recognizable as law.

Despite Bickel's growing hesitancy about the use of Court power, his conception of judicial review gained strong support, and over the years, its thrust expanded. Soon, the judicial defense of fundamental values extended to values neither identified in the text nor contemplated by the framers.[178] In this form, it constituted the basis for the revival of substantive due process and the Court's recognition of a constitutional right to privacy in the open-textured due process clause.[179] Proponents of the fundamental values approach also supported Court defense of principle beyond that of *The Least Dangerous Branch* by no longer confining judicial action, as had Bickel, to vindication of principle against unambiguous violation.

In seeing constitutional law as the broad defense of principled limits on power, this activist version of the fundamental values approach is faithful to the nature of a constitution and to the practice developed in acceptance of Marshall's innovations. But it shares the general failure to see that this practice is a new field of law and a new judicial responsibility. Fundamental values

177. See Alexander M. Bickel, *The Supreme Court and the Idea of Progress* (New York: Harper & Row, 1970).

178. See Grey, "Unwritten Constitution," 703–18, and Dworkin, *Taking Rights Seriously*, chap. 5.

179. Substantive due process originally took the form of liberty of contract and was a major vehicle through which the Court overturned attempts at governmental regulation of the economy. It arose in the 1880s and was abandoned in the Court crisis of the 1930s.

activism, consequently, suffers in its way from inappropriate reliance on ordinary law conceptions, including its enforcement model. It merged Bickel's new understanding of constitutional law's function with the only available conception of the Constitution, that of supreme ordinary law. As a result, it tends to see judicial review as enforcement of principle, rather than its augmentation or enhancement, and to support judicial implementation of principle with the same latitude with which judges enforce ordinary law. Constitutional principle is sufficiently different from ordinary law, however, to make such enforcement inappropriate. Judicial enhancement of principle must be accompanied by suitable restraint. Fundamental values analysis is on solid ground in rejecting the restraint of Frankfurter, Bickel, and interpretivism. But it still must address this issue systematically and make restraint an integral part of its constitutional law.

The Case for Restraint. The case for restraint in the judicial defense of fundamental values lies in the enduring differences in kind between fundamental and ordinary law, and in the novelty of the judicial responsibility to enhance principle that constitutes the modern practice. It lies, first, in the fact that now, as in periods 1 and 2, constitutional principles do not stand in need of authoritative exposition in order to maintain their integrity. For ordinary law, the absence of authoritative exposition means destruction of the rule of law, of the capacity to resolve human conflict in peace. Constitutional principle, in contrast, retains its vitality and integrity despite unresolved controversy over application in particular circumstances. It would lose that integrity only if constitutional law did, in fact, operate in a true enforcement context, upholding constitutional principle against unambiguous violation. As it is, public debate over the proper implementation of principle—of the First Amendment or the requirements of due process, for example—antedates and continues after Court pronouncements. Determination of when and how to make a court pronouncement is a political judgment, not a legal one as known in ordinary law.

Next, attempts to enforce principle with the same regularity with which ordinary law is enforced could easily become intolerable, even for the most principled of societies. As Bickel warned in first developing the idea of judicial review as the defense of principle: "No good society can be unprincipled; and no viable society can be principle-ridden."[180] Rigorous implementation of principle, moreover, invites an unsustainable judicial moralizing, one made so by the fallibility of human reasoning, including the best, and the absence of any need for finality in the application of principle. No matter how strong the contending interpretations of ordinary law and the degree of uncertainty over their relative merits, the judicial choice among them is commonplace, the fulfillment of an assigned, necessary function. In constitutional law, the stronger the contending principles governing particular circumstances, the more acute the political stakes and the more problematic the judicial choice among them.

180. *Least Dangerous Branch,* 64.

Restraint in the judicial application of political principle is indicated, last, by the fact that insistent judicial invocation of principle, necessarily lodged outside the text, undermines the Constitution's status as supreme ordinary law and threatens to move it back to that of fundamental law. It threatens to undo the fusion of principle and text, of politics and law, leaving us with an instrument whose restraints still bind, but with political, not legal force. It threatens to make challenges to the exercise of political power attacks on the moral legitimacy of the regime rather than legal errors.

The Interpretivist Response: An Inappropriate Restraint

Interpretivism dates from the 1970s. It shares the near-universal rejection of Frankfurter's self-restraint and accepts authoritative judicial exposition of the Constitution. To some extent, it even accepts the conceptualization of the Constitution as a statement of first principle. But it draws, predominantly, on constitutional law's ordinary law strand and insists that if the Constitution is a statement of first principle, it is a statement expressed in legal form. Judges, therefore, are properly confined to the defense of those principles or values identified in the constitutional text or demonstrably contemplated by the framers.[181] Interpretivism invokes text and intent because these are standard legal tools, and reliance on them will keep constitutional law limited, as law should be, to the execution of policy made elsewhere and expressed in legal text. Its chief aim is to keep judges from reading their own values into the open-textured clauses of the Constitution, as it argues the Court did in reviving substantive due process and establishing a constitutional right to privacy.

In its reliance on the ordinary law tools of text and intent, interpretivism is powerful testimony to the legalization of fundamental law achieved over the centuries. At the same time, its inability to resolve constitutional law's problems reveals the inadequacy of an exclusively legal conception. Text and intent are legal tools devised for ordinary law, where they provide substantial content for that law, and confine judicial action in a meaningful way to execution of policy made elsewhere. In constitutional law they cannot so function.

To the extent that interpretivism relies on a literal reading of intent, it is mistaken. Contemporary practice arose in repudiation of the framers' intent. By itself, intent cannot support any period 3 practice. That the framers never contemplated or intended modern judicial review also means that their specific intent with respect to substantive interpretation of particular constitutional provisions has no claim comparable to that of legislative intent in statutory interpretation. Whatever the difficulties of period 3 judicial review's search for substantive content for constitutional principle, it cannot be met by invoking a nonexistent intent.

Similar problems surround interpretivism's reliance on constitutional text. In moving beyond enforcement of the Constitution against unambiguous violation, period 3 judicial review can no longer draw on legal text. Even if it

181. See Bork, "Neutral Principles," 4–20; Linde, "Judges, Critics," 253–56; and Linde, "Constitutional Theory," 193–96.

were confined to defense of those values identified or implicit in the text, that text's generality would still leave constitutional law with a policy content unknown to ordinary law and suspect by democratic standards.

The most telling expression of the inability of constitutional text to function as does statutory text is that interpretivism's textual reliance is a selective one, limited largely to judicial defense of individual rights protections in the Bill of Rights, and the equal protection clause, confined to review of racial distinctions. But a selective textual reliance is not a textual reliance at all, but one that depends on the principle underlying selection. This text represents those aspects of Warren Court adjudication that have survived criticism to become part of a new consensus on the role of the courts. It is helpful, in this regard, to remember that whereas interpretivism regards *Brown* v. *Board of Education* as adequately supported by equal protection text and intent, *Brown*'s opponents did not share this view. Opposition to *Brown* was originally made in precisely the same terms used against substantive due process today. It was denounced as a politically directed, judicial choice of values, lacking in legal identity. The legal character that presumably attaches to *Brown* today does not, in fact, derive from a meaningful fidelity to text and intent, as interpretivism suggests, but from an extratextual consensus that has now developed supporting the decision. A judicial review limited to interpretation of the Bill of Rights and racial distinctions under the Fourteenth Amendment avoids a judicial choice of values only to the extent that it relies on an existing consensus on the values to be judicially protected and on the general contours of that protection. Interpretivism is a passable defense of the status quo, but it is unable to account for its own existence or to guide future practice. More seriously, in its focus on text and intent to the exclusion of first principle, it distorts the essence of American constitutional law.

Justice Harlan's Constitutional Law: Substantive Due Process and Self-Restraint

Without endorsing each or any particular decision, I believe Justice John Marshall Harlan has come closest of any modern judge or commentator to providing a successful model and working restraint for this new branch of law, which evolved from the unacknowledged assimilation of fundamental law into ordinary law. Harlan's constitutional law started from the premise that the Constitution's chief identity is as statement of first principle rather than legal text. It is, in his words, "the basic charter of our society, setting out . . . the principles of government."[182] Its text is "spare but meaningful."[183] In the due process clause, among the most spare but meaningful limits, it established "a freedom from all substantial arbitrary impositions and purposeless restraints."[184] This is the foundation for the revival of substantive due process, for judicial review as defense of principled limits on political power.

Harlan's substantive due process, like all his constitutional law, was pursued with an unmistakable self-restraint. As was Marshall's, it combined an unapologetic commitment to the use of judicial power over legislation with the

182. *Poe* v. *Ullman*, 367 U.S. 497, 540 (1961).
183. Ibid.
184. Ibid., 543.

realization that this authority could not be pursued as systematically as are ordinary law restraints on individual behavior. Marshall's judicial review was limited to reinforcement of one principle—vested rights—and exposition of one text—the contract clause. Harlan's self-restraint was visible in a substantial acceptance of popular and political implementation of principle, as represented in the governmental action before the Court.[185] Marshall's and Harlan's restraint was implicit recognition that judicial defense of principle is not its literal enforcement. At the same time, their readiness to exercise regular, routine control over legislation acknowledged the need to use judicial power if constitutional law was to retain its legal identity.[186] Underuse of judicial review destroys its character as a routine legal restraint on will; overuse brings the judiciary too far from the legal requirement that it not make law. Precisely where to draw the line involves political more than legal judgment.

In seeking content for the first principles to be judicially defended, Harlan turned to reason, disciplined by tradition, history, and societal values. Harlan's priorities reflected, first, the primacy of reason as a legal tool: "Precisely because it is the Constitution alone which warrants judicial interference in sovereign operations of the State, the basis for judgment as to the Constitutionality of state action must be a rational one."[187] Unlike text and intent, reason is a legal tool wholly applicable to constitutional law. It represents, in ordinary law and in constitutional law, the human striving for reason and principle over interest and will. It is the identifying characteristic of legal decision making through which the disinterestedness associated with law is sought and against which its achievement is measured.

As the reason of constitutional law is not meaningfully informed by legal text, Harlan supplemented it by appeal to history, tradition, and societal values. The content of due process, he argued, "represented [a] balance which our Nation . . . has struck between [individual] liberty and the demands of organized society."[188] It derives from "what history teaches are the traditions from which [the country] developed as well as the traditions from which it broke,"[189] and from "solid recognition of the basic values that underlie our society."[190]

185. See, for example, *Alberts* v. *California*, 354 U.S. 476, 496 (1959), and *Barenblatt* v. *United States*, 360 U.S. 109 (1959) (freedom of speech and association); *Wesberry* v. *Sanders*, 376 U.S. 1, 20 (1964), and *Reynolds* v. *Sims*, 377 U.S. 533, 589 (1964) (reapportionment); *Mapp* v. *Ohio*, 367 U.S. 643, 672 (1961), and *Miranda* v. *Arizona*, 384 U.S. 436, 504 (1966) (criminal procedures); *Harper* v. *Board of Elections*, 383 U.S. 663, 680 (1966), and *Shapiro* v. *Thompson*, 394 U.S. 618, 655 (1969) (fundamental rights and equal protection).

186. For Harlan, see, for example, *Roth* v. *United States*, 354 U.S. 476, 496 (1957), and *Cohen* v. *California*, 403 U.S. 15 (1971) (freedom of speech); *Poe* v. *Ullman*, 367 U.S. 497, 522 (1961), *Griswold* v. *Connecticut*, 381 U.S. 479, 499 (1965), and *Boddie* v. *Connecticut*, 401 U.S. 371 (1971) (fundamental rights and due process). See also *Katz* v. *United States*, 389 U.S. 347, 360 (1967), *Williams* v. *Illinois*, 399 U.S. 235, 259 (1970), and *Chambers* v. *Maroney*, 399 U.S. 42, 55 (1970) (criminal procedures).

187. *Poe* v. *Ullman*, 367 U.S. 497, 539–40 (1961). See also, ibid., 542 and 544.

188. Ibid., 542.

189. Ibid.

190. *Griswold* v. *Connecticut*, 381 U.S. 479, 501 (1965).

Harlan did not suggest that history, tradition, and societal values provided content for constitutional law comparable to that available to ordinary law from statutory text and common law precedent. Reliance on tradition and societal values would not "obviate all constitutional difference of opinion among judges"[191] nor remove the need for "judgement and restraint."[192] These were, however, the only proper sources for implementing the "spare but meaningful" constitutional text. Their invocation also reflects the need for popular involvement in this implementation. Reliance on tradition and societal values is the acknowledgment that although constitutional law evolved as the judicial defense of fundamental values, the people remain the ultimate source of constitutional implementation and, loosely, of the definition and redefinition of fundamental values. Changing conceptions of first principle, as they take place in society, are the closest counterpart in constitutional law to statutory text and intent in ordinary law. In this form they serve, simultaneously, as a form or restraint, one that Harlan contrasted to the "artificial and largely illusory" restraint of constitutional text.[193]

Ultimately, neither history nor tradition nor consensus can remove the need to inform judicial reason by the best human reasoning, by moral and political philosophy. But philosophy is not law, and judicial review cannot be the implementation of moral philosophy. Constitutional law, in its novel function of enhancing, not enforcing principle and in its absence of a need for finality, can and must check the lawyer's propensity to push reason to ultimate conclusions. Constitutional law's unique function allows it to acknowledge the fallibility of human reasoning and to leave resolution of some constitutional conflict outside the Judiciary. The need to keep constitutional law in conformity with the requirements of democracy compels such a course.

Harlan's constitutional law reflected all these considerations. His opinions exemplified the commitment to reason demanded by law; they were noteworthy for their genuine openness to contending conceptions of public and individual good, and their reasoned defense of the choices made, ones that took full account of the force of opposing arguments. This was so whether Harlan was accepting the popular and political implementation of values represented in the governmental action before the Court or overturning it in the name of constitutional principle. These same qualities kept his constitutional law from becoming the pursuit of a particular moral program or ideological agenda. Harlan clearly respected tradition and consensus, but recognized that within the confines of any popular consensus on values, there remained inescapable latitude. Included was the opportunity for judicial leadership in fostering particular implementations of that consensus and in challenging the status quo in the name of principle.

For Harlan, as for Marshall, constitutional law was a mixture of strong reasoning, sound political judgment, and keen sensitivity to the nature and limits of the legalization of principle. These combined to convey to their judgments

191. Ibid.
192. *Poe* v. *Ullman,* 367 U.S. 497, 542 (1961).
193. *Griswold* v. *Connecticut,* 381 U.S. 479, 501–02 (1965).

the commanding force of law. It was Marshall who introduced the lawyer's discourse into constitutional law, and it was Harlan who, of all contemporary justices, came to be regarded as a "lawyer's judge."[194] Harlan gained this reputation by the strength of his reasoning and by the avoidance of partisanship sufficient to give litigants a meaningful day in court. Yet it was also Harlan who revived substantive due process, and with it the insistence that judicial review is a check against all arbitrary impositions and purposeless restraints. His career stands as a demonstration of what it can mean for law to function as a restraint on popular power.

194. *New York Times*, September 20, 1971, 20.

RICHARD BENSEL
New School for Social Research

Southern Leviathan: The Development of Central State Authority in the Confederate States of America

War has probably been the single most important influence on the development of central state authority in the United States. Although the state-centered mobilization of economic resources and manpower that accompanies military conflict is commonly conceded to have had this effect throughout American history, the centralizing influence of the Civil War on the southern Confederate government has not been accorded the precedent-setting importance it deserves.[1] The consolidation of economic and social controls within the central government of the Confederacy was in fact so extensive that it calls into question standard interpretations of southern opposition to the expansion of federal power in both the antebellum and post-Reconstruction periods. Southern reluctance to expand federal power in those periods has been attributed variously to regional sympathy for laissez-faire principles, the "precapitalist" cultural origins of the plantation elite, and a general philosophical orientation hostile to state development. When the full expression of statist principles in the Confederate experience is examined, however, such

The author is indebted to Thomas Alexander, Kimberly Geiger, Ira Katznelson, Allan Lichtman, Elizabeth Sanders, Charles Tilly, and the editors of this journal for advice and criticism in the preparation of this article. An earlier version of this article was presented to the annual meeting of the Social Science History Association held November 21–24, 1985, in Chicago, Illinois.

1. Among those who have stressed the Civil War's influence on the strength of the Confederate state are Curtis Arthur Amlund, *Federalism in the Southern Confederacy* (Washington, D.C.: Public Affairs Press, 1966); Louise B. Hill, *State Socialism in the Confederate States of America*, no. 9 (Charlottesville, Va.: Historical Publishing, 1936); and Raimondo Luraghi, "The Civil War and the Modernization of American Society," *Civil War History* 18 (September 1972). See also Richard E. Beringer, Herman Hattaway, Archer Jones, and William N. Still, Jr., *Why the South Lost the Civil War* (Athens: University of Georgia Press, 1986), chap. 1.

explanations of southern hostility to the expansion of federal power seem, at best, incomplete. It would appear that southern opposition to northern industrial and commercial policies provided the impetus for both the region's opposition to a strong American state in the Union and support for a centralized Confederate regime after secession. Southern support for a strong Confederate and a weak American state (before and after the Civil War) can thus be viewed as a consistent strategy intended to minimize the anticipated deleterious impact of the northern industrial program for the national political economy on the plantation South.[2]

The existence of a comparatively strong Confederate state becomes, therefore, a central issue in evaluating the relative merits of political-economic and ideological-cultural explanations of American political development. It also provides a good opportunity to explore the implications of commonly held notions of statist principles for the practical organization and design of a central government. The Confederate experience is particularly appropriate for this purpose because the southern government began from scratch. Within a matter of months, the political elite of the Confederacy met and settled virtually every major question of central state authority and administrative organization. Many of these questions passed through the Confederate Congress where the expected effects of each alternative were debated in detail and brought to a vote of the membership. The resulting coalition patterns of statist and antistatist members underscore the unity of the southern white citizenry behind the Confederate nation and the executive-centered mobilization of southern economic resources and manpower.

This study is not a narrative account of the Confederacy nor is it intended to replace the now standard works on the Confederate Congress and the individual departments within the Confederate state. The interpretation put forward here does not assume any preexisting state-centered orientation on the part of the participants in Confederate public life, although a sampling of individuals' concern about the "despotic" growth of state power will be provided. As Stephen Skowronek has observed, state building in America has been, at best, a haphazard process in which most of the participants have not comprehended the statist implications of what they were doing.[3] In the Confederacy, this process was even more haphazard than it would become in the late nineteenth-century United States. The South did not have a natural reform elite such as the one that emerged from the cultural centers of the

2. For evidence of the continuity of the opposition of the South to northern economic policy, see Richard Franklin Bensel, *Sectionalism and American Political Development, 1880–1980* (Madison: University of Wisconsin Press, 1984) chap. 3–6. Also see Robert Royal Russel, *Economic Aspects of Southern Sectionalism 1840–1861*, University of Illinois Studies in the Social Sciences, vol. 11, nos. 1–2 (Urbana, Ill.: University of Illinois Press, March-June 1923), 164–66, and Elizabeth Sanders, "Industrial Concentration, Sectional Competition, and Antitrust Politics in America, 1880–1980," in *Studies in American Political Development*, vol. 1 : 142–214.

3. *Building a New American State: The Expansion of National Administrative Capacities, 1877–1920* (Cambridge: Cambridge University Press, 1982).

Northeast, nor did the region have the leisure to contemplate state-building proposals as an integrated policy.

Most of the evidence presented in the following pages will bear upon the legislative activity and coalitions that erected the Confederate state. This evidence is intended to demonstrate the underlying economic, political, and institutional bases of central state authority within the Confederacy, the fluid nature of legislative alignments on salient state-making measures, and the leadership effectiveness of the Davis administration. In describing the measures selected for analysis, many of the most important questions of implementation are addressed through reference to primary materials and the extensive literature on Confederate administrative performance. While this part of the discussion is intended to buttress the legislative analysis (by, for example, demonstrating that the Confederacy did not adopt policies that existed only on paper), the review of implementation must be, at best, incomplete. This review, however, does allow the construction of a model of the Confederate state that, in turn, provides a context within which the legislative decisions at the cutting edge of state formation took place. Near the end of the chapter, a summary discussion contends that the synergistic impact of individual state-enhancing measures made implementation even more statist than a consideration of legislative activity alone would suggest. In other words, the governmental whole was greater than the sum of its individual parts.[4]

ANALYTIC FRAMEWORK

Dimensions of Central State Authority

A theoretically consistent conception of the characteristics of a strong central state must guide this examination of the Confederacy. Although existing lit-

4. This interpretation of the Confederate experience does assume that a government designed in accord with commonly held statist principles is the most effective way to mobilize resources in a war (see, for example, Alan S. Milward, *War, Economy and Society: 1939–1945* [Berkeley: University of California Press, 1979], particularly chaps. 1–3). Obviously, this axiom should be applied to the inherently weaker of the parties involved in military conflict; the stronger side may pursue both guns and butter and still win the war (as did the Union). The best treatment of the North is still Leonard P. Curry, *Blueprint for a Modern America: Non-military Legislation of the First Civil War Congress* (Nashville, Tenn.: Vanderbilt University Press, 1968). In fact, the economic inferiority of the Confederacy was so great as to, in and of itself, impose limits on central state development. While this theme will resurface in the conclusion, other possible explanations of the failure of the South to win the Civil War will be touched upon only briefly.

The definition of a strong central state put forward here is concerned only with the concentration of authority and interior design of the central state. The political "efficacy" of a strong state—a matter related to state legitimacy, economic efficiency, and social cohesion—is not addressed. To include considerations of efficacy in the definition would implicate textual factors of the political environment that would ultimately reduce every instance of state development to idiosyncratic exceptionalism. While the definition advanced here thus gains in comparative and empirical applicability over more inclusive alternatives, the exclusion of efficacy considerations correspondingly limits the range of the concept. Some have argued, for example, that Confederate conscription policy was counterproductive in that,

erature on the state displays an apparent consensus on broad principles, that literature lacks a comprehensive definition and, as a consequence, fails to apply theoretical principles to specific aspects of central state organization.[5] The taxonomy of central state authority developed in this section is anchored loosely within that consensus and addresses both the structural design of the state and the substantive content of its policies.

Structural Design. The structural design of a strong state can be conveniently divided into two dimensions: centralization of authority and administrative capacity. The first dimension contains all measures that concentrate decision-making authority within one of the institutions of the central state (see figure 1). The administrative capacity dimension covers the interior design of the central state itself. Thus, a proposal to give the Confederate Supreme Court jurisdiction over cases that arise within the court systems of the individual states falls under the first, centralization of authority, dimension because it entails the subordination of individual state courts to the national tribunal. Similarly, measures that confer the power of appointment of military officers upon the president instead of lodging that authority with the individual states or with enlisted men fall under the centralization heading.

While the centralization dimension, in this formulation, subsumes all measures that concentrate authority in the central state, the administrative capacity dimension covers all proposals that favor the executive bureaucracy over the legislative and judicial branches. In this case, statist alternatives are those that further the autonomy and discretionary authority of the central state bureaucracy. From the perspective of strong-state advocates, the least attractive of the major central state institutions is the Congress. In fact, the perme-

---

according to these critics, the southern government lost more in civilian morale than it gained in manpower. In other words, these critics operate within a logic that can maintain that the Confederate state would have been "stronger" without conscription. Such a definition of a strong state allows them to identify and connect political "mistakes" to the effectiveness of the Confederate war effort. While the attractiveness of that logic should be clear, the problematic calculus should be equally obvious. The calculation of advantage in a trade-off between morale and manpower, if such a trade-off indeed existed, is hopelessly grounded in a specific historical context. For my limited purposes in this article, the above assumption (that a state designed according to statist principles maximizes the effectiveness of war mobilization) allows a full analysis of the Confederate performance, but implicitly rules out a consideration of contextual factors that may have influenced the efficacy of individual war measures.

5. Peter B. Evans, Dietrich Rueschemeyer, and Theda Skocpol, "On the Road toward a More Adequate Understanding of the State," in *Bringing the State Back In* (Cambridge: Cambridge University Press, 1985), 347–66. On the theoretical principles underlying state-centered approaches to political development, see Skowronek, *Building a New American State,* vii–x, 3–46; Theda Skocpol and Kenneth Finegold, "State Capacity and Economic Intervention in the Early New Deal," *Political Science Quarterly* 97, no. 2 (Summer 1982) : 256–78; Theda Skocpol, "Political Response to Capitalist Crisis: Neo-Marxist Theories of the State and the Case of the New Deal," *Politics and Society* 10, no. 2 (1980) : 155–201; and Stephen D. Krasner, *Defending the National Interest: Raw Materials Investments and U.S. Foreign Policy* (Princeton, N.J.: Princeton University Press, 1978), 5–34.

ability of Congress to the influence of private interests has consistently persuaded analysts to regard the national legislature as incapable of long-term
planning in the public interest and to consider statutory specification (the flip
side of legislative delegation) as inconsistent with technologically effective and
efficient administration.

The conception here has the president indistinguishable in most respects
from the executive bureaucracy. Thus, the interior design of a strong state
would favor presidential appointment of military officers over congressional
specification in statutory law. Presidential authority would be favored, also, in
questions involving the breadth of legislative delegation: the statist alternative
always confers greater administrative discretion. The comparatively few instances where a distinction must be drawn between the president and the
bureaucracy include civil service provisions and the formal designation of discretionary authority. Civil service rules governing recruitment and advancement further insulate the bureaucracy from the influence of the political

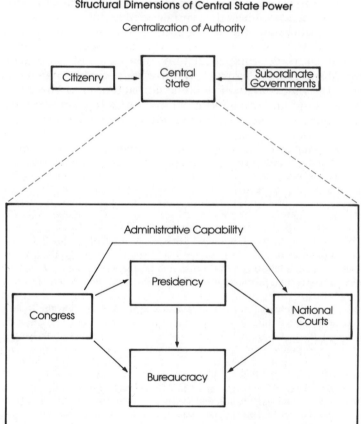

Figure 1.
Structural Dimensions of Central State Power

Centralization of Authority

branches (Congress and the president). The formal designation of career bureaucrats (instead of the president or political appointees) as the recipients of discretionary authority has a similar, insulating effect even though the executive may still influence any final administrative decision.

For parallel reasons, the national courts should, under this strong-state paradigm, give way to the central state bureaucracy. When, however, the judiciary is in direct competition with the president or Congress, the statist model favors the courts. Like the bureaucracy, the national court system is normally composed of career state officials who, aside from initial appointment, are insulated from political influence. Although the national courts share many of the characteristics of long-term planning, coordination, and administrative hierarchy that describe an ideal statist bureaucracy, judicial authority is, at best, redundant in a perfectly designed state and, at worst, in direct competition with the task-oriented design of the bureaucracy. Thus, the structural design of a strong state systematically favors the expansion of bureaucratic authority over that of the other three branches, the courts over the president and Congress, and the president when in competition with the legislative branch. Neither dimension of that design says anything, at this point, about the substantive content of central state policy. They are concerned only with the structural form of the state.

Substantive Content. A completely formulated conception of a strong state must move beyond structural design and encompass the substantive content of central state policy: specifically, policy dimensions delineating citizenship, property rights, client group formation, and involvement in the world system. The citizenship dimension takes in all the non-property-related rights and duties of individual citizens in their relations with the central state. Any narrowing in these rights, including the weakening of limitations on the authority of the central state to prescribe religious practice or political belief and to discriminate between ethnic groups implies an expansion of central state power. Similarly, policies that dictate the use of labor in service to the state or reduce the ability of individuals to resist such policies enhance central state power.

The control of property dimension includes all policy measures that increase the authority of the state over the use and ownership of property. All internal revenue measures fall under this category, as do all forms of state regulation of private economic activity and marketplace relations. Labor contracts between private parties (including subordinate governments) are also included when and if central state intervention does not, in itself, carry an obligation on the part of labor to service the needs of the state.

The creation of client groups dimension contains measures that create a dependency relation between individuals and the central state. Such measures can be subdivided into at least three subcategories. Those involving pensions, welfare payments, salaries from government employment, and income substitutes (such as price controls on commodities sold to specific groups in the population) generally insulate individuals from the marketplace. This insulation is the result of a reduction of their exposure to market forces by way of dependence on government-derived income. A different type of dependency is involved in the issuance and distribution of long-term debt securities by the central state. Acceptance of these securities involves individuals in the future viability and strength of the central state (but does not, in itself, reduce their exposure to market forces). Debt relationships are involved, again, in the currency policy of the central state. Manipulation of the definition of legal tender, as for the repayment of public and private debt, and government discretion over the inherent value of the currency—either through overt controls or participation in marketplace transactions—enhance the authority of the central state. Reliance on a gold standard and enforcement of a gold clause in contractual debt relations, by contrast, substantively reduce the dependence of private individuals on the discretionary exercise of central state authority.

The sixth and last dimension concerns those measures that describe the relationship of the central state with the remainder of the world system, including other central states. These policies include trade relations between national and world economies (for example, tariffs, import quotas, export subsidies, state-to-state economic aid and trading arrangements), diplomatic relations with foreign nations (treaty negotiations, military conflict, formal international alliances), and broadly conceived policies of internal development. Most measures in the last category involve the settlement of unoccupied territory, territorial expansion, or the administration of territorial possessions. Some, like the institution or manipulation of restrictions on immigration, involve the future composition of the citizenry and the permeability of national boundaries to noneconomic "alien" forces. Others promise to shape internal settlement patterns and to integrate disparate regional economies. In the late nineteenth century, the transcontinental railway and the Homestead Act were the two most prominent measures falling under this heading.

These categories are intended to be exhaustive in the sense that all policy choices that affect the scope of central state authority can be classified within one of the six dimensions. For the most part, the dimensions are also mutually exclusive, but several difficulties stand in the way of a full development of this property. In the first place, full mutual exclusivity would seem to depend upon the presentation of a completely articulated theory of both the political creation and the exercise of central state authority. In the absence of such a completely articulated theory of the state, mutual exclusivity between dimensions can be achieved only through an extensive, potentially endless cataloging of all conceivable policies involving the possible exercise of state power.

Despite the failure to achieve full mutual exclusivity, however, these dimensions will more than adequately play two roles in the following analysis. On the one hand, the taxonomy should facilitate comparison of legislative support, and, in turn, the support of specific groups and interests in the larger society, for the expansion of central state authority. Without some prior classification, such comparisons would be frustrated by the wide variety and apparent individuality of the hundreds, sometimes thousands of legislative measures considered annually. On the other hand, this taxonomy is not an a priori classification. Each element can be derived from theoretical concerns that find repeated expression in the literature on state formation (for example, administrative capacity), in the philosophical discussion of natural and constitutional rights (citizenship), or in conventional distinctions between the role of the state in different policy areas (the distinction between domestic and foreign policy). Several dimensions reflect a concern with more than one of these separate areas of theoretical discussion (see figure 2).

Figure 2.
Legislative Dimensions of Central State Authority

Centralization of Authority: Measures involving the transfer of decision-making authority from subordinate governments and the citizenry to the central state; in the case of individual citizens, such measures do not involve a substantive expansion of central state activity but, only, the allocation of influence and control over that activity; in the case of subordinate governments, such measures include the review of subordinate government decisions by central state institutions and the form of subordinate government participation in central state decision making.

Administrative Capacity: Measures involving a broadening or narrowing of bureaucratic discretion and long-term planning capacity within the central state; these measures affect only institutions within the central state itself; in analyzing policy, reference is made to a hierarchy based on relative insulation from societal or outside political influence (the state bureaucracy, national courts, presidency, and, last, congress).

Citizenship: Measures involving the religious practices, political beliefs, ethnic identity, and rights and duties of citizens in their relations with the state; this category excludes measures affecting property but includes all measures concerning the physical movement and labor of citizens (such as conscription).

Control of Property: Measures involving the control or use of property by individuals or institutions (other than the central state itself), including internal revenue policy, expropriation, regulation of the marketplace, and labor contracts between private parties.

Creation of Client Groups: Measures that increase the dependence of groups within society upon the continued existence and viability of the central state; includes only measures that provide income or income substitutes to individuals (e.g., pensions, employment by central state institutions, welfare, and price control programs for specific groups in society), that establish future-oriented obligations that depend on state viability (e.g., the issuance of long-term debt), and that control the value of the currency (e.g., the gold standard and redemption of paper money).

The Central State in the World System: Measures concerning the relationship of the central state and nation with other states and the world economy; these include access to foreign markets (e.g., licensing, import quotas, export subsidies, and tariffs), diplomatic relations (e.g., membership in international organizations, treaties, and military conflict), immigration restrictions, and broadly conceived policies of internal development (e.g., the Pacific Railroad, the Homestead Act, and administration of territorial possessions).

Selection of Confederate State-Building Decisions

As a focus for the study of Confederate state building, the southern Congress possesses one major liability—there is a paucity of information concerning the operation and internal politics of that body. Little is known about the Confederate Congress for a number of reasons. First, many, if not most, of its most important deliberations were conducted in secret session. The injunction of secrecy largely prevented contemporary coverage of legislative debates and may have discouraged members from setting down a more complete record of their participation in diaries or memoirs. The skimpiness of official records constitutes a second and equally serious limitation on historical knowledge of the Confederate Congress. Stringencies imposed by the war effort led the Congress to forgo a verbatim record of its proceedings. During the war, the Congress, along with many other Confederate institutions, delayed publication of many of its reports and even journals (which were later published by the U.S. Congress).[6] A third reason for the comparative lack of knowledge about the Confederate Congress is that body's inimical relations with the press. The hostility of the southern press was due, in part, to the Congress's practice of holding secret sessions and, in part, to the partisan involvement of newspaper editors as supporters or opponents of the Davis administration. Finally, the hectic pace of legislative deliberations, the trying conditions under which Confederate congressmen worked and lived, and even the dearth of good grades of paper resulted in a scarcity of personal documents such as diaries and personal letters. For all these reasons, Confederate congressmen are often seen as faceless, petty figures with relatively undeveloped political philosophies and worldviews.[7] Despite these deficiencies in the historical record, however, the information essential to an understanding of the statutory structure and administration of the Confederate state, as well as the voting behavior of congressmen on specific issues, can be retrieved from official documents.

The congressional decisions analyzed in the following pages were selected for a variety of reasons. One important criterion was the existence of information concerning the political and institutional context within which the decision was made. Because relatively little information (in the form of records, debates, and letters) has survived, this requirement is a fairly stiff test that precluded inclusion, for example, of many decisions made during the Provisional Congress. A second consideration favored selection of decisions that have been directly implicated by scholars in interpretations of Confederate

6. *Journal of the Congress of the Confederate States of America, 1861–1865*, 7 vols. (Washington, D.C.: U.S. Government Printing Office, 1904–05). Abstracts and summaries of the deliberations were printed in the Richmond *Examiner* and later collected by the Southern Historical Society (published as the "Proceedings of the Confederate Congress" in vols. 44–52 of the *Southern Historical Society Papers* [Richmond, 1923–59]). Those volumes are hereafter cited as *Proceedings*.

7. Bell Wiley cites similar reasons in his introduction to *Letters of Warren Aiken* (Athens: University of Georgia Press, 1959), 1–4.

defeat. This criterion in particular biased selection toward the structural design dimensions of central state power. A third requirement was the selection of a wide and representative range of the most important war measures considered by the Confederate Congress. The significance of some of these, such as conscription and suspension of the writ of habeas corpus, rests upon a consensus in the scholarly community. Others, such as the initial decision to publicly fund construction of a private railroad branch line, are less commonly discussed.[8]

The final considerations in the selection process favored inclusion of closely contested decisions in which congressmen divided fairly evenly and of decisions within a wide temporal spread. Both criteria particularly influenced the selection of specific decisions when more than one occurred in a narrowly defined subject area.

Analytic Categories. Similar considerations dictated the analytical categories through which support for the expansion of central state authority will be examined. The distinction made between exterior (Kentucky, Missouri, and West Virginia) and interior districts is a fundamental cleavage widely recognized in the literature on the Confederate Congress.[9] From almost the very beginning of the war, most thoughtful Confederates conceded Kentucky and Missouri (and, later, West Virginia) to the Union as a necessary outcome, barring miracles, of any negotiations attending independence. But despite these reservations, twenty-three congressmen (seven from Missouri, twelve from Kentucky, and four from western Virginia) continued to serve in the First and Second Confederate Congresses.[10] Contact with their constituencies was impossible: as John Crockett of Kentucky noted in debate, "In Kentucky every Southern man is marked. Six of the Kentucky delegation have been

8. One of the best general reviews of precedent-setting legislative decisions (and one upon which this study has relied) is in Amlund's *Federalism in the Southern Confederacy* (see, specifically, pp. 44–63).

9. The terminology is taken from Thomas B. Alexander and Richard E. Beringer, *The Anatomy of the Confederate Congress* (Nashville, Tenn.: Vanderbilt University Press, 1972), though they mean something different (all districts occupied by Union forces—a category that increases in size throughout the war; see p. 135). They find that the exterior-interior division is the single most important cleavage in the Confederate Congress. Wilfred Buck Yearns also emphasizes its significance in *The Confederate Congress* (Athens: University of Georgia Press, 1960), 225–26.

10. These members composed just over a fifth of the House of Representatives. The failure of officially sponsored conventions to ratify a secession ordinance prevented most objective observers from considering Kentucky and Missouri as integral parts of the Confederacy. Doubt concerning resolve over the retention of "West Virginia" led the Virginia General Assembly to request that the Confederate Congress formally commit the national government to such a policy. The resolution subsequently passed by Congress stated, "That in no event will this government consent to a division or dismemberment of the state of Virginia, but will assert and maintain her jurisdiction and sovereignty to the uttermost limits of her ancient boundaries, at any and every cost" (approved June 4, 1864), but it probably did little to allay the General Assembly's fears (*A Digest of the Military and Naval Laws of the Confederate States, Provisional and First Congresses*, 315–16).

indicted for treason by the Northern Government."[11] Interior congressmen viewed these delegates as representing rotten boroughs and thus diluting representation from the remaining, legitimate areas of the Confederacy. In 1864, for example, Josiah Turner of North Carolina wrote to his wife that he "would rather plough and feed hogs than legislate . . . with Missouri and Kentucky to help me."[12] Later, near the end of the war, the House of Representatives formally debated resolutions questioning the legitimacy of representation in Congress of areas overrun by Union armies.[13]

Congressmen from occupied areas, particularly from Kentucky, Missouri, and what later became West Virginia, were the strongest adovcates of a dominant central state role in the new southern nation. Their more or less consistent support for the expansion of central state authority arose, in part, out of the realization that only a convincing, clear-cut southern victory would lead to an incorporation of their constituencies into the Confederacy.[14] In addition, northern occupation of their homes cut off almost all private sources of income for these members and thus produced a dependence upon congressional salaries and other support from the Confederate government. This dependence led them to resist adjournment resolutions (which reduced per diem income), to support substitution of an annual salary for per diem reimbursement of expenses, and to favor generally an active professionalization of the role of congressmen in the Confederate state.

Members from occupied districts also had two electoral reasons that allowed or encouraged them to disproportionately support the growth of central state power. Since their constituents were behind Union lines, these members heard few, if any, complaints concerning the substance of Confederate measures or the way in which they were implemented. On the other hand, the electorate that sustained these congressmen was almost solely drawn from

11. *Proceedings*, 44 : 117. By 1863, major portions of the Confederacy had fallen under the control of Union armies and the normal conduct of elections became impossible in these areas. In the states of Arkansas, Kentucky, Louisiana, Missouri, and Tennessee the Confederate Congress ordered "general ticket" elections by which means refugees and residents of unoccupied territory could cast a vote for a candidate in each of the individual districts of the state. The candidate receiving the greatest number of votes was then declared eligible to serve in the Confederate Congress as the representative from the district in which he was a candidate (Yearns, *Confederate Congress*, 43). The text of the separate acts appears in *Public Laws of the Confederate States of America, Third Session, First Congress (1863)*. The Louisiana act (pp. 157–58) provided for voting by refugees from districts occupied by the enemy but did not specify a general ticket. In Tennessee (pp. 164–65), Missouri (pp. 173–74), and Arkansas (pp. 189–90), however, use of the general ticket format was specified. The acts providing for elections in the last two states appear in *Public Laws of the Confederate States of America, Fourth Session, First Congress (1863–1864)* (Richmond: R. M. Smith, 1864).

12. Quoted in Yearns, *Confederate Congress*, 225.

13. Alexander and Beringer, *Anatomy of the Confederate Congress*, 66–67, and *Proceedings*, 52 : 266–69 (January 31, 1865). For an example of the bitterness between members engendered by the representation of occupied areas, see the exchange between Lafayette McMullen and Robert Montague, both of Virginia, in *Proceedings*, 51 : 229–31 and 246 (June 9 and 11, 1864).

14. See, for example, Yearns, *Confederate Congress*, 39, 225.

the ranks of the Confederate military (soldiers who formerly resided in the occupied states) and, of much less significance, from refugees. Although the electoral record is incomplete, what is known suggests that the soldier vote strongly favored more extreme war measures and, consequently, a stronger central state.[15]

Within the group of interior districts, further distinctions can be drawn between constituencies with varying levels of slaveholding and value-added in manufacturing. Slaveholding has frequently been considered the most significant ecological correlate of secession sentiment and, later, southern nationalism, and the distinction drawn here touches on many previous interpretations of antebellum Confederate politics.[16] The classification of districts according to per capita value-added in manufacturing (above and below ten dollars) relates to the widely accepted argument that the industrialization process generates social and economic demands for the expansion of central state authority and administrative capacity.[17]

Congressmen, in this case including exterior members, are further categorized into their respective committee assignments. The three most important committees organized in the Confederate House were the committees on the Judiciary, Military Affairs, and Ways and Means. Together, the membership of these three committees, which rarely overlapped, accounted for between a quarter and a third of all congressmen. During the life of the Confederate Congress, however, these panels accounted for approximately two-thirds of all committee reports filed in the House of Representatives (see table 1). With a usual complement of thirteen—one drawn from each state in the Confederacy—Military Affairs alone accounted for nearly a third of all committee reports.[18] The heavy work load of that committee led to complaints by members on and off the panel and to sporadic, largely ineffective efforts to distrib-

15. On the reasons that explain the disproportionate support of congressmen from occupied areas for a stronger central state, see Alexander and Beringer, *Anatomy of the Confederate Congress,* 320–28, 336–37. On North Carolina troops (the soldiers' vote) favoring an expanded war effort and stronger central state, see Georgia Lee Tatum, *Disloyalty in the Confederacy* (Chapel Hill: University of North Carolina Press, 1934), 132. On support by Georgia troops for Governor Brown's reelection, see I. W. Avery, *History of the State of Georgia: 1850–1881* (New York: Brown & Derby, 1881; reprint, New York: AMS Press, 1972), 261. For an example of the arrangements made to accommodate voting by soldiers, see General Order No. 38 (April 7, 1863) which relays "an act of the legislature of Virginia, passed March 26, 1863," in R. H. P. Robinson, *General Orders of the Confederate States Army, 1863* (Richmond: A. Morris, 1864), 39–40.

16. In their exhaustive analysis, Alexander and Beringer consider only the slaveholding characteristics of the members themselves (*Anatomy of the Confederate Congress,* 59–65).

17. Antebellum party allegiance is not studied here both because Alexander and Beringer have intensively analyzed its influence and because their findings are generally inconclusive. In an important sense, the decision not to study party allegiance concedes the absence of formal party organizations (or effective surrogates) in the Confederacy—a concession that not all Confederate scholars would be willing to make.

18. The total number of standing committees in the Confederate House ranged from twenty-two to twenty-eight in the various sessions. The membership of the permanent House of Representatives was 106.

Table 1. Legislative Activity in the Confederate House of Representatives: Committee Reports, 1861–1865

Committee	Provisional Congress (Unicameral) (Feb. 4, 1861–Feb. 17, 1862)		First Congress 1st and 2nd Sessions (Feb. 18–Oct. 13, 1862)		First Congress 3rd and 4th Sessions (Jan. 12, 1863–Feb. 17, 1864)		Second Congress 1st and 2nd Sessions (May 2, 1864–Mar. 18, 1865)	
	%	N	%	N	%	N	%	N
Judiciary	14.7	(79)	16.0	(83)	16.7	(72)	12.2	(53)
Military Affairs	32.5	(175)	35.9	(186)	31.2	(135)	26.2	(114)
Ways and Means	17.8	(96)	12.5	(65)	13.0	(56)	26.0	(113)
All other	34.9	(188)	35.5	(184)	39.1	(169)	35.6	(155)
All reports	100.0	(538)	100.0	(518)	100.0	(432)	100.0	(435)

Source: Computed from the subject index to the respective volumes of the *Journal of the Confederate Congress.*

Note: Reports originating from the committees on Engrossment, Printing, and Enrolled Bills are excluded from this table.

ute portions of its jurisdiction to newly created committees.[19] Of the thirty decisions analyzed in the following pages, nineteen (63 percent) originated in one of these three committees.

EVIDENCE

Citizenship in the Confederate State

The decisions, first, to conscript men into the Confederate military and, second, to grant to the president the authority to suspend the writ of habeas corpus were by far the most significant state-power-enhancing measures ever adopted by the Confederate Congress. The only other measure that might compete in importance was embodied in legislation that regulated the already existing practice of impressment. Both conscription and suspension of habeas corpus were similarly viewed by the southern citizenry as the strongest war measures enacted during the life of the Confederacy. Referring to conscription, for example, Representative Henry Foote of Tennessee claimed that Jefferson Davis and his cabinet promoted "this rank centralizing measure" in order "to put down all opposition to their scheme of despotic domination."[20]

The first conscription act was passed by the Confederate House of Representatives on April 14, 1862, and enacted by Congress as a whole two days later. This act declared all able-bodied, white males between the ages of eighteen and thirty-five subject to service in the Confederate military and retained those already enrolled in the army for an additional three years. As high state policy, conscription dramatically centralized control over the organization of the military forces of the Confederacy by eliminating or severely reducing most aspects of participation by individual state governments. The implications of this step were not lost on states' rights advocates. Conscription also enmeshed the individual citizen in a direct and subordinate relation to central state authority.[21]

19. On recognition of Military Affairs' heavy work load, see *Proceedings,* 45 : 185 (August 20, 1862). To more widely distribute the jurisdiction, the House created committees on the Medical Department, Ordnance and Ordnance Stores, and Quartermaster's and Commissary departments, and Military Transportation. None of them filed more than 3 percent of all committee reports in the House.

20. Henry Stuart Foote, *War of the Rebellion* (New York: Harper & Brothers, 1866), 370n. For a general history of conscription in the Confederacy, see Albert Burton Moore, *Conscription and Conflict in the Confederacy* (New York: Hillary House Publishers, 1963). A briefer account appears in John Christopher Schwab, *Confederate States of America: 1861–1865* (New York: Burt Franklin, 1968), 193–202. Ironically, perhaps, the closest the Confederate government came to using conscription for despotic purposes was when congressmen advocated an end to the exemption of newspaper editors. Otho Singleton of Mississippi, for example, was quoted (paraphrased) by the Richmond *Examiner* as saying that "he was for smoking out some disreputable little fellows who were fonder of spilling ink than of blood, and whose occupation it was to bark at the heels of gentlemen" (*Proceedings,* 48 : 48 [February 3, 1863]).

21. The vulnerability of the individual citizen to central state controls was immeasurably enhanced by the suspension of the writ of habeas corpus in combination with conscription (Moore, *Conscription and Conflict,* 86–87).

From the very beginning, most governors of the individual states opposed conscription and sought outright repeal or limitations on the exercise of associated powers, such as the commissioning of officers, by the central government.[22] The attitude of these state executives was best reflected in the message Governor John Letcher sent to the Virginia Legislature on May 5, 1862:

> Since your adjournment, the confederate congress have passed a conscription bill, which relieves the general assembly, in a great measure, from the necessity of further legislation in regard to military matters. This bill divests the state authorities of all control over the troops of Virginia, and vests in the confederate government the power to enroll all persons between the ages of eighteen and thirty-five, organize them, commission the officers, call them into service, and dispose of them in such manner as they may deem advisable.
>
> It is my deliberate conviction that this act is *unconstitutional;* but taking into consideration the peculiar condition of affairs existing at the time of its passage, I forbear to debate the question at present. When the war is ended, we can discuss these questions, and so settle them as to preserve the rights of the states.[23]

Many congressmen similarly considered conscription of doubtful constitutionality but, like Governor Letcher, they forwent criticism. One of the most important members in this group was William Miles of South Carolina, chairman of the Committee on Military Affairs which held jurisdiction over conscription measures.[24]

Because the Confederate Congress never provided for a Supreme Court, judicial challenges to the constitutionality of the conscription acts were heard in the state and local courts.[25] The most influential of these cases was *Jeffers* v. *Fair,* decided by the Supreme Court of Georgia. As this and similar cases were decided in favor of conscription, "the great powers of the Confederate Gov-

22. Ibid., 228–304, and Yearns, *Confederate Congress,* 83–85. Many states had previously or subsequently enacted their own conscription acts. See, for example, "An Act: To render certain persons subject to military service (December 6, 1862)," no. 42 in State of Alabama, *Acts of the Called Session, 1862 and of the Second Regular Annual Session of the General Assembly* (Montgomery: Montgomery Advertiser Book and Job Office, 1862), 63–64. For more on the Alabama militia, see Walter L. Fleming, *Civil War and Reconstruction in Alabama* (New York: Columbia University Press, 1905), 90.

23. *Journal of the Senate of the Commonwealth of Virginia, Extra Session* (Richmond: James E. Goode, 1862), 16–17. Governor Francis Pickens sent a similar message to the South Carolina legislature (Richmond *Dispatch,* November 26, 1862).

24. *Proceedings,* 45 : 203–11 (August 22, 1862) and 48 : 88 (February 9, 1863). For other examples of congressional debate on the constitutionality of conscription and its relation to states' rights, see *Proceedings,* 45 : 382 (August 19, 1862); 46 : 25–28, 38–40, 49–54, 68–72, 83–85, 95–97, 108–11, 136, 148–52, 167, 252 (September 3–26, 1862).

25. The Richmond *Dispatch,* for example, reported a decision by the Elbert County Superior Court in Georgia in which the conscription act was declared unconstitutional and a conscript liberated from the enrolling officer (October 1, 1862). For similar cases in Alabama, including those in which it was determined that "the right of the Confederacy to the military service of a citizen was paramount to the right of the state" (see Fleming, *Civil War and Reconstruction in Alabama,* 96–97).

ernment were unsheathed by the courts" and "the new government looked so much like the old one that it was painful to the ultra-States' rights men."[26]

In supporting conscription, the Richmond *Examiner* argued that Confederate policy "would be similar to that enforced by probably every government of Europe, except that of Great Britain. . . . The experience of Europe is the experience of all ages and all military powers."[27] But, even so, the original Confederate conscription act predated a much weaker Union policy by over a year and was the first military draft in American history. And it was extensively enforced. By the beginning of 1864, the chief of the Confederate Bureau of War noted, "The conscription is now being pressed mercilessly. It is agonizing to see and hear the cases daily brought into the War Office, appeal after appeal and *all* disallowed. Women come there and weep, wring their hands, scold, entreat, beg, and almost drive me mad. The iron is gone deep into the heart of society."[28] The unrelenting necessities of the war effort, however, demanded an even harsher manpower policy. In November of the same year, the secretary of war advocated an end to all exemptions except those "officers actually essential to the conduct of the Confederate and State Governments" and that all other able-bodied men "without distinction, be at once devoted to the sacred study [of] defending their country in the field."[29]

Richard Goff has referred to conscription as "one of the more efficient war policies" implemented by the Confederate government. In describing the improvements embodied in the 1864 revision, he observed that from "an administrative viewpoint the act left little to be desired, except for the exemption of officialdom and professionals."[30] Charles W. Ramsdell praised the same act because it abolished previously protected exemptions and "authorized the Secretary of War to detail men for certain necessary civil services" which left "factory owners . . . entirely at the mercy of some government bureau."[31] The final report of the Bureau of Conscription, issued in 1865, estimated that 177,000 men had been enrolled from areas east of the Mississippi. In his

26. Moore, *Conscription and Conflict*, 162–63, 170. For an account of the *Asa Jeffers (conscript)* v. *John Fair (enrolling officer)* case, see the Richmond *Dispatch* (November 18, 1862), which contains abstracts from the defendant's brief, the court's decision, and a long quote from Judge Jenkins's majority opinion. The state of Georgia subsequently provided further assistance to Confederate efforts to enforce conscription. In particular, see "An Act to Punish Any Person who May Hereafter Conceal, or Assist any Deserter in Resisting a Legal Arrest in this State" (December 15, 1863), printed in *Acts of the General Assembly of the State of Georgia* (Milledgeville: Boughton, Nisbet & Barnes, 1863), 63. See also Sidney D. Brummer, "The Judicial Interpretation of the Confederate Constitution," in *Studies in Southern History and Politics* (New York: Columbia University Press, 1914), 109–11.

27. From Frank Moore, ed., *Rebellion Record* (New York: G. P. Putnam, 1864–71), 1 : 325 (no date).

28. Robert Kean, *Inside Confederate Government*, ed. Edward Younger (New York: Oxford University Press, 1957), 174.

29. Confederate States of America, War Department, *Report of the Secretary of War* (Richmond, 1864), 7.

30. Richard Goff, *Confederate Supply* (Durham: Duke University Press, 1969), 95, 163.

31. Charles W. Ramsdell, *Behind the Lines in the Southern Confederacy* (Baton Rouge: Louisiana State University Press, 1944), 102.

Conscription and Conflict, Albert Moore concludes that the bureau's estimate should be raised to at least 300,000 (effectively accounting for between 30 to 50 percent of all enlistments). When allowance is made for "voluntary" enlistments, which were, in fact, the result of the imminence of conscription, Moore estimates that "most of the military population was reached and allocated" and that conscription "rendered a distinct service by systematizing and centralizing the military system."[32]

Conscription, particularly discretionary authority over the granting of exemptions, gave the Confederate government almost complete command over the labor force throughout the southern economy. In turn, the Confederate government's control over the supply of labor gave the central state indirect control over industrial and agricultural production, including profit margins on government contracts and price ceilings on agricultural produce.[33] The Confederate government seems to have most actively exercised this power in relation to controls on wool, cotton, leather, shoe, and general ordnance production.[34] The most extensive use of exemption authority was, however, in relation to Confederate direction of railroad operations.[35] Control of railroad traffic, in turn, complemented exemption-derived influence over industrial production because, given the shortfall in railway capacity, control of railroad operations was roughly equivalent to control over the allocation of raw materials. Compliant factories were systematically favored by Confederate quarter-

32. Pp. 355–58. Moore also notes that early Confederate conscription policy "had many imperfections," the most important of which were class or categorical exemptions in which the government was left with little or no discretion and the system of substitution under which conscripts could hire substitutes to serve in their place (pp. 354–55). Both defects were remedied, for the most part, by 1863.

33. Amlund, *Federalism in the Southern Confederacy,* 63, 71, and Charles W. Ramsdell, "The Control of Manufacturing," *Mississippi Valley Historical Review* 8, no. 3 (December 1921) : 235. As an example of agricultural price controls, see Goff, *Confederate Supply,* 162. Goff adds that the "broad exemption-and-detail provisions" of the third conscription act (February 17, 1864) "put the government in a general position to control farm and factory labor, and in the face of mounting subsistence shortages, the act, together with subsequent War Department rulings, spelled out government controls over agriculture with even greater precision."

34. Ramsdell, "The Control of Manufacturing," 234–40, 245–46. For an example of military enforcement of labor in detailed or exempted occupations, see R. H. P. Robinson, *General Orders of the Confederate States Army, 1863* (Richmond: A. Morris, 1864), no. 30 (March 18, 1863): "conscripts or detailed men leaving their employment without written permission, shall be reported to the nearest enrolling officer, to be tried and punished as deserters" (p. 28).

35. Goff, *Confederate Supply;* Amlund, *Federalism in the Southern Confederacy:* "A railroad bill enacted in 1863 gave Davis the power to require 'any carrier to devote its facilities to the support of the army'; under the law Richmond could prescribe railroad adherence to through train schedules. By 1865 the central government was no longer threatening companies that would not cooperate with it; rather it was indicating that the government would place the employees of uncooperative roads into military service" (pp. 47–48); Francis B. C. Bradlee, *Blockade Running during the Civil War: And the Effect of Land and Water Transportation on the Confederacy* (Salem, Mass.: Essex Institute, 1925), 255; and Charles W. Turner, "The Virginia Central Railroad at War, 1861–1865," *Journal of Southern History* 12, no. 4 (November 1946) : 513.

masters. Outside the conscription-centered system of industrial and agricultural controls, the provisions of an Act to Lay Taxes for the Common Defence and Carry on the Government of the Confederate States, amended February 17, 1864, effectively conferred upon the central government potential licensing authority over all major trades, businesses, and occupations.[36] Together, Confederate direction of railway operations, taxation, and conscription conferred upon the central government almost absolute control over the southern economy. At all times, however, the manpower authority embodied in the conscription and exemption acts was far and away the most important source of central state influence.[37]

Another policy that carried comparable implications for the position of the citizen within the Confederate state was the suspension of the writ of habeas corpus. Congress passed legislation authorizing suspension on four separate occasions. A first law was approved February 27, 1862, which, after a second act passed April 19, was set to expire on October 13, 1862 (thirty days after the next meeting of Congress). On that date, Congress approved a third suspension act, which, again, was set to expire thirty days after the next meeting of Congress. On February 13, 1863, the authority expired, only to be renewed one year later, on February 15, 1864, under a fourth and final law. The renewal expired ninety days after the next meeting of Congress, August 1, 1864. Under the first and subsequent laws, authority to suspend the writ was given for all arrests made by the central government for offenses against the Confederacy. The fourth statute detailed these offenses, including treason, desertion, sabotage, and unlawful intercourse with the enemy, but, in practice, it was almost as broad a grant of authority as the original.[38]

Congressmen assumed more consistent and philosophically coherent posi-

36. Dozens of different occupations and businesses were assigned specific taxes which could have easily become prohibitive. For example, Section 4, Part IX, stated: "Brewers shall pay one hundred dollars, and two-and-a-half per centum on the gross amount of sales made. Every person who manufactures fermented liquors, of any name or description for sale, from malt, wholly or in part, shall be deemed a brewer under this act" (*Laws of Congress in Regard to Taxes, Currency, and Conscription* [Printed by Order of the Virginia Senate] [Richmond: James E. Goode, 1864], 3–20).

37. The enforcement of conscription also threatened to turn the Bureau of Conscription into a central manpower agency for employment within the Confederate government itself. For General Order No. 7 (January 19, 1863) which recognized the exempted status of Post Office Department employees, see *General Orders of the Confederate States Army, 1863*, 8. For the implications of conscription enforcement on Ordnance Bureau operations, see Frank E. Vandiver, "Makeshifts of Confederate Ordnance," *Journal of Southern History* 17, no. 2 (May 1951) : 190. For a conscription-induced shortage of clerks in the Treasury Department, see Richard Cecil Todd, *Confederate Finance* (Athens: University of Georgia Press, 1954), 10–11. On the relationship between departmental operations and conscription enforcement generally, see Goff, *Confederate Supply*, passim.

38. Schwab, *Confederate States of America: 1861–1865*, 187; Frank Lawrence Owsley, *State Rights in the Confederacy* (Chicago: University of Chicago Press, 1931); Amlund, *Federalism in the Southern Confederacy*, 106. Texts of the various acts can be found in *A Digest of the Military and Naval Laws of the Confederate States, Provisional and First Congresses* (Columbia, S.C.: Evans & Cogswell, 1864), 132ff.; the text of the February 15, 1864, act can be found in *Public Laws of the Confederate State of America, Fourth Session, First Congress*, 187–88.

tions on suspension of the writ than on almost any other issue that repeatedly confronted the Congress.[39] Yet, considering their profound implications for individual liberty and for the relative influence of the judicial systems of the individual states, suspension acts passed the Confederate Congress with relative ease.[40]

The opponents of suspension focused attention on the ways in which the authority seriously, perhaps irremediably, reshaped citizen–central state relations. During debate on the third (October 13, 1862) bill, one opponent accused a supporter of suspension of advocating a "doctrine" comparable to that adopted by the "Duke of Alma, one of the bloodiest tyrants of ancient or modern times." He then "protested against the doctrine that our Government was framed only for peace or the sunshine of political existence. . . . This idea of living under such a law oppressed him almost with a sense of suffocation. . . . men were imprisoned in this city under circumstances which no British ministry of modern times would have dared to sustain or sanction."[41]

In an open letter to a Virginia colleague, John Gilmer of North Carolina argued that suspension was "a severe blow on the main pillar of all constitutional government" and plaintively asked "whether the judgment of a Confederate court, upon a Confederate law, is inferior to the mere official whims and ministerial pertinacity of the Secretary of War?"[42] This and similar complaints recognized that the suspension acts, in addition to circumscribing individual liberty and delegating extensive legislative authority to the executive branch, also consolidated power in central state institutions that otherwise was lodged in the judicial systems of the individual states. In the absence of a fully integrated national judiciary, the suspension acts, in effect, allowed Confederate officials to ignore the otherwise definitive rulings of local and individual state courts. In Georgia and North Carolina, in particular, suspension of the writ was thus viewed as a direct assault on states' rights.[43]

On March 2, 1862, three days after enactment of the first suspension bill,

39. Alexander and Beringer, *Anatomy of the Confederate Congress*, 180.

40. For a general history of suspension of the writ in the Confederate state, see Schwab, *Confederate States of America*, 186–92; William M. Robinson, Jr., *Justice in Grey* (Cambridge, Mass.: Harvard University Press, 1941), 389–415; Yearns, *Confederate Congress*, 150–60; Alexander and Beringer, *Anatomy of the Confederate Congress*, 166–73.

41. Richmond *Dispatch*, October 8, 1862. For other examples of congressional debate on suspension, see *Proceedings*, 45 : 242–47 (August 26, 1862); 46 : 175 (September 17, 1862); 51 : 77–80, 101–04, 110–13, and 118–27 (May 16–21, 1864).

42. *Letter Addressed to Hon. William C. Rives: On the Existing Status of the Revolution, etc.* (Richmond, 1864), 2–3.

43. See, for example, the text of "Resolutions on the Suspension of Habeas Corpus" (March 19, 1864) in *Acts of the General Assembly of the State of Georgia*, 152–54. As has been noted, local judges were often as nationalistic as Confederate officials. In order to ensure judicial conformity with the legislature's interpretation of the suspension acts, the latter passed an Act to Amend the Habeas Corpus Laws of this State (December 14, 1863) which imposed a fine of $2,500 upon a judge of a superior or inferior court who refused to grant a writ of habeas corpus to any individual who applied. The fine was made payable to the applicant (p. 45).

President Davis declared martial law in Richmond and all areas within ten miles of the city. His proclamation suspended the writ of habeas corpus, replaced all civil authority (the mayor excepted) with military rule, and closed all distilleries and liquor stores. Similar proclamations under the first act later included other areas of Virginia, the city of Memphis, the Department of East Tennessee, and much of the territory surrounding Charleston, South Carolina.[44] Proclamations issued by either the president or individual military commanders extended suspension to the cities of Mobile, New Orleans, Atlanta, and Salisbury, North Carolina; the entire states of Arkansas and Texas; and portions of Louisiana and Mississippi.[45] Even so, most arrests under martial law were probably related to the sale of liquor by civilians to enlisted men, usually in camps.[46]

Most civil and military officers within the Confederate state considered suspension of the writ and martial law inextricably connected and virtually identical policies. Even before the first suspension act reinforced presidential authority to suspend the writ,

> numerous arrests were made in the Confederate States by the civil and military authorities, both State and federal, on charges of treason and on suspicion of aiding and abetting the enemy. Many of the arrests made by military commanders were, to say the least, extraconstitutional. Some were in the broad twilight zone between war crimes and treason. The Army usually refused to yield a prisoner on a writ of habeas corpus on the ground that no civil court had power to inquire into the detention of prisoners of war . . . on the theory that upon the dissolution of the Old Union every citizen had the right to determine whether he would remain a citizen of the United States or go with his State to the new Confederacy.[47]

Within Congress, strenuous but ultimately unsuccessful efforts were made to disentangle martial law and suspension. Thomas Jones of Tennessee, for example, declared that, whereas the Confederate Congress had the power to

---

44. Schwab, *Confederate States of America*, 186–87. See Moore, *Rebellion Record*, for the text of proclamations extending martial law to Norfolk, Virginia (February 27, 1862; 4 : 216), to East Tennessee (April 8, 1862; 3 : 502), and to Buchanan, Lee, McDowell, Wise, and Wyoming counties in the southwestern corner of Virginia.

45. Owsley, *State Rights in the Confederacy*, 151–52, 157–60.

46. See, for example, the summary of "Sentences by Court-Martial" carried in the Richmond *Dispatch*, December 5, 1862; a separate case in which a civil court intervened, December 15, 1862; and another in which the adjutant and inspector general of the Confederate army ordered the release of detained civilians while allowing the confiscation of contraband liquor, November 28, 1862.

47. This interpretation, related in the last portion of the passage, was supported by a U.S. Supreme Court decision originally handed down in 1830 in a case arising out of the American Revolution (Robinson, *Justice in Grey*, 385). The Alabama secession convention defined citizenship as including only those born in the state of Alabama and those, if born outside the state, who swore an oath of allegiance to the state of Alabama and an oath renouncing allegiance to any other government (Fleming, *Civil War and Reconstruction in Alabama*, 50). This definition effectively gave all individuals the kind of choice anticipated in the text.

authorize suspension of the writ, martial law was "nearly what General Van Dorn had defined it in Mississippi—the will of the officer who declares it" and "whoever declared it did so unconstitutionally." He maintained that even Congress could not impose martial law.

The writ of habeas corpus was formally suspended by congressional action for only eighteen months. In other periods, however, Confederate military officers often acted as if the writ were formally suspended by resorting to martial law. By thus acting, the military filled the breach in periods when the Confederate Congress failed to pass enabling legislation and President Davis was unwilling to suspend the writ by executive proclamation. Thomas Alexander and Richard Beringer have argued that legislative authorization constituted prima facie evidence of "serious internal oppostion" to the Confederate war effort and of the reluctance of at least some judges to "render decisions acceptable to executive authority."[48] But under both conscription and suspension of the writ the formal authority granted to the central state apparently matched the comparative requirements of the war effort in both the Union and the Confederacy. Manpower shortages forced the South to adopt a fully developed conscription program and, through it, a more or less comprehensive, centrally controlled allocation of labor throughout the southern economy. In contrast, the relative absence of disloyalty in the South allowed the Confederacy to adopt less rigorous measures to suppress dissent and suspend civil judicial process.[49]

The patterns of support for conscription and suspension within the Confederate Congress were remarkably similar (see table 2).[50] Both drew much greater support from congressmen who represented exterior districts (Missouri, Kentucky, and West Virginia), although a majority from the interior also backed each policy. As was the case for most state-enhancing measures, the slaveholding characteristics of the constituency had little or no effect on congressional support for an extension of central state authority; members from the black belt plantation districts were no more likely to favor conscription or suspension of the writ than were members from upland white districts. Interior districts with modest levels of manufacturing (over ten dollars value-added per capita) provided comparatively greater backing. This category includes many of the leading cities of the South: Mobile, Alabama; Columbus and Savannah, Georgia; New Orleans, Louisiana; Wilmington, North Carolina; Charleston, South Carolina; Chattanooga, Nashville, and Memphis, Tennessee; and Arlington, Lynchburg, Petersburg, and Richmond, Vir-

48. *Anatomy of the Confederate Congress,* 166.

49. One of the primary reasons for suspending the writ was, of course, the fact that it inhibited the interference of local and individual state courts in the implementation of conscription. See, for example, Moore, *Conscription and Conflict,* 238–39.

50. The conscription vote chosen for this table was recorded the first time the policy passed the Confederate House of Representatives. The suspension vote was taken on passage of the legislation that renewed authority originally granted on February 27, 1862 (*Journal of the Confederate Congress,* 5 : 228, 518).

ginia.[51] With the exception of a few cities such as Atlanta and Augusta, Georgia, and Norfolk, Virginia (which had little industry), the value-added in manufacturing category divides the South along both an urban-rural and an industrial-agrarian dimension. Southern manufacturing, however, was only a very pale shadow of northern industrialization. Almost all southern interior districts would have fallen in the lowest tier of industrial capacity in the Union Congress.

On these crucial decisions, the members of the leading committees of the Confederate House of Representatives also provided a disproportionately higher level of support for the state-enhancing position. Members serving on the Military Affairs Committee, in particular, almost unanimously favored both conscription and suspension of the writ. In no category, however, did members provide greater support for state expansion in these policy areas

Table 2. Citizenship in the Confederate State

Type of Member/District	Support for a Stronger State (House Votes Cast)			
	Conscription (April 14, 1862)		Suspension of Habeas Corpus (October 9, 1862)	
	%	N	%	N
ALL CONGRESSMEN	67.1	(79)	56.7	(67)
Exterior districts	92.9	(14)	85.7	(7)
Interior districts	61.5	(65)	53.3	(60)
Slave population				
0–24%	61.5	(13)	75.0	(8)
25–49%	58.1	(31)	41.9	(31)
Over 50%	66.7	(21)	61.9	(21)
Value-added in manufacturing (per capita)				
Over $10	80.0	(15)	57.1	(14)
Under $10	56.0	(50)	52.2	(46)
Major committees				
Judiciary	71.4	(7)	75.0	(8)
Military Affairs	88.9	(9)	81.8	(11)
Ways and Means	85.7	(7)	71.4	(7)

51. One additional district in Louisiana and Tennessee, both Florida districts, and two from Virginia are also included in this category. In all, nineteen interior districts produced a total value-added in manufacturing greater than ten dollars per capita according to the 1860 census. Maps of counties included in Confederate districts can be found in John Brawner Robbins, "Confederate Nationalism: Politics and Government in the Confederate South, 1861–1865" (Ph.D. diss., Rice University, 1964).

than did those congressmen representing exterior regions of the Confederacy.

Centralization of Authority

In the spring of 1861, Montgomery, Alabama was filled with devoted proponents of states' rights and individual liberty, armed with a philosophical rhetoric sharpened and polished from long years passed in political combat in the halls of the federal Congress.[52] Among other things, the Constitution they drafted prohibited internal improvements subsidized by the Confederate government, barred a protective tariff, and allowed the legislature of an individual state, under certain circumstances, to impeach an officer of the national government. By the middle of 1862, the Confederate government had practically vitiated the first two prohibitions on grounds of military necessity and, apparently, no Confederate official was ever impeached.[53]

In other areas, such as the term of office and authority of the chief executive, Confederate practice and the Constitution were much more centralized that those of the Union. Although isolated phrases could be attributed to the states' rights ideology and doctrine of minimal central state power with which southerners left the Union, other passages proved more than an adequate base for an expansion of Confederate authority into all aspects of southern life. Among the most important were a necessary and proper clause, an injunction concerning faithful execution of the laws, a modified supremacy clause, and an oath of allegiance to the Confederacy imposed upon the officers of the individual states. Much of this, as was true of most of the entire document, was taken verbatim from the antebellum Constitution. Thus, although it is true that the framers of the fundamental law of the Confederacy "were antipathetic toward the expansive interpretation given the federal Constitution by nationalists who favored a viable, centralized government in Washington," the most striking feature of the new framework was that it "prescribed for the Confederacy much the same kind of union which the Southerners had dissolved"—a document that under the pressure of civil war proved fully as expansive as that in the North.[54]

In the remainder of this section, six major tests of legislative sentiment on the centralization of authority in the Confederate state are discussed. The first of these tests arose not in the Congress but during the Constitutional Convention when the framers included appeals from the highest tribunals of the individual states in the jurisdiction of the Supreme Court. This decision was challenged from the floor by Christopher Memminger of South Carolina who

52. About a third (85 of 267) of all Confederate congressmen and senators had previously served in the United States Congress. The percentage was higher in the Senate (55 to 48 percent in the First and Second Confederate Congresses) than in the House (39, 32, and 21 percent in the Provisional, First, and Second Congresses, respectively) (Alexander and Beringer, *Anatomy of the Confederate Congress*, 24–25).

53. Amlund, *Federalism in the Southern Confederacy*, 22.

54. Ibid., 17–18 (and, generally, 17–27); Emory M. Thomas, *The Confederate Nation: 1861–1865* (New York: Harper & Row, 1979), 64; Charles R. Lee, Jr., *The Confederate Constitution* (Chapel Hill: University of North Carolina Press, 1963), 82–140.

offered an amendment to bar Confederate review of decisions handed down by state courts. In a significant endorsement of centralism, the convention rejected Memminger's amendment.[55]

Despite the apparent victory for the advocates of a strong national judiciary, Charles Lee has called this decision the "key" to understanding the ultimate failure of the Confederacy to actually establish a Supreme Court because the motion "indicated a strong state rights persuasion" among southern statesmen.[56] Congressional debate later over the establishment of the court in 1863 underscores Lee's interpretation. There Henry Foote argued what, in effect, might have been the majority position in 1861:

> The establishment of the court, with appellate power over the supreme courts of the States, would be utterly subversive of States' rights and State sovereignty; and instead of securing the desired harmony between the Confederate Government and the Government of the States, would tend to bring them immediately into conflict. No reasonable man could expect that the supreme judicial tribunals for the States would submit to the exercise of appellate power on the part of the supreme court of the Confederate states upon constitutional questions. No, sir, the establishment of the court would have the inevitable effect of bringing the sovereign States of our system in dire conflict with the central government.[57]

Even so, the two issues must be kept distinct. The establishment of a national supreme court, even without jurisdiction over the state courts, would have improved the administrative capacity of the Confederate judiciary by increasing the coherence and coordination of an otherwise decentralized system. The extension of jurisdiction to include decisions of the higher courts of the individual states would have, on the other hand, immeasurably centralized authority in the Confederate state and formally written into fundamental law that power necessary for national supremacy. To repeat, the Confederate Constitution granted national supremacy but the Congress refused to establish the court.

As has been noted, Congress is considered here to be the least statist-oriented of the major branches of American and Confederate government, owing primarily to the permeability of the national legislature to public influence through elections. Any measure that insulates individual members of Congress from public pressure and electoral competition increases the autonomy of the institution and furthers the development of internal relations between the legislature and the other, more statist-oriented branches. The most important such measure adopted by the Confederate state was the institution, through congressional resolution, of secret sessions from which the public and members of the press were excluded and concerning which congressmen

---

55. Louisiana, South Carolina, and Texas supported Memminger's restriction; Alabama, Georgia, and Mississippi voted for an expansive jurisdiction; and Florida's delegation split evenly (*Journal of the Confederate Congress*, 1 : 880–81 [March 7, 1861]).

56. *Confederate Constitution*, 108.

57. *Proceedings*, 50 : 68 (December 16, 1863).

were enjoined from discussion outside the chamber. Most major Confederate policies were discussed and adopted in secrecy, and secret sessions were convened throughout the life of the Confederate Congress. Many members complained that secret sessions made a mockery of the "representation" role of elected representatives. Foote, for example, "quoted Macaulay to prove the 'absurdity' . . . of sending members to Congress and keeping their actions secret," and he periodically offered resolutions that would have made it more difficult for the House to invoke secrecy.[58] The vote on one of these resolutions—requiring that one-fifth of the members in attendance approve a motion to go into secret session—is the second test of congressional sentiment on centralization.

Aside from conscription, the most difficult issue frustrating professionalization of the Confederate military concerned the appointment of officers. The statist position was presidential appointment, which faced competition from two alternatives: commissions to be granted by the individual states and election by enlisted men; both applied only to relatively junior officers. Two clear tests of congressional sentiment occurred during the life of the Confederacy. The first occurred on the adoption of an amendment to the 1862 conscription bill. As approved by the House, the amendment gave to the individual states the authority to commission officers who had been elected by enlisted men. The original provision, to be struck out by the amendment, had given commissioning authority to the president. Both alternatives contemplated a system that relied primarily on election by enlisted men. The chief difference between them lay in the location of the formal commissioning authority and, thus, in the relative centralization of the military hierarchy.[59]

A second test of congressional sentiment took place two years later on an amendment that would have allowed enlisted men to elect regimental, battalion, and company, as well as lower-ranking, officers. This amendment, which was rejected, would have replaced presidential appointment and, in that way, decentralized the military toward the citizenry.[60]

Another decision involving citizen participation in wartime governance was considered by the Confederate House of Representatives when it took up legislation intended to eliminate fraud and speculation in the purchasing and manufacturing activities of the government. To the clause providing that any person "who shall violate any of the provisions of the foregoing sections shall be liable to indictment, and fined in a sum not less than one thousand dollars, and imprisoned not less than one year, at the discretion of the jury trying said case," Lucius Gartrell of Georgia offered an amendment to strike the word *jury* and substitute *judge*. The amendment was rejected on a voice vote and a

58. *Proceedings*, 177–78 (August 18, 1862). For other debate on the propriety of secret sessions, see 44 : 20 (February 19, 1862); pp. 44–45 (February 24, 1862); pp. 91–93 (March 4, 1862); 45 : 180–81 (August 18, 1862). On April 8, 1862, the House of Representatives appointed members to a "Joint Committee on Conference" to "decide what matters shall be considered in secret session" (45 : 96).

59. *Journal of the Confederate Congress*, 5 : 224 (April 14, 1862).

60. Ibid., 6 : 684 (January 25, 1864).

later motion to reconsider was defeated in a roll call, 36–41. Adoption of the amendment would have taken authority from the citizenry to try the case and impose sentence and have lodged it in the district court judges of the Confederacy. Such an arrangement would have established a procedure through which the actions of purchasing officials were reviewed by other central state officers and further insulated administrative performance from public influence. This is the fifth test of centralizing sentiment.

Other than instituting secret sessions, one of the most significant ways in which the central state can reduce or shape the influence of the citizenry on governmental decisions is by providing for an internal screening of elected officials. A mechanism that imposes conditions set by central state officers, besides popular election, in effect declares some types of popular influence illegitimate. This can be done through electoral law, constitutional requirements such as age, residence, and citizenship, and loyalty oaths. The most rigorous method used by the Confederate Congress was the expulsion of duly elected members; two members were expelled from the House of Representatives for disloyalty to the Confederate state. In the first case, W. R. W. Cobb of north Alabama was expelled because, in the words of the committee appointed to consider the issue, he

> had taken the oath of allegiance to the enemy; that he could have attended the meeting of the last Congress and claimed his seat in that body if he had so desired; that he went voluntarily into the enemy's lines; that when the enemy penetrated into his country he was not within their lines, but went of his free will and joined them, representing to them that he was a "good Yankee"; that he has the reputation among his own people of being a disloyal man; that it appears that he had no sympathy with our cause, and is unfit to be the Representative of a Southern constituency.[51]

Cobb was expelled on November 17, 1864, by a unanimous vote of the House of Representatives. Because Cobb never took his seat, expulsion was largely a symbolic decision with little direct impact on the range of permissible representation. The expulsion of Henry Foote was an entirely different matter. As has been noted, Foote was one of the most active and vocal members of the House. He was also a leading critic of administration policy and the foremost advocate of a war effort that would depend upon the uncoerced nationalism of the citizenry.

As the war progressed, Foote became increasingly strident and on December 17, 1864, "intimated that he intended soon to withdraw from Congress. He would never legislate under a despotism. . . . He saw that it was the deliberate intention of Congress to suspend the habeas corpus—to break up the press—to invest the President with the most extraordinary powers—to give over to the President and the Secretary of War the powers of 'details'—and rather than have a part in such legislation he should resign." Three days later he stepped down from the Committee on Foreign Affairs and on January 12 attempted to cross into Union lines. After Davis notified Congress of Foote's

61. *Proceedings*, 51 : 310 (November 15, 1864); *Journal of the Confederate Congress*, 7 : 277.

apprehension by Confederate troops, a House committee appointed to study his detention urged Foote's release, but the full membership sent the subject back to the president "for his action." On January 19, a resolution to expel Foote was referred to the Committee on Elections, which, five days later, recommended expulsion for his attempt "to pass into the enemy's lines and to the capital of the United States without permission, which was in violation of law and disregard of his duty as a member of this body." The committee concluded that Foote had "been guilty of conduct incompatible with his duty and station as a member of the Congress." The House voted 51 to 25 to expel Foote, but abstentions prevented passage because the Constitution required the approval of two-thirds of all members; this vote is shown in table 3. The House then, on a voice vote, censured him. Foote subsequently passed through the lines on the way to Washington and the House of Representatives expelled him outright.[62]

Care must be exercised in drawing conclusions from these tests of congressional sentiment on centralization. Congressmen from exterior districts again provided consistently greater support for the statist alternative than did those from the interior. The differences between the two groups are large and in the indicated direction in four of the five roll calls; the exterior states had not yet joined the Confederacy when the first vote was recorded. Second, slaveholding in the districts exhibited almost no relationship to support for centralization. Whereas plantation district representatives strongly backed the last four state-enhancing measures, they were the most numerous opponents of an expanded supreme court jurisdiction and secret sessions. Urban manufacturing districts sent representatives who, as a group, provided greater support on four of the six centralization measures. Only four congressmen from these districts, however, voted on the supreme court amendment, and the differences in support between manufacturing district congressmen and other members are generally small. The Judiciary Committee was once more a center of statist sentiment. Compared to the entire membership of the Confederate House of Representatives, congressmen serving on the committee provided greater support for a stronger central state on all but one roll call, and the percentage differences are uniformly large. The record of the Military Affairs and Ways and Means committees is mixed, with the latter panel exhibiting slightly lower levels of support than the entire House. The clearest pattern that emerges from these tests of congressional sentiment on centralization accentuates the relative statist sympathies of exterior district representatives. Within the larger group of interior members—on the whole, weaker supporters of a strong Confederate state—congressmen representing plantation or manufacturing districts and serving on the Judiciary Committee also leaned toward a greater centralization of authority.

62. *Proceedings*, 52 : 22 (December 17, 1864); p. 32 (December 20, 1864); pp. 144–45 (January 13, 1865); p. 176 (January 19, 1865); pp. 215–16 (January 24, 1865). See *Letters of Warren Akin* for one member's account of the first vote on expulsion (p. 96) and *War of the Rebellion*, 374–415, for Foote's own account of his peace trip to the North and his expulsion.

Table 3. Centralization of Authority in the Confederate State

	Support for a Stronger State (House Votes Cast)											
Type of Member/District	Supreme Court Jurisdiction over State Cases[a] (March 7, 1861)		Secret Sessions of Congress (March 4, 1862)		Officers Commissioned by States (April 14, 1862)		Trial by Judge instead of Jury (Feb. 19, 1863)		Officers Elected by Enlisted Men (Jan. 25, 1864)		Expulsion of Foote from Congress (Jan. 24, 1865)	
	%	N	%	N	%	N	%	N	%	N	%	N
ALL CONGRESSMEN	47.6	(42)	62.5	(88)	48.1	(81)	46.8	(77)	62.2	(82)	67.1	(76)
Exterior districts	—[b]		75.0	(16)	76.5	(17)	40.0	(15)	69.2	(13)	84.2	(19)
Interior districts	—[b]		59.7	(72)	40.6	(64)	48.4	(62)	60.9	(69)	61.4	(57)
Slave population												
0–24%	75.0	(4)	55.6	(18)	38.5	(13)	30.8	(13)	62.5	(16)	50.0	(12)
25–49%	47.1	(17)	70.0	(30)	38.7	(31)	50.0	(28)	51.6	(31)	50.0	(26)
Over 50%	42.9	(21)	50.0	(24)	45.0	(20)	57.1	(21)	72.7	(22)	84.2	(19)
Value-added in manufacturing (per capita)												
Over $10	50.0	(4)	58.8	(17)	43.7	(16)	53.3	(15)	70.6	(17)	54.5	(11)
Under $10	47.4	(38)	60.0	(55)	39.6	(48)	46.8	(47)	57.7	(52)	63.0	(46)
Major committees												
Judiciary	66.7	(6)	88.9	(9)	57.1	(7)	42.9	(7)	75.0	(8)	100.0	(8)
Military Affairs	20.0	(5)	50.0	(6)	40.0	(10)	50.0	(8)	90.0	(10)	81.8	(11)
Ways and Means	40.0	(5)	55.6	(9)	71.4	(7)	66.7	(9)	57.1	(7)	44.4	(9)

[a] Vote in Provisional Congress sitting as Constitutional Convention.
[b] When this vote was taken, none of the states in which exterior districts were located had been admitted into the Confederacy.

Administrative Capability

In creating the administrative apparatus necessary to orchestrate the industrial production needed to support a major war effort, the Confederate state started from scratch.[63] Two practices made the process easier than it might have been: the provisional adoption of all U.S. laws and the intact absorption of the southern branches of the federal bureaucracy. Both the individual states and the Confederate government passed legislation providing for the enforcement of U.S. laws and the continued employment of federal officials despite secession of the South from the Union. In many respects the Confederate state was a carbon copy of the Union government. The Confederate Constitution was almost identical to the U.S. Constitution; the Confederate Congress initially adopted, until "altered or repealed," all the then-existing laws of the United States; and the administrative departments of the Confederate state unabashedly mimicked their northern counterparts.[64]

The establishment of the Post Office Department of the Confederacy, for example, entailed tacit cooperation with the Union in the transfer of control to the southern nation, a vigorous campaign to bring federal employees into the new department, the use of federal equipment and supplies (including stamps), and the adoption, with minor changes, of the previous administrative organization of mail delivery. By 1862, the Confederate government was maintaining 8,300 local post offices, of which number 8,228 had been previously established by the U.S. government. By 1863, postal service was provided throughout the Confederacy with regular delivery to all territory under southern control.[65]

63. For a general account of Confederate administration, see Amlund, *Federalism in the Southern Confederacy,* chap. 6.

64. A comparison of the texts of the two constitutions is provided in Jefferson Davis, *The Rise and Fall of the Confederate Government,* vol. 1 (Reprint, New York: Thomas Yoseloff, 1958), app. K. On congressional adoption of U.S. laws, see Yearns, *The Confederate Congress,* 32, 36. The rules and organization of the Confederate Congress were also largely taken from procedures used in the North (pp. 34–35). On similarities between Confederate and Union administrative design, see Paul P. Van Riper and Harry N. Scheiber, "The Confederate Civil Service," *Journal of Southern History* 25, no. 4 (November 1959): 448–70. Robert C. Black described the Confederate quartermaster bureau as a "photographical reproduction of the old United States organization," in *The Railroads of the Confederacy* (Chapel Hill: University of North Carolina Press, 1952), 50. On the adoption of Union judicial precedents and practice by the Confederacy, see Amlund, *Federalism in the Southern Confederacy,* 65, 83, and Robinson, *Justice in Grey.*

65. "The Postmaster-General's Report," in *Confederate States Almanac for 1863,* 51–52. The Confederate Post Office Department absorbed the existing Union administration in the South without change. See Walter F. McCaleb, "The Organization of the Post Office Department of the Confederacy," *American Historical Review* 12, no. 1 (October 1906) : 66–74. See also the following publications of the Post Office Department of the Confederacy: *Instructions to Post Masters* (Richmond: Ritchie & Dunnavant, 1861); *A List of Establishments, Discontinuances, and Changes in Name of the Post Offices in the Confederate States since 1861; Report of the Postmaster-General, April 29, 1861* (Montgomery, Ala., 1861); *Report of the Postmaster-General, November 27, 1861* (Richmond, 1861); *Advertisement of December 31, 1862, Inviting Proposals for Car-*

Where the South deviated from the model set by the United States, Confederate innovations often strengthened administrative capacity. Noting that the Confederate Department of Justice was the first bureau of its kind in America, William Robinson also observed that it was "the first such subdivision of government in an Anglo-Saxon country. . . . In 1861 no department of justice existed in the United States and the attorney general simply presided over a small office consisting of one assistant and three clerks."[66]

At high tide, the civil service of the Confederacy totaled over 70,000 employees. Over 80 percent of all civil servants were employed in the War Department. The Post Office Department employed about 9,000 (13 percent) and the Treasury about 2,800 (4 percent). Most of the remaining civil employees worked for the Navy Department (about 1,000). Only 125 were employed in the Department of Justice and even fewer (29) in the State Department.[67] The dominance of the War Department was also expressed in overall expenditures—over 90 percent of all expenses in 1864, outside those related to debt service, were incurred by the War Department.[68]

Most departments employed far more civil servants in the field than they did in the capital. The War Department, for example, employed between 260 and 281 clerks and messengers in the city of Richmond. These clerks composed less than .5 percent of all civilian employees in the department. John L. Preston, superintendent of the Bureau of Conscription (itself a part of the War Department), estimated expenditures in Richmond at $44,772 for the first six months of 1865, less than 2 percent of total spending for the bureau. In addition, Robert Kean reported in his diary that about 2,000 able-bodied male employees of the Confederate government resided in Richmond in 1863. His estimate, if accurate, suggests that slightly more than 2 to 3 percent of all civilian employees worked in the capital. If conscripts detailed to noncombatant bureaucratic tasks in Richmond are included, total administrative employment in the capital would have been marginally higher.[69]

---

rying the Mails . . . from July 1, 1863 to June 30, 1867 (Richmond, February 28, 1862); *Report from the General Post Office Department to the Postmaster General* (Richmond, November 22, 1861).

66. *Justice in Grey,* 27.

67. Despite the progressive innovations and imitative development of the administrative apparatus, the Confederate Congress sought to control bureaucratic expansion—at least at the beginning and in the capital. See, for example, the itemized appropriations for clerks in the appropriations acts of August 24 and 29, 1861, in *Acts and Resolutions of the Third Session of the Provisional Congress,* 41–43, 47–48.

68. Van Riper and Scheiber, "The Confederate Civil Service," 450. For a description of the creation, structure, and operation of the Treasury Department, see Todd, *Confederate Finance,* 1–24; Confederate States of America, Treasury Department, *Report of the Secretary of the Treasury* (Richmond, n.d.), 2. The reporting period was April 1 to October 1, 1864. For estimated expenses in the first six months of 1865, see p. 44.

69. Confederate States of America, War Department, *Report of the Secretary of War* (Richmond, November 3, 1864), 23; Goff, *Confederate Supply,* 127; for a description of War Department structure and operations, see pp. 127–58 (*Report of the Secretary of War* [November 3, 1864], p. 36). The estimate is misdated as 1864 when it describes projected expenses

Because of both its sheer size and the policies it carried out, the Department of War came to symbolize the oppressive future that some citizens foresaw for the Confederacy and, for that reason, became the most important target of public hostility. In his open letter, for example, John Gilmer implored:

> Read General Orders, (army) current series, 1862, Nos. *Nine, eleven, fifteen, eighteen, twenty-one, thirty-three, thirty-five, forty-two, fifty-five, fifty-six* and *sixty-six.* Read them, consecutively, and your mind will stand aghast at the concrete evidence of absolute, arbitrary, irresponsible, tryannizing dominion over the civil rights of the people, the courts, and personal franchises. . . . You will discover all civil remedies suppressed, the courts closed, except in such cases as they are *"permitted" to sit by military orders.*

Of the secretary of war, Gilmer asked, "Is his mere volition to silence the laws, fetter the courts, enslave the citizen?"[70]

As was previously discussed, the administrative capability of a central state is improved by any expansion of the discretionary authority lodged within its bureaucracy and by an arrangement that insulates the bureaucracy from purely political influence. Among the four branches, the bureaucracy is the most statist, followed by the national courts, the presidency, and Congress, respectively. Thus, two primary kinds of legislative choice fall under the administrative capability rubric: those that transfer decision-making authority between the branches of the central state in a statist direction and those that promise to increase the autonomy of any branch from the influence of a less statist branch (for example, the autonomy of the president with reference to Congress). Legislative measures that enhance hierarchial organization and bureaucratic specialization, however, tend to blur this distinction between decision-making authority and structural autonomy.

The largest and most important bureaucracy in the Confederate state was, of course, the army, and one of the most pressing tasks associated with constructing an efficient and more insulated state apparatus was the depersonalization of military appointments and promotions. The first clear test of legislative sentiment in this area arose on an amendment offered by John Baldwin of Virginia to a bill "to amend an act for the establishment and organization of a general staff for the Army." His amendment, adopted by the House on a roll call vote (37–22), added the language: "Adjutants appointed by the President shall be deemed officers of the general staff, shall be regarded as part of the commands to which they are attached and not as belonging to the personal staff of the officer [under] whose orders they may be serving for the time being, and shall, where competent, be promoted in their several army corps as assistant adjutant and inspector generals to fill vacancies according to

---

These projections do not include estimates for the trans-Mississippi region of the Confederacy but, interestingly, do include estimates of $100,000 each for Kentucky and Tennessee—states entirely lost by 1864 (Kean, *Inside the Confederate Government,* 77; Van Riper and Scheiber, "The Confederate Civil Service," 452).

70. *Letter Addressed to Hon. William C. Rives,* 2.

seniority."[71] Although there were other attempts to professionalize the officer corps, few were so focused on the problem of transforming a military structure that originated largely in the personal recruitment efforts of individual members of the landed aristocracy into a permanent bureaucracy in which the separate organization units, not their leaders, provided administrative continuity.[72]

Although necessary to bureaucratic professionalization, depersonalization is not sufficient. As bureaucratic functions specialize, personnel can no longer transfer so freely between units, and demonstrated expertise becomes a critical factor in recruitment and promotion. Thus arose the second legislative test on administrative capability. On March 11, 1863, Muscoe Garnett of Virginia offered an amendment to a bill "to provide and organize engineer troops to serve during the war," which presented the Confederate House with a clear legislative choice along this dimension. The amendment would have specified that "no officer shall be appointed or promoted under authority of this law until his qualifications have been tested by examination under rules to be prescribed by the War Department, and appointment shall be made from those passing such examination in the order of merit."[73] The impetus for the amendment came from the reputed poor training of officers in the engineering corps. In a letter to his wife (dated October 12 and 16, 1862), the head of the Confederate Engineer Bureau complained, "Of the one hundred officers allowed—twenty-four have been given to worthless men of broken down Virginia families—about twenty to South Carolinians, no better than the aforesaid Virginians. Out of the whole, we have thus far gotten no more than a dozen good men—men who can lay any claim to be called engineers."[74]

Seen from a slightly different perspective, the civil service test amendment promised to transfer influence over the recruitment of engineers from the president (and, indirectly, the Senate) to the bureaucracy. In this sense, the amendment was unusual because most legislative measures of this type involved choices between presidential and congressional prerogatives. The clearest and perhaps most hotly contested struggle between executive and legislative

71. *Journal of the Confederate Congress*, 5 : 533–34.

72. For other examples of legislation relating to the organization of a general staff of the army, see R. C. Gilchrist, *General Orders of the Confederate States Army* (Columbia, S.C.: Evans & Cogswell, 1864), 86–87, 92–97. A related but separate issue involved the appointment of a "commanding general" to administer the Confederate military and serve just below President Davis. Because of the president's strong opposition, a commanding general was not created until the war was almost over (Yearns, *Confederate Congress*, 108).

73. *Journal of the Confederate Congress*, 6 : 172. The amendment was rejected on a roll call vote (24–45). For the text of the law ultimately passed by Congress (without a civil service test), see *Public Laws of the Confederate States of America, Third Session, First Congress* (Richmond: R. M. Smith, 1863), 98–99. For the military regulations that implemented the statute, see General Order No. 66 (May 22, 1863) in *General Orders of the Confederate States Army, 1863*, 70–71.

74. James L. Nichols, *Confederate Engineers*, Confederate Centennial Studies, no. 5 (Tuscaloosa, Ala.: Confederate Publishing, 1957), 32. For a general account of the administration of the Engineer Bureau, see chap. 2.

appointment arose late in the life of the Confederacy over the appointment of midshipmen to the naval academy. When the Confederate Congress passed a bill reallocating authority over appointments to each individual representative and senator, President Davis vetoed the measure. In his veto message, he emphasized the formal allocation of powers under the Confederate Constitution. These he interpreted as assigning all appointments of officers to the executive, and he averred that congressional control of appointment "is repugnant to the whole theory of our republican institutions, which are based on the fundamental idea of independent and distinct function in each of the departments of Government—the legislative, executive, and judicial; and evil consequences must result from any departure from this principle." After vigorous debate, the House of Representatives sustained the veto.[75] Although this decision was not debated in terms of an enhancement of central state authority, the implicit positions of the actors with reference to the development of the Confederate state were remarkably clear and provided another important test of legislative sentiment.

In an earlier contest over the determination of exemptions from conscription, the legislative alternatives had also turned on the relative scope of central state authority. The decision involved passage of legislation that would have lodged all authority over exemptions with the secretary of war. The bill was very short and the most important clause read, "the Secretary of War shall, upon such terms and conditions as may be prescribed by him, and with the approval of the President, exempt from all military service, or detail for specified purposes, such person or persons as, with the approval of the President, he may deem essential for the good of the service or the general interests of the country."[76] Debate on the bill went heavily against the administration and provided yet another instance in which the positions of the Davis administration and the statist alternative were the same. Criticism was roughly divided into three general themes. First, opponents charged that the bill unlawfully delegated legislative authority to the executive. In this vein, Charles Collier of Virginia charged that, "the duties appertaining to the President should be discharged by the President, and the duties appertaining to Congress should be discharged by Congress. . . . If exemption laws are to be enforced, let Congress signify by law, as far as it can, who shall be exempt, and then let a discretion be lodged in the Executive to mitigate its harshness in those cases, exceptional it may be, which Congress may have overlooked."

Another Virginian, Walter Preston, opposed the bill because "its adoption would place in the hands of the President and Secretary of War the entire control of every white male inhabitant between the ages of eighteen and forty-five years, and he never could, in view of his responsibility as a representative of the people, consent to the delegation of any such extraordinary power. . . . The bill reported by the Committee on Military Affairs he regarded as a monstrosity." Preston's objections originated in the sheer magnitude of power over

75. *Journal of the Confederate Congress,* 7 : 500–02 (January 26, 1865); *Proceedings,* 52 : 232 (January 26, 1865). A majority (40–36) of the House of Representatives voted to override the veto but fell short of the two-thirds required by the Constitution.

76. *Journal of the Confederate Congress,* 6 : 36–37, 40–41 (January 21–22, 1863).

the southern economy that would accompany the bill. Not only would the legislation transfer authority from Congress to the president; implicit in his description is the recognition that discretionary power in the hands of the state carried much more coercive potential than categorical statutory exemptions. Discretion allowed the state to grant exemptions as an inducement for compliance in other governmental policies and, thus, further the complete mobilization of resources behind the southern war effort.

Other members cited the adverse impact of the bill on states' rights. As William Clark of Georgia remarked, this was conscription in its "most odious form" and "swept away the last vestige of States rights and State sovereignty."[77] The legislation would have enhanced central state authority for all three reasons: the aggrandizement of the executive, the centralized mobilization of resources, and, least important, the detrimental impact on the prerogatives of the individual states.

It is worth remembering that throughout the life of the Confederacy, the judicial branch was hampered by the failure of Congress to organize the Supreme Court provided for in the Constitution. Although that failure carried important implications for states' rights, the decision also prevented the judiciary from successfully competing with the executive and legislative branches for influence over the course of the Confederate state. The absence of a supreme court probably liberated, on occasion, the more statist bureaucracy, but its absence also almost certainly had a negative effect on overall administrative capability.[78]

The provisional constitution stipulated that judges of the district courts would, sitting together, compose the Confederate Supreme Court. Congress passed the necessary implementing legislation on March 16, 1861, but, before the court could convene, it passed a second statute providing that the court would not meet until organized under the permanent Constitution by the first Confederate Congress. The only serious subsequent attempt to establish the court came in the spring of 1863. At this time, however, the House of Representatives voted (39–30) to suspend consideration of the bill until the next session of Congress. With this postponement, serious efforts to organize the court ceased.[79]

Despite the failure in this instance of the Congress to adopt the statist alternative, it should be noted that the absence of a supreme court was not a serious hindrance to the *administrative* performance of the Confederate state for a number of reasons. In the first place, both the national district courts and the courts of the individual states were largely staffed by judges who had renounced their allegiance to the Union, resigned their federal posts, and

77. For this and other debate on exemptions, see *Proceedings*, 47 : 173, 181, 183, 205, 211–12 (January 21–27, 1863); 50 : 189, 204–07 (January 6–8, 1864).

78. For background on the decision not to organize the court, see Schwab, *Confederate States of America*, 219–20. On the structure and operation of the Confederate courts generally, see Robinson, *Justice in Grey*, 39–69.

79. Brummer, "The Judicial Interpretation of the Confederate Constitution," 107; for the text of the act postponing organization of the court, see *Acts and Resolutions of the Third Session of the Provisional Congress*, 6–7; Robinson, *Justice in Grey*, 420–34, 474–91.

been reappointed to the Confederate judiciary. Both these judges and those newly appointed were aware of and followed precedents established by the antebellum Supreme Court of the United States. Despite the absence of a supreme tribunal in the Confederacy, this practice unified constitutional interpretation throughout the South, minimized differences between the constitutional law of the two nations, and generally strengthened the claims of the central government. Second, on his own initiative, the attorney general of the Confederacy reviewed laws enacted by the individual states for conformity with the Constitution, advised the government not to respect those that he considered unconstitutional, and generally consolidated some of the functions of a supreme court in the executive branch.[80] Although the attorney general became less assertive in the later years of the Confederacy, his decisions consistently favored central state power.

A pervasive tendency by the highest courts of the individual states to sustain the exercise of national authority also minimized any difficulties that otherwise might have arisen from the failure to establish a Confederate supreme court. Most of the cases implicating national sovereignty related in one way or another to conscription, and here the record of the individual state courts almost universally favored Richmond.[81] In fact, the courts were so compliant that some scholars have cited their record as one reason the Confederate Congress failed to establish a national tribunal. For all these reasons, the absence of a Confederate supreme court probably was not a serious impediment to Confederate interests.[82]

Less indicative of statist sentiments than the supreme court decision was passage of a bill to establish "a bureau for special and secret service." Covert espionage permanently housed in its own bureaucratic structure epitomizes activities associated with a strong central state. In this instance, President Davis was evidently to be given wide discretionary authority "as to what service and business . . . shall be placed under the control" of the bureau.[83] Approved by the House on February 25, 1865 (34–26), the measure apparently died in the Confederate Senate.

Congressional sentiment on these six decisions followed substantially the same pattern exhibited in the citizenship and centralization roll calls (see table 4). Members from exterior districts again provided significantly greater sup-

80. Amlund, *Federalism in the Southern Confederacy*, 83; Brummer, "Judicial Interpretation of the Confederate Constitution," 132; Rembert W. Patrick, ed., *The Opinions of the Confederate Attorneys General* (Buffalo: Dennis, 1950), xx.

81. Brummer, "Judicial Interpretation of the Confederate Constitution," 133; Robinson, *Justice in Grey*, 436; J. G. de R. Hamilton, "The State Courts and the Confederate Constitution," *Journal of Southern History* 4, no. 3 (November 1938) : 425–48; Amlund, *Federalism in the Southern Confederacy*, 88–92; Moore, *Conscription and Conflict*, 162–90. But also see congressional debate on a Georgia Supreme Court decision that struck down the impressment law as unconstitutional (*Proceedings*, 50 : 53–55 [December 15, 1863]).

82. Robinson, *Justice in Grey*, 435–36; Amlund, *Federalism in the Southern Confederacy*, 84, 93.

83. Although the text of the bill seems to have been lost, some of the provisions can be deduced from amending activity on the floor. See *Journal of the Confederate Congress*, 7 : 652 (February 25, 1865).

Table 4. Administrative Capability in the Confederate State

| | Support for a Stronger State (House Votes Cast) | | | | | | | | | | | |
| | General Staff for the Army (Oct. 11, 1862) | | Presidential Exemptions from Conscription (Jan. 22, 1863) | | Civil Service Test for Army Engineers (Mar. 11, 1863) | | Establish Confederate Supreme Court (April 9, 1863) | | Presidential Appointment of Midshipmen (Jan. 26, 1865) | | Establish Secret Service Bureau (Feb. 25, 1865) | |
Type of Member/District	%	N	%	N	%	N	%	N	%	N	%	N
ALL CONGRESSMEN	62.7	(59)	47.3	(74)	34.8	(69)	43.5	(69)	47.4	(76)	56.7	(60)
Exterior districts	85.7	(7)	57.1	(14)	27.3	(11)	46.2	(13)	68.8	(16)	85.7	(14)
Interior districts	59.6	(52)	45.0	(60)	36.2	(58)	42.9	(56)	41.7	(60)	47.8	(46)
Slave population												
0–24%	62.5	(8)	30.8	(13)	36.4	(11)	16.7	(12)	25.0	(12)	58.3	(12)
25–49%	73.1	(26)	46.4	(28)	32.1	(28)	55.6	(27)	34.5	(29)	38.1	(21)
Over 50%	38.9	(18)	52.6	(19)	42.1	(19)	41.2	(17)	63.2	(19)	53.8	(13)
Value-added in manufacturing (per capita)												
Over $10	58.3	(12)	43.8	(16)	58.3	(12)	55.6	(9)	50.0	(12)	50.0	(14)
Under $10	60.0	(40)	45.5	(44)	30.4	(46)	40.4	(47)	39.6	(48)	46.9	(32)
Major committees												
Judiciary	85.7	(7)	75.0	(8)	28.6	(7)	80.0	(5)	62.5	(8)	57.1	(7)
Military Affairs	33.3	(9)	66.7	(6)	12.5	(8)	40.0	(10)	36.4	(11)	50.0	(8)
Ways and Mcans	71.4	(7)	44.4	(9)	25.0	(8)	50.0	(8)	77.8	(9)	33.3	(6)

port for the enhancement of central state power. Among interior districts, congressmen from plantation constituencies were no more favorable to statist alternatives than representatives in the other slaveholding categories. A pattern was more clearly established for manufacturing districts. These members comparatively favored—in most instances by wide margins—an enlargement of central state capacity. Members of the Judiciary Committee again gave a disproportionately high percentage of their votes to a strengthening of the Confederate government; the membership gave greater support (than did the entire House) to the statist alternative on five of the six measures. The record of the Ways and Means Committee was mixed and that of Military Affairs was noticeably weak. On the whole, then, the same two patterns emerge: exterior members favored a stronger state more than did interior congressmen, and slaveholding, manufacturing, and Judiciary Committee memberships were weakly to moderately associated with support for an enlargement of central state capacity.

Many of the most common criticisms lodged against the administrative capability of the Confederate state have been addressed in this section. An additional defect has been cited by Paul Van Riper and Harry Scheiber. In their analysis of the Confederate civil service, they maintain that "Lincoln and the North were more competent in controlling and utilizing civil personnel, especially toward the goal of gaining political and administrative support for the military effort," adding that "in the South the patronage was regarded as a nuisance rather than a possible source of strength." It should be noted, however, that from a statist perspective, political patronage is a primitive means of recruiting administrative talent. In his attempts to wrest appointing authority from the Confederate Congress, Jefferson Davis was progressive. In his use of that authority to recruit personnel to the general staff, naval academy, and army engineers on the basis of expertise, he was ahead of his time.[84]

Control of Property

The Confederacy sought and gained control over the use and disposition of private property in many sectors of the southern economy. Most of these sectors bore an immediate, direct relation to the requirements of military supply. Some government policies, such as the production of salt and the impressment of gold coin and plate, were less directly connected to the war effort (although by no means unrelated).[85] Almost all central state activities had parallels administered by the governments of the individual states. In most cases these parallel activities complemented, rather than competed with,

84. "The Confederate Civil Service," 470.
85. For example, see the following descriptions of salt production in the Confederacy: on activity by national and individual state governments, Schwab, *Confederate States of America*, 267–68, and Goff, *Confederate Supply*, 78–128; on Confederate salt works in Florida, William Watson Davis, *Civil War and Reconstruction in Florida* (New York: Columbia University Press, 1913), 205–10. The best overall treatment is Ella Lonn, *Salt as a Factor in the Confederacy* (New York: Columbia University Press, 1933).

the central government's mobilization effort.[86] Confederate control of the southern economy was most complete in quartermaster stores (other than food) and munitions.[87] Perhaps the best example of such control was the operations of the Confederate Nitre and Mining Bureau. Faced with severe shortages of ordnance, the Confederate state through the bureau granted advances of 50 percent toward the capital cost of private production of nitre and the mining of coal and iron, in addition to claiming authority over the production and operations "of any mine or manufactory" necessary "to secure an adequate supply." As a consequence of these activities, Confederate bureaus came to underpin the southern economy. Throughout the South, "country and city teemed with officious agents of the new bureaucracy who sometimes impressed into service what they could not buy."[88]

In this section, six of the legislative decisions that set important precedents in the extension of central state control over the southern economy are discussed. Although they are generally representative, these decisions do not include a few of the most significant aggrandizing actions of the Confederate state—such as the entry of the government into large-scale manufacturing activity—because the latter decisions were so consensual that congressmen did not record their votes on these issues. Perhaps no decision more clearly revealed the precipitate renunciation of antebellum political tradition than the passage of a bill to extend Confederate aid to the Richmond and Danville Railroad. In the federal Congress, most southerners had consistently opposed government assistance in the construction of internal improvements because they viewed such activity as unconstitutional and interpreted aid as an enhancement of the power of the central government at the expense of the states. This opposition carried over into the first formative months of the Confederacy, and as a consequence, the Provisional Congress-as-Constitutional-Convention adopted a provision prohibiting almost all types of government assistance.[89]

Despite this constitutional prohibition, Jefferson Davis advocated Confederate aid in the construction of a rail connection between Danville, Virginia, and Greensboro, North Carolina, as early as the fall of 1861. Arguing that government assistance would be premised on military necessity rather than commercial advantage, the administration gained congressional approval on

86. For general accounts of individual state activity, see May Spencer Ringold, *Role of the State Legislatures in the Confederacy* (Athens: University of Georgia Press, 1966), 39–56, and Amlund, *Federalism in the Southern Confederacy*, chap. 9.

87. Amlund, *Federalism in the Southern Confederacy*, 68–74; and Ramsdell, "Control of Manufacturing by the Confederate Government," 231–49.

88. Lester J. Cappon, "Government and Private Industry in the Southern Confederacy," in *Humanistic Studies in Honor of John Calvin Metcalf* (Charlottesville: University of Virginia, 1941), 187. For a description of the manufacture of munitions and other war matériel by Confederate arsenals, see pp. 163–68, 172–74, and 177–78. On the extent of Confederate control of economic production, see Goff, *Confederate Supply,* 32, 103; General Order No. 85 (June 16, 1863), *General Orders of the Confederate States Army, 1863,* 96–97; Ramsdell, *Behind the Lines in the Southern Confederacy*, 73–74.

89. Lee, *Confederate Constitutions*, 95, 179.

February 7, 1862, with almost two-thirds of those voting supporting government aid (see table 5). But the decision continued to be heatedly debated. For example, the *Richmond Semi-Weekly Examiner* pointed out that the "precedent of government aid to railroads . . . is dangerous, difficult to be confined within proper limits, and liable to abuses and corruptions, especially in a legislative body which envelopes its proceedings with secrecy." Once the precedent had been set, however, the Confederacy engaged in numerous construction projects, but it limited government assistance to loans and rail extensions of military value. The nature of military operations during the Civil War and of Confederate strategy (with its emphasis on perimeter defense) conferred upon almost all construction projects some military relevance. The real limitation on Confederate-sponsored rail expansion was not ideological opposition but a chronic shortage of iron.[90]

Like government construction assistance, Confederate control of railroad operations significantly expanded central state authority. The House of Representatives passed legislation that would have established "consultations" between railroad officials and the secretary of war as early as April 17, 1862, but the Senate failed to consider the bill. As reported by the Committee on Military Affairs, the bill would have invested all railroad officials with military rank and subjected them to military discipline—thus centralizing control over all operations within the Confederate military.[91] Floor amendments, however, systematically stripped the measure of its strongest provisions and left the bill only a pale shadow of the form in which it was introduced. Even so, passage provoked a petition protesting that the Confederate Constitution nowhere "authorizes or justifies Congress in appropriating or seizing the property of States or persons. . . . On the contrary, we believe that the Constitution expressly prohibits and denies such power." In addition, the signers believed that the bill subverted "the great and fundamental principles of State sovereignty," largely because so many railroads were owned and operated by the individual state governments. Finally, they argued that Confederate intervention was unnecessary because the railroads were already well managed and operated. They ended their petition with the observation that the reasons for their opposition must be apparent "to every intelligent mind not unreasonably depressed by exigencies and vicissitudes, through which Providence has decreed that we should pass in our progress to national independence."[92]

A law enacted on May 1, 1863, gave the executive branch wide discretionary authority over operations, schedules, and the impressment of railroad property either as a penalty for noncooperation or wherever necessary to maintain more essential lines. Although Robert Black contends that this law

90. Robert C. Black III, *The Railroads of the Confederacy*, 148–49, 162, 200; *Journal of the Confederate Congress*, 1 : 781–82, 819, 821 (February 10, 1862); 5 : 260, 480.

91. Black, *The Railroads of the Confederacy*, 97–98.

92. *Proceedings*, 45 : 162–63 (April 19, 1862). In December 1862, the Alabama legislature passed a similar but more moderate protest concerning Confederate operation of the railroads (see *Acts of the Called Session, 1862 and of the Second Regular Session of the General Assembly*, 200–01).

Table 5. The Confederate State and the Control of Property

	Support for a Stronger State (House Votes Cast)											
	Government Subsidy to Railroads (Feb. 7, 1862)		Destruction of Property (Mar. 5, 1862)		Government Control of Railroads (Apr. 17, 1862)		Impressment of Property (Feb. 13, 1863)		Prohibit Trade in U.S. Securities (Apr. 30, 1863)		Slaves as Soldiers (Feb. 20, 1865)	
Type of Member/District	%	N	%	N	%	N	%	N	%	N	%	N
ALL CONGRESSMEN	64.2	(67)	53.6	(84)	54.2	(72)	88.1	(59)	76.5	(68)	61.3	(75)
Exterior districts	100.0	(11)	64.3	(14)	66.7	(12)	100.0	(9)	78.6	(14)	73.7	(19)
Interior districts	57.1	(56)	51.4	(70)	51.7	(60)	86.0	(50)	75.9	(54)	57.1	(56)
Slave population												
0–24%	81.8	(11)	47.1	(17)	61.5	(13)	88.9	(9)	77.8	(9)	57.1	(14)
25–49%	51.9	(27)	56.7	(30)	41.9	(31)	85.0	(20)	62.5	(24)	50.0	(28)
Over 50%	50.0	(18)	47.8	(23)	62.5	(16)	85.7	(21)	90.5	(21)	71.4	(14)
Value-added in manu-facturing (per capita)												
Over $10	58.3	(12)	43.7	(16)	66.7	(12)	80.0	(10)	58.3	(12)	64.7	(17)
Under $10	56.8	(44)	53.7	(54)	47.9	(48)	87.5	(40)	81.6	(12)	53.8	(39)
Major committees												
Judiciary	71.4	(7)	37.5	(8)	42.9	(7)	100.0	(6)	83.3	(6)	55.6	(9)
Military Affairs	60.0	(10)	16.7	(6)	75.0	(8)	81.8	(11)	66.7	(9)	41.7	(12)
Ways and Means	60.0	(5)	44.4	(9)	40.0	(5)	87.5	(8)	62.5	(8)	80.0	(10)

remained unused for the remainder of the war, General Order No. 15 (February 15, 1864) indicated complete Confederate control of private rail operations: "As the various railroads of the Confederacy for the transportation of troops, supplies, and munitions of war are under the control of Quartermaster's department, the orders of commanding generals, and other officers, relating to such transportation by railroad, will be immediately furnished to the Quartermaster-General, in order that arrangements may be made in time to harmonize the various routes so as to prevent accidents and delays."

The prospect of possible impressment of both employees and rolling stock gradually brought the railroads under the domination of the War Department. On November 3, 1864, the secretary of war requested even stronger measures to further centralize rail operations, and on February 28, 1865, Congress enacted legislation giving the secretary absolute control over all rail operations and subjecting employees to military discipline.[93] Although these two acts (of May 1, 1863, and February 28, 1865) were more powerful measures than the bill that passed the House on April 17, 1862, the latter measure established the original and probably more significant precedent concerning central state control over the operations and property of private business.

One of the extreme measures that a central state can undertake with reference to the private economy is to forcibly take or destroy property without compensating the owners. An amendment to that effect—striking the language "and the owners thereof shall receive just compensation therefore from the Confederate Government under such laws and regulations as may hereafter be established by Congress"—was offered to a bill providing statutory authority for the burning of cotton, tobacco, and other property likely to fall into Union hands. William Miles, the chairman of the Committee on Military Affairs, contended that the "destruction of the cotton was the first consideration, and the compensation a matter of detail." Jabez Curry followed with one of the most violent declarations of southern nationalism ever heard in the halls of the Confederate Congress: "If there was any man in Alabama who was so avaricious that he would not, with his own hands, put the torch to every lock of cotton rather than that the Lincoln Government should get it, he hoped the Yankees would burn him." Roger Pryor, a Virginian, warmed to Curry's theme: "Away then with all temporizing policy, with all palliations, with all anxious reservation of individual interest, with all trembling solicitude for property." After adopting the amendment, the House of Representatives subsequently backtracked a bit and passed a Senate bill providing for both the destruction of property and compensation.[94]

93. Black, *The Railroads of the Confederacy*, 121–22, 164–75, 280–81. The 1863 act gave administrative control to the quartermaster-general (*General Orders of the Confederate States Army, 1864*, 17). By contrast, see General Orders No. 2 (January 3, 1863) and No. 26 (March 7, 1863) issued before the May 1, 1863 law (*General Orders of the Confederate States Army, 1863*, 4–5, 24–25), and Goff, *Confederate Supply*, 105, 110–11; Ramsdell, *Behind the Lines in the Southern Confederacy*, 97; *Report of the Secretary of War*, 14.

94. *Journal of the Confederate Congress*, 5 : 60 (March 5, 1862); *Proceedings*, 44 : 99–104, 117 (March 5 and 7, 1862).

Another, more significant practice was the systematic impressment of private property as the primary means of supplying the Confederate military. Large-scale impressment began in the autumn of 1861 when inflation and shortages in the marketplace drove prices to prohibitively high levels. By the fall of 1862, the Confederate government had vastly expanded the scope of impressment activities:

> Authorities took medical supplies from blockade runners and from speculators; they seized quarter-master hardware, forage, and horses in the hands of uncooperative sellers; and the Secretary of War authorized the impressment of such major items as railroad iron, distilleries, and niter caves. The government attempted to make its confiscatory actions as palatable as possible. Officials paid on the spot the high prices prevailing on the market, handed out receipts and certificates in profusion, and theoretically made out reports to superiors.[95]

For the first two years of the war, impressment was a practice outside the law. Only in the spring of 1863, beginning with passage of legislation in the House of Representatives, did Congress embody authority for impressment in the statutory code. Arguing for congressional action, Muscoe Garnett observed:

> that the merest agents, the lowest subordinates, were armed with a power to go through the Confederacy, to invade the homes of the people, and to impress as they pleased the stock and produce of the country. The people of this country may well object to a system of impressment under which they are the victims of the discretion, and perhaps sometimes the spite, of mere petty agents. . . . The fact that [the power of impressment] was confided to mere agents of the lowest degree, and the practices that had been perpetuated under this system, were sufficient to shock and startle the country . . . the interest of the government and integrity of our constitutional law claimed the attention of Congress to the present practice of seizing private property.[96]

On February 12, 1863, the House overwhelmingly passed the impressment measure (52–7; see table 5).

On March 26, Congress gave final approval to legislation establishing price-setting boards of assessment to regulate impressment activity. Appointed by President Davis and governors of the individual states, these boards published official price schedules to be followed by officers doing the impressment. The schedules invariably set prices below marketplace levels and, as the war continued, evolved into a national system of price controls.[97] Later, the Confed-

---

95. Goff, *Confederate Supply*, 41–42, 97. For a general history of impressment, see Schwab, *Confederate States of America*, 202–09. See also General Order No. 31 (March 19, 1863) (*General Orders of the Confederate States Army, 1863*, 29–30).

96. *Proceedings*, 47 : 127 (January 15, 1863); *Journal of the Confederate Congress*, 6 : 107 (February 13, 1863).

97. For the text of the March 26, 1863, act and an April 27, 1863, amendment, see *Public Laws of the Confederate States of America, Third Session, First Congress*, 102–04, 127–28. Implementing orders can be found in General Order No. 161 (December 10, 1863) which set out

erate Congress enacted a tax "in kind" on farmers that required payment of "one tenth of the wheat, corn, oats, rye, buckwheat or rice" produced.[98] In practice, this tax largely routinized impressment activities as it also reduced the internal revenue system to barter.

The southern state's reliance upon impressment as a procurement practice has sometimes been attributed to the weakness of the Confederate currency.[99] That weakness, in turn, has been attributed to the failure of the Confederate state to pass sufficiently comprehensive tax legislation and to enact legal tender laws. In the North, the Legal Tender Act of February 25, 1862, conferred legal tender status on U.S. greenbacks and was justified, on constitutional grounds, as a "necessary and proper" means of supporting the Union armed forces. In the South, both the Confederate secretary of the treasury and Jefferson Davis opposed legal tender legislation, and the issue, as a consequence, was never tested in the courts. A dearth of precious metals, an unwillingness to impose heavy taxes in addition to impressment, and the absence of legal tender legislation combined to drive the value of Confederate currency ever lower. As inflation accelerated, U.S. greenbacks began to penetrate the southern economy and circulate behind Confederate lines.[100]

---

regulations concerning procedures for the appeal of the decisions of impressing officers (*General Orders of the Confederate States Army, 1863*, 223–24. For examples of price schedules used by impressment officers, see, for Georgia, *General Orders of the Confederate States Army, 1863*, 65–70; for Virginia, Ibid., 114–18, 139–44, 158–64, 203–04, 217–22; for South Carolina, Ibid., 154–58; for Virginia, *General Orders of the Confederate States Army, 1864*, 8–13, 75–80, 92–97; and for North Carolina, Wilmington *Daily Journal*, October 13, 1864. For the activities of the impressment board in Florida, see Davis, *Civil War and Reconstruction in Florida*, 186. For evidence that price schedules and impressment practices evolved into a fairly centralized form of price control, see Goff, *Confederate Supply*, 98; General Order No. 34 (April 1, 1863), *General Orders of the Confederate States Army, 1863*, 32–33 (setting prices for beef hides to be paid by the army); and General Order No. 10 (January 30, 1864), *General Orders of the Confederate States Army, 1864*, 13 (which extended impressment authority "to the Impressment of ore, timber, all materials essential to the production and manufacture of iron"—in addition to iron itself).

98. *Laws of Congress in Regard to Taxes, Currency, and Conscription*, 14.

99. See, for example, Alexander and Beringer, *Anatomy of the Confederate Congress*, 140.

100. Outside the government, however, broad support for legal tender legislation existed. Both the Richmond *Dispatch* and Charleston *Courier* backed legislation "as an accommodation to the loyal and a check to the disloyal" and interpreted refusal to accept Confederate notes as evidence of a "latent infidelity to the Southern cause" (Schwab, *Confederate States of America*, 86–101, 161). The state of Alabama made Confederate notes a legal tender for all future debts (p. 100). An Alabama law also set a ceiling of .25 percent on the annual interest of any debt for which payment in Confederate notes was refused by the creditor (see *Acts of the Called Session, 1862 and of the Second Regular Session of the General Assembly*, 68–69). For a sample of congressional sentiment on Confederate legal tender proposals, see *Proceedings*, 47 : 45 (October 3, 1862), and 49 : 27–28 (March 25, 1863); Eugene M. Lerner, "Money, Prices, and Wages in the Confederacy, 1861–1865," in Ralph Andreano, ed., *The Economic Impact of the American Civil War* (Cambridge, Mass.: Schenkman Publishing, 1967), 31–60; William J. Shultz and M. R. Caine, *Financial Development of the Untied States* (Englewood Cliffs, N.J.: Prentice-Hall, 1937), 287.

The Confederate House of Representatives first passed legislation prohibiting acceptance of U.S. greenbacks on April 30, 1863. As approved by the House, the prohibition was considerably broader than a simple prohibition on Union currency, as it included a ban on the securities of northern state governments and private corporations chartered under northern law. The recorded vote analyzed below arose on a motion to table the bill (16–52); the measure subsequently cleared the chamber on a voice vote but failed in the Senate. A second bill, narrower in scope, moved through the House on December 24, 1863 (again on an unrecorded voice vote), and became law on February 6, 1864. This legislation prohibited the circulation of U.S. currency but exempted postage stamps and the activity of authorized Confederate officials.[101]

Of all the legislation passed by the Confederate Congress, the one law that most perfectly demonstrated the depth of southern nationalism and its new life independent of the slave culture that had originally given birth to the Confederacy was the bill providing for the arming and, implicitly, the freeing of the slaves. Prior to congressional action that would be taken in the last months of the war, the state of Louisiana had organized a regiment of free blacks in April 1861 and Alabama had enlisted Creoles for the defense of Mobile in November 1862. The Confederate Congress first authorized the impressment of slaves as laborers in military operations in 1863 and significantly expanded that authority the following year.[102]

Serious congressional debate on the possible arming of slaves appears to have begun with the *Report of the Secretary of War* (November 3, 1864). In his

---

101. For the text of the earlier measure, see *Journal of the Confederate Congress*, 6 : 466–67 (April 30, 1863). For congressional debate on the second bill, see *Proceedings*, 50 : 102, 105 (December 22, 1863), and 147–48 (December 29, 1863). The text of the later bill appears on pp. 125–26 (December 24, 1863).

102. The two general accounts of the background of this legislation are N. W. Stephenson, "The Question of Arming the Slaves," *American Historical Review* 18, no. 2 (January 1913) : 295–308, and Thomas R. Hay, "The South and the Arming of the Slaves," *Mississippi Valley Historical Review* 6, no. 1 (June 1919) : 34–73. See also Moore, *Conscription and Conflict in the Confederacy*, 343–49. The state of Alabama impressed slaves as laborers as early as 1862, and the legislature authorized enlistment in "An Act: To authorize the enrollment of the Creoles of Mobile" (November 20, 1862), which provided that "certain persons of mixed blood" would be enrolled in the "militia . . . if in the opinion of the mayor of the city it is expedient" (*Acts of the Called Session, 1862 and of the Second Regular Session of the General Assembly*, 37–40, 162). For military regulations relating to slave impressment, see *General Orders of the Confederate States Army, 1863*, 190–92. Also see South Carolina, State of, *Journal of the House of Representatives: Session of 1863*, 72, for a brief account of Confederate impressment of slave labor in the defense of Charleston. For the text of the second impressment act (February 17, 1864), see Robert F. Durden, *The Grey and the Black* (Baton Rouge: Louisiana State University Press, 1972), 51–53. The secretary of war called the impressment of slaves as laborers a success but urged further centralization of impressment authority in order to "relieve authorities from dependence on the State agencies" in his *Report of the Secretary of War* (November 3, 1864), 6, 14–15. See also Harrison A. Trexler, "The Opposition of Planters to the Employment of Slaves as Laborers by the Confederacy," *Mississippi Valley Historical Review* 27, no. 2 (September 1940) : 211–24.

message, the secretary observed that conscription or impressment of slaves as soldiers "would of course require the concurring legislation of each State . . . because to the States belong exclusively the determination of the relations which their colored population, or any part of them, shall hold." This position conceded to the central state the power to impress slaves into the army and to arm them but gave to the individual states exclusive authority to emancipate slaves from bondage. Because emancipation was believed—evidently by all who considered the matter—to be an essential feature of the proposal to arm slaves, the cooperation of the individual states would be required. But, the secretary added, "while it is encouraging to know this resource for further and future efforts is at our command, my own judgment does not yet either perceive the necessity or approve the policy of employing slaves in the higher duties of soldiers." In his annual message to Congress on November 7, President Davis stopped short of advocating the impressment of slaves as soldiers but added "should the alternative ever be present of subjugation or of the employment of slaves as soldiers, there seems no reason to doubt what should be our decision." [103]

For the next four months, Congress and the southern nation argued the case for and against arming slaves. During this period most congressmen made the transition from "the Confederate States of America *and* slavery" to "the Confederate States of America *without* slavery." Henry Chambers of Mississippi said he was "ashamed to debate the question. All nature cries out against it. The negro race was ordained to slavery by the Almighty. Emancipation would be the destruction of our social and political system. God forbid that this Trojan horse should be introduced among us. The negro . . . will not fight. All history shows this." [104] On January 7, 1865, E. A. Pollard's Richmond *Examiner* held that the objection to enlisting slaves as soldiers was "not so much to the employment of the negro in itself, as the shock to the rights of property which is involved" and continued, "On this kind of possession the South has concentrated all its proprietary feeling, and the man who would submit without a murmur to the impressment of his horses or his crops may very likely shrink back with a species of superstition however from the attempt by his own government to deprive him of these very slaves for whom he had already fought a long and desperate war." [105] Thomas Gholson of Virginia spoke for those who resisted arming the slaves until the very end: "To fight the negro and give him his freedom at the close of the war was abolition, and was in express violation of every declaration of the South. It differed only from the

103. Hay, "The South and the Arming of the Slaves," 52.

104. On the difficulty of this transition, see *Letters of Warren Akin*, 32–33, 40 (letters dated October 31 and December 16, 1864); *Rebellion Record*, vol. 11, Document 68, pp. 475–76. Chambers spoke on November 10, 1864.

105. Quoted in Trexler, "Opposition of Planters to the Employment of Slaves," 213. See also *Rebellion Record*, 11 : 476–79. That the employment of slaves as soldiers was viewed as equivalent to the abolition of slavery was evident from congressional debate; *Proceedings*, 51 : 276 (November 8, 1864); 52 : 241–42 (January 27, 1865). See also 52 : 329–31 (February 10, 1865).

Yankee policy in this respect—the Yankee gave him his freedom at once, we gave it to him prospectively."[106]

On February 11, 1865, the Confederate House of Representatives appointed a special committee of thirteen members (one from each state) to consider legislation enabling slaves to serve as soldiers. That committee brought back to the House a bill providing for the conscription of "300,000 troops . . . to be raised from such classes of the population, irrespective of color, in each state, as the proper authorities thereof may determine." Nothing in the bill mandated emancipation "except by consent of the owners and of the states," although all expected emancipation to follow. With the strong backing of President Davis, Governor Smith of Virginia, and General Robert E. Lee, this bill cleared the House on February 20, 1865. The best test of congressional sentiment, however, occurred on an amendment adopted just prior to passage. Offered by Charles Conrad of Louisiana, the amendment inserted presidential authority to call for troops under the terms discussed above and isolated the issue of arming the slaves from the remainder of the bill. Approved by a wide margin (46–29), the amendment demonstrated the depth of nationalist sentiment in the House—and its detachment from the preservation of slavery. As such, the bill presented the Confederate House with the chamber's stiffest challenge—whether or not the "rights" of private property in slaves should be violated, both individually and as a system, as part of the military effort directed by the central state of the Confederacy.

The Confederate Congress finally forwarded the slaves-as-soldiers legislation to Davis on March 13, 1865, and the Confederate president immediately signed it into law. General Order No. 14, the implementing bureaucratic directive, specified first that "No slave will be accepted as a recruit unless with his own consent and with the approbation of his master by a written instrument conferring, as far as he may, the rights of a freedman." The directive added further that "All officers . . . are enjoined to a provident, considerate, and humane attention to whatever concerns the health, comfort, instruction, and discipline of these troops, and to the uniform observance of kindness, forbearance, and indulgence in their treatment of them, and especially that they will protect them from injustice and oppression." As Emory Thomas notes, this paternalistic injunction implies a standard of "equal treatment" for black soldiers in the ranks.[107]

By the end of the war (and, in most cases, from almost the beginning), the

---

106. *Proceedings*, 52 : 276–77 (February 1, 1865).

107. *Proceedings*, 52 : 337; *Journal of the Confederate Congress*, 7 : 611–12 (February 20, 1865). For the complete text of the bill as enacted, see Durden, *The Grey and the Black*, 202–03. Passage came too late for implementation. On April 28, 1865, for example, "the major-general commanding in Florida directed ten prominent citizens of Florida each 'to proceed at once to raise a company of negroes to be mustered into the service of the Confederate States for the War' but Lee had already surrendered at Appomattox on the ninth, nearly three weeks previously" (Davis, *Civil War and Reconstruction in Florida*, 227–28). Durden, *The Grey and the Black*, 249–50, 268–69; Emory M. Thomas, *The Confederate Nation, 1861–1865* (New York: Harper & Row, 1979), 296–97.

Confederate state could exercise authority over the use and disposition of every form of private property anywhere in the South. The impressment acts allowed outright seizure in return for deferred compensation at rates far below market levels. Various bills conferred control over the structure and operation of the railroads—the most massive and complex industrial system in the South. Although the full potential authority that lay in these railroad bills was not administratively realized, enough control of rail operations was achieved, in practice, to convert that authority into an extralegal means of controlling the activities of private manufacturers.[108] With the prohibition of trade in U.S. securities, the Confederate state moved toward government regulation of investment decisions and securities markets. Of course, direct Confederate investment in manufacturing operations and outright socialization of individual firms were even more significant evidence of central state capacity. Finally, the Confederate state turned on the property system that had given rise to its separate existence and enacted legislation that contemplated the liquidation of slavery as a means of supplying the front with additional troops. Administrative shortcomings there may have been, but there was no failure of will.

Congressional voting on the six property measures followed the, by now, familiar pattern (see table 5). Members from exterior districts favored the statist alternative by a greater margin than did those from the remainder of the Confederacy on all six roll calls—by far the most impressive showing of any group in this category of legislation. Slaveholding again seemed to play little special role in the building of state-enhancing legislative coalitions. On the other hand, congressmen from plantation districts delivered a surprisingly large 71.4 percent of their ballots in favor of slaves-as-soldiers—a surprising fact both because of the common observation, at the time, that slaveholders constituted the most important source of opposition to the proposal and because adoption struck at the very basis of the plantation system and culture. Members from manufacturing districts were no more willing to expand central state authority over private property than were congressmen from rural, nonmanufacturing constituencies. The membership of the Judiciary Committee again provided greater backing for statist proposals than the other two leadership panels, but no committee, including Judiciary, gave more support than did the House as a whole. Everything considered, only the exterior-interior distinction appears to have been as influential in this category of legislation as it had been in the previous three (see tables 2, 3, and 4).[109]

---

108. Ramsdell, "Control of Manufacturing," 239–40.

109. Inevitably, this selection of measures affecting the control of private property omits other enactments almost as important, if not equally so. One such act, passed in August 1861, provided for the confiscation and sale of property owned by "aliens" residing within the Union (Amlund, *Federalism in the Southern Confederacy,* 61–62). Another sequestered the property of individuals who evaded conscription (*Journal of the Confederate Congress,* 7 : 366–67 [December 20, 1864]). For congressional debate on sequestration power, see *Proceedings,* 49 : 199–200 (April 22, 1863); 51 : 445, 456, 464 (December 10–13, 1864); 52 : 31 (December 20, 1864).

Creation of Client Groups

Client groups are those segments of the general population that are dependent upon the central state for a major fraction of their total income. Government policies that create client groups include those that provide income or income substitutes to individuals (for example, pensions, employment by central state institutions, welfare, and price control policies that benefit specific targeted groups in society), that establish future-oriented obligations that depend on state viability (for example, long-term debt or land warrants for frontier settlement), and that control the value of the currency (for example, the gold standard and redemption of paper money). Of the six legislative dimensions of central state authority, Confederate policies under this heading were the least developed.

Very early in the life of the southern nation, the Provisional Congress of the Confederacy adopted a motion to postpone indefinitely consideration of an invalid pension bill and, thus, refused to support southerners who had been on the pension rolls of the United States (see table 6). Although debate on this early measure has been lost, a similar proposal was made in 1863. This second bill would have continued "in pay all soldiers discharged by reason of wounds and injuries in the service." In debate, William Boyce of South Carolina favored "a system of pension, as part of the great military system which the South must adopt. She must say to every soldier who fought her battles—you shall be cherished with the care which a fond mother extends to her children."[110] On the whole, however, those favoring the creation of client groups (the statist alternative as defined here) fairly consistently opposed the adoption of state-enhancing measures along the other dimensions. In contrast, those who favored a stronger state in other areas were relatively unsympathetic to the creation of client groups.

For budgetary reasons, President Davis opposed the creation of a pension system and even vetoed legislation to establish a veteran soldiers' home. When the president's veto message was received in the House, Jeremiah Clapp of Mississippi contended, "we should be following the example of civilized nations. The *Hospital des Invalides,* of Paris, was the glory of the French nation." Other backers emphasized that wounded veterans from areas overrun by Union armies had nowhere to go. The soldiers' home bill first passed the House by a margin of over eight to one (59–7), but after the veto, supporters mustered fewer than 40 percent of the ballots on a motion to override (table 6).[111]

In initiating programs of assistance to soldiers' families, the governments of individual states were not nearly as reluctant to create client groups.[112]

110. *Proceedings,* 49 : 52–53 (March 30, 1863).

111. *Proceedings,* 50 : 242–43, 256 (January 15, 18, 1864). For the text of the president's veto, see *Journal of the Confederate Congress,* 6 : 808–10, and on the override vote, 848–49 (February 17, 1864).

112. The largest such group was composed of the families of soldiers who, if impoverished by the absence of their father and husband, were eligible for state-supported indigent relief. These programs spread rapidly throughout the South and by the end of the war

Table 6. Creation of Client Groups in the Confederate State

			Support for a Stronger State (House Votes Cast)							
	Invalid Pensions (May 13, 1861)		Redistribution of Income (Oct. 1, 1862)		Nontransferable Bonds (Jan. 25, 1864)		Price Control for Soldiers' Families (Feb. 3, 1864)		Veteran Soldiers' Home (Feb. 17, 1864)	
Type of Member/District	%	N	%	N	%	N	%	N	%	N
ALL CONGRESSMEN	27.8	(36)	34.4	(64)	31.4	(70)	62.7	(67)	39.1	(64)
Exterior districts	0.0	(1)	0.0	(4)	20.0	(10)	87.5	(8)	28.6	(14)
Interior districts	28.6	(35)	36.7	(60)	33.3	(60)	59.3	(59)	42.0	(50)
Slave population										
0–24%	0.0	(3)	50.0	(10)	26.7	(15)	61.5	(13)	44.4	(9)
25–49%	43.7	(16)	28.6	(28)	40.0	(25)	57.1	(28)	47.8	(23)
Over 50%	18.7	(16)	40.9	(22)	30.0	(20)	61.1	(18)	33.3	(18)
Value-added in manufacturing (per capita)										
Over $10	—[a]		23.1	(13)	29.4	(17)	53.3	(15)	25.0	(12)
Under $10	—[a]		40.4	(47)	34.9	(43)	61.4	(44)	47.4	(38)
Major committees										
Judiciary	37.5	(8)	14.3	(7)	71.4	(7)	42.9	(7)	50.0	(6)
Military Affairs	40.0	(5)	66.7	(12)	0.0	(8)	85.7	(7)	14.3	(7)
Ways and Means	0.0	(3)	0.0	(8)	14.3	(7)	57.1	(7)	12.5	(8)

[a]None of the members from districts with value-added in manufacturing over $10 at the time voted on this issue.

Likewise, in support of local efforts to provide indigent relief, the Confederate government instituted a tax on slave overseers who were exempted by statute from conscription. The proceeds of this levy were then turned over to the relief agencies of the individual states—in effect, a redistribution of income from the owners of plantations to the large, yeoman-farmer class of the South. On October 1, 1862, Robert Trippe of Georgia proposed to include within the scope of this tax all exempted men—not just overseers—except those employed in a civilian or military capacity by the individual states and those physically or mentally incapacitated. Each man so exempted would be asked to pay "five dollars on every hundred dollars" worth of real and personal property and "five dollars on each hundred dollars of salary or fees or pay for personal services he may have received during the present year." Although Trippe's amendment failed, his sweeping proposal drew the support of more than a third of those voting (see table 6).[113]

A different kind of redistribution was involved in the price control policy of the Confederacy. There, plantations run by exempted overseers were compelled to sell surplus agricultural production to the government or soldiers' families at prices set by the impressment boards. Adopted as an amendment to the Act to Organize Forces to Serve during the War on February 3, 1864, the price control provision effectively covered all plantations employing twenty or more slaves and many with less than that number (see table 6).[114] Since the

---

constituted a large fraction of all individual income. In Alabama, for example, 10,263 families were on relief during 1862 (10.6 percent of all families). This total rose to 31,915 (33.3 percent) in 1863 and to 37,521 (37 percent) in 1864. In one rural hill county, 59 percent of all families were on indigent relief in 1863. Most indigent families, in fact, held no slaves, and the absence of their father and husband deprived them of their primary source of income (Bessie Martin, *Desertion of Alabama Troops from the Confederate Army* [New York: Columbia University Press, 1932], 128–34, 174–87). The suffering of their families, Martin argued, was the major cause of desertion among Alabama soldiers. See also State of Alabama, *Acts of the Called Session, 1862 and of the Second Regular Session of the General Assembly*, 17–18, 26–29; *Acts of the Called Session of the General Assembly of Alabama, 1861*, 76–80; *Acts of the General Assembly of the State of Georgia, 1862–1863*, 49–52, 66–74; *Acts of the General Assembly of the State of South Carolina: December, 1861*, 15–16. South Carolina relief was later expanded to include the "families of free negroes who have been employed in the military service of [either South Carolina or the Confederacy], as laborers or otherwise . . . at the discretion of the respective [local] Boards" (*Acts of the General Assembly: Sessions of 1864–1865* [Columbia: Julian A. Selby, 1866, 239–44). Through relief to soldiers' families, the state of Florida "was contributing to the support of approximately one non-combatant for every soldier in the field" by 1863–64 (Davis, *Civil War and Reconstruction*, 188–89). On the general response of state governments, see Ringold, *Role of the State Legislatures in the Confederacy*, 77–80.

113. An attempt to eliminate the tax on overseers was overwhelmingly defeated in the House of Representatives on the same day (*Journal of the Confederate Congress*, 5 : 474–77). For executive and administrative actions undertaken by the Confederacy in support of local relief efforts, see Paul D. Escott, " 'The Cry of the Sufferers': The Problem of Welfare in the Confederacy," *Civil War History* 23, no. 3 (September 1977).

114. As offered by John Goode of Virginia, the amendment read, *"Provided further,* That the owner of such farm or plantation shall sell all his surplus provisions hereafter raised for

price schedules regulating impressment were set far below market levels and since food was the major form of civilian expenditure during the war, this provision was, in all probability, an even more effective means than the 1862 tax of redistributing income from the owners of plantations to indigent families.

Another method of creating a client group is the issuance of government bonds—a strategy pursued by the Confederacy out of necessity. Bonds drawn on the credit of the government create, as Alexander Hamilton knew, an interest in the general viability and extractive (revenue) capacity of the state. One common difficulty with bonds, from a statist perspective, is that they can be marketed, and, once they are sold, the seller no longer has an enduring interest in the welfare of the state. An unusual solution to this problem was offered by John Atkins of Tennessee as an amendment to a bill "to continue in service all troops now in the military service" of the Confederacy. The bill already provided that all men who enlisted would receive a bounty of one hundred dollars in bonds, thereby guaranteeing a wide distribution. To this provision, Atkins offered the amendment, "That said bonds shall not be transferable," which would have ensured that the original owners would retain possession.[115] Although the thrust of the restriction was, perhaps, a little too obviously Machiavellian when applied to soldiers already at the front, Atkins's proposal still drew over 30 percent of all votes cast (see table 6).

These five measures, all of which sought to expand the client base of the Confederate state, display voting patterns radically different from those that held in the other legislative dimensions of central state authority. Members from exterior districts, for example, gave less support than interior congressmen on four of the five proposals and, although the numbers were small, the percentage differences were fairly wide. Members from plantation constituencies were also comparatively unsympathetic; in no instance did congressmen from districts over half slave provide greater backing for the statist alternative than colleagues from areas less dependent on the plantation economy. Similarly, congressmen from rural, nonmanufacturing constituencies comparatively favored client group formation (on the four applicable votes). On the other hand, the "normal" pattern held for the memberships of the leading committees. Both Judiciary and Military Affairs gave greater backing to the

the use of soldiers' families and for the use of the Government at prices not greater than those fixed for the time being by the commissioners appointed under the impressment acts" (*Journal of the Confederate Congress*, 6 : 742–43 [February 3, 1864]). In its final, statutory form, the section read, "Such person shall further bind himself to sell the marketable surplus of provisions and grain now on hand, and which he may raise from year to year, while his exemption continues, to the government, or to the families of soldiers, at prices fixed by the commissioners of the state under the Impressment act: *provided,* that any person exempted as aforesaid shall be entitled to a credit of twenty-five percent on any amount of meat which he may deliver within three months from the passage of this act" (General Order No. 26 [March 1, 1864], *General Orders of the Confederate States Army, 1864,* 35). On the relationship between conscription and price control in Florida, see Davis, *Civil War and Reconstruction,* 214–15.

115. *Journal of the Confederate Congress,* 6 : 688 (January 25, 1864).

establishment of client groups than the House as a whole on three of the five votes. Ways and Means, however, was comparatively hostile. This committee may have been disproportionately sensitive to the impact of client group policy on revenue and expenditures because of the panel's jurisdictional responsibility for taxation and spending. Such an explanation would account, in part, for the relative sympathy Ways and Means members exhibited for the price control proposal because it entailed an off-budget redistribution of wealth. On the whole, the voting patterns on client group legislation indicate that this dimension of central state authority was the one least well integrated, by Confederate legislators, into a comprehensive design for the Confederate government.

The World System

In a perfectly designed state, the relationship of the nation to the remainder of the world system would be determined by a professional career foreign service insulated from the distracting and relatively parochial concerns of internal domestic politics. In such a government, the service could base the foreign policy of the country on the national interest, free from the short-term political interests that otherwise divide the polity, restrict bureaucratic freedom of action, and debilitate long-term planning capacity. Needless to say, no American state has ever approached this ideal and the Confederacy was no exception.

The first task facing the Confederate Congress was the establishment of relations with the European powers and the related question of whether Confederate representatives would be responsible to Congress or the president. In a very early test, the Provisional Congress overrode the objections of Robert Barnwell Rhett, then chairman of the Foreign Affairs Committee, and gave wide discretionary authority over commissioners (in effect, unrecognized ambassadors) to President Davis. On March 15, 1862, this decision was reaffirmed by the House of Representatives when it passed a joint resolution "authorizing the President to send additional commissioners to foreign powers" (see table 7).[116]

An even more sensitive foreign policy topic concerned relations with the northern Union. Here the most pressing issue, aside from the war itself, involved the treatment of prisoners. Both sides, with some justification, believed the other to be intentionally mistreating prisoners of war. Very early in the conflict the Provisional Congress granted Davis extraordinarily wide authority to "retaliate" for Union abuse of captured southerners. An Act Authorizing the President to inflict Retaliation upon the Persons of Prisoners, adopted August 30, 1861, read: "That the President be, and he is hereby, authorized to select such prisoners taken from the United States, and in such numbers as he may deem expedient, upon the prisoners of whom he may inflict such retaliation, in such measure and kind as may seem to him just and proper." The act carried implicit authority and responsibility for negotiations with the

116. Yearns, *Confederate Congress*, 165. *Journal of the Confederate Congress*, 5 : 104–05 (March 15, 1862).

Table 7. The Confederate State in the World System

	Support for a Stronger State (House Votes Cast)									
	Authorization of Foreign Commissioners (Mar. 15, 1862)		Duty-Free Imports (April 2, 1862)		Retaliation on Prisoners (May 1, 1863)		Blockade-Runner Cargo (Jan. 28, 1864)		Negotiated Peace (May 23, 1864)	
Type of Member/District	%	N	%	N	%	N	%	N	%	N
ALL CONGRESSMEN	56.1	(82)	19.3	(83)	61.4	(57)	84.7	(72)	74.7	(83)
Exterior districts	58.8	(17)	43.7	(16)	75.0	(12)	100.0	(8)	90.9	(11)
Interior districts	55.4	(65)	13.4	(67)	57.8	(45)	82.8	(64)	72.2	(72)
Slave population										
0–24%	40.0	(15)	9.1	(11)	33.3	(9)	85.7	(14)	68.7	(16)
25–49%	63.3	(30)	19.4	(36)	45.5	(22)	83.3	(30)	58.1	(31)
Over 50%	55.0	(20)	5.0	(20)	92.9	(14)	80.0	(20)	92.0	(25)
Value added in manufacturing (per capita)										
Over $10	56.2	(16)	23.5	(17)	50.0	(12)	66.7	(18)	88.2	(17)
Under $10	55.1	(49)	10.0	(50)	60.6	(33)	89.1	(46)	67.3	(55)
Major committees										
Judiciary	60.0	(6)	33.3	(9)	80.0	(5)	85.7	(7)	88.9	(9)
Military Affairs	60.0	(5)	9.1	(11)	75.0	(8)	75.0	(8)	90.0	(10)
Ways and Means	37.5	(8)	0.0	(8)	57.1	(7)	62.5	(8)	88.9	(9)

Union over the treatment of prisoners. These negotiations did not go well, and in the spring of 1863 the Confederate Congress again took up the subject.[117]

When it did, the governments of the individual states—rather than Congress—emerged as the most important alternative to executive authority. The best account of the statist position was delivered by Edmund Dargan of Alabama who "did not think that the office of retaliation could be transferred to the [individual states], as it was a right exclusively incident to the nationalities that were at war. . . . The states which had no power to declare war were not only legally incapable of exercising the rights of belligerents in this matter of retaliation" but were otherwise not competent to do so. In the end the Confederate Congress adopted legislation providing that "the President of the Confederate States is hereby authorized to cause full and ample retaliation to be made for every such violation [of the usages of war of civilized nations] in such manner and to such extent as he may think proper." The law further specified that enemy officers leading black troops would be tried for "inciting servile insurrection" by the "military court attached to the army or corps" that captured those officers.[118] Adoption reaffirmed executive preeminence in negotiations with the Union.

Presidential control of foreign relations was challenged from yet another quarter before the end of the war. As the prospects for an outright Confederate military victory diminished, a fairly substantial "peace movement" developed within the South. Always a distinct minority, the goal of this movement was conservative: a negotiated peace in which the South would gain the practical equivalence or substance of independence. As many scholars and contemporary observers have noted, it was not entirely clear—particularly after Lincoln's victory over McClellan in the 1864 presidential election—why the Union would negotiate such a peace. The most serious attempt to propose negotiations was made in the form of a joint resolution offered by James T. Leach of North Carolina, a member, as Alexander and Beringer put it, of the "lunatic fringe." Leach proposed that delegations from the individual states request that President Davis offer a ninety-day armistice to the U.S. government as a precondition to negotiations concerning a peace in which individual state sovereignty and independence would be secured. Although not explicitly binding on Davis, the resolution was correctly seen as an infringement upon the president's foreign policy prerogatives. After brief debate, the joint resolution was tabled by a large majority (see table 7).[119]

The Confederate Constitution prohibited "any duties or taxes on importa-

---

117. *Acts and Resolutions of the Third Session of the Provisional Congress,* 53–54. Moore, ed., *Rebellion Record,* 1 : 359–60.

118. *Proceedings,* 48 : 65 (February 5, 1863). For additional debate, see 47 : 152–53, 167–68 (January 19, 21, 1863). For the text of the act, see *Public Laws of the Confederate States of America, Third Session, First Congress (1863),* 167–68. For the vote, see *Journal of the Confederate Congress,* 6 : 488 (May 1, 1863).

119. *Anatomy of the Confederate Congress,* 295; *Journal of the Confederate Congress,* 84–85 (May 23, 1864); Yearns, *Confederate Congress,* 176, and generally, 171–83.

tions from foreign nations" intended "to promote or foster any branch of industry." This provision, with its limitations on the discretionary authority of the central state to shape internal development through manipulation of the terms of foreign trade, weakened the formal structure and power of the Confederate government. Prior to its adoption on February 9, 1861, the Provisional Congress had continued the existing U.S. tariff. Later, the Congress provided, on February 22 and March 15, for free navigation of the Mississippi from the river's mouth to the northern border of the Confederacy, repealed, on February 26, U.S. navigation laws, with their hated monopoly on the coastal trade for American vessels, and, on February 28, imposed an export tax on cotton of one-eighth of a cent per pound. Although the early decision to establish a tariff and continue in force existing schedules was motivated by the desire of representatives of border states (for example, North Carolina, Tennessee, and Virginia) to protect their home industries, later reductions and modifications, adopted May 21 and August 3, 1861, removed most duties in excess of those required for revenue.[120] In adopting the new tariff schedules, the Confederacy in effect revised the U.S. tariff of 1857. Included among the few changes the South made in that revision was a section providing for the duty-free admission of "breadstuffs" from the Northwest, a special treatment that had been intended to reduce opposition to southern independence in the western half of the Union. In order to entice imports of war matériel and encourage those willing to run the blockade, the Confederacy also reduced duties in other schedules.[121] As one of the last acts of the first session, the Provisional Congress prohibited the exportation of cotton to the North. Since, as the Richmond *Daily Examiner* noted, the naval blockade prevented exports to Europe, the sale of cotton to the Union would have damaged southern interests by stimulating the northern economy.[122]

In spite of the constitutional ban on import duties, protectionist sentiment was strong in some quarters. On March 8, 1862, for example, Augustus Wright of Georgia presented to the House of Representatives

> a communication from Colonel Wade S. Cottran, President of the Bank of the Empire State, in reference to the iron interests. The leading idea of the communication was that the iron interest has suffered for the want of tariff for permanent protection. The iron interest was sufficiently remunerative, but parties declined to take any steps in the matter for fear that, in case of a

120. Russel, *Economic Aspects of Southern Sectionalism*, 259–60, 273–74. Although important as a precedent, the export duty produced almost no revenue for the government (about $6,000 total in specie during the war) (Schwab, *Confederate States of America*, 240–42; Todd, *Confederate Finance*, 123–24. For Confederate tariff schedules, see the Richmond *Daily Examiner*, April 12 and June 18, 1861).

121. Richmond *Daily Examiner*, May 25, 1861. On May 28, the paper published an analysis of why the Northwest should allow the South to secede. See also Yearns, *Confederate Congress*, 162–67.

122. May 27, 1861. The text of this law was published June 5.

termination of the war, foreign iron would be brought in, and thus destroy all remuneration. The parties pray for a protective tariff for a limited number of years.[123]

Such efforts, however, proved counterproductive as they ultimately provoked an even larger movement to repeal the tariff entirely and open up the South to unrestricted free trade involvement in the world economy.

During debate on a free trade bill, John Perkins of Louisiana noted that the measure had been "recommended by the Legislatures of Georgia, Texas, and South Carolina . . . by a very large number of the merchants of New Orleans, and by the chamber of Commerce of Charleston . . . [and] by the Commercial and Planters convention that met in Georgia," adding that the secretary of the treasury's "statement showed that the revenue collected from imports [since July, 1861] was just about equal to the expense of collection. . . . we surrender nothing whatever of the revenue in point of fact."[124] The House of Representatives subsequently adopted the bill, which would have entailed an ideological commitment to free trade by the Confederate state (see table 7); however, the Senate failed to consider the proposal and Confederate tariff policy remained focused on revenue—though, as Perkins observed, most customs offices probably operated at a loss.

The free trade bill was a potential blow to the foreign policy powers of the Confederate state because it neither yielded revenue to the government nor created dependent economic sectors protected by a state-maintained tariff wall. In creating these dependent sectors, it should be noted, the state would have also provided central direction and encouragement to internal economic development. Between the twin goals of revenue raising and economic development, a theory of central state authority cannot choose; each contributes to the authority and influence of the state in a different way. A theoretically consistent endorsement of free trade principles, however, entails the renunciation of both statist alternatives. Adoption of such principles not only weakens the revenue capacity of the government and forgoes one of the most powerful means of directing the shape of internal economic development, but also leaves the situation open to the exploitation by other central states through their own trade policies.

In the end, the Confederate state both repudiated pure free trade principles and vitiated most of the significance of the constitutional ban on protectionism. The first policies that turned the state in an interventionist direction were those that prohibited cotton exports to the Union except where conducted by authorized Confederate officials. This prohibition was later expanded to include all staple crops, but it was almost impossible to enforce. Trade with nations other than the Union primarily took the form of blockade running, through the northern navy, and was much easier to monitor and

123. *Proceedings*, 44 : 123. See, more generally, Todd, *Confederate Finance*, 128.

124. *Proceedings*, 45 : 59–61 (April 2, 1862). For the roll call on this bill, see *Journal of the Confederate Congress*, 5 : 170–71. See also Todd, *Confederate Finance*, 128.

control.[125] In 1863, the Confederacy sought to compel vessels running the blockade to dedicate one-third to one-half of all cargo space to government imports. This statute, however, exempted vessels chartered or owned by the individual states, a measure that frustrated Confederate efforts to centralize control of the export-import trade.

In February 1864, the Confederate government assumed control of 50 percent of the export-import trade upon adoption of a law prohibiting the importation of luxuries and another giving the president wide discretionary power over exports. Under the latter, enacted February 6, 1864, the "exportation of cotton, tobacco, military and naval stores, sugar, molasses, and rice from the Confederate States, except under such uniform regulations as might be made by the President was prohibited; and the President was authorized to employ any portion of the military and naval forces of the Confederacy in order to prevent the departure of any vessels or vehicles that might be employed in carrying on a commerce in these articles contrary to law." (The House originally approved the law January 28, 1864; see table 7). President Davis aggressively utilized the discretionary authority granted him under the act, and an effective centralization of much of the foreign trade of the Confederacy was achieved. In fact, executive control was viewed with so much alarm that the Confederate Congress subsequently passed two measures intended to weaken presidential authority. Each of these measures, however, Davis stopped with vetoes.[126]

These tests of sentiment on the world-system powers of the Confederate state provide substantial confirming evidence of the tentative patterns found on the other dimensions. Members from exterior districts gave greater support to the expansion of state authority than congressmen from the interior. Members from manufacturing districts also favored greater central state mediation of foreign relations. District dependence on a plantation economy appears, however, to have exercised little influence on the positions of congressmen. Although members from constituencies containing large slave populations came down solidly for presidential discretion in prisoner retaliation and peace negotiations, they also were disproportionately opposed to tariffs and Confederate control of blockade running. The free trade vote, in particular, dis-

125. Yearns, *Confederate Congress*, 135–38. On the importance of blockade running to the Confederate war effort and its scale in general, see Bradlee, *Blockade Running during the Civil War;* Gordon Wright, "Economic Conditions in the Confederacy as Seen by the French Consuls," *Journal of Southern History* 7, no. 2 (May 1941) : 200–02; and in Florida, Davis, *Civil War and Reconstruction,* 198–203; Hill, *State Socialism in the Confederate States of America,* 8–9.

126. General Order No. 43 (April 16, 1864), *General Orders of the Confederate States Army, 1864,* 84–86 (includes implementing regulations). For the text of the statute, see *Public Laws of the Confederate States of America, Fourth Session, First Congress,* 181–83; *Journal of the Confederate Congress,* 6 : 703; Hill, *State Socialism in the Confederate States of America,* 14–23. These vetoes indicate once again that the legislative decisions analyzed in the text are at the cutting edge of Confederate state formation. The fact that the southern Congress attempted at times to retreat from the major advances attained earlier should not constitute a major qualification of the state-building achievement as a whole.

plays clear differences within the southern political economy. Manufacturing districts and regions near the northern border, which were particularly vulnerable to trade competition from the Union, were less favorable to duty-free imports than the export-dependent constituencies of members from plantation districts. The Judiciary Committee once again turned in a sterling statist performance while, as before, the memberships of the Military Affairs and Ways and Means committees were less enthusiastic about the expansion of central state authority. The members of all three panels, however, emphatically rejected an infringement of executive prerogatives with regard to a negotiated peace.

THE "POLITICAL FAILURE" THESIS OF CONFEDERATE DEFEAT

The Question of Organized Opposition

Scholars who contend that the root cause of Confederate defeat can be traced to purely political defects in governmental organization and ideological obstinacy base their argument on the alleged inadequate centralization of authority within the southern political system. In one direction, this criticism invokes the texture of relations between the central government and the individual states, emphasizing in particular the role of the latter both as a bulwark against extensions of central state power and as a platform for states' rights resistance to administration policy. In another direction, advocates of the political failure hypothesis contend that the more or less libertarian beliefs of the southern citizenry led them to reject those centralizing measures necessary for military success. This ideology, amounting in some versions to short-sighted stubbornness and not shortages in manpower or matériel, was, it is maintained, responsible for southern defeat.[127]

The most prominent political failure theme is perhaps the lack of open competition by organized political parties.[128] First articulated by David Potter,

127. On the most general level, see Roy F. Nichols, "The Operation of American Democracy, 1861–1865: Some Questions," *Journal of Southern History* 25, no. 1 (February 1959) : 31–52. David Donald cited southern reliance on the election of military officers by enlisted men, excessive leniency in controlling dissent, and civil libertarian obstacles to effective administrative performance as aspects of broader cultural defects in the structure of southern society ("Died of Democracy," in David Donald, ed., *Why the North Won the Civil War* [Baton Rouge: Louisiana State University Press, 1960], 89–90). See also Donald's "The Confederate as a Fighting Man," *Journal of Southern History* 25, no. 2 (May 1959) : 192–93.

128. Within the political failure thesis, four additional distinct themes can be identified: (1) that the Confederacy collapsed because of the decentralizing impetus of states' rights sentiment; (2) that the political talent available to the Confederacy—particularly Jefferson Davis and his cabinet—was inadequate to the challenge presented by the war and generally inferior to the administrative and political ability of Union leaders; (3) that the administrative performance of the Confederate state, for a wide variety of reasons, fell short of what reasonably might have been expected and was the proximate cause of military failure; and (4) that the incompetence and political immaturity of the Confederate Congress frustrated the executive branch in the latter's effort to centralize mobilization of the South's resources and manpower. The first three are not directly addressed in this article. The fourth is

who suggested that "the Confederacy may have suffered real and direct damage from the fact that its political organization lacked a two-party system," the thesis was fully elaborated by Eric McKitrick in 1967. Among the several arguments McKitrick advances, two best illustrate this general position: first, that formal party organizations and widespread popular identification with them serve as indispensable referents for the political strategy of any political leader, and second, that party organizations in the North mobilized loyalist elements behind the prosecution of the war while isolating the disaffected into a separate, easily identifiable, and, as long as it remained a minority of the electorate, relatively impotent group. The thesis has been most effectively advanced, for example, when connected to the distribution of executive patronage.[129]

Perhaps inadvertently, the lack-of-political-parties theme challenges one of the most fundamental tenets of conventional political wisdom: that political minorities must organize in order to counter the greater power of their opponent's numbers. McKitrick and others concentrate their attention on the majority side of the state-centered equation: the supporters of the Davis and Lincoln administrations. From this perspective, the Davis administration chose not to organize. However, from the perspective of the minority side of the same equation, the thesis implicitly contends that northern Democrats chose not to disband while opponents of the Davis administration in the South chose not to channel their activity into a formal party. Viewed this way, the thesis contends that opposition to the policies of the Confederate state was more effective (than, say, the Democratic opposition in the Union) because it was unorganized. By failing to assume a formal organization or to adopt a common platform, opponents of a strong central state were able to blend indistinguishably into the ranks of loyal Confederate nationalists and frustrate the latter's efforts to mobilize the citizenry. Thus, while the nationalists could have reaped immense political dividends by assuming a formal organizational identity and should have imposed—it seems to be implied—at least a "negative" identity upon those who could not subscribe to the nationalist program, it is

---

approached, albeit indirectly, through evidence that the Confederate Congress did respond to the urgent state-building requirements presented by the Civil War. See Owsley, *State Rights in the Confederacy;* Marc Kruman, "Dissent in the Confederacy: The North Carolina Experience," *Civil War History* 27, no. 4 (December 1981) : 293–313; Alexander and Beringer, *Anatomy of the Confederate Congress,* 54–58, 332, 342.

129. David M. Potter, "Jefferson Davis and the Political Factors in Confederate Defeat," in Donald, ed., *Why the North Won the Civil War,* 113; Eric L. McKitrick, "Party Politics and the Union and Confederate War Efforts," in William Nisbet Chambers and Walter Dean Burnham, eds. *The American Party Systems: Stages of Political Development* (New York: Oxford University Press, 1967), 117–51; Van Riper and Scheiber, "The Confederate Civil Service," 470. Patronage, as pointed out above in the text, is a relatively primitive mode of recruitment and, because of the incompetence and corruption that often attends its use, can be employed in wartime only by a relatively resource-rich state. Compared to the well-endowed Union (where administrative corruption and incompetence were rampant), the South could not afford to draw loyalty through a calculated squandering of limited national resources.

contended that the opponents of centralization would have gained no advantage through organization.[130]

Both the Davis and Lincoln administrations practiced co-optation of opposition members—a classic state-centered strategy not available to opponents. Davis attempted to maintain a broad societal consensus by frustrating the development of a coherent opposition. Lincoln, by contrast, isolated an already existing and relatively extreme opposition in the minority party. Both are optimal strategies for a central state under different initial conditions. A broad southern consensus both existed in fact and provided a major justification for Confederate separatism. Because opponents of the Davis administration, by and large, differed over how, not whether, the war should be fought, the Confederate state could tolerate dissent and still mobilize the southern nation. A significant segment of the northern Democratic party, on the other hand, opposed the Union war effort outright. The abundance of matériel and manpower available to the Union allowed the Lincoln administration to forgo a full mobilization of the North and, instead, exploit the political advantage of branding the minority as traitorous. Even a brief excursion into this line of explanation shows how quickly it slides into a contextual morass.[131]

One way out is to examine the formal policy products of the two political systems. From the perspective of administrative structure and central state power, the viability of the lack-of-political-parties thesis rests upon the relative strength of the Confederate state. If the formal structure and powers of that state were as fully developed as those in the Union, then the absence-of-political-parties thesis would be hard-pressed to explain the failure of the Confederacy by way of state design. In this instance, parity, not perfection, is the test of relative state performance in the mobilization of resources and manpower in support of a war effort.

More immediately, the thesis calls into question the leadership ability of

130. This line of argument strongly implies that northern Democrats should have disbanded for the duration in order to more effectively frustrate the Union war effort and that Lincoln's strategy of creating a nonpartisan "Union" party was counterproductive. See McKitrick, 141–42.

131. Other variants of the thesis experience similar difficulties. For example, an organized administration party might have better served the propaganda needs of the Confederacy or better calculated the trade-off between coercive efficiency and civilian morale. While not directly addressed here, upon inspection these variants would also almost certainly degenerate into idiosyncratic exceptionalism. Whether propaganda needs are better served by an organized administration party (and an organized opposition) or a fluid, co-opting consensus in which all major societal groups alternately participate can probably be answered only through a consideration of specific contextual factors. Similarly, questions addressing implementation of formal policy decisions must consider the effect upon the South of the serious decentralizing forces of communication difficulties, transport deterioration, and local anxiety over invasion. (Even conceding that such factors operated upon the Confederate state, their broad effect seems to have been to increase the autonomous discretion of national officials in the field: for example, Kirby Smith's administration of the trans-Mississippi region after the fall of Vicksburg.)

Jefferson Davis: whether, on the one hand, the Confederate president recognized the state-enhancing potential of enlargements of his own authority and whether, on the other hand, he correctly identified and effectively led a congressional coalition in pursuit of that objective. In examining these questions an additional query will emerge concerning the sophistication of the putative executive coalition: whether President Davis and his supporters recognized the state-enhancing potential of measures that insulated bureaucratic decison making from executive influence or that strengthened the judiciary. An executive-led coalition, even while constituting the most effective force in building a strong state, may ultimately limit administrative capacity by maximizing executive prerogatives at the expense of the more statist bureaucracy and judiciary. As it turns out, the evidence strongly supports the existence of a relatively sophisticated statist coalition led by Jefferson Davis, thus demonstrating both the president's administrative vision and his leadership effectiveness in the absence of a formal party system.

In order to pursue this line of investigation, independent identification of presidential supporters is required. Previous work on the Confederate Congress yields at least two such identifications. Wilfred Buck Yearns published a list of supporters as a part of his appendix ("Biographical Notes on Confederate Congressmen") to *The Confederate Congress* (see the notes to table 8). His identification of presidential supporters is broken down by individual Congress (Provisional, First, and Second) but omits about half of all members, primarily for their failure to vote on a sufficient number of issues. Yearns does not indicate the roll call decisions upon which he relied in identifying supporters and opponents, and as a result, it is not known which, if any, of the decisions analyzed here also entered into his own calculations. The second listing has been taken from Alexander and Beringer's *The Anatomy of the Confederate Congress* and moves closer than Yearns did to a "statist-nonstatist" dimension. They identified members who favored or opposed "the objective of establishing an independent Confederacy with a central government adequate to the tasks imposed upon it in war or peace" and computed an "Average Adjusted Scale Position" for all congressmen regardless of how long or when they served.[132]

132. Chapter 11 and pp. 7, 409–18. Alexander and Beringer do not expand the theoretical basis of their roll call assignments beyond this quote. Their scores, which run from 0 through 9, are based on roll calls that include six of the thirty studied here. In each case, the "stronger war effort" alternative is the same as the statist option. In the course of their analysis they indicate a "strong" position on an additional fifteen decisions analyzed in this chapter and the statist and "strong" sides agree on all but two measures: the imposition of a civil service test for military engineers and, inexplicably, the legislation proposing the elimination of import duties. From a statist perspective, their identification of the first measure with a weaker war effort indicates a tendency to pull their dimension toward "executive dominance" where that differed from "state capacity." Indeed, Alexander and Beringer favor executive discretion on all measures where they indicate a "strong" position and omit two of the three roll calls where executive interests and state capacity conflict: the creation of a general staff and the veterans' home veto (the other is the civil service test). In addition to the partial identification of administration interests with a "stronger war effort," they omit

Table 8. Loyalty to the Davis Administration, Support for a Stronger War Efffort, and Voting on State-building Measures, 1861–1865

Dimension	Measure	Relation to	
		David Administration Loyalty[a]	Support for a Stronger War Effort[a]
Citizenship	Conscription	.86	.95
	*Habeas corpus	.85	.76
Centralization	Court jurisdiction	−.33	.78
	Secret sessions	.36	.47
	*Officers by states	.57	.82
	Judge or jury	−.35	.26
	*Officer election	.60	.64
	Expel Foote	.71	.92
Administrative	*General staff	−.27	−.20
	*Exemptions	.88	.63
	*Civil service test	−.55	−.71
	Establish court	.66	−.01
	*Midshipmen	.88	.86
	Secret service	.49	.71
Property	Railroad subsidy	.59	.53
	Destroy property	−.36	−.09
	Control railroads	−.06	.09
	Impressment	.11	.13
	U.S. securities	.44	.08
	*Slave soldiers	.82	.60
Client groups	Pensions	−.65	.11
	Redistribution	.49	−.00
	Bonds	.29	.02
	Price control	.66	.60
	*Veterans' home	−.55	−.80
World system	*Commissioners	.61	.30
	Duty-free imports	.15	.39
	*Retaliation	.78	.47
	Blockade Cargo	.16	.56
	*Negotiated peace	.81	.89

Notes and Sources: Figures represent the association between voting in favor of the statist alternative on each of the measures (see text) and (1) "David Administration Loyalty"—either support of or opposition to the administration (see Wilfred Buck Yearns, *The Confederate Congress,* Appendix, pp. 236–44) and (2) "Support for a Stronger War Effort"—either "high": scale positions 5 through 9, or "low": scale positions 0 through 4 (see Thomas B. Alexander and Richard E. Beringer, *The Anatomy of the Confederate Congress,* Average Adjusted Scale Position, pp. 398–405).

Measures marked with an asterisk significantly affected the scope of executive discretion or, in the case of the veterans' home bill, were vetoed by President Davis.

[a] The association is measured by the statistic Yule's Q.

By and large, those members identified as supporters of the Davis administration strongly backed legislation that expanded executive discretion (see table 8 and note asterisked measures).[133] In all twelve instances, including the three cases in which the interests of the central state and executive conflict, the direction of the relationship between support for the statist alternative and "Davis administration loyalty" is the same as that holding for "support for a stronger war effort." On nine of the twelve, administration supporters were relatively favorable to a stronger central state, *but* on all twelve they favored executive discretion. This relationship, of course, is to be expected (although it does substantiate the conflation of "support for a stronger war effort" with presidential backing). Even so, such results could not have arisen in the absence of an effective and consistent application of executive influence and leadership. In addition, the data strongly suggest that those members who followed Davis's leadership did not recognize bureaucratic autonomy as a desirable feature of the state when that autonomy conflicted with executive authority. The vision of central state design of the president's supporters was thus limited.

The interesting results, however, relate administration supporters to central state enhancement in areas that less directly implicated presidential interests. Here the two designations produce different outcomes. Yearns's formulation, for example, positively connects administration supporters to backing for the statist alternative on thirteen of the eighteen nonexecutive measures. Alexander and Beringer's listing does the same on fifteen of the eighteen. The direction of the relationship is inconsistent on seven measures (two more than necessary to explain the difference in overall backing) and generally suggests a certain ambiguity in administration attitude. Taken all together, however, these results indicate a degree of sympathy for the interests of the central state that has not been commonly attributed to either Jefferson Davis or Confederate congressmen who backed his administration.

Another way to examine the impact of presidential leadership and the enhancement of executive authority is to analyze the voting patterns of the major state-building groups. As has been noted previously, the most consistent advocates of expanded central state power came from exterior districts. Within

---

any analysis of client group legislation apart from the amendment redistributing income to soldiers' families. Thus, although more broadly conceived and empirically grounded than Yearns's formulation, the Alexander and Beringer list of scale positions is still, more or less, a proxy for administration support. Unlike Yearns, their scale includes all members of the House of Representatives. For the purpose of analysis here, the scale has been reduced to a dichotomous identification of "supporters" and "opponents" of a stronger war effort.

133. These twelve measures are those in which expanded executive discretion constituted a major issue in legislative consideration. Outside "administrative capacity" and "centralization of authority" dimensions, however, the scope of executive discretion was ultimately less important, overall, than the substantive content of central state expansion. The comparatively statist orientation of Davis and his supporters conforms to an almost universal American experience: every American president has urged a more state-centered war mobilization (with the possible exception of that for the Spanish-American War) on a reluctant Congress.

the House of Representatives, the most consistent institutional group was composed of members of the Committee on the Judiciary. When all thirty decisons are considered, the Judiciary Committee's role as one of the strongest institutional advocates of central state expansion is self-evident; the panel's membership provided greater support than the remainder of the House for the statist alternative in twenty-two (73 percent) of the decisions. The record is less clear for Military Affairs and Ways and Means. The former gave relatively greater support in only thirteen cases (43 percent) and the later in only nine (30 percent).[134]

Inconsistent support came from congressmen from interior plantation and manufacturing districts (see table 9). More often than not, these members gave less support to the statist alternative than the remainder of the House membership (which includes exterior districts not categorized by slave owning or manufacturing). When compared to other interior members alone, plantation districts gave more support to the statist alternative on seventeen (57 percent) decisions. Manufacturing members gave greater backing on sixteen (55 percent). Thus, while interior plantation and manufacturing districts turned in a relatively poor showing compared to the entire House, nonplantation and nonmanufacturing interior districts were even, in this analysis, less statist-oriented. The state-enhancing tendencies of exterior districts were so pronounced as to make all other groupings appear weak by comparison. The decision to allow members from exterior districts to sit in the House thus appears to have significantly enhanced the statist tendencies of the Confederate Congress.

In every case the members of these separate groupings more consistently favored the expansion of central state authority on measures involving the president than on legislation that had a relatively unimportant or no discernible impact on the prerogatives of the executive. The differences were particularly pronounced for plantation and manufacturing members. Plantation members, for example, cast a greater percentage of their ballots in favor of

134. The statist tendencies of the Judiciary Committee were well recognized in the House of Representatives as a whole. Nationalist members, for example, attempted to enlarge the panel's jurisdiction by sending the midshipmen appointment bill to that committee after Davis had vetoed it. The proposed referral would have prevented the House from considering (and possibly overriding) the veto (*Journal of the Confederate Congress*, 7 : 502 [January 26, 1865]). The bill would have denied President Davis the authority to appoint midshipmen to the naval academy, giving that prerogative to individual congressmen. See also *Proceedings*, 44 : 110 (March 6, 1862), where Charles Conrad of Louisiana hoped the bill to authorize the destruction of cotton and tobacco would "not be referred to that committee [Judiciary]; he knew very well what their report would be" concerning the compensation of property owners. The predilections of the committee are relatively silent evidence of the statist orientation of the speaker of the House of Representatives. Although no other corroborating information has been discovered, the speaker appointed a disproportionately large number of Confederate centralists to this strategic committee, which held jurisdiction over authority to retaliate on Union soldiers captured by Confederate forces for abuses suffered by southern prisoners, the creation of a Confederate supreme court, suspension of the writ of habeas corpus, and the impressment of property.

Table 9. Presidential Leadership, State Enhancement, and Congressional Coalition Formation in the Confederacy

Grouping[b]	Support for the Statist Alternative[a]						Support for the President[a]	
	All Measures		Not Involving the Executive		Involving the Executive		Executive-Enhancing Measures	
	%	N	%	N	%	N	%	N
Exterior districts	75.9	(29)	70.6	(17)	83.3	(12)	91.7	(12)
Plantation districts	43.3	(30)	27.8	(18)	66.7	(12)	75.0	(12)
Manufacturing districts	44.8	(29)	35.3	(17)	58.3	(12)	66.7	(12)
Judiciary Committee members	73.3	(30)	66.7	(18)	83.3	(12)	75.0	(12)

Note: Figures in parentheses indicate the number of roll calls in which the position of the group was recorded.

[a] *Support for* means that members in the indicated category cast a greater percentage of their votes in favor of the statist alternative or presidential-power enhancement, respectively, than did all members in the House of Representatives.

[b] *Exterior* includes all members from Kentucky, Missouri, and what became West Virginia. *Plantation* includes all members from interior districts containing a population more than half slave. *Manufacturing* includes all members from interior districts producing more than $10 value-added per capita in manufacturing. *Judiciary* includes all members on the committee at the time the respective votes were recorded.

the statist alternative on only 27.8 percent of the eighteen decisions not involving the executive. When executive prerogatives were involved, however, the plantation grouping outperformed the rest of the House on two-thirds of the decisions examined.

As was noted, in three of the decisions involving executive prerogatives the statist position and the position that promised to enhance executive authority did not coincide (the general staff, civil service test, and veterans' home cases; see table 9). In these three instances, backing the statist alternative implies opposition to the president and vice versa. On the other nine decisions involving the executive, the statist and executive-enhancing positions are the same. When examined solely from the perspective of executive enhancement, all four groupings gave much more frequent support to an enlargement of President Davis's authority than the remainder of the House, and, in each case except the Judiciary Committee, this support was greater than that given to statist alternatives. Thus, when the choice lay between expanding state capacity or enhancing executive power, the major state-building groups tended to favor executive power—yet another indication of the salience and effectiveness of presidential leadership.

In sum, the voting patterns of these thirty decisions provide significant and sometimes strong evidence for (1) the existence of a general statist orientation among members previously identified with loyalty to the Davis administration or support for a stronger war effort; (2) the importance of the rotten borough exterior districts to the state-building process within the Confederacy and, incidentally, the importance of the political decision to give them representation in Congress; (3) the statist predilections of the Judiciary Committee and, incidentally, of the speaker who appointed the members of this strategically important panel; and (4) the existence of a statist coalition, led by President Davis, that drew support from plantation regions of the slave economy, manufacturing cities (usually ports), and exterior districts. This coalition came together most often and most effectively on legislation enhancing executive prerogatives at the expense of the citizenry, the individual states, or Congress itself. Given the evidence of strong presidential leadership, the absence of intense and consistent internal divisions within the southern nation is remarkable. The president appears to have worked within a broad consensus that allowed strong executive leadership without producing massive internal dissension. It is difficult to believe that a formal party system, in the midst of a war for independence in which social unity was imperative, could have produced superior results.

Conclusion: The Confederate State and Southern Society

The most impressive evidence that the Confederacy did not fail politically is, of course, the impressive state apparatus that the South created to prosecute the war. Even though the analysis of statist measures in Congress has unavoidably emphasized legislative action and coalition patterns at the expense of pure description of the structure and operation of the central state itself, much of that apparatus has already been described. In this section, the synergistic impact of some of the most salient features of the Confederate state are discussed.

Considered as a whole, the Confederate state attempted to direct a mobilization of men and matériel as complete and as centrally directed as any in American history. Based primarily on conscription and impressment policies, Confederate control of manpower and property brought the southern factory, railroad, and plantation into the war effort even where explicit statutory authority was lacking. Conscription, for example, not only sent men to the front but also, through military details and categorical exemptions, allocated labor throughout the southern economy. During the first year, suspension of the writ of habeas corpus rendered opposition ineffective in those areas that came under presidential proclamations. Later, after the courts of the individual states had ruled in favor of conscription, local judiciaries supported effective administration of the Confederate draft.

Impressment reached units of production from below through the outright confiscation of property. Impressment dated from the very beginning of the war as an integral part of the martial law powers of an army in the field. The practice was later bureaucratized through an explicit statutory grant of authority to the military and price control boards. Even more detailed provisions affecting railroads, slave labor, and factory production followed. Control of railroad operations, in turn, centralized the supply of raw materials to manufacturers. By the time these twin policies (conscription and impressment) met in the city or countryside, the susceptibility of manufacturers and the great plantations to Confederate command was complete.

Although many other features of the Confederate state further demonstrate the level of statist sentiment and sophistication within the southern nation, this emphasis on the synergism between conscription and impressment concisely describes the core policies of the Confederate war effort. Although some aspects were specified in law, most authority conferred upon the central state was subject to executive or bureaucratic discretion. And, although this discretion could theoretically have been used to enhance the planning capacity and centralizing tendencies of the state, in practice both technological deficiency (primarily in telegraphic communication but later extending to transportation) and chronic shortages in matériel and manpower forced a much more decentralized control apparatus upon the Confederacy. Before these twin policies of conscription and impressment, the individual was almost entirely helpless. Armed with immense and largely unappealable discretionary power, Confederate civilian and military agents improvised temporary solutions to the problem of supplying and arming a military force capable of holding at bay an army backed by one of the world's leading industrial powers.[135]

From this perspective, it becomes clearer that the failure of the Confederate

135. Four nations—the United Kingdom, China, India, and France—had a total manufacturing output greater than the United States in 1860. Without the South, the manufacturing output of the North may, in addition, have fallen below that of Russia. See Paul Bairoch, "International Industrialization Levels from 1750 to 1980," *Journal of European Economic History* 11, no. 2 (Fall 1982) : 269–334. In terms of "modern" industrial capacity, the United States may have ranked as high as third, after the United Kingdom and, possibly, France.

state was the product of matériel and manpower shortages. As these shortages became more acute, individual bureaus assumed control over resources essential to their operations and allocated commodities to other departments within the government. The Nitre and Mining Bureau socialized mineral extraction and iron production by taking over mines and foundries or by so dominating their operations that outright confiscation was unnecessary. The Subsistence and Quartermaster's departments obtained exclusive purchasing rights in the domestic market through the power of impressment and thus became the sole agent in the allocation of cotton textile production. As the war continued, all agencies became increasingly dependent on blockade running as the domestic economy, sundered by invasion and cavalry raids, failed.[136]

Significantly, the Union state apparatus appears relatively anemic when compared to the Confederacy. Northern experiments with conscription and internal economic controls never approached the all-encompassing Confederate operation in the South. The Confederate Congress was more insulated from popular control (for example, exterior districts and secrecy) and had much less influence over bureaucratic appointments and patronage (with less attendant debilitating corruption and incompetence). In the North, however, recruitment and promotion of military officers ultimately became more professional than in the South. A relatively prosperous economy also allowed the Union to create and expand client group policies, whereas the South gave only passing attention to this dimension of state enhancement. In spite of these deviations, however, the Confederate state was a much more pervasive and encompassing presence in the daily life of southern society than the Union government was in the North.[137] Toward the end, one North Carolina congressman was led to lament (in debate summarized by the Richmond *Examiner*): "There was too much of brass button and bayonet rule in the country. The land was alive with them [Confederate officials]. They were as thick as locusts in Egypt. Richmond was full of them. Even in his little town they were so thick that he could not walk without being elbowed off the streets by them."[138]

By then southern nationalism had immeasurably strengthened centralizing forces within the Confederate state. This nationalist sentiment led one Georgia judge to write:

> It [is] not only the right but the duty of a nation to protect itself, and that any contract or right flowing out of the operation of law which came in conflict with the preservation of the State [is] an unconstitutional act, not obligatory

136. Goff, *Confederate Supply*, 157–58. Once established, the Confederate bureaucracy rapidly became a disciplined and statist-oriented institution. Even after the evacuation of Richmond just days before Appomattox, instructions were sent to an impressment officer in Louisiana informing him that "the duty intrusted to you is a delicate one, and care will be taken not to interfere with any planter so as to curtail the provision crop which he may be cultivating" (Trexler, "The Opposition of Planters to the Employment of Slaves," 218).

137. A comprehensive comparison of the Confederate and Union states will be undertaken in *Yankee Leviathan: The Origins and Exercise of Central State Authority in America* (in preparation).

138. *Proceedings*, 52 : 242 (January 27, 1865).

on the law-making power, and within the constitutional power of the government to repeal. . . .

All rights, all property, all persons who are citizens of a government, may be used by the government in time of war, and it [is] the duty of the courts to sustain the government in the appropriation of the means exercised rightfully by the legislature to protect the whole people from subjugation and ruin.[139]

The single most important "political failure" of the Confederacy was the fact that secession did not occur in 1850 instead of 1860. Then the South might have won the war.[140]

---

139. Paraphrased in Moore, ed., *Rebellion Record,* 8 : 393–94. This decision upheld the right of the Confederate state to end substitution practices in conscription.

140. David M. Potter, *The Impending Crisis: 1848–1861* (New York: Harper Torchbooks, 1976), 118–20.

EDWIN AMENTA
ELISABETH S. CLEMENS
JEFREN OLSEN
SUNITA PARIKH
Center for the Study of Industrial Societies, University of Chicago
THEDA SKOCPOL
Harvard University

The Political Origins of Unemployment Insurance in Five American States

The last decade has been a time of rapid development in comparative social scientific research on modern welfare states—or more concretely, research on social insurance, pensions, and public assistance policies. Synchronic studies, using highly aggregated measures to make causal inferences about policy developments in all the nations of the world, have declined in favor of longitudinal comparative studies of up to eighteen advanced industrial capitalist democracies. Concomitant with this shift, analytic interest has moved away from industrialization and urbanization and toward more political explanatory variables—including class power and class alliances, the structures of political regimes, political parties, and party systems, and the activities of administrators and policy intellectuals.[1]

For helpful comments and criticisms, we thank David Menefee-Libey, Lloyd I. Rudolph, Elizabeth Sanders, anonymous reviewers, and the Workshop of American Society and Politics at the Center for the Study of Industrial Societies.

1. For arguments concerning class power and class alliances, see John D. Stephens, *The Transition from Capitalism to Socialism* (London: Macmillan; Atlantic Highlands, N.J.: Humanities Press, 1979); Gosta Esping-Andersen, *Politics against Markets: The Social Democratic Road to Power* (Princeton: Princeton University Press, 1985). For arguments concerning the structures of political regimes, political parties, and party systems, see Francis G. Castles, *The Social Democratic Image of Society* (London: Routledge & Kegan Paul, 1978); Francis G. Castles, "The Impact of Parties on Public Expenditures," in *The Impact of Parties* (Beverly Hills, Calif.: Sage Publications, 1982), 21–96; Peter Flora and Jens Alber, "Modernization, Democratization, and the Development of Welfare States in Western Europe," in Peter Flora

As scholars have turned toward longitudinal research designs focusing on smaller numbers of nations, interest has grown in the contents of different kinds of policies—for example, the substantive provisions of unemployment insurance laws[2] or old-age pensions[3]—rather than simply the aggregate amounts spent on all policies or the proportions of a national population convered by them. What is more, scholars have discovered that the determinants of the origins of social policies may be quite different from the determinants of their subsequent expansion.[4]

The research reported here—a comparative analysis of the political origins of unemployment insurance in five states of the United States—builds upon some of these trends in recent scholarship, showing that comparative historical analysis and attention to policy origins and contents can also improve our understanding of social policy development in the United States. Although grounded in a tradition that emphasizes state structure—therefore branding the United States as exceptional because of its federal political system—our approach demonstrates that the United States can play more than a residual role in comparative research and theorizing on the origins of modern social policies.

A RATIONALE FOR COMPARATIVE ANALYSIS WITHIN THE UNITED STATES

At the national level, the United States failed to initiate or even seriously debate modern social insurance and pension programs between the 1880s and the 1920s, when many other industrializing capitalist nations in Europe, Aus-

---

and Arnold Heidenheimer, eds., *The Development of Welfare States in Europe and America* (New Brunswick, N.J.: Transaction Books, 1981), 37–80; Harold Wilensky, *The 'New Corporatism,' Centralization, and the Welfare State* (Beverly Hills, Calif.: Sage Publications, 1976); Harold Wilensky, "Leftism, Catholicism, and Democratic Corporatism: The Role of Political Parties in Welfare State Development," in Peter Flora and Arnold Heidenheimer, eds., *The Development of Welfare State in Europe and North America* (New Brunswick, N.J.: Transaction Books, 1981), 341–78; Ann Shola Orloff and Theda Skocpol, "Why Not Equal Protection? Explaining the Politics of Public Social Spending in Britain, 1900–1911, and the United States, 1880s–1920," *American Sociological Review* 49 (1984) : 726–50. For arguments concerning the role of administrators and policy intellectuals, see Hugh Heclo, *Modern Social Politics in Britain and Sweden: From Relief to Income Maintenance* (New Haven: Yale University Press, 1974).

2. For a comparative small-nation study of unemployment insurance, see Jens Alber, "Government Responses to the Challenge of Unemployment: The Development of Unemployment Insurance in Western Europe," in Peter Flora and Arnold Heidenheimer, eds., *The Development of Welfare States in Europe and America* (New Brunswick, N.J.: Transaction Books, 1981), 151–83.

3. For a comparative small-nation study of old-age pensions, see John Myles, *Old Age in the Welfare State: The Political Economy of Public Pensions* (Boston: Little, Brown, 1984).

4. For research on the differential determinants of the origins and expansion of social policies, see Peter Flora and Arnold Heidenheimer, "The Historical Core and the Changing Boundaries of the Welfare State," in *The Development of Welfare States in Europe and America* (New Brunswick, N.J.: Transaction Books, 1981), 17–34.

tralasia, and Latin America instituted such policies. Thus many comparative studies of social policy origins either have left the pre-1930s United States out of the analysis[5] or have treated it as a special case because of the strength of liberal values of the hegemony of capitalists in American society and politics.[6] Social scientists have paid little attention to early policy developments in the American states.

Social scientists do recognize that the United States eventually launched a nationwide welfare state with the passage of the Social Security Act of 1935; for the period after the 1930s and 1940s the United States is routinely incorporated into cross-national studies of the relative expansion of social spending and social programs across the advanced industrial capitalist democracies. But the Social Security Act tends to be treated as a "big bang" of national policy innovations, coming in response to the wrenching effects of the Great Depression.[7]

This perspective overlooks crucial facts. The states, not the federal government, were the units that debated health and unemployment insurance bills and passed workers' compensation and mothers' pension laws during the Progressive Era and after.[8] Moreover, during the 1920s, some states passed laws enabling localities to offer pensions to the impoverished elderly. The U.S. Social Security Act of 1935 was not the first or the only American social policy innovation during the Great Depression; many state policies were instituted between 1929 and 1935. Furthermore, state politicians involved in some of the earliest debates and successful legislation moved to Washington with the New Deal in 1932–33 and shaped the proposals that became embodied in federal legislation.[9]

Perhaps most important, the 1935 federal Social Security legislation scrupulously worked around and built upon state-level laws in areas where they already existed or were close to passage. Only contributory old-age insurance was enacted as a purely national program. The public assistance and unemployment insurance titles of the Social Security Act were (in different ways) "federal" measures, leaving the states in charge of benefits and administra-

5. For instance, Flora and Alber, in "Modernization, Democratization, and the Development of Welfare States in Western Europe," omit any discussion of the United States.

6. For research that emphasizes the strength of liberal values or the hegemony of capitalists, see David Collier and Richard Messick, "Prerequisites versus Diffusion: Testing Alternative Explanations of Social Security Adoption," *American Political Science Review* 69 (1975) : 1299–1315; Gaston Rimlinger, *Welfare Policy and Industrialization in Europe, America, and Russia* (New York: Wiley, 1971); Stephens, *The Transition from Capitalism to Socialism.*

7. Christopher Leman, "Patterns of Policy Development: Social Security in the United States and Canada," *Public Policy* 25 (1977) : 261–91.

8. For state-level social policy developments, see Elizabeth Brandeis, "Labor Legislation," in John R. Commons, ed., *History of Labor in the United States, 1896–1932* (New York: Macmillan, 1935), 3 : 399–700; Roy Lubove, *The Struggle for Social Security, 1900–1935* (Cambridge: Harvard University Press, 1968).

9. Theda Skocpol and John Ikenberry, "The Political Formation of the American Welfare State in Historical and Comparative Perpective," *Comparative Social Research* 6 (1983) : 120–31.

tion. In institutional terms, therefore, unemployment insurance provides a useful case through which to explore state-level variations that were eventually built into the federal Social Security system.

Apart from its significance for the historical development of U.S. social policy, the debates surrounding unemployment insurance provide considerable insight into the political dynamics of industrial society. More than any other component of welfare policy, the states' response to unemployment politicized antagonisms between capital and labor. Moreover, the emergence of unemployment as a legitimate target for state action entailed both the development of a politically viable interpretation of the cause of unemployment and decisions concerning the appropriate extent of the government's intervention in the economy.

In the United States, these questions were debated simultaneously in a number of political arenas. The recognition that state-level processes were central to the shaping of U.S. public social provision suggests new research questions to comparative social scientists interested in the origins of social policies. Comparisons among states, rather than narratives concerning one peculiar nation, provide the analytical leverage needed to explore causal arguments. The research reported here addresses a variety of theoretical perspectives by examining the historical roots, the relative timing of adoption, and the programmatic contents of the unemployment insurance laws passed in five American states between 1932 and 1937.

RESEARCH DESIGN AND CASE SELECTION

If our purpose were to explore the direct and indirect effects of industrialization and urbanization on social policies, then choosing to study a small set of industrialized states would be inappropriate; nothing less than a full forty-eight-state study would suffice. But we have decided against such an analysis and have opted in favor of a comparative historical study of five urban-industrial states, since findings in recent cross-national research show the weakness of economic determinants and the strength of political determinants of social policy developments among industrialized nations.[10] Furthermore, preliminary analyses indicate that levels and processes of industrialization were not the major determinants of unemployment insurance outcomes across American states in the 1930s.

A perspective that we call the "logic of industrialism" emerged from aggregate-quantitative studies of the emergence and growth of social insurance programs across a large number of nations.[11] This approach posits that ur-

10. For a literature review, see Theda Skocpol and Edwin Amenta," States and Social Policies," *Annual Review of Sociology* 12 (1986) : 131–57.

11. For the logic of industrialism approach, see Phillips Cutright, "Political Structure, Economic Development, and National Social Security Programs," *American Journal of Sociology* 70 (1965) : 537–50; Robert W. Jackman, *Politics and Social Equality* (New York: John Wiley, 1975); Harold Wilensky, *The Welfare State and Equality: Structural and Ideological Roots of Public Spending* (Berkeley and Los Angeles: University of California Press, 1975), chap. 2.

banization and industrialization create social dislocations that governments must alleviate with social policies, regardless of the type of political system or ruling party. Empirically, when dozens of nations ranging from the highly industrial to the most agricultural are analyzed together, logic of industrialism variables have sometimes worked moderately well to explain the origins of social policies. But this perspective has been found wanting in longitudinal quantitative studies of social policy origins.[12] And within the subset of rich industrialized nations, variables referring to industrialization, urbanization, and economic growth have far less explanatory power than do political factors.[13]

Within the United States, similar relationships among findings hold true. In a multivariate analysis of forty-eight states, Amenta and Carruthers found that the level of industrialization in 1929 had only a modest effect on the timing of adoption of legislation for unemployment insurance, whereas administrative and political variables had strong explanatory effects. An examination of the top twenty industrial states, similar in design to studies of rich industrialized nations, revealed no significant relationships between the timing of unemployment insurance and a number of variables representing levels and trends in industrialization.[14] Similarly, for the five states compared here, we found that logic of industrialism variables do not explain the timing of unemployment insurance legislation.[15]

It is often claimed that U.S. social policies in the 1930s were enacted in response to the Great Depression. Without question, that economic crisis was the occasion for state-level social policy debates that led to the passage of measures, including unemployment insurance, that had been stalemated or not considered at all before the 1930s. But across forty-eight states, the varying severity of economic crisis does *not* predict how soon unemployment insurance policies were enacted.[16] And across our five states, the severity of economic depression fails to predict either how quickly each state enacted unemployment insurance or how favorable the provisions of its law were for

12. See Collier and Richard Messick, "Prerequisites versus Diffusion"; Flora and Alber, "Modernization, Democratization, and the Development of Welfare States in Western Europe."

13. Wilensky, *The Welfare State and Equality*, chap 3; Stephens, *The Transition from Capitalism to Socialism*; Castles, "The Impact of Parties on Public Expenditures."

14. Edwin Amenta and Bruce G. Carruthers, "The Formative Years of U.S. Social Policy: Theories of the Welfare State and Social Policies in the American States during the Great Depression" (Paper presented at the Annual Meeting of the American Sociological Association, New York, 1986; revised 1987).

15. We looked at relative levels of industrialization and urbanization (in cities over 20,000) in 1929 and also examined the ordering of the states in terms of changes in industrialization from 1923 to 1929 and urbanization from 1910 to 1930 and from 1920 to 1930. Illinois, the last state to legislate unemployment insurance, comes out first or second (with Wisconsin) on all rank orderings. And Ohio, the next-to-last state to legislate, outranks Massachusetts on all measures and New York on all but the 1929 level of industrialization. Precise measures and results are available upon request, as are those for the top twenty industrial states.

16. Amenta and Carruthers, "The Formative Years of U.S. Social Policy."

unemployed workers.[17] In short, political conditions and forces—not urbanization, industrialization, or the severity of economic crisis—mediated the effects of the Great Depression to produce varying policy outcomes at the state level. The need to discover and analyze what noneconomic variables were at work is apparent.

For purposes of such an analysis, a close comparison of a limited number of states, chosen to reveal full variation on the aspects of policy we seek to explain, is preferable to a quantitative study of all or many of the states, for several reasons. A detailed analysis of a few well-documented cases can be undertaken even when data and measures are not easily available, and it can explore processes over time that connect causal conditions and the outcomes of interest. Although results are not automatically generalizable, a small-scale comparative investigation can generate new hypotheses worthy of further research. Moreover, it can probe for configurations of causes and allow for the possibility of alternative routes to policy outcomes.

Wisconsin, New York, Massachusetts, Ohio, and Illinois are the five states we explore in depth. As table 1 shows, these states all fell within the top third or fourth of standard rankings of wage earners in 1929 or 1930 in manufacturing, value added in manufacturing, percentage of population that was urban, and total size of the population; all but Wisconsin fell within the highest ranks of these measures. The socioeconomic similarities of the five states were not decisive for this study, however; rather, we chose to focus our analysis upon the political conditions in these states that affected the relative *timing* and *contents* of the unemployment insurance laws they passed in the 1930s. On these dependent variables, our five states exhibit wide variations. The par-

Table 1. Rankings with Respect to Forty-eight States

	Wage Earners in Manufacturing (1929)	Value-Added by Manufactures (1929)	Percent Urban (1930)	Total Population (1930)
New York	1	1	3	1
Ohio	3	3	8	4
Illinois	4	4	5	3
Massachusetts	5	7	2	8
Wisconsin	10	10	15	12

Source: Statistical Abstract of the United States, 1932 (Washington, D.C.: U.S. Government Printing Office, 1932). Manufactures: pp. 762–65; percent urban: p. 46; population: pp. 7–8.

17. We investigated the decline of "value added by manufactures" and the decline of "wage earners in manufacturing," measuring each from 1929 to 1933. Wisconsin was the hardest hit state on both measures, but Illinois was next hardest hit, which probably meant more overall economic difficulty for the state, since it was more industrial than Wisconsin in 1929. And New York (which legislated unemployment insurance next after Wisconsin) was the least hardest hit by the depression of all our states. Exact measures and results are available upon request, as are those for the top twenty industrial states.

ticular policies to be explained for the five are summarized in table 2, and their provisions can be situated in relation to the characteristics of all state laws passed in the 1930s.[18]

The five states we have chosen encompass the full range of legislative timing for unemployment insurance. In retrospect, the five-year span from 1932 to 1937 may not seem particularly significant, but this judgment assumes that action by the national government was only a matter of time. A more accurate description of events would portray a series of policy debates and innovations in the states that was abruptly truncated by an unprecedented act of national politics. Although it is unlikely that any of these states would have taken action in the absence of an economic crisis, the onset of the depression in no way guaranteed that unemployment insurance would be adopted by all states of the Union. More important, in light of the considerable federal pressure needed to pass legislation in such states as Ohio and Illinois, it is unreasonable to assume these laggard states would have adopted unemployment insurance in the absence of such federal pressure.[19] In short, it is with respect to their varying potential for proactive policy formative that the five states are comparable with the nation-states of Europe. The relative timing of adoption and the contents of legislation provide important indications of this potential.

The first American unemployment benefits law passed in Wisconsin in 1932, well before any other state and more than three years before the federal government acted. New York passed the second pioneering law in April 1935, clearly ahead of the signing of the Social Security Act on August 14, 1935. Massachusetts, which passed its law in August 1935, acted roughly in tandem with the federal government. Ohio passed its law in December 1936. As table 3 shows, Ohio falls within a group of eighteen lagging states that passed legislation in the same month, soon after the Supreme Court refused to overturn the New York law and just before federal business taxes were imposed (the taxes would not be remitted to states until they had established unemployment compensation).[20] Illinois was the last state in the nation to enact a law. Its legislature passed a bill when opponents no longer had any reason to fight it—in June 1937, after the collection of federal taxes had begun and the Supreme Court in May had found the Social Security Act constitutional.

A comparison of these five states also allows the examination of important variations in the substantive content of unemployment insurance laws and

18. For the provisions of state unemployment compensation legislation, see Bryce M. Stewart, *The Planning and Administration of Unemployment Compensation in the United States* (New York: Industrial Relations Counselors Inc., 1938).

19. Under the tax-offset plan built into the unemployment insurance provisions of the Social Security Act of 1935, the federal government gave the states an overwhelming incentive to legislate and took away most of the incentives for businesses to veto unemployment insurance. A 3 percent tax was levied by the federal government on all employers with eight or more employees. A state would forfeit all the money taken in taxes on its employers if it did not pass an acceptable unemployment compensation program. In the event that the state passed a plan, businesses were credited 90 percent of the federal tax.

20. Robert Ingalls, *Herbert Lehman and New York's Little New Deal* (New York: New York University Press, 1975), 85.

Table 2. Provisions of State Unemployment Insurance Policies

	Wisconsin	New York	Illinois	Massachusetts	Ohio	Ohio Plan
When passed	January 29, 1932	April 25, 1935	June 30, 1937	August 12, 1935	December 17, 1936	—
Type of contribution	Individual reserves	Pooled fund	Pooled fund	Pooled fund	Pooled fund	Pooled fund
Who contributes	Employers 2.0%	Employers 3.0%	Employers 2.75%	Employers: 2% Employees: 1%	Employers: 2.7%	Employers: 2% Employees: 1%
Merit-rating ranges	1.0–2.0%	None	0.0–3.6%	None (possible later)	1.0–2.7%	1.0–3.5%
Benefits	$5–$10 per week, 10 weeks	$5–$15 per week, 16 weeks	$5–$15 per week, 16 weeks	$5–$15 per week, 16 weeks	$0–$15 per week, 16 weeks	$0–$15 per week, 16 weeks
Waiting period	2 weeks[a]	3 weeks (10 weeks if misconduct or strike)	3 weeks (8 weeks if misconduct)	4 weeks (8 weeks if misconduct)	3 weeks (6 weeks if misconduct)	2 weeks
Form of commission	Administered by existing Industrial Commission	9 members: 3 business, 3 labor	Administered by director of labor	3 members: 1 business, 1 labor	3 members: 1 business, 1 labor	3 members: 1 business, 1 labor

[a] Unless otherwise noted, loss of employment through misconduct or strike disqualifies individuals from receiving unemployment compensation.

plans. For the early 1930s, we investigate the "Wisconsin plan" and the "Ohio plan," taking these as intellectually self-conscious alternatives. These were the legislative proposals that had the greatest nationwide visibility and prestige in shaping state and national debates during the 1930s.[21] We also examine the specific modifications and innovations in each of the five states' bills in order to detect the relative strength and varying concerns of the political actors involved.

Wisconsin was the only state in which a continuous debate on unemployment insurance took place throughout the 1920s. The Huber bill was introduced into the state legislature in 1921. During the remainder of the decade, the central concerns of the advocates of unemployment insurance moved from state- or industrywide proposals to the system of unemployment reserves that came to be nationally known as the Wisconsin plan. Each business enterprise was to be taxed in order to build up an unemployment reserve from which to

Table 3. The Timing of Passage of State Unemployment Compensation Legislation

1. WISCONSIN	January 29	1932	25. West Virginia	December 17	1936
2. NEW YORK	April 25	1935	26. Maine	December 18	1936
3. New Hampshire	May 29	1935	27. Tennessee	December 18	1936
4. California	June 25	1935	28. Virginia	December 18	1936
5. MASSACHUSETTS	August 12	1935	29. New Jersey	December 22	1936
6. Alabama	September 14	1935	30. Vermont	December 22	1936
7. Oregon	November 15	1935	31. Iowa	December 24	1936
8. Indiana	March 18	1936	32. Michigan	December 24	1936
9. Mississippi	March 23	1936	33. Minnesota	December 24	1936
10. Rhode Island	May 5	1936	34. South Dakota	December 24	1936
11. South Carolina	June 6	1936	35. Kentucky	December 29	1936
12. Louisiana	June 29	1936	36. Arkansas	February 26	1937
13. Idaho	August 6	1936	37. Wyoming	February 26	1937
14. Utah[a]	August 29	1936	38. Montana	March 16	1937
15. Texas	October 27	1936	39. North Dakota	March 16	1937
16. Colorado	November 20	1936	40. Washington[a]	March 16	1937
17. Connecticut	November 30	1936	41. Nevada	March 24	1937
18. Arizona	December 2	1936	42. Kansas	March 26	1937
19. Pennsylvania	December 5	1936	43. Georgia	March 29	1937
20. Oklahoma	December 12	1936	44. Nebraska	April 30	1937
21. New Mexico	December 16	1936	45. Delaware	April 30	1937
22. North Carolina	December 16	1936	46. Florida	June 9	1937
23. Maryland	December 17	1936	47. Missouri	June 17	1937
24. OHIO	December 17	1936	48. ILLINOIS	June 30	1937

Source: Bryce M. Stewart, *The Planning and Administration of Unemployment Compensation in the United States* (New York: Industrial Relations Counselors Inc., 1938), 28.

[a] The dates for passage of Utah and Washington refer to legislation that was found constitutional. Both had previously passed legislation that was declared unconstitutional.

21. For a discussion of these plans, see Daniel Nelson, *Unemployment Insurance: The American Experience, 1915–1935.* (Madison: University of Wisconsin Press, 1969).

compensate its own workers if they were laid off. The idea was to induce businessmen to prevent unemployment, since they would pay lower taxes if they did so. Although the Wisconsin debate profoundly influenced other state and national legislation, few states enacted a similar system of unemployment reserves. Elsewhere the individual reserves idea was criticized for its failure to ensure sufficient benefits to unemployed workers across all enterprises and industries.[22] Inspired by Wisconsin's preventive approach, however, "merit-rating" provisions, which adjusted a firm's taxes to it employment record, were incorporated into the unemployment insurance laws of most states.

The Ohio plan emerged in the early 1930s as an alternative to the Wisconsin plan.[23] Proponents of the Ohio plan, whose views both influenced and reflected those of many reformers as the depression deepened, did not believe that unemployment could be prevented by individual businesses. Concerned to provide adequate relief for all the unemployed, not just those laid off by companies with funds in their unemployment account, they advocated taxes on both employers and employees and the establishment of a statewide pooled insurance fund. The Ohio plan, however, failed to pass in its home state in 1933, and the 1936 Ohio legislation did not fully embody the plan's ideas.

By the mid-1930s, a standard unemployment insurance model of sorts—basically the Ohio plan without taxes on employees—prevailed in many states. From then on, it is less valid to treat laws as entirely independent plans. Instead, we can compare the basic provisions of state laws in terms of their relative advantages for industrial workers or business. We do not assume that workers or business directly shaped these policy patterns. Nevertheless, it is important to explain the relative advantages for both groups since political debates addressed the trade-off between workers' needs for adequate unemployment benefits and businessmen's desires to avoid taxes. (The term *workers* refers here to nonagricultural workers only, for agricultural workers were excluded from all unemployment compensation plans.)

The four states in our set that legislated from 1935 to 1937 present important variations in legal provisions of concern to business and labor. In comparison to all other state laws, New York's 1935 law was unusually favorable to the needs and preferences of industrial labor; benefits were financed through high fixed business taxes without merit-rating provisions, and the legislation allowed unemployment benefits to be paid to workers on strike. In comparison, Massachusetts made concessions to business by requiring employee contributions, imposing a moderate business tax, and providing for the future administrative application of merit rating to adjust business taxes above a fixed minimum. Finally, Ohio and Illinois passed laws incorporating steep merit-

22. In Wisconsin itself, a pooled balancing account was created in 1937 to provide benefits to unemployed workers from companies whose individual accounts had been depleted (Myers, Employment Stabilization and Wisconsin Act," 35).

23. See Issac M. Rubinow, "The Movement toward Unemployment Insurance in Ohio," *Social Service Review* 7 (1933) : 186–224; Ohio Commission on Unemployment Insurance, *Report of the Ohio Commission on Unemployment Insurance* (Columbus: F. J. Heer, 1932).

rating provisions that promised to keep taxes very low for many businesses and, in Illinois, to reduce taxes to zero for some others. Overall, business won the most important advantages in the substantive provisions of the Ohio and Illinois laws.

In the following sections, we seek to explain the variations in timing and content of unemployment insurance laws in the five states by exploring arguments about the political origins of social policies—arguments that appear in the cross-national social science literature as well as in debates among students of American history. We begin with a "political learning" perspective that stresses the roles of administrative traditions and reformist policy intellectuals in shaping policy. Next we examine arguments about the class-based political actions of business and industrial labor. Finally we turn to discussions about the effects of the activities and structures of political parties on social policies.

As the analysis proceeds, we retain arguments that are at least partly effective in order to identify a combination of conditions that best accounts for the variations in timing and contents of unemployment compensation legislation across our five states. Although certain political variables—especially those that refer to administrative arrangements and political parties—emerge from our analysis, socioeconomic and class relations do not drop out altogether. But although urban-rural cleavages and the activities of business organizations and industrial unions do matter, we have found that their effects must be specified in relation to features of political party structure and party competition that more directly influenced policy outcomes in the five states. The evidence for this study has been assembled from a large number of secondary and primary sources—published books and articles, organizational reports (such as labor federation proceedings), reports of state commissions set up to investigate unemployment insurance, governmental statistical compilations, and legislative records. Measures of particular variables are discussed where appropriate. Otherwise, the footnotes document specific points.

POLITICAL LEARNING: ADMINISTRATIVE CAPACITIES AND REFORM TRADITIONS

The political learning perspective on social policy development advanced by Hugh Heclo provides an alternative to arguments that stress socioeconomic developments and crises.[24] According to Heclo, although socioeconomic conditions—including major crises like the Great Depression—may encourage social policy breakthroughs, the actual policy innovations are likely to be shaped directly by civil administrators and reformist policy intellectuals who puzzle over new problems on the basis of, and in reaction to, previously institutionalized governmental policies for dealing with similar problems.

Although this approach has never been defined in an analytically rigorous way, it does suggest that we should attend to the preexisting social and labor policies in the five states, and to the parts of state civil administration involved

24. Heclo, *Modern Social Politics in Britain and Sweden.*

in their formulation and implementation. In addition, we examine the networks of policy intellectuals who were directly involved in political debates over unemployment policy. The established relationships, if any, of these intellectuals to civil administrators and political leaders are important determinants of policy innovations, according to the political learning perspective.

American debates over social insurance and labor regulations did not originate with the Great Depression. Rather, they can be traced back to the Progressive Era. Although many proposed reforms failed to pass,[25] between 1911 and 1913, twenty-one states enacted workers' compensation laws requiring business to insure employees against accidental injuries, and other states soon followed.[26] The administrative arrangements through which workers' compensation and other Progressive labor and social regulations were implemented varied considerably across the states, these differences reflecting in part the prior progress of general civil service reform in each state.

In addition, variations in administrative arrangements reflected the fate of Progressive proposals for the creation of omnibus industrial commission, staffed by trained professional experts. The establishment of these commissions was advocated by the American Association for Labor Legislation (AALL) and other reform groups. Ideally, they would superintend the administration of all new labor regulations and propose further legislation based on administrative experience and studies by experts.[27] By the 1920s, however, only Wisconsin had a full-blown version of this sort of administrative-academic complex. Consequently, Wisconsin provided an ideal setting for continuous political learning in Heclo's sense.

The Administrative-Academic Complex in Wisconsin

The Wisconsin Industrial Commission, created in 1911 to administer workers' compensation and virtually all other labor laws, was the point of reference for policy debates about unemployment insurance and social reforms throughout the Progressive Era and the 1920s. This administrative commission had powers to implement laws and to investigate needs for new legislation, and it drew on a history of public management that was relatively nonpartisan, centralized, and well financed. This broad mandate reflected the relative autonomy of state agencies from party politics and factional struggles in Wisconsin.

In the 1880s, Wisconsin had passed its first civil service law, and by the turn of the century charges of public corruption, although far from rare, were directed primarily at the lower levels of government.[28] Wisconsin took unusu-

---

25. On the failure of reforms, see Orloff and Skocpol, "Why Not Equal Protection?"

26. On workers' compensation, see Brandeis, "Labor Legislation"; Robert Asher, "Workmen's Compensation in the United States, 1880–1935" (Ph.D. diss., University of Minnesota, 1971).

27. John R. Commons, "Constructive Investigation and the Industrial Commission of Wisconsin" *Survey* 29 (1913) : 440–48; John B. Andrews, *Labor Problems and Labor Legislation* (New York: American Association for Labor Legislation, 1919).

28. Robert S. Maxwell, *La Follette and the Rise of the Progressives in Wisconsin* (Madison: State Historical Society of Wisconsin, 1956), 64.

ally early steps toward the establishment of centralized administrative bodies such as the State Board of Control.[29] Also, the passage of one of the nation's earliest income tax bills in 1911 provided financial stability for the administration.[30] The special character of Wisconsin public life also reflected a tradition of public involvement and faculty participation on government boards begun in the 1880s by the president of the University of Wisconsin, John Bascom.[31] The relationship between academics and state legislators was strengthened by the establishment of the Legislative Reference Library in 1901, and the close association between academics and administrators was apparent in the operations of the Wisconsin Industrial Commission from 1911 onward.

Members of the Wisconsin Industrial Commission were appointed as representatives neither of parties (as in New York) nor of economic interests (as in Ohio). Instead, the first members were associated with existing state agencies or the university; the remarkable stability of the commission's membership, despite the changing fortunes of the Republican factions, suggests that the administration was protected from pure partisan politics.[32] Financial autonomy was given in the form of blanket appropriations that complemented the commission's broad mandate. Rather then enumerating specific regulations, the legislature charged the commission to adhere to what Commons called "the noblest and the most practical of legal doctrines—'reasonableness.' "[33] Advisory boards made up of industrialists, labor leaders, and technical experts were created to help the commission negotiate the specific content of regulations and devise new legislative proposals. Over the course of the next decades, the commission's activities were increasingly integrated.

During the 1920s, when proposals for unemployment insurance began to be discussed in the state, the commission's practice of negotiation over laws and their practical implementation influenced organized labor's perception of what reforms were politically possible and substantively effective.[34] Furthermore, the Industrial Commission had been a training ground for well-educated administrators committed to expert-based, formally nonpartisan, incremental reform of the capitalist system. Throughout the 1920s, members of the commission addressed interest groups and served on committees concerned with social reform. Although full-time academics such as Elizabeth Brandeis and Paul Raushenbush were more visible in the drafting of legisla-

29. Samuel E. Sparling, "State Boards of Control with Special Reference to the State of Wisconsin," *Annals of the American Academy of Political and Social Science* 17 (1901) : 74–91.

30. W. Elliot Brownlee, Jr., "Income Taxation and the Political Economy of Wisconsin, 1890–1930," *Wisconsin Magazine of History* 57 (1973) : 123–40.

31. Merle Curti and Vernon Carstensen, *The University of Wisconsin, 1848–1925* (Madison: University of Wisconsin Press, 1949), 1 : 247.

32. Arthur J. Altmeyer, *The Industrial Commission of Wisconsin: A Case Study in Labor Law Administration,* University of Wisconsin Studies in the Social Sciences and History, no. 17 (Madison, 1932).

33. Commons, "Constructive Investigation and the Industrial Commission of Wisconsin," 441.

34. Charles A. Myers, "Employment Stabilization and the Wisconsin Act" (Ph.D. diss., University of Chicago, 1939), 20.

tion, university-trained administrators, including Arthur J. Altmeyer and Edwin Witte, held key positions on the legislative committees. Thus, the Wisconsin Industrial Commission was a source of continuity in two important senses: it was consistently available as a means for implementing legislation, and it stood at the focal point of a larger arena for the discussion and development of industrial policies.

Wisconsin's unique conception of unemployment insurance—as a regulatory measure to induce business to prevent unemployment rather than as a way to give adequate relief to laid-off workers—had its roots in the Wisconsin Industrial Commission's approach to workers' compensation. In implementing workers' compensation, the commission enjoyed, by law, considerable administrative discretion and negotiated with employers about rules and their implementation.[35] The commission came to favor adjustable insurance rates that could be tailored to the conditions of given industries and raised or lowered according to the accident records of particular enterprises. Wisconsin regulators aimed to reward cooperation and good practices by employers, and thus to promote workplace safety. This so-called preventionist approach, which became the operating ideology of the commission as well as of numerous University of Wisconsin policy intellectuals, also informed proposals for unemployment insurance. The earliest proposals argued that by forcing firms to pay the social costs of irregular employment practices, bankers would be less willing to overextend credit during expansionary phases of the business cycle.[36] Preventionist strategies included imposing adjustable taxes on business, but not on labor, and setting up compulsory insurance reserves. These provisions were intended to give the Wisconsin Industrial Commission the regulatory power to prod capitalists into enlightened behavior. This approach embodied the essence of the Wisconsin administrative and intellectual tradition of capitalist regulation from the Progressive Era onward.

The Absence of a Policy Debate in Illinois

On the variables of interest from the political learning perspective, Illinois provides a sharp contrast to Wisconsin. Unlike the latter state, Illinois did not have a continuous policy debate on unemployment insurance going into the 1930s, and it was the last state to pass unemployment insurance. When the Illinois law did pass, it included no significant contributions from, and envisaged no strong role for, public administrators.

To the extent that policy experts were present in Illinois, they were concentrated in Chicago, especially at the University of Chicago, and were isolated from state politics. This was understandable given Illinois's laggard performance in civil service reform and administrative autonomy. Even when merit-based civil service and administrative reorganization were introduced in 1917, politicians circumvented the law by installing so-called temporary appointees

35. Altmeyer, *The Industrial Commission of Wisconsin.*

36. John R. Commons, *Unemployment Insurance: The Road to Prevention* (Madison: Wisconsin Association for the Prevention of Unemployment, 1923), 5.

who neither took examinations nor were replaced by permanent civil servants.[37]

Established in 1913 to administer a state workers' compensation act, the Illinois Industrial Board was not an omnibus industrial commission. Consisting of three "nonpolitical" members, the board had virtually no power and generally failed to make use of what little it had. In practice, discretion on policy issues lay with an advisory board made up of representatives of the Illinois Manufacturers' Association and the Illinois State Federation of Labor. Any legislative improvements had to be approved by the advisory board, but its members were rarely able to agree. An attempt in 1915 to create a Wisconsin-style labor commission was opposed by the Illinois State Federation of Labor and defeated in the legislature. Even the Civil Administrative Code of 1917, which centralized labor administration overall, kept the (renamed) Industrial Commission and workmen's compensation separate from each other and from other labor-related agencies. Consequently, factory inspectors had little access to accident reports filed with the Industrial Commission.[38] In general, politicians and socioeconomic interest groups supported an administrative structure fragmented to the point of inefficiency, with the result that Illinois administrators had all they could handle just enforcing existing laws, much less formulating proposals for new ones.

Municipal Reform and the Indigenous Failure of the Ohio Plan

At the level of state government, Ohio resembled Illinois. There was neither a continuous tradition of autonomous labor law administration nor close involvement of reformist intellectuals with state politics. In the cities, however, a strong network of policy intellectuals developed in conjunction with Progressive movements combating social ills and patronage politics. The Ohio movements were more successful than similar efforts in Chicago, New York, or Boston and laid the basis for an enduring urban reformist debate about new social policies throughout the 1920s.[39] In contrast, the state government was generally dominated by conservative Democrats and Republicans, who were opposed to administrative autonomy.

Until the Ohio Constitutional Convention of 1912, reformers had few opportunities to influence the state-level policy process.[40] Therefore, when merit-based civil service and Ohio's far-reaching workers' compensation Illinois were passed in 1913, there was no administrative tradition upon which to draw. Temporary political circumstances made it easy to establish an omnibus industrial commission; Democrats dominated the legislature and James Cox, a progressive Democrat, was governor. Although less powerful than its coun-

37. Earl Beckner, *A History of Illinois Labor Legislation* (Chicago: University of Chicago Press, 1929), 425–26.

38. Ibid., pp. 500–04.

39. Kenneth Finegold, "Progressivism, Electoral Change, and Public Policy: Reform Outcomes in New York, Cleveland, and Chicago" (Ph.D. diss., Harvard University, 1985).

40. Hoyt L. Warner, *Progressivism in Ohio, 1897–1917* (Columbus: Ohio State University Press, 1964), 326–27.

terparts in New York and Wisconsin, the Ohio commission had the power to adjudicate issues and set rules.[41] Yet even when administrative operations were successful, the commissioners made no attempt to initiate policies. As in New York, the Ohio commission was circumscribed in its membership; there could be no more than one member representing labor and one representing business on a three-man commission. Ohio also resembled New York in that there were no advisory boards to provide channels for new policy initiatives.

Just as favorable political conditions originally empowered the Ohio Industrial Commission, a change in political climate circumscribed it. Upon regaining power from the Democrats in 1921, the Republicans moved quickly to limit its autonomy, along with the power of other new administrative agencies. The commission was divided, with the one part responsible for the administration of workmen's compensation and the other for the adjudication of claims. This turned an effective commission into two organizations that were in constant conflict.[42] With its diminished mandate and powers, the Ohio Industrial Commission was not an important participant in the debates over unemployment insurance in the early 1930s. Instead, these debates were initiated and shaped by reformers and policy intellectuals outside state government.

Progressivism in Ohio had always been a predominantly municipal rather than state-level affair. Many cities had well-developed public employment agencies as well as middle- and upper-class social service groups (often staffed by women) that were perhaps more open to labor and social reforms than were good government or social service groups in other states. Even before the depression began to strain the resources of cities and social workers, unemployment insurance became an issue for Ohio reformers. Policy study was organized by the Consumer League of Ohio, whose prime movers were social service workers and Jewish community agencies in the many Ohio cities.[43]

Policy-oriented intellectuals at Antioch and other small Ohio colleges joined with social service workers to consider possibilities for unemployment insurance. The most notable expert was William Leiserson, who had helped establish public employment agencies in New York City, Wisconsin, and Ohio. Because the issue of unemployment insurance did not emerge directly from the administration of preexisting state labor laws, there was no continuity of policy debate linking the new proposals to workers' compensation. Ohio reformers stressed differences rather than similarities between the purposes and methods of the two kinds of laws. Unemployment insurance was seen chiefly as a way to deliver adequate relief to suffering unemployed workers and only

41. Walter F. Dodd, *Administration of Workmen's Compensation* (New York: Commonwealth Fund, 1936), 286–88.

42. F. W. Coker, "Dogmas of Administrative Reform as Exemplified in the Recent Reorganization in Ohio," *American Political Science Review* 16 (1922) : 399–411.

43. Papers of William M. Leiserson, "Elizabeth Magee to Leiserson, April 4, 1929" (Madison: State Historical Society of Wisconsin, Box 25). Magee was a member of the Consumer League.

secondarily as a way to further general economic recovery.[44] Such, of course, were the predictable concerns of reformers and intellectuals oriented to urban social services.

Eventually, the newly elected Democratic governor, George White, responded to labor pressures, the initiatives of the reformers, and a joint resolution of the legislature by appointing the ad hoc Commission on Unemployment Insurance in December 1931. This special commission was so dominated by social service people and intellectuals that the one business representative soon stopped participating in the general debate and filed a minority report. Predictably, perhaps, this body did not work out a pragmatic compromise acceptable to both organized labor and business. Nor did it work with the state legislature. Instead, the leading intellectuals on the commission—William Leiserson, the commission's chairman, and Isaac Max Rubinow—saw themselves as influencing debates across the nation by providing a clear alternative to the Wisconsin plan.[45]

In Wisconsin, both the administrative Industrial Commission and the various academic policy experts linked to state government negotiated with business, labor, and state legislators until an unemployment compensation law was passed. In contrast, the ad hoc Ohio commission of 1931–32 counted on Governor White to do the political work necessary to turn their proposals into law. In the end, the governor disappointed them.[46]

Administration and Reform in Massachusetts and New York

In Massachusetts and New York, conditions were not as unfavorable to administrative policy debates at the state level as they were in Illinois and Ohio. Special investigatory commissions set up to consider unemployment insurance in the early 1930s included policymakers serving in, or working closely with, the Massachusetts Commission of Labor and Industries and the New York Industrial Commission. But in neither state did administrators of labor laws or reformers succeed in shaping new legislation. Breakthroughs on unemployment insurance in the two states did not come on the basis of the measures proposed by investigatory commissions in the early 1930s, but had to await new conditions in party politics and the direct involvement of state legislators in working out policy packages.

Massachusetts was an early leader in labor legislation, labor administration,

44. J. Michael Eisner, *William Morris Leiserson* (Madison: University of Wisconsin Press, 1967); Papers of William M. Leiserson, "Minutes of the Ohio Commission on Unemployment Insurance" (1932) (Madison: State Historical Society of Wisconsin, Box 31); Ohio Commission on Unemployment Insurance, *Report of the Ohio Commission on Unemployment Insurance.*

45. Rubinow, "The Movement toward Unemployment Insurance in Ohio."

46. See the correspondence between William M. Leiserson and Isaac M. Rubinow, and the correspondence between Leiserson and Elizabeth Magee, the commission's secretary, from October 1932 through March 1933 (Papers of William M. Leiserson [Madison: State Historical Society of Wisconsin, Boxes 35 and 25]).

and civil service reform. It instituted the first state factor inspection system and the first state bureau of labor statistics.[47] But these developments occurred mostly before the Progressive Era, establishing state boards with powers of investigation but not of direct administration. In the Progressive Era some new labor regulations were enacted, but much of the enforcement machinery was adapted from the past rather than created anew as it was in New York and Wisconsin. Although the Massachusetts Commission of Labor and Industries did gain rule-making authority over regulations concerning working conditions, no omnibus authority was established. Workers' compensation was implemented by a special seven-member Industrial Accident Board that remained independent of other labor agencies.

Continuing a nineteenth-century tradition, the ad hoc investigatory commission was the mechanism by which Massachusetts's governors and sociopolitical establishment reacted to possibilities for new kinds of social legislation. The state's commissions tended to be set up at moments of perceived emergency—in the case of unemployment insurance, in the wake of industrial downturns in 1914–15 and 1921–22—and their recommendations usually lacked political clout and soon faded from public view. Thus policy debates in Massachusetts took a choppy course, as successive ad hoc commissions ignored or reversed earlier recommendations. The U.S. debate on unemployment insurance began in Massachusetts with the introduction in 1915–16 of a bill modeled on British unemployment insurance.[48] A 1916–17 gubernatorial commission commented favorably on this proposal and recommended further study,[49] but a subsequent ad hoc commission in 1922–23 rejected this approach and endorsed voluntary business plans.[50] Debate then ended for the rest of the 1920s.

The Massachusetts debate resumed in earnest with the appointment of a special commission in June 1931 by Democratic governor Joseph Ely. The commissioner of labor and industry was the secretary of the group, which included three members from universities and two representatives each from business and labor. The December 1931 preliminary report called for legislation concerning public employment offices, the regulation of private em-

47. Richard Abrams, *Conservatism in a Progressive Era: Massachusetts Politics, 1900–1912* (Cambridge: Harvard University Press, 1964), 1–13; James Lieby, *Carroll Wright and Labor Reform* (Cambridge: Harvard University Press, 1960); Sarah Whittlesey, "Massachusetts Labor Legislation: An Historical and Critical Study," *Annals of the Academy of Political and Social Science* (supp.) 17 (1901).

48. Massachusetts Committee on Unemployment, "Unemployment Insurance for Massachusetts: Draft of an Act with an Introduction and Notes," *Bulletin*, no. 2 (1916).

49. Massachusetts Special Commission on Social Insurance, *Report of the Special Commission on Social Insurance*, Massachusetts House Document no. 2075 (Boston: Wright & Potter, State Printers, 1917).

50. Massachusetts Special Commission on Unemployment, Unemployment Compensation, and the Minimum Wage, *Report of the Special Commission on Unemployment, Unemployment Compensation, and the Minimum Wage*, Massachusetts House Document no. 1325 (Boston: Wright & Potter, State Printers, 1923).

ployment offices, and the establishment of a public works planning board.[51] The final report of December 1932 called for compulsory unemployment reserves on the Wisconsin model.[52] But bills written by this 1931–32 commission failed to pass the Massachusetts legislature in 1933 and 1934.

From the Progressive Era to the 1930s, administrators and policy intellectuals in Massachusetts were only loosely incorporated into the political processes that transformed policy proposals into laws. The eventual passage of unemployment insurance in Massachusetts did not come until after a new commission devised an approach that differed substantially from the Wisconsin-style ideas advocated in 1931–32. This later commission was not dominated by administrators and policy intellectuals. Instead, it included primarily state legislators, who worked with Governor James M. Curley to pass their law in 1935.

Like Wisconsin, New York introduced merit-based civil service in the 1880s, but it did not develop the same tradition of administrative autonomy. The result was strong administrative organs subject to partisan control, and reformist professionals and intellectuals lacked the necessary access to state government until the late 1920s. The New York civil service law of 1883 made it possible for the governor to circumvent restrictions when desired. This combination of official autonomy and political control was evident in the New York Industrial Commission established to administer workers' compensation. The state legislature created an omnibus commission almost as powerful as Wisconsin's, suggesting that politicians were not afraid to create a strong administrative body. The organization of New York's commission, however, precluded involvement in the agitation for new programs and legislation. Reflecting the close competition of Democrats and Republicans in state politics, the New York commission was divided by law along partisan lines; three members were appointed by the governor's party and two by the opposition. Moreover, labor legislation in New York tended to be more specific than laws passed in Wisconsin, leaving less room for administrative discretion and innovation.[53]

During the Progressive Era and the 1920s, implementation of social reforms in New York was managed by party politicians despite the presence of

51. Massachusetts Special Commission on the Stabilization of Employment, *Preliminary Report of the Special Commission on the Stabilization of Employment,* Massachusetts House Document no. 1100 (Boston: Wright & Potter, State Printers, 1932).

52. Massachusetts Special Commission on the Stabilization of Employment, *Final Report of the Special Commission on Stabilization of Employment,* Massachusetts House Document no. 1200 (Boston: Wright & Potter, State Printers, 1933).

53. Irwin Yellowitz, *Labor and the Progressive Movement in New York State, 1897–1916* (Ithaca: Cornell University Press, 1965), 109; Joseph Zimmerman, *The Government and Politics of New York State* (New York: New York University Press, 1981); Henry Bischoff, "The Reformers, the Workers, and the Growth of Positive Government: A History of the Labor Legislation Movement in New York State" (Ph.D. diss., University of Chicago, 1964), 649–50.

numerous reformers and policy-oriented intellectuals in the major universities and private charitable organizations based in New York City. Foremost among these groups was the American Association for Labor Legislation (AALL), the academic and professional association promoting labor laws and social insurance. The period of Progressive reform prior to the First World War was the high point of political participation by New York City intellectuals and reformers, but their failure either to capture the leadership of a political party or to secure greater administrative autonomy ensured that these successes would be short-lived.[54] Continually at odds with the patronage parties that dominated New York State politics through the 1920s, New York City reformers failed to establish close connections with the state legislature or with state-level administrative agencies.[55]

After the election of reform-minded Democratic governor Franklin Roosevelt, an event soon followed by the start of the depression, policy debates proliferated among New York reformers and intellectuals. Roosevelt and his industrial commissioner, Frances Perkins, took a direct interest in the subject of unemployment insurance. The state quickly became a focal point for the AALL and other policy experts supporting Wisconsin-style plans for unemployment reserves, and their efforts appeared to have the edge in 1930–31. Roosevelt and Perkins even sponsored a special interstate commission to encourage similar unemployment compensation legislation across states.[56]

At first, business resistance and Republican strength made it impossible for Roosevelt, Perkins, and their supporters (including policy experts led by AALL secretary John Andrews) to establish compulsory unemployment reserves. Yet this advocacy persisted as the deepening depression generated ever more interest in unemployment insurance. But confronted with so many reformers, many of whom were more oriented to national debates than to politics in Albany, Roosevelt, Perkins, and Andrews could not hold together a state coalition favoring Wisconsin-style legislation. Policy intellectuals soon became fragmented as strong proponents of Ohio-type ideas spoke out against the Wisconsin plan advocates from 1932 onward.

The successful New York legislation of 1935, one of the most liberal unemployment insurance plans in the nation, did *not* reflect the plans put forward by investigatory commissions or debated by reformist intellectuals in the early 1930s. A new political dynamic took hold in 1933, breaking the continuity of the preceding policy debates and allowing the New York State Federation of Labor to write its own ideas about unemployment insurance into law. Policy experts in New York were bypassed, especially those who had ini-

---

54. Finegold, "Progressivism, Electoral Change, and Public Policy."

55. Yellowitz, *Labor and the Progressive Movement in New York State*, 111; J. Joseph Huthmacher, "Charles Evans Hughes and Charles Francis Murphy: The Metamorphosis of Progressivism," *New York History* 46 (1965) : 25–40; Robert F. Wesser, *Charles Evans Hughes: Politics and Reform in New York* (Ithaca, N.Y.: Cornell University Press, 1967), 306; Richard McCormick, *From Realignment to Reform: Political Change in New York State, 1893–1910* (Ithaca, N.Y.: Cornell University Press, 1981).

56. Nelson, *Unemployment Insurance*, 165–68.

tially seen Roosevelt's governorship as the ideal platform for the extension of the Wisconsin plan.

The Limits of the Political Learning Perspective

The political learning perspective contributes to an explanation of the variations in timing and contents of unemployment insurance legislation across our five states, but it does not provide a complete explanation. Only one state, Wisconsin, had the institutional context that the perspective suggests is necessary for administrative-led policy innovation: an authoritative industrial commission and established ties among reformist intellectuals, administrators, and political leaders. In contrast, Illinois entirely lacked these conditions. Thus the political learning perspective sheds light on why Wisconsin legislated first and developed a law whose contents reflected administrative analogies to workers' compensation. It also helps explain why in the early 1930s Illinois was virtually devoid of state-level policy debates over unemployment insurance.

Yet the case histories of all the states—especially Ohio, Massachusetts, and New York—suggest that the analysis must extend beyond administrative capacities and reform traditions. Developed by Heclo in a study of European parliamentary systems, the political learning perspective tends to assume that ministerial authority allows administrators and reformers to enact their ideas. But in the United States, where legislatures operate independently of political executives, reforms cannot be pushed through simply by intellectuals allied with top administrators and executives. Our evidence shows that reformers could not rely on governors to engineer majorities in state legislatures. By the early 1930s, reformist intellectuals dominated or gained prominent access to ad hoc commissions appointed by governors to investigate unemployment insurance, but none of the legislative proposals for unemployment insurance made by the initial investigatory commissions in Ohio (1931–32), New York (1930–31, 1931–32), and Massachusetts (1931–32) was enacted into law. Practical progress toward unemployment insurance awaited broader shifts in political alignments. Looking for additional factors, we now examine the political actions of business and organized labor.

CAPITALISTS, ORGANIZED LABOR, AND THE POLITICS OF UNEMPLOYMENT INSURANCE

Class-based arguments about the politics of social policy-making are prominent in the recent scholarly literature. Some students of the United States have stressed the role of enlightened welfare capitalists in initiating and shaping new public social policies.[57] This perspective takes capitalist domination

57. Ibid.; Edward Berkowitz and Kim McQuaid, *Creating the Welfare State: The Political Economy of Twentieth-Century Reform* (New York: Praeger, 1980); James Weinstein, "Big Business and the Origin of Workmen's Compensation," *Labor History* 8 (1967) : 156–74; Jill S. Quadagno, "Welfare Capitalism and the Social Security Act of 1935," *American Sociological Review* 49 (1984) : 632–47.

of U.S. politics for granted and looks for splits among capitalists as the key to periods of reform. Meanwhile, other scholars attend to politicized conflicts over social policy between capitalists and industrial workers. Many of them presume that business influence in the political process either blocks new policies or renders their provisions ungenerous to workers, whereas labor influence in politics causes or facilitates new social policies beneficial to workers.

In this section, we consider evidence from our five states about the roles of welfare capitalists, organized business, and organized labor in the struggles over the passage of unemployment compensation. We find that welfare capitalists influenced some policy debates, but failed to get the results this perspective suggests. In contrast, both organized business and organized labor influenced the timing and contents of legislation, and did so in the directions class-conflict theories would predict. The influence of business and, especially, of organized labor, however, depended on the agenda-setting and legislative roles of political parties, whose characteristics, organization, and electoral strength need to be analyzed in their own right.

Welfare Capitalists, Organized Business, and Unemployment Benefits

According to the welfare capitalism thesis, progressive capitalists were in a position to shape new social policies in the 1930s for the following reasons. In the early twentieth century, certain American businesses preceded the public sector in evolving principles of modern organizational management, including policies for stabilizing and planning employment and for protecting the social welfare of loyal employees. Henry Dennison of Massachusetts's Dennison Manufacturing, Marion Folsom of Eastman Kodak, Gerard Swope of General Electric, and others pressed their ideas upon policy experts and public officials. The leaders of the American Association for Labor Legislation, the Wisconsin policy experts of the Commons school, and the New York politicians surrounding Franklin Roosevelt supposedly accepted welfare capitalist ideals and devised preventive plans of unemployment insurance accordingly. This thesis postulates that when public social insurance policies were shaped in the states and at the federal level during the 1930s, they were modeled upon welfare capitalist precedents and were designed to meet the needs of such progressively managed business corporations.

The welfare capitalism thesis addresses both the content of unemployment insurance legislation and the processes by which laws developed. It contends that business influence on debates over unemployment insurance often took the form of positive attempts to promote laws congenial to progressive business practices. The thesis also predicts that where welfare capitalists were most politically active, the enacted laws embodied their preferences. Welfare capitalists, however, did not shape unemployment insurance legislation in the 1930s.

Of all the American states, Massachusetts was the one where liberal welfare capitalists were best organized and most active on the issue of unemployment insurance, so this state offers a crucial test for the welfare capitalism thesis. Events before the 1930s look promising for the thesis. Massachusetts welfare capitalists strongly influenced policy debates through a 1922–23 commission that sidetracked earlier proposals for British-style unemployment insurance and advocated purely voluntary schemes of corporate benefits.[58] Moreover, in the early years of the depression, a Special Commission on Stabilization of Employment was assembled by conservative Democratic governor Ely. This commission included the prominent liberal capitalists Henry Dennison and Henry Kendall, and its December 1932 report, with its rhetorical emphasis on the prevention of unemployment, called for individual company reserves on the Wisconsin model.[59] Yet this was the high-water mark of welfare capitalism in Massachusetts. One unemployment proposal, the King bill, was based on the 1932 commission report, but was defeated handily in 1933 and 1934. The kind of legislation that ultimately passed in Massachusetts resembled the Ohio plan more closely than either the purely voluntarist schemes of the 1920s or the Wisconsin brand of legislation advocated by some liberal Massachusetts businessmen in the early 1930s. In short, the welfare capitalism thesis appears on track for Massachusetts only through 1932, when developments took a turn not explained by this perspective.

If welfare capitalist influence was visible in Massachusetts, it was virtually absent in our other states, including Wisconsin. We argued in the previous section that the pioneering Wisconsin unemployment benefits law embodied the tenets of a long-standing administrative regulatory tradition in that state. Contrary to the view of welfare capitalism proponents, this tradition was necessarily at odds with the desire of businessmen to leave unemployment insurance as a private voluntary matter. In Wisconsin, as elsewhere, capitalists were especially opposed during the depression to any kind of compulsory unemployment compensation. This attitude was shared even by employers who had previously established voluntary unemployment benefits schemes in their own firms because they wanted the option to drop them; Dennison Manufacturing, General Electric, and many others did just that during the early depression. Wisconsin administrators and policy intellectuals aimed to cooperate with employers in implementing unemployment benefits, but in order to get those benefits they had to overcome the opposition of the Wisconsin Manufacturers' Association.[60] Wisconsin policymakers advocated compulsory individual company reserves not because businessmen supported them but because such reserves were considered the best way to use public regulatory power to encourage firms to avoid layoffs.

An analysis that emphasizes class conflict, positing organized business opposition to unemployment insurance, is far more in accord with the historical evidence than the welfare capitalism thesis. Except in Massachusetts, the influence of business associations on the political debates about unemployment insurance was uniformly negative: they opposed *all* forms of compulsory unemployment compensation. Sometimes this opposition was registered through

58. Massachusetts Special Commission on Unemployment, Unemployment Compensation, and the Minimum Wage, *Report of the Special Commission on Unemployment, Unemployment Compensation, and the Minimum Wage;* Nelson, *Unemployment Insurance,* 174.

59. Massachusetts Special Commission on the Stabilization of Employment, *Final Report of the Special Commission on Stabilization of Employment,* 23–29.

60. Nelson, *Unemployment Insurance,* 124–28.

investigatory commissions. In Wisconsin, Ohio, and New York, for example, commissions with representatives from organized business were assembled in 1930 to suggest ways to combat the depression; all recommended reliance on voluntary approaches.[61] Otherwise, business associations pressured politicians to reject proposals for mandatory unemployment insurance. In addition to the opposition of the Wisconsin manufacturers mentioned above, the Ohio Manufacturers' Association fiercely opposed the 1932 report of the Ohio Commission on Unemployment Insurance. In Illinois there were no study commissions for organized business to undermine, and the Illinois Manufacturers' Association pressured state legislators to delay any action.[62] Many Massachusetts business people opposed compulsory unemployment insurance, also. Thus, even though its welfare capitalist members managed to line up the nominal support of the Boston Chamber of Commerce for unemployment compensation, the 1931–32 Massachusetts special commission was unable to gain the backing of the Associated Industries of Massachusetts.[63]

Finally, New York business organizations took an especially intransigent stand against unemployment insurance, despite the fact that this state was the home base of some notable individual welfare capitalists. Organized business in New York opposed a bill (Mastick-Steingut) promoted by John Andrews of the AALL and the Interstate Conference on Unemployment, which included governors or their representatives from seven northern states. When the conference report was released on February 12, it was immediately countered by the negative recommendations of the Joint Legislative Committee on Unemployment, the so-called Marcy committee. This committee was dominated by Republican legislators, whose positions reflected the views of organized business. The Republicans in the General Assembly later killed the bill. When it came up again in 1933, the Marcy committee once more reported unfavorably, and the bill died again.

Ironically, the fact that New York organized business worked so closely and effectively with Republican legislators to block unemployment insurance helped undermine the ability of businessmen to influence the New York unemployment insurance law of 1935, which was passed by Democratic majorities in the Assembly and Senate.[64] In the other four states, however, the political opposition of organized business did not preclude its influence on the provisions of laws that passed. In Wisconsin, the 1932 law included the administration of unemployment insurance by the Industrial Commission, as advocated by the business-supported minority report of the legislative interim committee. More significantly, in Massachusetts the views of business were taken into account with the tax on employees and the provision giving the administrator

61. Ibid., 164, 181. Don Lescohier and Florence Peterson, *The Alleviation of Unemployment in Wisconsin* (Madison: Industrial Commission of Wisconsin, 1931), 103–15.

62. Alfred H. Kelly, "A History of the Illinois Manufacturers' Association" (Ph.D. diss., University of Chicago, 1938), chap. 29.

63. Nelson, *Unemployment Insurance*, 175–78.

64. Ingalls, *Herbert Lehman and New York's Little New Deal*, 73–85; Nelson, *Unemployment Insurance*, 162–73.

the power to apply merit rating. In Ohio and Illinois, organized business was able to delay legislation and, eventually, to write steep merit-rating schedules in the laws.

Organized business pressures against unemployment insurance laws—or in favor of certain substantive provisions when laws passed—were much more consequential than welfare capitalist influences. Yet we cannot predict either the timing of state legislation or the pro-business provisions of the laws that eventually passed solely as a function of business pressures. Business organizations opposed unemployment insurance everywhere, and the effectiveness of that opposition depended on shifting electoral balances and on the openness of state Republicans and Democrats to business influence. As we shall see, the characteristics of the political parties in each state had much to do with their ties to business or labor, or both.

The Political Capacities of Organized Labor

In the recent cross-national literature on the development of welfare states, class conflict ideas have chiefly appeared in the influential social democratic model, which asserts that the organizational capacities of the industrial working class best predict how early and how extensively public social provision will develop.[65] For European nations, especially since World War II, the working-class organizational capacities stressed by this perspective include both trade unions and a labor-based political party able to govern at the national level. In the United States, labor-based political parties, at least in the strict sense, have not controlled state or national governments.[66] We can still inquire, however, about the political capacities of the unionized working class.[67]

In all our five cases, state federations of labor affected the relative timing and form of unemployment insurance. We will consider several factors in order to understand how this labor influence operated. One is the strength of the state federations. According to the logic of the social democratic model, the stronger unions are, the more effectively they can work for public policies favorable to the working class. A second factor, unique to the U.S. context, is the relationship between each state federation and the national leadership of

65. Michael Shalev, "The Social Democratic Model and Beyond," *Comparative Social Research* 6 (1983) : 315–51.

66. Populist or loosely social democratic farmer-worker parties (for example, the Minnesota Farm Labor party) have gained statewide electoral power in the United States, but not strictly labor parties as such. In the states studied here, victories of "labor" parties were limited to scattered representation in state legislatures and control of some city governments. Even when American Socialists based in a city gained some influence in state politics—as did the Milwaukee Socialists in Wisconsin and Morris Hillquit's group of Socialists in New York City—they had to take very moderate reformist approaches and compromise with non–social democratic forces (as the Wisconsin Socialists did) in order to make any legislative headway.

67. For cross-national research concerning the political capacities of the working class, see Stephens, *The Transition from Capitalism to Socialism.* For research in the United States concerning the political capacities of the working class, see J. David Greenstone, *Labor in American Politics* (New York: Knopf, 1969).

the American Federation of Labor (AFL), which refused to endorse unemployment insurance until December 1932. The most important factor, however, was the degree to which organized labor, regardless of its strength or independence, directly cooperated with mainstream party politicians, and which particular politicians, in each state.

In order to examine the strength of state federations, we measured their fiscal strength as indicated by federation receipts per wage earner in 1933. Table 4 gives the relevant findings. Our measure of fiscal strength taps the relative ability of the state federations to extract money from their potential supporters. It is a more political measure of the strength of unionized labor than the usual indicator, union density, because the latter measures only the number of workers in trade unions and cannot say anything about the capacities of unions to influence the political process.

Differences in fiscal strength among state federations are not, however, associated in any meaningful way either with the timing of laws passed in the various states or with the substance of their debates and legislation on unemployment insurance. Wisconsin, the first state to pass legislation, was second among the five states in federation fiscal strength, but Illinois, whose labor federation was the strongest, fiscally speaking, was the last state to adopt unemployment insurance. Especially surprising is the relative weakness of the New York federation, given the extraordinarily pro-labor unemployment insurance law enacted in 1935. Similarly, despite the relative weakness of organized labor in Ohio, the Ohio plan gave greater benefits to unemployed workers than the Wisconsin approach.

Ties between state federations and the national AFL are more helpful in explaining the timing and content of unemployment insurance laws. Those state federations that broke with the AFL position and allied themselves on unemployment policy with state political parties saw legislation enacted sooner

Table 4. Fiscal Strength of State Federations of Labor: State Federation of Labor Revenues as Percentage of Wage Earners in Manufacturing

	Revenues (1933)	Wage Earners (1933)	Revenues/Worker
Illinois	$30,940	420,334	$0.0736
Wisconsin	$11,165	158,730	$0.0703
Ohio	$18,424	472,699	$0.0390
Massachusetts[a]	$13,638	442,649	$0.0308
New York	$21,198	733,452	$0.0289

Sources: ISFL, 51st Annual Proceedings, 1933, pp. 52–53; WSFL, 41st Annual Proceedings, 1933, p. 102; NYSFL, 70th Annual Proceedings, 1933, p. 98; OSFL, 49th Annual Proceedings, 1932, pp. 68–69; MSFL, 51st Annual Proceedings, 1936, p. 57.

[a]The figure for Massachusetts SFL revenues is based on information for 1936. Since unions were gaining strength in these years, the 1936 figure should be higher than the 1933. Thus the relative ranking for Massachusetts on this table should be the same or lower for 1933.

than state federations that went along with the official AFL position. Thus, by coming out strongly for unemployment legislation when the AFL was still opposed, the Massachusetts and Wisconsin federations were able to participate actively in the legislative process. The Ohio and Illinois federations, on the other hand, remained closely tied to the AFL leadership. William Green, president of the AFL, was from Ohio, and he did not endorse unemployment insurance legislation until December 1932, nor did the Ohio federation officially support the Ohio plan until the end of that year.[63] Illinois labor was similarly constrained; the secretary-treasurer of the Illinois federation led the old guard opposition to unemployment insurance within the AFL's resolutions committee. New York offers a more ambiguous example. While the rank and file supported legislation, the state leadership was constrained to follow the AFL line, and thus was unable to enter fully into the debate until the AFL finally endorsed insurance.[69] However, once the AFL decided, a strong and long-established labor–Democratic party alliance produced the most pro-labor bill among the states.

In Wisconsin, the State Federation of Labor was dominated by so-called constructivist Milwaukee Socialists.[70] The Socialists were willing to work with Republican progressives and the Wisconsin Industrial Commission on reform legislation. They helped initiate and sustain debates over unemployment insurance in the 1920s and, after failing to get a better alternative, supported the 1932 Groves bill.[71] The lack of a pooled fund meant restricted benefits, but the Socialists agreed in order to get legislation passed early in the depression. Organized labor's stance did not directly cause or fashion unemployment insurance, but it helped keep unemployment insurance continually on the agenda and facilitated the early passage of an unemployment insurance law—although not exactly the law Wisconsin labor preferred.[72]

Among the other four states, New York had by far the longest standing and closest ties between the State Federation of Labor and the Democratic party. Cooperation started early in the 1900s when the Tammany machine controlled the party,[73] and in the 1920s it carried over as organized labor consistently endorsed Democratic governors Smith and Roosevelt. Numerous pro-labor measures were passed during the second Lehman administration (1935–37) including a strong measure to supplement the National Labor Relations Act of 1935.[74]

68. Ohio State Federation of Labor, *Forty-seventh Annual Convention Proceedings, 1930* (Columbus, 1930), 72, 135; Ohio State Federation of Labor, *Forty-eighth Annual Convention Proceedings, 1931* (Columbus, 1931), 54, 91; Ohio State Federation of Labor, *Forty-ninth Annual Convention Proceedings, 1932* (Columbus, 1932), 56, 76–87, 100.

69. Nelson, *Unemployment Insurance,* 169–71.

70. Robert W. Ozanne, *The Labor Movement in Wisconsin: A History* (Madison: State Historical Society of Wisconsin, 1984).

71. Nelson, *Unemployment Insurance,* chap. 6.

72. Thomas W. Gavett, *Development of the Labor Movement in Milwaukee* (Madison: University of Wisconsin Press, 1965), chap. 2.

73. Yellowitz, *Labor and the Progressive Movement in New York State,* 109.

74. Ingalls, *Herbert Lehman and New York's Little New Deal,* chap. 6.

The Massachusetts Federation of Labor was less fully or consistently allied with Democrats in the 1920s than was the New York federation. Indeed, there were some areas of the state in which cooperation with Republicans prevailed. But the Massachusetts federation worked more closely with the Democrats than the Ohio or Illinois federations, and ties between organized labor and the Massachusetts Democrats became much closer from the late 1920s through the election in 1934 of Governor Curley, who had the federation's endorsement.[75]

In Ohio, the state federation reached the peak of its willingness to ally with Democrats and push directly for labor legislation during the 1913–15 period. After that, the Ohio federation had to contend with factionalized parties and often-ascendent conservative Republicans. Throughout the 1920s and into the 1930s, the Ohio federation adhered to a policy of nonendorsement of candidates or parties. In 1930, an attempt was made to change the nonendorsement policy, but its opponents were unable to garner enough support to succeed. Because the Ohio federation failed to form any party alliance to advance the cause of labor legislation after 1914, it had no organizational means beyond its own bargaining power to affect the passage of unemployment legislation.[76]

Finally, the Illinois State Federation of Labor shows how a *relatively strong* state federation made a series of political choices in the 1910s and 1920s that left it without strong ties to the Democrats (or any mainstream nonconservative political party) by the 1930s. Not only was the Illinois federation fiscally strong; the state had a long history of working-class organizational strength. During the Progressive Era, Illinois had one of the strongest and most radical federations of labor. But unlike its counterparts in New York and Wisconsin, the Illinois federation did not ally consistently with either major political party. Indeed, the federation went so far as to support the scandal-ridden administration of the Republican governor Len Small (1921–29) because he agreed to back a federation-sponsored bill that limited the use of the injunction to halt labor disputes.[77] The Illinois federation's president served as a downstate *Republican* legislator in the 1930s and introduced most of the key labor legislation. The alliance with Small prevented the Illinois federation from throwing in its lot with the rising Democratic party, even in 1932.[78] The emerging Democratic boss of Chicago and Illinois, Anton Cermak, enjoyed the enthusiastic support of business, rather than organized labor, in his successful 1931

75. Harold Gorvine, "The New Deal in Massachusetts," in John Braeman, Robert H. Bremner, and David Brody, eds., *The New Deal: The State and Local Levels* (Columbus: Ohio State University Press, 1975), 3–44.

76. Ohio State Federation of Labor, *Forty-first Annual Convention Proceedings, 1924* (Columbus, 1924), 148–63; Ohio State Federation of Labor, *Forty-seventh Annual Convention Proceedings, 1930*, 77, 140.

77. Eugene Staley, *The History of the Illinois State Federation of Labor* (Chicago: University of Chicago Press, 1930), 461–73.

78. Illinois State Federation of Labor, *Weekly News Letter*, October 29, 1932, p. 1.

mayoral race, and Cermak's successor, Edward Kelly, continued this tilt toward business.[79]

In all five states, both the capacity and the willingness of organized labor to promote unemployment insurance legislation depended upon relationships to political parties. The state federations of labor made choices concerning political alliances and their relationship with the national labor movement, but these choices occurred neither as a simple function of their own strength nor in a political vacuum. The characteristics of political parties and electoral competition in each state strongly influenced what organized labor (as well as business, reformers, and others) tried to achieve in public policy-making, what they could achieve, and when. It is crucial, therefore, to understand how political parties themselves contributed to shaping the timing and contents of unemployment insurance legislation.

THE ROLE OF POLITICAL PARTIES

How did political parties and electoral alignments affect the passage and contents of unemployment insurance legislation in Wisconsin, New York, Massachusetts, Ohio, and Illinois? These legislative achievements were not the direct result of the electoral realignment of the 1930s, when the Democratic party gained ground everywhere at the expense of Republicans. Indeed, the first state to pass unemployment insurance, Wisconsin, continued to be dominated by Republicans. Across the other four states, moreover, the attainment of nominal Democratic control in legislatures or governorships, or even both together, was *not* sufficient either to cause the immediate passage of unemployment insurance or to ensure that labor would gain more advantages than business from laws passed under Democratic aegis. In Illinois and Ohio, during the 1933 legislative sessions, the Democrats had nominal control of the lower and upper houses of the legislature as well as the governor's office. Illinois retained this dominance during the 1935 session, when New York Democrats first gained control. If Democratic control were sufficient, Ohio and Illinois would have preceded New York in passing unemployment insurance, and their laws would have favored labor, not business.

In this section, therefore, we look beyond electoral outcomes to focus on issues of political party organization and partisan cleavages: Did patronage-oriented parties frustrate or further social policies? Did intraparty factionalism matter? How did patterns of party organization and competition line up with urban-rural cleavages? Initially, we consider those four states—New York, Massachusetts, Ohio, and Illinois—where the Democrats were becoming the stronger party in the early 1930s. For these states, we find that unemployment insurance passed sooner and in a form more amenable to the expressed preferences of organized labor where—as in New York and Massachusetts—the

79. Harold Gosnell, *Machine Politics: Chicago Model* (Chicago: University of Chicago Press, 1937), 11–12; Alex Gottfried, *Boss Cermak of Chicago: A Study of Political Leadership* (Seattle: University of Washington Press, 1962), 210–18.

Democrats were more centrally disciplined and they were urban-based, bridging the various cities in the state. The degree and timing of Democratic dominance in state government also mattered, but Democratic incumbency was not sufficient to ensure early passage of generous unemployment insurance if—as in Ohio and Illinois—the Democrats were factionalized and represented both urban and rural constituencies. At the end of this section, we assess the special case of Wisconsin, a state governed by moderate Republicans from the Progressive Era through the New Deal.

Patronage Parties and Social Policy-making

When political parties are discussed in the cross-national literature on the origins and development of modern social policies, it is usually assumed that they are disciplined and unitary. But for the United States such an assumption is untenable. From the nineteenth century into the twentieth, American politics was typically conducted by decentralized, mass-based patronage parties, oriented toward the delivery of divisible benefits to complex coalitions including various businesses and locally based popular groups.[80] Any historical analysis of the politics of social policy must take into account the special characteristics of U.S. political parties.

The role of urban patronage political parties in U.S. social reform from the Progressive Era into the New Deal has been portrayed in two contrasting ways by interpreters of American social politics. One interpretation might be called the "patronage versus reform" thesis offered by political scientist Martin Shefter. Briefly, he sees an obstacle to reform in the existence of the strong, disciplined, patronage-based political machines that flourished in the industrial Northeast. Such machines, in this view, tended to be conservative for two reasons: first, the patronage-based parties made deals with businessmen and were therefore unable to deliver certain policies in the collective interest of working-class and other popular constituencies; second, the electoral strength of the patronage parties made it difficult for third parties in general and reformist parties in particular to contend for power.[81]

A contrasting perspective on the role of patronage parties is the "urban liberalism" thesis advanced by historian John Buenker. According to Buenker, there are only a few types of forces involved in reformist politics: middle-class reformers, who devise social legislation; representatives from urban and mining areas, who make no proposals but who form the basis of support for social legislation; and small-town and rural representatives, who ally with business groups to block social legislation, typically under the auspices of the Republican party. Buenker underscores the role played by urban Democrats and discounts heavily the role of social workers, professional economists, and reform

---

80. See Ira Katznelson, *City Trenches: Urban Politics and the Patterning of Class in the United States* (New York: Pantheon, 1981); Martin Shefter, "Party and Patronage: Germany, England, and Italy," *Politics and Society* 7 (1977) : 404–51; Martin Shefter, "Regional Receptivity to Reform: The Legacy of the Progressive Era," *Political Science Quarterly* 98 (1983) : 459–83; McCormick, *From Relignment to Reform*.

81. See Shefter, "Regional Receptivity to Reform."

organizations, which at best aided in "fostering the proper climate of opinion" for social legislation. The urban-Democratic "new stock" lawmakers "provided much of the sponsorship, legislative skill, and the votes necessary to launch the welfare state."[82]

The case of Wisconsin is consistent with Shefter's argument. In that state, mass-based patronage parties never took hold, and civil service reform and antipatronage political reforms triumphed in the Progressive Era. Wisconsin engaged in continual debates over unemployment compensation and other social policy innovations during the 1920s and was the first state to enact unemployment compensation. But in New York, where unemployment insurance passed next and in a form especially favorable to labor, politics was dominated by patronage-oriented party machines throughout much of the period leading into the New Deal. Indeed, because of the strength of its party machines into the 1920s, New York was the last of our states to institute the direct primary, a progressive reform that was anathema to Democratic and Republican patronage politicians alike. Shefter is right to see patronage machines as obstacles to such *political* reforms as the direct primary, short ballots, and civil service professionalization, for these threatened the organizational life of the machine. On questions of social reform, however, the picture is more complicated.

Buenker would respond that the existence of patronage parties does not rule out social reforms. Mobilization by machine parties may entail the formation of broad and diverse political alliances. The larger and more diverse its constituency, the more a patronage-based party needs to take into account the demands of disparate groups in selecting public policies. Machines might be forced to embrace social legislation that aided their popular constituents, while tailoring the policies to avoid offending business supporters. In New York in the early twentieth century, the Tammany Democrats facilitated some social and labor reforms that were opposed by business yet appealed to both working-class constituents and middle-class reformers.[83] Moreover, the electoral strength of New York's originally patronage-based Democratic machine paved the way for the eventual passage of more comprehensive reforms by Governors Smith, Roosevelt, and Lehman from the late 1920s into the 1930s. Yet Shefter could rightly counter that the New York Democratic party simultaneously moved away from patronage principles of internal organization and localistic, piecemeal ties and toward businesses and working-class ethnics. Under Smith and especially Roosevelt and Lehman, the New York Democratic party became less patronage-oriented, and it moved into closer *programmatic alliances* with independent reformers and organized mass constituencies such as the New York State Federation of Labor.

Across our states we find that the receptivity of Democratic parties to prolabor unemployment insurance legislation varied according to a logic that can be synthesized from both Shefter and Buenker. As Shefter would have it,

82. John Buenker, *Urban Liberalism and Progressive Reform* (New York: Charles Scribner's Sons, 1973), 43–44.

83. Yellowitz, *Labor and the Progressive Movement in New York State.*

patronage-oriented Democratic parties were not as willing to court organized labor's support or agree to its full program as were Democrats who did not rely as heavily on patronage. Yet as Buenker points out, patronage-oriented parties had eclectic constituencies and consequently had to make some gestures to labor groups as well as to business and other supporters. All in all, the degree to which Democrats were patronage-based affected the *contents* of the social legislation, including unemployment insurance legislation, that passed under Democratic leadership in New York, Massachusetts, Ohio, and Illinois. Democrats in New York were not so reliant on patronage by the 1930s, but the Democrats in the other three states remained highly patronage-oriented. Only New York passed a form of unemployment insurance unequivocally favorable to organized labor; the other three states all enacted bills that compromised the preferences of business and labor.

For the case of New York, moreover, we can discern a telling temporal contrast between the patronage-based Democratic party run by the Tammany bosses that passed a compromise workers' compensation measure in 1913 and the reformed Democratic party led by Governor Herbert Lehman that put through the nation's most pro-labor unemployment insurance measure in 1935. Although the New York workers' compensation bill of 1913 was a clear gain for workers, Tammany had to balance both labor and commercial business interests; thus it ignored organized labor's demand for a monopolistic state fund.[84] Governor Lehman, however, could dismiss business interests with impunity and enact a comprehensive program of labor legislation, including an unemployment insurance bill written in part by Federation of Labor leaders.[85] The resulting New York unemployment insurance law taxed business at an unusually high rate and provided benefits to strikers that could help unions prolong strikes.

The patronage-based administration of the Massachusetts Democrat James Michael Curley passed an unemployment insurance law soon after New York, yet the character of the Massachusetts legislation was less in accord with organized labor's needs and interests. Rather than attempting to cement his alliance with organized labor through reform, as did Lehman, the former Boston mayor fought the depression primarily through labor-intensive public works and work-sharing measures. Both increased the state patronage at his disposal and the spoils available to local Democratic organizations.[86] Like Lehman, Curley was able to act quickly to put many antidepression measures, including unemployment insurance, through the state legislature; the New York and the Massachusetts leaders were both strong governors in control of their parties. Yet Curley faced Republican majorities in the legislature and so, aside from his own indifference to a programmatic alliance with labor, he might have gotten nowhere with unemployment insurance had he insisted on a one-sided measure like New York's. Curley was willing and able to add into the legislative equation some of the preferences of Republicans and their busi-

84. Ibid., 116; Wesser, *Charles Evans Hughes: Politics and Reform in New York,* 366–70.
85. Ingalls, *Herbert Lehman and New York's Little New Deal,* chaps. 4–6.
86. Gorvine, "The New Deal in Massachusetts."

nessmen allies. He adopted a bill previously worked out in a 1933–34 commission that had brought together Democrats and Republicans in the legislature with representatives of business and organized labor. The resulting Massachusetts unemployment insurance law had a pooled fund and promised relatively generous benefits to workers, yet provided for employee contributions, something that organized labor opposed in every state and accepted only reluctantly in Massachusetts. It also allowed eventual administrative discretion in the application of merit rating, which might adjust business taxes above a fixed minimum.[87]

As in Massachusetts, the Democratic parties of Ohio and Illinois remained patronage-oriented in the 1930s. Thus, when their unemployment insurance laws finally passed in 1936 and 1937, they were eclectic compromises and (for further reasons about to be specified) made greater concessions to conservative and business preferences than did the Massachusetts law. Although both the Ohio and the Illinois laws had statewide pooled funds, they had merit-rating provisions so steep that businesses in many industries could soon end up paying very low taxes, necessarily constricting benefits to workers.

The Importance of Party Cohesion

The timing of unemployment insurance across our states, as well as its relative generosity to labor, was not simply a function of patronage-orientation of the various Democratic parties. It also mattered whether Democratic parties were cohesive or factionalized. During the 1920s, all four states had patronage-oriented parties, but there were significant variations in their cohesiveness.

Ohio and Illinois had strong factional divisions within both major parties, and those divisions continued into the 1930s.[88] During the 1920s, moments of reform in these states were episodic, and attempts at sustained administration were soon rolled back. During the 1930s, the previous shortcomings of reform and continuing patterns of party factionalization undercut the reform potential of the politically ascendant Democrats.

New York and Massachusetts differed markedly from Ohio and Illinois in party cohesion, although only in New York was Democratic cohesion a long-standing reality. In Progressive Era New York, the ability of Tammany Democrats to pass strong state labor legislation depended in part on effective party discipline in the legislature. Even after Tammany had weakened, strong Democratic party discipline carried over into the administration of the reformist Lehman, helping him pass unemployment insurance and other labor re-

87. Massachusetts Special Commission to Make an Investigation of Unemployment Insurance, Reserves, and Benefits, *Second and Final Report of the Special Commission to Make an Investigation of Unemployment Insurance, Reserves, and Benefits,* Massachusetts House Document no. 2225 (Boston: Wright & Potter, State Printers, 1935).

88. For Ohio, see Thomas Flinn, "The Outline of Ohio Politics," *Western Political Quarterly* 13 (1960) : 702–21; John Fenton, *Midwest Politics* (New York: Hold, Rinehart & Winston, 1966). For Illinois, see Charles E. Merriam, *Chicago: A More Intimate View of Urban Politics* (Chicago: University of Chicago Press, 1929); Barry Karl, *Charles Merriam and the Study of Politics* (Chicago: University of Chicago Press, 1974); Roger Biles, *Big City Boss in Depression and War: Mayor Edward J. Kelly of Chicago* (DeKalb: Northern Illinois University Press, 1984).

forms.[89] Similarly, in Massachusetts during the mid-1930s, Curley effectively controlled the Democratic legislative delegation during his brief tenure as governor and could also swing some Republicans to his side.[90] This allowed him to pass his various antidepression measures, including unemployment insurance. Yet Democratic cohesion was new (and temporary) in Massachusetts; prior to Curley's governorship, Massachusetts Democrats had been factionalized and ineffective.

During the 1930s, a Curley-style attempt to make the Illinois Democrats more cohesive was frustrated by the assassination of the chairman of the Cook County Democratic party, Anton Cermak, who caught a bullet meant for President-elect Roosevelt. In an attempt to gain control of the state Democratic party, Cermak had been elected mayor of Chicago in 1931 and his choice, Henry Horner, elected governor in 1932. But Cermak was dead soon after the 1933 legislative session began. Instead of centralized control, chaos reigned among the Democrats, as a bitter power struggle broke out between the new Chicago mayor, Edward Kelly, and Governor Horner. This conflict raged throughout the summer of 1935, immediately before unemployment insurance was to be considered by the legislature in a special session, and Kelly's bloc of legislators refused to follow Horner's lead on unemployment insurance.[91]

Conditions Promoting Party Cohesion

If party cohesion is such a powerful factor in explaining the ability of Democrats to put through unemployment insurance in the 1930s, then what—aside from chance events such as the shooting of Mayor Cermak—accounts for party cohesion? Our evidence suggests that there were at least three factors at work. The first two had long-term roots, based in the political history of each state and shifting patterns in the 1930s: first, how consistently competitive with the Republicans were the state's Democrats, and second, how cleanly did urban-rural divisions line up with the party split? The third factor affecting Democratic party cohesiveness in the 1930 was much more immediate: the impact on state politics of the Roosevelt administration, which distributed large amounts of money to the states for relief and other purposes. In deciding how and where to spend the money, the administration became embroiled in factional struggles in the state and local Democratic parties, sometimes at the expense of centralized control.[92]

With respect to party competitiveness, the New York Democrats had long

89. Ingalls, *Herbert Lehman and New York's Little New Deal,* 12.

90. Gorvine, "The New Deal in Massachusetts."

91. Biles, *Big City Boss in Depression and War,* 50–51; Gene DeLon Jones, "The Origin of the Alliance between the New Deal and the Chicago Machine," *Journal of the Illinois State Historical Society* 67 (1974) : 253–74.

92. For a discussion of the role of administration in state political struggles, see James T. Patterson, *The New Deal and the States: Federalism in Transition* (Princeton: Princeton University Press, 1969).

been able to compete more effectively with Republicans than could their counterparts in Illinois, Ohio, and Massachusetts, and long-standing Democratic party cohesiveness in New York was aided by, and in turn furthered, state-level electoral prowess. As table 5 shows, although Illinois Democrats won larger percentages of seats in the lower house and although Ohio regularly elected Democratic governors in the 1920s, only in New York were the Democrats consistently competitive in all three arenas. In New York two powerful parties squared off against each other in hard-fought close contests. Throughout the 1920s the New York Democrats always came close to winning both houses of the legislature and the governor's office, and actually did so in 1934.

As for urban-rural divisions, Democrats in New York and Massachusetts were more homogenously urban than in Ohio and Illinois during the 1920s. Moreover, in the early 1930s, both the New York and the Massachusetts Democratic parties expanded beyond New York City and Boston by gaining support in other urban areas. Democrats in New York State had typically carried only New York City in legislative elections, but during the Democratic upheavals the New York–upstate split turned into a genuine urban-rural split, as counties with cities such as Buffalo and Albany began to return Democrats. The already cohesive New York Democrats became still more able to promote the legislative agendas of urban reform interests, including organized labor. Although the Massachusetts Democratic party was much less politically competitive with Republicans in the 1920s and remained relatively weak in the 1930s, it also unified urban representatives. Democratic legislators usually carried only Boston in the 1920s, but the smaller industrial cities of Massachusetts returned Democrats to the Massachusetts General Court (legislature) in the 1930s, and Governor Curley forged the unusual (for Massachusetts) Democratic unity that aided the passage of many antidepression measures.

In Ohio and Illinois, it was more difficult for Democratic party leaders to crack the whip, partly because those parties included many rural members

Table 5. Democratic Representation in Four State Governments, 1921–1936

	Governor[a]	Senate[b]	House[b]
New York	55.1% (14)	45.9%	42.3%
Illinois	45.3 (4)	33.8	44.9
Massachusetts	46.2 (6)	23.4	33.7
Ohio	50.1 (12)	18.3	27.1

Sources: New York Red Book, 1921–1935; Illinois Blue Book, 1921–1935; Ohio Election Statistics, 1921–1935; Manual of The General Court 1921–1935.
[a] Governor: Average Democratic percent of two-party vote, 1920–1934 elections (Number of years Democrats held office, 1921–1936).
[b] House, Senate: Average percent of Democratic seats, 1921–1936.

who resembled conservative Republicans in spirit and in action.[93] In addition, Republicans had considerable urban strength. During the 1920s Ohio cities were represented in the legislature primarily by Republicans. By the 1930s, only a few cities, mainly the ones in the northern part of the state, such as Cleveland, went Democratic, while others, such as Cincinnati, remained in the Republican camp.[94] In the case of Illinois, matters were aggravated by the system of minority representation, which assured the smaller of the two major parties one of three lower-house seats in legislative districts where the smaller party had no chance to win a Senate seat.[95] Even though the Republicans dominated the state in the 1920s, minority representation assured the Democrats a foothold both in Chicago and downstate. The pockets of rural Democratic strength prevented the imposition of party discipline by Chicago Democrats even in the 1930s when Democrats were in the majority. Moreover, although the Democrats in Chicago won a series of elections starting in 1931, the Republicans controlled nearly one-third of the Chicago delegation in the lower house because of minority representation.

The third factor, the impact of the Roosevelt administration, pinpoints how the new federal forays into state-level Democratic politics sometimes reinforced the strength of state-level Democratic party leaders and sometimes undermined them. In New York, the administration's actions helped strengthen the governor in his bid to centralize the party. In Massachusetts, the administration did little to aid the governor's cause, but did not aid or create a major opponent. In Illinois and Ohio, the Roosevelt administration encountered serious difficulties with the governors and actively propped up the governors' factional enemies instead.

There was little question of who the administration would support in New York; Roosevelt sided with his former lieutenant governor Lehman and his faction of the Democratic party in opposition to the New York City Tammany machine. Roosevelt ran an independent Democratic candidate in the 1933 New York mayoral election, splitting the Democratic vote, throwing the elec-

93. For Ohio, see Flinn, "The Outline of Ohio Politics"; Fenton, *Midwest Politics,* 132. For Illinois, see William B. Phillip, "Chicago and the Downstate: A Study of Their Conflicts, 1870–1934" (Ph.D. diss., University of Chicago, 1940).

94. Flinn, "The Outline of Ohio Politics," 705.

95. The minority representation system was in effect in the lower house of the Illinois General Assembly. Each of the fifty-one legislative districts for the General Assembly sent one senator to the upper house and three representatives to the lower house. Each voter could cast three votes in any combination for the election of representatives; one could give all three votes to one candidate. This made it easy for one of the two major parties to salvage one seat in a district where the minority party was badly outnumbered because the minority party would usually nominate only one candidate, who would then receive all three votes from each of the minority party's followers. This generally led to larger-than-expected delegations of Democrats in the 1920s and to larger-than-expected delegations of Republicans in the 1930s (Ernest L. Bogart and John Mabry Mathews, *The Centennial History of Illinois,* Vol. 5, *The Modern Commonwealth, 1893–1918* [Chicago: A. C. McClurg & Co., 1922]; Fenton, *Midwest Politics,* 209).

tion to the Republican, Fiorello La Guardia (who won by a plurality), and depriving the Tammany machine of city patronage.[96] At the level of state government, the Roosevelt administration cooperated closely with the Lehman administration and channeled resources to state agencies.

In Illinois, the Roosevelt administration sided with Boss Kelly of Chicago in his factional battle with Governor Horner. Although Horner was closer to the New Deal in ideology than was Kelly, Horner did not act quickly enough in passing taxes for emergency relief to suit Harry Hopkins, the Federal Emergency Relief administrator. The administration also respected the Chicago Democratic machine's vote-getting powers, as exhibited in the fall 1934 and spring 1935 elections. Roosevelt did not put up a challenge to Kelly in 1935, and when Kelly began his unsuccessful attempt to unseat Horner in 1935, Kelly had the backing of the administration.[97] The Roosevelt administration thus helped aggravate the already serious split among Illinois Democrats.

In Ohio, too, the Roosevelt administration ended up at odds with a Democratic governor and actively sought to undercut him. Governor Martin Davey (1935–39) placed a premium on keeping state expenditures as low as possible even in the midst of the depression and was unwilling to finance state relief programs or to match federal ones. In addition, Davey denounced Hopkins for naming Republicans to relief posts. Afterward Hopkins followed up reports of corruption and authorized an investigation of the Ohio relief program. When the investigation showed that Davey's relief appointments were patronage-based, the Roosevelt administration assumed direct control of the program, making Ohio one of only six states where relief was directly administered by the federal government.[98] Governor Davey had liberal Democratic rivals, including former governor Vic Donahey from Cleveland, and the Roosevelt administration backed the rivals whenever it could.

Massachusetts fell between the extremes of New York on the one hand and Illinois and Ohio on the other. Roosevelt did not ally with the Curley administration of 1935–37, even though Curley had led the Roosevelt Massachusetts forces in his battle against Smith for the 1932 nomination. Roosevelt cut off much of Curley's federal patronage.[99] Pursuing a strategy unlike that in Illinois, however, Roosevelt did not line up with Curley's main opponents, the Joseph Ely–David Walsh faction of western Massachusetts.[100] Instead, he made an abortive attempt to establish a third force in Massachusetts politics led by

96. Arthur Mann, *La Guardia Comes to Power, 1933* (Chicago: University of Chicago Press, 1965), chap. 4.

97. Biles, *Big City Boss in Depression and War*, chap. 3.

98. Carl Wittke, *The History of the State of Ohio* (Columbus: Ohio State Archaeological and Historical Society, 1942), 11 : 459–60; David J. Maurer, "Relief Problems and Politics in Ohio," in John Braeman, Robert H. Bremner, and David Brody, eds., *The New Deal: The State and Local Levels* (Columbus: Ohio State University Press, 1975), 76–102; Patterson, *The New Deal and the States*, 61–62.

99. Patterson, *The New Deal and the States*, 62.

100. Duane Lockard, *New England State Politics* (Princeton: Princeton University Press, 1959), 127–28.

James Roosevelt.[101] Although the Roosevelt administration did not aid Curley, it did not try as hard as in Illinois and Ohio to undermine him.

In sum, Democrats in New York moved further from patronage methods at the state level than the other Democratic parties and enjoyed a unique combination of conditions favoring state party cohesion: they had been competitive with the Republicans in the 1920s, they went from dominating New York City to representing all important cities in the state, and the governor had powerful support from the Roosevelt administration. For these reasons the New York Democrats passed the nation's second unemployment insurance law as part of an antidepression program deliberately tailored to meet urban needs and uniquely oriented to the policy preferences of organized labor. In the United States, the New York experience in the mid-1930s most closely resembled the social democratic scenario of public policy-making, with the Democratic party allied to organized labor as a functional equivalent of a true labor-based political party.[102] Yet it is worth emphasizing that it took a special intersection of social and political conditions furthering the unity and discipline of a Democratic party to make this scenario possible. For as we demonstrated above, the fiscal strength of the Federation of Labor, the unionized arm of the industrial working class, was *not* what set New York apart from the other states.

Party Politics in Wisconsin

Where does Wisconsin fit in our analysis of party influences on social policy breakthroughs? Clearly, the Republican-dominated politics of Wisconsin contrasted strongly with the politics of the other cases, but within the Republican party the La Follette Progressive faction frequently held sway. In Wisconsin, any politician hoping to dominate the Republican party, a prerequisite for successfully sponsoring progressive legislation, faced a special set of facilitating and impeding political conditions. Special as they were, these conditions can be analyzed in the same terms—patronage, urban-rural cleavages, and party cohesion—identified above as important for the other four states.

Wisconsin politics was relatively patronage-free by the time of the Progressive Era. Thus a progressive Republican governor would not be bound to honor business preferences to sustain party organization. Nor were urban ethnic–based political machines of particular concern. Only the relatively weak Democrats had such a constituency, and it was overshadowed by the Milwaukee Socialists. Instead, Wisconsin's Progressive Republicans tended to promote reformist measures, such as tax revisions or consumer regulations, designed to favor farmers and middle-class urbanites. In the process, they often made cooperative gestures to workers, partly in order to attract direct electoral support but also to win practical cooperation from the unions and the Socialists.

For the other four states, we have argued that urban-rural differences

101. J. Joseph Huthmacher, *Massachusetts People and Politics* (New York: Atheneum, 1959), 235–36; Gorvine, "The New Deal in Massachusetts."
102. See Greenstone, *Labor in American Politics.*

impeded Democratic cohesion unless Democratic control was aligned with these cleavages. In Wisconsin, however, urban and rural differences were mediated politically by the willingness of the Progressive Republicans and the moderate Milwaukee Social Democrats to compromise farmer and worker interests at the fiscal expense of business; both workers' compensation and unemployment reserves shifted the cost of relief from property taxes to the payrolls of business but not to those of commercial agriculture, which was often exempted from labor legislation. In addition, there is reason to believe that patterns of urbanization in Wisconsin made that state less prone to urban-rural conflicts.

Wisconsin was far less urbanized than the other states, whether one uses the census measure of 2,500 (as in table 3) or the 20,000 limit more characteristic of cross-national research (table 6) as the standard for "urban." In addition, as table 7 reveals, Wisconsin's urban population in the 1930s was located mainly in cities of 20,000 to 50,000 people, with 35.7 percent in that category. Moreover, Wisconsin had proportionately fewer urbanites in cities of 100,000 or more residents, only 49.3 percent of its urban population, as compared to 58.1 percent for Massachusetts, 74.8 percent for Ohio, 76.2 percent for Illinois, and 88.3 percent for New York.

The concentration of urban populations in larger cities may help explain the urban-rural splits we noted in the other states. These splits could impede the social reform potential of the Democratic parties in contradiction of economic determinist theories that stress the positive effect of large-scale urbanization (and industrialization) on social policy. In Wisconsin, however, the absence of a strong urban-based Democratic party did not preclude innovative social policies, since urban-rural conflicts were mediated by compromises between the Socialists and the Progressive Republicans. Moreover, urban-rural splits in Wisconsin life were less stark in strictly socioeconomic terms.

During the 1930s, Wisconsin Republicans were not as disciplined as the Democrats of New York or Massachusetts. Wisconsin Republicanism after 1900 was marked by jostling and uneasy compromises between two factions, Progressives and Stalwarts. As the depression deepened, intraparty compromises degenerated into open warfare. The Progressive Philip La Follette captured the governor's chair in 1930, but he did not control enough state legislators to impose his will upon the Stalwarts and the reviving Democratic party. This

Table 6. Percentage of Urban Population in Five States, 1910, 1920, 1930 (Cities of 20,000 or More Residents)

	New York	Massachusetts	Illinois	Ohio	Wisconsin
1910	70.5%	66.8%	48.5%	39.3%	26.3%
1920	73.9	68.2	53.6	49.7	31.4
1930	74.7	71.9	59.9	52.9	39.9

Sources: The Fourteenth Census of the United States (Washington, D.C.: U.S. Government Printing Office), 3:261–64, 690–95, 784–88, 1131–33; The Fifteenth Census of the United States vol. 3, part 1, pp. 628–31; vol. 3, part 2, pp. 288–92, 491–95, 1333–34.

situation prevented the passage of La Follette's plan for a state-financed centralized system of economic management and planning.[103] Instead, political compromises capable of attracting some conservative Republican and farm-area support were worked out for more limited measures, including unemployment insurance, by academic reformers working through the Wisconsin Industrial Commission. In 1934, the La Follette faction finally abandoned the Republicans, establishing the Progressive party, which was the primary recipient of New Deal largesse.[104]

In short, the Wisconsin Industrial Commission and not a unified party was the key to Wisconsin's system of unemployment compensation. The politically influential commission, along with the university reformers and labor leaders tied to it, kept debates on unemployment insurance going through the 1920s. Understandably, the commission and the John R. Commons school intellectuals kept their preventionist ideas of unemployment compensation at the forefront.[105] The coming of the depression heightened organized labor's interest in getting some sort of unemployment insurance, but it also encouraged labor and the Socialists to press for pooled-fund-type plans that would deliver more generous benefits. Perhaps, if the Progressive faction of the Wisconsin Republican party had been fully dominant in the early 1930s, a deal might have been struck among Progressive politicians, the Federation of Labor, and the Socialists—a deal that would have produced something like the New York unemployment insurance law three years earlier. But the Wisconsin Progressives did not consolidate themselves until 1934, by which time the Industrial Commission had been able to use its skills of interest group mediation and its

Table 7. The Structure of Urbanization in Five States in 1930 (Number of Cities and Percentage of Total Urban Population in Selected Categories of Population)

	20,000 to 50,000		50,000 to 100,000		100,000 to 200,000		200,000 to 400,000		400,000+	
	N	Percent	N	Percent	N	Percent	N	Percent	N	Percent
Wisconsin	14	35.7%	3	15.0%	0	0.0%	0	0.0%	1	49.3%
Massachusetts	25	26.8	7	15.1	8	32.5	0	0.0	1	25.6
Ohio	19	18.2	4	7.0	2	7.8	4	29.6	2	37.4
Illinois	19	13.2	7	10.6	1	2.3	0	0.0	1	73.9
New York	20	6.6	6	5.1	3	5.0	1	3.5	2	79.8

Source: See table 6.

103. Wisconsin Legislative Interim Committee on Unemployment, *Report of the Wisconsin Legislative Interim Committee on Unemployment* (Madison: Industrial Commission of Wisconsin, 1931).

104. Donald R. McCoy, "The Development and Dissolution of the Wisconsin Progressive Party of 1934–1946" (M.A. thesis, University of Chicago, 1949), 41.

105. John B. Ewing, *Job Insurance* (Norman: University of Oklahoma Press, 1933), 36–38.

influence with legislators to get its preferred approach enacted. This happened *despite* the Republican feuding that kept many antidepression measures favored by Governor La Follette from passing the legislature.[106]

The Groves Unemployment Reserves Act, the Industrial Commission's proposed legislation, was, of course, a politically tailored compromise. Wisconsin farmers, including dairymen concerned to protect workers' income, insisted that farm workers not be covered and that business or labor pay the bills.[107] Proscribing agricultural workers and any contributions from general state revenues was the price of support from Republicans with rural constituents.[108] The academic and Industrial Commission reformists accepted these conditions, which complemented the regulatory style of the commission: to use taxes on business to create incentives for unemployment prevention. Finally, Wisconsin labor leaders and Socialists cooperated, as long as workers were not taxed, in the hope that the Groves bill would be the first step in developing an effective response to the depression.

In sum, Wisconsin's relative freedom from patronage, the tradition of moderate Republican dominance through the 1920s, and the nonpolarization and special mediations of urban and rural interests laid the foundation for continuous policy debates and early legislation. Nevertheless, it is hard to imagine either the continuous debates or the early breakthrough occurring without the vision and political effectiveness of the Wisconsin Industrial Commission. And certainly the *contents* of the 1932 Wisconsin law would be inexplicable without knowing the Industrial Commission's history as an omnibus administrative agency and the ideas that John R. Commons and his University of Wisconsin associates developed to inspire and inform the Industrial Commission from the Progressive Era to the New Deal.

EXPLAINING THE POLITICAL ORIGINS AND UNEMPLOYMENT INSURANCE IN FIVE STATES

No single variable accounts for the relative timing and various contents of unemployment insurance legislation in the five states. We can, however, point to regular relationships among administrative traditions, characteristics of political parties, and patterns of socioeconomic conflict, on the one hand, and the timing and contents of unemployment insurance laws, on the other. We can also identify an explanatory principle that encompasses Wisconsin's and New York's alternative routes to the strikingly different first and second unemployment insurance laws.

The evidence shows that early and indigenous state initiatives on unemployment insurance in the 1930s required an alliance between reformers or organized labor or both and a cohesive political organization that could engineer a majority in the legislature. Wisconsin and New York had such alliances,

---

106. Robert C. Nesbit, *Wisconsin: A History* (Madison: University of Wisconsin Press, 1973), 487.

107. Ewing, *Job Insurance*, 45–46.

108. Nesbit, *Wisconsin: A History*, 488.

but the partners differed in ways that corresponded to the contents of the pioneering laws passed in Wisconsin in January 1932 and in New York in April 1935.

In Wisconsin the legislative majority for the nation's first unemployment compensation law was engineered by the Wisconsin Industrial Commission, which drew on its long-standing capacities for policy investigation, legislative maneuvering, and interest group bargaining. The commission worked closely with university-based reformers, and the contents of the unprecedented law directly reflected the policy perspective of the labor law administrators themselves and their university allies. Moreover, since the Industrial Commission had no direct presence in the legislature, its measure necessarily avoided provisions that would prompt farmers or organized labor to join business in pressuring legislators to vote against it. The willingness of the Industrial Commission to avoid such provisions allowed the Wisconsin legislation to pass early in the depression, even though political turmoil among the Wisconsin Republicans threatened to unsettle the well-established relations among moderate, non-patronage-oriented Republicans, organized labor, and "constructivist" Socialists. In addition, the relative absence of sharp urban-rural cleavages facilitated the compromises engineered by the Industrial Commission.

In New York, as in the states other than Wisconsin, administrative, intellectual, and political circumstances did not sustain debates on unemployment insurance through the 1920s. Thus the state was not poised to arrive quickly at a consensual proposal when the depression hit. Instead, after a few years of divided policy debates and shifting electoral alignments, a strengthened Democratic party, programmatically allied with organized labor, put the nation's second unemployment insurance law through the state legislature in April 1935. From the Progressive Era onward, New York had a cohesive and disciplined Democratic party, which gained the balance of power over upstate Republicans in the 1930s—just at the time when Democratic patronage politics was giving way to independent reformist governors, when all of New York's urban areas fell into the party's camp, and when the growing New York Federation of Labor unions, spurred by the depression, became willing to demand and draft unemployment insurance proposals. Although the unemployment insurance law put through by the Democratic-labor alliance in New York postdated Wisconsin's, the New York law was also pioneering. Not only did it precede Social Security, its unusually pro-labor content was distinct from the Wisconsin and Ohio plans. This law ignored business preferences altogether by mandating a pooled fund and a high fixed tax on business to generously finance benefits for the unemployed and by including provisions that could help unions sustain strikes.

Massachusetts, Ohio, and Illinois all legislated in the shadow of the federal Social Security Act—although a case could be made for an indigenous initiative in Massachusetts, since Governor Curley sponsored a bill devised during 1933 and 1934. All these states had patronage-oriented Democratic parties that gained ground in tandem with the depression. Yet there were also important differences among them, reflecting the extent of factionalism. The more factionalized the Democratic party, the longer it took to get unemployment insurance through the legislature and the greater the concessions to business when the law was finally passed.

As in New York, the law in Massachusetts was the product of a cohesive Democratic party. Yet the Democrats of Massachusetts did not match the electoral predominance of those of New York and never abandoned patronage methods. Indeed, the Boston-based Governor Curley brought only temporary and partial cohesion to Massachusetts Democrats through the exuberant use of patronage methods. Under Curley, Massachusetts Democrats and organized labor were loosely but not programmatically allied. In the brokered politics of Massachusetts, Curley agreed to tax workers and to allow the eventual administrative application of the merit ratings to adjust business taxes—ideas that made unemployment insurance more palatable to some Massachusetts Republicans and businessmen.

Both Ohio and Illinois had highly factionalized Democratic parties, partly because party divisions cut across rural and urban differences. Traditions of autonomous administration and continuous reform debates at the level of state government were also lacking. Despite the eventual cooperation between organized labor and both state Democratic parties—parties that captured both houses of the legislature and the governor's office during the 1930s—there was no strong political institution upon which to build a coalition. For unemployment insurance, the result was tardy legislation—under the gun of the federal government—and eclectic compromises between the expressed preferences of business and labor, weighted in favor of business.

Ohio generated the nationally prestigious Ohio plan, which failed to pass in 1933. That plan grew out of reform networks in several Ohio cities, some of which had been at the forefront of social and political reform during the Progressive Era. Because of its emphasis on adequate relief for the unemployed, this reformer-fashioned plan eventually won the support of organized labor and some Democratic legislators, but parts of the internally divided Ohio Democratic party remained subject to conservative business and rural interests. Ultimately, an Ohio law more cautious than the original Ohio plan, a law embodying tax provisions favorable to business, passed in December 1936.

Contrary to the standard imagery that has the southern states lagging in the rear of U.S. social policy developments, Illinois was the last state in the nation to pass unemployment insurance, in spite of its high levels of urbanization and industrialization, its fiscally strong labor federation, and its growing Democratic electorate. Favorable as these conditions would seem, Illinois Democrats had so many party factions engaged in such shifting and cut-throat rivalries that organized business or organized labor could veto reforms of all sorts. Because of administrative weaknesses and the bitter internal disputes within the Democratic party, there were neither party leaders, nor reformers tied to state government, nor authoritative state-level administrators who could take the initiative in fashioning and enacting unemployment insurance. Accordingly, Illinois did not enact a law until June 1937, after Social Security taxes were being collected and the Supreme Court had declared the federal law constitutional. At that point the factionalized and patronage-ridden Illinois Democrats brokered a compromise that gave something to labor and even more, through tax breaks, to business. Some Illinois businesses escaped taxes altogether.

CONCLUSION

This research has demonstrated the need to reframe analyses of U.S. social policy to take account of developments in the states. Our findings about Wisconsin and New York demonstrate that it is misleading to assume that the 1935 Social Security Act constituted the starting point of the U.S. welfare state, even for unemployment insurance, a policy area that did not witness any legislative enactments before the 1930s. More important, one's sense of how and why U.S. social policy innovation occurred in the 1930s shifts markedly when these pioneering states are moved to the center of analysis.

Scholars have concluded that the Social Security Act was shaped from the top down by business leaders and groups[109] or by New Deal state managers understood in various ways.[110] Neither organized labor nor political parties have been identified as important shapers of Social Security. But, as we have seen, a programmatic political alliance between organized labor and the Democratic party did shape generous unemployment insurance in New York, and the influence of labor, mediated by Democratic parties, also mattered in Massachusetts, Ohio, and even Illinois. Moreover, in Wisconsin, the 1932 unemployment benefits law grew out of patterns of administrative-led political bargaining established in the Progressive Era. This bargaining included organized labor and its political allies, the Milwaukee Socialists; it also occurred in a partisan context marked by the strong influence of Progressive Republicans. In short, if we examine politics at the state level, we discover that organized labor and political parties (as actors and as organizational structures) played a much more important role in the shaping of American unemployment insurance than nationally focused research reveals. This finding places the U.S. case on the same analytical ground covered in recent studies of other capitalist democracies that attribute social policy outcomes to socioeconomic interests as mediated by state structures and political party systems.[111]

This study also contributes to debates about the effects of U.S. federalism on social policy. Scholars have long understood that the division of sovereignty among levels of American government leaves considerable room for variation in policies; yet the relations of processes operating at the different levels have not always been fully explored or correctly specified. Two ideas about the effects of U.S. federalism that are questioned by this research are,

---

109. Quadagno, "Welfare Capitalism and the Social Security Act of 1935."

110. For two very different accounts emphasizing the role of New Deal state managers, see Skocpol and Ikenberry, "The Political Formation of the American Welfare State in Historical and Comparative Perspective"; Frances Fox Piven and Richard A. Cloward *Regulating the Poor: The Functions of Public Welfare* (New York: Random Housed, 1971).

111. See, for instance, Castles, "The Impact of Parties"; Esping-Andersen, *Politics against Markets*.

first, the belief that conservative influence within U.S. federalism are overwhelmingly attributable to southern exceptionalism and, second, the notion
that states are sites for policy experimentation, laboratories for national policies that later supersede the less viable state policies.

Obviously, U.S. federalism is not simply a means by which conservative
southern influences have been registered in American policy-making. The
five states discussed here were all relatively advanced within the United States
of the 1930s in levels of urbanization and industrialization, yet they include
the full range of timing and contents for unemployment compensation laws.
Moreover, in this policy area, the southern states were not all laggards; indeed, Alabama, Mississippi, and Louisiana passed unemployment insurance
relatively early.[112] Because agricultural workers were everywhere excluded
from the original U.S. unemployment insurance laws, these measures did not
impinge upon the southern agricultural system or race relations. Instead, unemployment insurance affected relations among business, industrial labor, and
each state's political system. And, as the cases of Illinois and Ohio indicate,
disunified, patronage-oriented Democratic parties in states with weak administrative structures and sharp urban-rural and class cleavages could produce
the greatest constraints on the passage and generosity of unemployment insurance.

Even more clearly, this research shows that state-level policy developments
are not adequately understood as mere experiments for future national action. The unemployment insurance policies we examined were deeply rooted
in prolonged political struggles and policy debates specific to each state. The
policies can be understood only through an analysis of state-level variations in
administrative arrangements, relations of experts to government, prior policies, patterns of political party organization, electoral outcomes, and configurations of organized class interests. Moreover, once some states have acted,
national policymakers do not necessarily choose the best of the many state
policies available and then impose that policy on the other states. During the
mid-1930s, versions of the Ohio plan became the most prestigious in the eyes
of the many experts and interest groups who were loosely consulted during
the drafting of the Social Security proposals.[113] Certain Wisconsin ideas, however, originally fashioned in predepression conditions, prevailed over Ohio
ideas as well as post-1932 New York ideas in the fashioning of the Social
Security Act, but even the Wisconsin plan was not imposed on everyone. The
unemployment insurance provisions of the Social Security Act preserved the
prerogatives of all the states to determine taxes and benefits. Moreover, when
the Social Security Board led by Wisconsin's Arthur Altmeyer attempted to
nationalize unemployment insurance in the late 1930s and early 1940s, such

112. See table 3.
113. Although Roosevelt's Committee on Economic Security eventually recommended
the tax-offset plan, which allowed the states to decide the shape of unemployment compensation, the experts on the staff and the Technical Board of the committee were overwhelmingly in favor of the principles embodied in the Ohio plan. See Edwin E. Witte, *The Development of the Social Security Act* (Madison: University of Wisconsin Press, 1962), 111–28.

attempts not only were defeated in Congress but were also fought by the administrators of Wisconsin's peculiar unemployment compensation law.[114]

In short, the timing and variety of state-level policies and policy debates, the matters we have explored in this comparative historical research of five key American states, created important constraints on the vision and capacities of even the best positioned of national policymakers in the United States. Future analytic historical studies of American social policy-making should proceed not only at the national level but also through systematic comparisons across sets of states.

114. For Altmeyer's wartime views on the inadequacy of the federal-state unemployment compensation system, see Arthur J. Altmeyer, "War and Post-War Problems," in Wilber J. Cohen, ed., *War and Post-War Social Security* (Washington, D.C.: American Council on Public Affairs, 1942), 20–30. On the opposition of Wisconsin administrators to national standards in unemployment compensation, see "Statement of Paul A. Rauschenbush," in U.S. Congress, Senate, Committee on Finance, *Hearings on H.R. 6635, 76th Congress, 1st session* (Washington, D.C.: U.S. Government Printing Office, 1939), 209–28.

JOHN MARK HANSEN
University of Chicago

Choosing Sides: The Creation of an Agricultural Policy Network in Congress, 1919–1932

In 1930, Congress passed the Smoot-Hawley Tariff Act, the last of the major tariff bills that redistributed millions of dollars from consumers to domestic manufacturers. The Smoot-Hawley bill, E. E. Schattschneider observed, arose not from a process that was open and attentive to all but from "a free private enterprise in pressure politics which administered itself," a process accessible only to protected industrialists and their congressional and bureaucratic allies. The outlines of public policy, he concluded, mirrored the membership of this "private enterprise": "The nature of public policy is the result of 'effective demands' upon the government."[1]

Schattschneider's characterization rang so true that his "private enterprises" became a centerpiece in the study of American politics. The tight relationships among legislators, administrators, and lobbies—dubbed iron triangles, subgovernments, and issue networks—figure prominently in accounts of Washington activities ranging from agenda setting to legislation to administration. They form the foundation of theories of public policy. According to J. Lieper Freeman, for instance, "the relations among members of a subsystem are basic determinants of the kind of public policy that comes into being." Still other observers also find in policy networks a distinguishing feature of American politics. "What emerges as the most important reality is an array of relatively separated political systems. . . . Taken together," Grant McConnell

I owe many thanks to Brian Balogh, Jeffrey Berry, Robert Browning, Michael D. Cohen, Louis Galambos, Karen Orren, Steven J. Rosenstone, Stephen Skowronek, Jennifer Sosin, Edward R. Tufte, Peter VanDoren, R. Kent Weaver, a reviewer, seminar participants at numerous universities and meetings, and especially David R. Mayhew. I owe thanks, too, to the Brookings Institution for its generous support.

1. E. E. Schattschneider, *Politics, Pressures and the Tariff* (New York: Prentice-Hall, 1935), 30–31, 4.

claimed, "they constitute the characteristic form of power in the United States."[2]

Policy networks, then, are institutions central to our understanding of American politics. We lack, however, a coherent theory of their origins, their causes, and the precise range of their occurrence. Instead of an explicit set of propositions about why these networks come into being in some places and at some times, we have only scattered and generally unsystematic notions about political exchange, about the absence of effective centralized control, and about deeply held beliefs in decentralization and self-government.[3] We point to a dynamic of interest group ascent and political party decline, but we do not really know whether it is a description or a cause of this "characteristic form of power."

This essay specifies the link between the rise of national pressure groups, the decline of political parties, and the development of policy networks. It offers one part of a general theory of network creation, a theory derived from postulates about how goal-oriented legislators react to interest groups and parties in an uncertain environment. In order to explicate this historic shift in congressional allegiances, I leave to another time a parallel investigation of bureaucratic agencies in policy networks. In the first part of this essay I will outline the general conditions under which lawmakers will develop close ties with interest groups at the expense of their established ties with parties and local elites. Policy network relationships, I contend, will develop only (1) when groups serve the electoral, policy, and political intelligence needs of representatives better than parties or other intermediaries, and (2) when members of Congress expect their dealings with particular groups under particular circumstances to recur. From these considerations we can begin to elaborate the specific institutional logic of congressional responses to the rise of interest groups.

The second part of this essay recounts the history of the celebrated agricultural price policy network, exploring the interplay of farm group initiatives and congressional responses in 1920s farm politics. Close relationships be-

2. J. Lieper Freeman, *The Political Process* (New York: Random House, 1965), p. 33; Grant McConnell, *Private Power and American Democracy* (New York: Alfred A. Knopf, 1966), 244, 211; Jack L. Walker, "Setting the Agenda in the U.S. Senate," *British Journal of Political Science* 7 (August 1977) : 423–45; John W. Kingdon, *Agendas, Alternatives, and Public Policies* (Boston: Little, Brown & Co., 1984); Theodore J. Lowi, *The End of Liberalilsm*, 2nd ed. (New York: W. W. Norton & Co., 1979); Douglass Cater, *Power in Washington* (New York: Random House, 1969); Randall A. Ripley and Grace B. Franklin, *Congress, the Bureaucracy and Public Policy* (Homewood, Ill.: Dorsey Press, 1980); Ernest S. Griffith, *Congress* (New York: New York University Press, 1951); Hugh Heclo, "Issue Networks and the Executive Establishment," in Anthony King, ed., *The New American Political System* (Washington: American Enterprise Institute, 1978), 87–124; Lawrence C. Dodd and Richard L. Schott, *Congress and the Administrative State* (New York: John Wiley & Sons, 1979).

3. David B. Truman, *The Governmental Process*, 2nd ed. (New York: Alfred A. Knopf, 1971), 322–40; Dodd and Schott, *Congress*, chap. 2; Freeman, *Political Process*, 1–26; Cater, *Power;* McConnell, *Private Power;* Lowi, *End of Liberalism.* For a good review, see Keith E. Hamm, "Patterns of Influence among Committees, Agencies, and Interest Groups," *Legislative Studies Quarterly* 8 (August 1983) : 379–426.

tween the farm producer groups and midwestern lawmakers arose in the mid-1920s, but only after the farm groups had proven superior to parties in furthering the electoral goals of plains representatives and only after the agricultural economy indicated that midwesterners were going to see a lot more of the issue of price supports. Likewise, close relationships between the farm groups and southern members awaited the realization that the issue of intervention to support southern crops would recur and the recognition that the aid of the farm lobby was indispensable if southern committee leaders were to secure a farm relief policy.

The conclusion, finally, extends the theory to other policy domains and closes with a consideration of the relationship between the party system and the pressure system

A THEORY OF NETWORK FORMATION

Policy networks are close, regular working relationships among congressional committees, executive agencies, and interested groups. They are important to theories of legislation, administration, and policy-making because some policy advocates—those with "access"—are taken more seriously by committees and agencies than others. Advocates with access enjoy consistent serious consideration of their views by formal policymakers. Those lacking access find that conveyance of their positions and information is more often an idle exercise.[4]

Members of Congress grant regular access to interest groups when two conditions prevail: (1) when lobbying organizations enjoy a competitive advantage over other Washington-to-district intermediaries, and (2) when members of Congress expect groups, issues, and circumstances to recur.

These two conditions are a direct result of congressional strategies for dealing with uncertainty. Say that:

1. Legislators for the most part desire reelection.
2. Lawmakers are uncertain about what their constituents think on issues, about how aroused constituents are on issues, about which policies will work for constituents, and about how constituents judge their performance.

4. Truman, *Governmental Process*, chap. 9. Consequently, my definitions, methods, and theoretical approach differ from recent treatments of policy networks as information-passing and -consuming structures. See Edward O. Laumann, David Knoke, and Yong-Hak Kim, "An Organizational Approach to State Policy Formation," *American Sociological Review* 50 (February 1985) : 1–19; David Knoke and Edward O. Laumann, "The Social Organization of National Policy Domains," in Peter V. Marsden and Nan Lin, eds., *Social Structure and Network Analysis* (Beverly Hills: Sage Publications, 1982), 255–315; and Thomas L. Gais, Mark A. Peterson, and Jack L. Walker, "Interest Groups, Iron Triangles and Representative Institutions in American National Government," *British Journal of Political Science* 14 (April 1984) : 161–85. The theory draws heavily on the economics literature on agency problems. For good introductions, see Terry M. Moe, "The New Economics of Information," *American Journal of Political Science* 28 (November 1984) : 739–77; and Oliver E. Williamson, *Markets and Hierarchies* (New York: Free Press, 1975), chap. 2.

3. Some outsiders—for example, parties, interest groups, local elites—offer to reduce uncertainty by guiding representatives' decisions. They give lawmakers information about constituent preferences and perceptions, provide technical assistance on policy questions, and help shape constituent evaluations to the advantage of cooperative members.
4. The reliability of intermediaries is not known to representatives without cost.
5. Lawmakers adopt strategies for dealing with uncertainty that work and discard those that do not. Representatives whose strategies are unsatisfactory either fail to be reelected or learn from their own close scrapes and the travails of colleagues who have chosen a similar course.

A policy network relationship—that is, a close consultative tie between members and lobbies—is one strategy for dealing with uncertainty. It is a policy of reliance on interest groups for advice and assistance. This dependence on interest group cues naturally limits how responsive lawmakers can be to the demands of others, like parties and local elites. Consequently, close ties between legislators and lobbies await the fulfillment of the two conditions listed above. Representatives need, first, an indication that interest groups can serve their information and propaganda needs better than other intermediaries or a set of intermediaries that does not include interest groups; that is, they need evidence of lobbies' competitive advantage. Second, legislators need an indication that group advantage is sustainable, that is, that the group, the issues and the circumstances will recur. Let us consider both in greater detail.

Competitive Advantage

For legislators to prefer consultation with lobbying groups to consultation with other intermediaries, interest groups must be able to offer greater advantages at lower cost. This is not an astonishing point, of course. As many others have noted, policy networks are based on mutual assistance. Interest groups provide technical information on policy questions. They supply political intelligence on the receptivity of constituents and policy elites to different policy options. And they propagandize to create better images for their friends.

But interest groups have no monopoly on these resources. Nearly every political organization in Washington offers "advantages" to legislators who pay them heed. Members of Congress, naturally enough, would rather not choose between intermediaries, and in most cases they need not. But frequently they receive conflicting advice from interest groups, parties, and local elites. In this sense, then, interest groups are in competition with other intermediaries, and lawmakers must ask when interest groups are the better go-between.

Interest groups are superior intermediaries when they can perform the role of intermediary at lower cost and when interest group ties work "better" than party ties in furthering legislators' electoral and policy aims.

Minimizing Costs. One intermediary has an advantage over others if it can minimize the costs to legislators of gathering information about the preferences and passions of their constituents and propagating accounts of their loyalty and effectiveness.[5] The direct costs of creating these communications links vary widely. Whatever their governmental structure, formal organizations like parties and pressure groups already have centralized lines of communication. Moreover, interest groups, unlike parties and district loyalists, are highly specialized. The most salient common concerns of group members are easily discerned from the group's purpose. Thus, by employing interest groups as go-betweens members of Congress gain nearly costless access to targetable publics within their constituencies.

In contrast, reliance on local elites (or the local press) for gathering and disseminating political information, once a common practice, is inordinately expensive. Legislators must build local contacts at their own expense, either by inheriting them from mentors after long apprenticeships or by spending years in tedious positions (like county courts and prosecutors' offices) that present opportunities for meeting local elites. Once in Washington, lawmakers must bear the cost of keeping in touch with a diffuse, decentralized crowd. Finally, local elites are seldom united on any single purpose, necessitating a legislator's having to pay close attention to a catalog of special interests and quirks. Interest group intermediaries promise much less bother.

Finally, interest groups are more likely to enjoy a competitive advantage by minimizing costs when they are extensive, both within districts and between districts and Washington. An organization that is extensive within a district promises greater return for any given expenditure of members' resources. An organization that is extensive between the capital and the constituency promises lower up-front costs of intelligence and propaganda.

In sum, lobbying groups perform the role of intermediary at lower cost when they are formally organized, specialized, and extensive. Lobbies need do no more than make their already-established communications networks available to cooperative lawmakers. Groups give politicians an efficient means to come in contact with people who may, depending on the legislators' acumen, be useful to them in furthering their political ambitions.

Promoting Goals. Some intermediaries—party organizations come to mind—can do more for representatives, however, than act merely as conduits for intelligence and propaganda. They can mobilize voters and Washington elites. Thus, in order for interest groups to enjoy competitive advantage over intermediaries with resources in the district and in Washington, ties to lobbying groups must work better in furthering the reelection or policy aims of members of Congress. How do lawmakers (and researchers) know when pressure groups do better in promoting their goals? Mostly they learn by experience.

Lobbies promote the policy goals of members more effectively than parties when groups can build coalitions where parties cannot. The attractiveness of interest group aid in brokering policy alliances depends first on its strategic usefulness. Groups that control blocs of committee votes are more important

5. Cf. Michael C. Jensen, "Organization Theory and Methodology," *Accounting Review* 58 (April 1983) : 319–39.

to senior committee members than to junior members and are more important to majority party members than minority members. Senior majority
members simply have greater strategic use for the group's services, since they
are responsible for obtaining policy. Second, the ability of a lobbying group
to further policy goals depends on its prior claim on the loyalties of a set of
committee members. Committee leaders need some basis for believing that
the group can indeed deliver, a reason easily deduced if a group has visibly
aided the election efforts of other committee members.

In furthering representatives' electoral goals, groups can provide direct
electoral assistance in the form of money, personnel, and exposure. Perhaps
more important, they can provide identifiable constituencies that dissuade
challenges to incumbents if they declare themselves satisfied and encourage
opposition if they proclaim themselves disaffected. The importance of group
favor is greatest when close associations with political parties become uncom-
fortable—when the economy is sluggish, when the top of the ticket is unpopular, when the policies championed by the party are irksome to constituents.
When this happens, politicians seeking reelection deemphasize party affiliations and stress interest affiliations, substituting new, less controversial lines
of cleavage for old, controversial ones.[6]

Thus, testing new alliances with interest groups is encouraged when there
are negative party images from which lawmakers wish to dissociate themselves
and when group constituencies cut across party cleavages. The success of this
strategy, of course, hinges on the ability of lawmakers to substitute group
support for party associations without antagonizing other important interests.
It makes sense in districts where interests are either homogeneous or not
conflictual. In heterogeneous districts with antagonistic interests, legislators
tread more lightly and may cautiously prefer to maintain party ties. On the
other hand, if the group is inclusive of the heterogeneous elements, alliances
with lobbies lose none of their luster; legislators can rely on group leaders to
achieve consensus for them.

Whether alliances with groups hold depends finally on whether elections
bear expectations out. Politicians read elections like soothsayers read cards,
and the verity of their interpretations is not nearly as important as their belief
in them. If members of Congress become convinced that party regularity has
failed to help them, they are more likely to turn to other sources of support.
If they think that close ties to interest groups aided them or helped colleagues
in similar circumstances, they will begin to favor group ties over party ties.

Summary. In sum, interest groups enjoy competitive advantage over other intermediaries:

6. Close association with lobbying groups is not only a means of transcending interparty
competition, however. In times when parties are riven by faction, developing bases of support independent of parties and ideologies is an obvious survival tactic. See Gary C. Jacobson
and Samuel Kernell, *Strategy and Choice in Congressional Elections*, 2nd ed. (New Haven: Yale
University Press, 1983); E. E. Schattschneider, *The Semi-sovereign People* (New York: Dryden
Press, 1960).

1. When interest groups perform the role of intermediary at lower cost: Groups that are organized, specialized, and extensive reduce the cost to legislators of political intelligence and propaganda.
2. When group ties work better in promoting the policy or reelection goals of members of Congress: Groups that can deliver blocs of votes advance the policy goals of committee leadership more effectively than a party. Groups whose constituencies cross ideological boundaries allow lawmakers to transcend inter- and intraparty competition. Thus, close relationships with lobbies are encouraged by elections interpreted as endorsements of group viewpoints instead of party regularity.

If these conditions obtain, representatives can mitigate uncertainty about the preferences of their constituents and gain a greater measure of control over their destinies by consulting interest groups rather than other intermediaries. But competitive advantage is useful to lawmakers only if it will carry over into the future. Reliance on interest groups for advice and assistance depends, too, on whether groups, issues, and circumstances recur.

Recurrence

Accommodating political interests can be a dangerous business. Legislators cannot always take care of all interests whose blessings they might want, but lawmakers who refuse to cooperate risk retribution either at the polls or when coalitions are built. Attention to interest group cues requires that representatives anticipate dealings with a group to recur on similar issues and under similar circumstances.

Because a good turn for one intermediary might cost members of Congress the amity of others, members want to be sure their favor will be and can be reciprocated. Legislators who look to groups for electoral assistance, for instance, are strategically disadvantaged: they make policy decisions in advance of their bids for reelection. The value of the district information and propaganda that go-betweens provide is uncertain at the time representatives make up their minds. If lawmakers and lobbies know they will meet again, however, legislators can potentially retaliate for a group's negligent performance. The incentive to act in good faith provided by recurrent dealings protects lawmakers from exploitation of their strategic handicap.[7]

If consultative relationships with groups are to come about, then, lawmakers must anticipate the durability of the groups they deal with. Establishing a formal organization with offices in Washington is one important way a group indicates its durability to representatives. Less obviously, legislators must expect issues and circumstances to persist. When representatives encounter an issue they learn how reliably the lobby informs them about their constituents' perceptions and wants, how important the issue is to the lobby and how im-

---

7. Robert Axelrod, *The Evolution of Cooperation* (New York: Basic Books, 1984), 126–32. Thus, the development of policy networks was closely related to the devolution of authority from congressional leadership to committees. Before the creation of a jurisdictional committee system with seniority rights to seats, the possibilities for group and issue recurrence, and by implication for close relationships between legislators and groups, were remote.

portant the issue is to others. To the degree that the problem can be expected to recur—either because of systemic factors, like reauthorizations, or because of exogenous factors, like the economy—legislators can predict how dependably the lobby will inform them and how committed the lobby and others will be.[8]

If recurrence cannot be expected, lawmakers cannot judge a group's future commitment and future ability. New circumstances might cause the group to lose interest in a policy it had been pushing intently; new issues might inspire it less. New situations might give a lobby less stake in legislators' reelections, leaving them vulnerable to retaliation from those whose advice they had ignored. More important, a group might not be able to influence and mobilize its members as effectively if the problem changes too radically. New circumstances might make old issues less salient to constituents. The group's word might be less authoritative on new questions. If issues and situations seem unlikely to recur, then, legislators cannot be sure a lobby will maintain its superiority into the future, when they need it.

Committee leaders who look to pressure groups for aid in building coalitions are not subject to such acute strategic disadvantages, of course. The value of the lobby's assistance is obvious immediately. Still, recurrent groups, issues, and circumstances heighten the incentives for leaders to rely on interest groups, and, to the degree that the situation repeats itself, the lobby will be as important to a leader's success in the future as it is now. Accommodating an interest group, even if it alienates others, becomes an investment in its future goodwill.

Summary. Before members of Congress will adopt as a policy reliance on interest groups for advice and assistance, they must be sure they will continue to need lobbies and lobbies will continue to need them; otherwise accommodation of group interests exposes members to risks of future retaliation from others. Recurrence of groups ensures that legislators and lobbies will meet again. Recurrence of issues and circumstances ensures that groups will and can come through for representatives when they need the help in the future.

Conclusion

Two circumstances must prevail before close relationships between lawmakers and pressure groups come about: competitive advantage of lobbies over other intermediaries and recurrence of groups, issues, and circumstances. When these conditions hold, representatives will have minimized uncertainty about their reelection and the reliability of those they depend on for reelection. Not only does this view stress the contingency of network formation on political interpretation; it also helps to illuminate the relationship between the strategic calculations of institutional elites and pressure politics.

8. Williamson, *Markets*, 9, 28, 39–40; Oliver E. Williamson, "The Economics of Organization," *American Journal of Sociology* 87 (1981) : 548–77; Michael T. Hannan and John Freeman, "The Population Ecology of Organizations," *American Journal of Sociology* 82 (1977) : 949–64.

After a brief explication of my methods, I put the theory up against the history of the agricultural price support policy network. The congressional-group interactions that arose around farm price policy in the 1920s are uniformly cited as a paradigm case of policy networking. "Farm policy," according to Ripley and Franklin, "has long been synonymous with the presence and dominance of subgovernments."[9] The origin of this exemplary policy network, then, is a particularly instructive test case. What is more, the farm price policy network is a particularly stringent test of the choice theory. This network did not arise because no one really cared outside of those most affected. As we will see, the agricultural pricing network arose despite the continued and widespread contentiousness of the issue.

In broad outline, the analysis goes as follows. The competitive advantage of the farm lobbies over parties and local elites in the Midwest was ambiguous until about 1926, despite the creation of the farm bloc in 1921, despite agrarian unrest in the 1922 elections, and despite the advent in 1923 of a well-orchestrated pressure campaign for the McNary-Haugen subsidy bill. The 1924 elections, however, signaled that identification with either faction of the Republican party was quite dangerous, and the 1926 elections were a stunning victory for the farm lobbies. By 1926 the competitive advantage of organized agriculture in the Midwest was established.

Expectations of issue recurrence originated about the same time. Although a severe depression put the issue of price supports on the agenda in 1921, the downturn was seen as temporary. There was, after all, a long history of such sporadic outbursts from farmers and no clear indication that this was not simply more of the same. In 1926, however, agricultural prices again collapsed after a short rally, and midwestern representatives began to perceive the crisis and the organizational demand for price supports as something durable. With both conditions satisfied in the mid-1920s, midwestern Agriculture Committee members strengthened their ties with the agricultural lobbies.

Southern members followed suit only five years later. Cotton and tobacco prices were strong until 1926, and when the collapse came it too was seen as temporary. In the early 1930s, though, prices fell to historic lows, and the conclusion was inescapable that the organized demand for price supports for southern crops was not going to go away. The farm groups never proved their competitive advantage in elections, since the southern Democrats were not as faction-ridden as midwestern Republicans and the southern farm organizations were weaker. Instead, in 1931, when Democrats assumed control of Congress, the sizable bloc of committee midwesterners the farm groups did control suddenly became a vital strategic resource for the new leadership. The discovery of the competitive advantage of the farm groups in promoting southern leadership goals, coupled with expectations of recurrence, led southern lawmakers to join midwesterners in the agricultural price policy network.

9. Ripley and Franklin, *Congress*, p. 94; McConnell, *Private Power*, chap. 7; Lowi, *End of Liberalism*, chap. 4; Theodore J. Lowi, "How the Farmers Get What They Want," *Reporter*, 21 May 1964, 34–37.

STUDYING NETWORK FORMATION

Although observers have spoken of policy networks with great confidence networks have proven elusive empirically. Most often, they have been identified by their consequences—certain types of policies are produced by certain types of networks. An explanatory theory of public policy, however, should not do double duty as a theory of measurement. Consequently, I start by identifying policy networks as institutions, as sets of relationships, and try to specify the key dimensions of those relationships.

What matters about policy networks is their form, which can be described in terms of three variables: structure, character, and constraints. Network structure is distinguished by *who* takes part in communications about legislation, the *who* being thought of as a descriptive noun, not a proper name. The actors in policy networks include both formal actors—congressional committees and the executive agencies they oversee—and "outsiders"—legislative and executive superordinates and peers, parties, interest groups, and promoters of causes. Network character refers to the status of outside actors within the network structure; it describes which actors have "access." [10] The interests and viewpoints of some outsiders are considered legitimate by formal actors and are given respectful hearings. Representatives of other viewpoints, seen as less legitimate, are excoriated or simply ignored. Finally, policy networks are characterized by the constraints network participants think they face. The barriers to network action might be internal or external: the primary worry of participants might be securing agreement among themselves, or it might be keeping those who are already outside excluded.

I gauge the nature of congressional-group interactions in the 1920s by monitoring the exchanges between lawmakers and groups, mostly in the hearings conducted by the House Committee on Agriculture on the major omnibus price support legislation in the post–World War I era. The hearings are the only *consistent* documentation of the nature of congressional-group interactions. By now, few could give an insider's report, and the infrequent personal papers of committee members are not, judging by the collections I have seen, overly illuminating.

This method makes use of one of the early discoveries of political science—that hearings often are less a forum for gathering information than a ritual for legitimizing decisions. Hearings are in part a stage show, and lawmakers are keenly aware of their role as actors. Legislators curry favor of the people important to them; they go through the motions of interest when witnesses can safely be ignored; and they beat up, so to speak, on the people they are expected to beat up on.

Again, that they behave in this way should come as no surprise to an academic audience. Schattschneider noted in 1930 that "the questions asked [during hearings on the Smoot-Hawley tariff bill] were remarkably tender to the sensibilities of protected interests." Neither would it surprise those who have spent time in a witness chair. To illustrate, in 1965 lobbyist Reuben Johnson told a House panel that "we in the Farmers Union feel like we are a part

10. Truman, *Governmental Process*, chap. 9.

of the Government. We feel very kindly toward this committee because we feel welcome here. You always listen to our comments, even though you may not act on them." Others are not so fortunate. For example, Benjamin Marsh, head of the People's Lobby, a left-leaning prototype of the public interest groups, grumbled that "I appeared frequently at committee hearings . . . but could merely make the record."[11] Because lawmakers are on display at hearings, their reactions to witnesses yield important clues about their relationships with those groups.

In examining the hearings, then, I looked for evidence of three developments. First, if network structure changes, then the cast appearing before the committee should change. New interests should be represented for the first time or should be represented in greater number. Second, if network character changes, then the nature or number of policy views accorded serious consideration should change. The behavior of legislators toward particular types of witnesses should move from contentiousness to attentiveness to solicitousness, and from no interest to interest in information to interest in general policy views. Finally, if constraints on policy networks change, then members' perceptions of the nature and degree of the threats to network autonomy should change.

Once I have sketched a portrait of legislator-group relations, I turn to an examination of evidence bearing on the two conditions identified above. In particular, I look for indications of two things: (1) a realization on the part of legislators that groups enjoy competitive advantage (elite interpretations of elections are especially important in this regard); and (2) the nature of the agenda—whether lawmakers consider their dealings with lobbyists as being temporary or recurrent.

My focus in the pages to come is on what happened in the House Agriculture Committee rather than on what happened in Congress. Readers who wish to gain an appreciation of events in the broader legislative context are referred to a number of fine treatments by historians, economists, and political scientists.[12] My concern here is not legislative coalitions, which are related but larger and usually more ephemeral. It is policy networks.

THE CREATION OF THE AGRICULTURAL PRICE POLICY NETWORK

By the end of World War I, what seemed to be the political potential of farmers had come to naught. Numerical strength, overrepresentation in Congress, and a succession of farmer parties had brought few tangible benefits to agri-

11. Schattschneider, *Tariff*, p. 39; *Hearings before the House Committee on Agriculture*, "Wheat and Feed Grains," 89th Congress, 1st sess., 1965, 1136; Benjamin C. Marsh, *Lobbyist for the People* (Washington: Public Affairs Press, 1953), 166.

12. Murray R. Benedict, *Farm Policies of the United States, 1790–1950* (New York: Twentieth Century Fund, 1953); Gilbert C. Fite, *George N. Peek and the Fight for Farm Parity* (Norman: University of Oklahoma Press, 1954); Alice M. Christensen, "Agricultural Pressure and Governmental Response in the United States, 1919–1929" (Ph.D. diss., University of California at Berkeley, 1936); James H. Shideler, *Farm Crisis, 1919–1923* (Berkeley and Los Angeles: University of California Press, 1957); Grant C. McConnell, *The Decline of Agrarian Democracy* (Berkeley and Los Angeles: University of California Press, 1953).

culturalists, especially compared to tariff-protected manufacturers. In the 1920s, however, that situation began to change. By the end of the decade, a Congress that had periodically rebuffed agrarian demands for direct intervention in the agricultural marketplace approved price-fixing measures twice. Not coincidentally, it was also in the 1920s that the current structure in agricultural policy-making began to take shape. Lawmakers began to establish close ties with farm lobbying groups. As Blaisdell put it in 1940, "Congress in recent years has become more and more solicitous of farmer opinion."[13]

In more than one respect, this chronology is not surprising. On the congressional side, a jurisdictional committee system built upon seniority was firmly in place, the House leadership had been weakened, and party organization was hamstrung by restrictions on patronage. As a result, the battle for congressional loyalties was met on terms more favorable to interest groups than ever before. Things had changed in the field of interest organizations as well. With the Great War came a permanent farm group presence in Washington. The Populist fiasco had convinced farm leaders of the futility of partisan politics, and War War I price controls underscored the need for a voice in the Capital. By 1920, four general farm organizations had opened offices there: the Farmers National Council, the National Board of Farm Organizations, the National Grange of Patrons of Husbandry, and the American Farm Bureau Federation. Of the two now defunct, the first, the Farmers National Council, was a federation of several regional farm groups and the remnants of the "progressive Grange" movement, six state Granges disenchanted by the Patron's political timidity. Because of the council's history, its designation as Washington spokesman for the National Nonpartisan League (NPL), and its leader's passion for the single tax, the council had a Washington reputation for radicalism.[14] The National Board of Farm Organizations was a more ambitious alliance. Its sponsor and patron was the National Farmers Union, whose president, Charles S. Barrett, dreamed of forging "an AFL of agriculture." The board was formed in 1917 by the Farmers Union, the National Milk Producers Federation and a half dozen minor groups. The Grange, although recruited vigorously, declined to join but maintained close contacts. In the end, however, the board functioned mostly as the lobbying arm of the Farmers Union and Milk Producers.[15]

The establishment of offices in the Capital was an important step in the

13. Donald C. Blaisdell, *Government and Agriculture* (New York: Farrar & Rinehart, 1940), 36; McConnell, *Agrarian Democracy*, chaps. 1–7. Cf. James T. Bonnen, "Observations on the Nature of National Agricultural Policy Decision Processes, 1946–76," in Trudy Huskamp Peterson, *Farmers, Bureaucrats, and Middlemen* (Washington: Howard University Press, 1980), 309–27.

14. Christensen, "Agricultural Pressure," pp. 13–15; J. Clyde Marquis, "The Radical Minority," *Country Gentlemen* (hereafter *CG*), 24 April 1920, 26; McConnell, *Agrarian Democracy*, chaps. 1–6.

15. Shideler, *Farm Crisis*, p. 24; Commodore B. Fisher, *The Farmers' Union* (Lexington: University of Kentucky Press, 1920); Edward Wiest, *Agricultural Organization in the United States* (Lexington: University of Kentucky Press, 1923); James L. Guth, "The National Board of Farm Organizations," *Agricultural History* 48 (July 1974), 418–40.

development of congressional-group relations. Before 1917, lawmakers seeking to target appeals to farmers faced a bewilderingly large number of organizations they might contact, including, at least on paper, 559 in Illinois, 449 in California, 93 in North Dakota, and 2,203 in New York.[16] Establishing ties with farm groups was hardly more efficient than building a network of local contacts. But with the largest of the farm groups now based in Washington, a clear and more accessible channel for congressional communications was close at hand.

From the standpoint of the groups, permanent offices were an important step as well. Prior to 1917, farm lobbying in Washington occurred only when a crying need arose and group leaders could tear themselves away from their farms. After 1878, for example, "the legislative task [of the Grange] was effectively promoted through the work of an annually-created legislative committee of the National Grange (usually the executive committee)." The committee, according to member T. C. Atkeson, "made a close study of all the bills which dealt with agricultural questions . . . [and] kept in touch with Congress through personal friends in Washington. . . . When any matters in which the farmers were interested were pending before congressional committees, they arranged for a date when we could be heard. Then the members of the committee would go to Washington." A permanent legislative director in Washington made better monitoring possible, with corresponding benefit to group members and leaders. Commented one observer, "National legislation is to the average agricultural citizen something afar off. . . . Hence, he relies for his information upon organizations like the Grange, the Farm Bureau, and similar bodies with representatives at Washington and to a degree acts on their advice."[17]

The Grange, however, was not the organization to make the most of its opportunity. The move to Washington in 1919 did not cause Atkeson, its legislative director, to become any more aggressive, and the "lobby acted as a mere clearing house of information and not as a pressure on Congress." In fact, Atkeson had little freedom to be more militant. The Grange's decision to locate in Washington had been a matter of contention for years, and the argument that finally prevailed over those who felt its mission was mostly social was that an office was needed to keep "unauthorized persons"—probably the progressive Granges—from besmirching its name.[18] Further, the Grange lacked a broad geographical base; its membership was concentrated in the Northeast and Ohio. The Farmers Union, although more insistent politically, was, on the other hand, confined in its membership to the Great Plains.

The American Farm Bureau Federation, gathered in 1919 into a group

16. J. Clyde Marquis, "Farmers Can Have What They Want," *CG*, 1 November 1919, 9.

17. Charles M. Gardner, *The Grange* (Washington: National Grange, 1949), 93; T. C. Atkeson, "Pioneering in Agriculture," *CG*, 14 February 1925, 49; Charles Moreau Harger, "Mr. Farmer Considers His 'Bloc,'" *Independent*, 24 June 1922, 541.

18. William G. Carleton, "Gray Silver and the Rise of the Farm Bureau," *Current History* 28 (June 1955) : 343; T. C. Atkeson, "Pioneering in Agriculture," *CG*, 21 February 1925, 12; "The Grange on Politics," *Hoard's Dairyman*, 6 August 1920, 92.

317,000 strong, faced none of these problems. Its membership, although concentrated in the Corn Belt, was national in scope, and its rapid growth in a period marked by little upheaval lent it stability and inclined it toward conservatism. The Farm Bureau was also politically bold. When a 1920 bill to retool the Muscle Shoals dam for production of fertilizer lost on a voice vote, for instance, the bureau asked representatives to report how they had voted to federation lobbyist Gray Silver. That impertinence caused Silver and President James R. Howard to be called before the House Banking and Currency Committee, where a litany of Farm Bureau crimes was recited to them. One consequence of this uproar was a change in federation tactics. "What will take the place of the lobby?" a *Country Gentleman* reporter asked prophetically. "Contact with the member of Congress through his own people—his constituents. . . . The Washington representative can act as a go-between on occasion. The Farm Bureau Federation has the means to establish this line of communication between Washington and the people at home."[19]

Although Silver's methods seem commonplace today, in 1921 they were an innovation. There were interest groups at the time with lots of money but few members and others with members but no money. The Farm Bureau was one of the few with both, and Silver put them to good use. As J. R. Howard's son put it:

> The technique for exerting political pressure from the grass roots might have been devised earlier . . . but credit for perfecting it goes to [Gray Silver]. At his disposal were district-by-district tabulations of responses to public sentiment polls taken by county farm bureaus at the request of the headquarters in Chicago. . . . If a congressman seemed to be wavering in advance of an important roll call or if someone had the temerity to challenge the Farm Bureau's position, Silver did not hesitate to show him the poll results. In an emergency, he would telegraph directly to state and county offices and know that a flood of wires would pour into his office as evidence that the grass roots were informed and aroused.[20]

The Farm Bureau's pressure was not always as blatant as this implies. The efficiency of its political intelligence and propaganda was impressive enough. In 1921, the federation held hearings in counties throughout the farm belt and presented the transcripts to the Joint Commission of Agricultural Inquiry. The hearings were marvelous in their extent and detail. "To one acquainted with agricultural conditions," a reporter wrote, "much of the matter contains nothing new. But as human interest documents these county hearings are unique."[21] The constituency resources at the AFBF's disposal were remarkable and unprecedented among agricultural interest groups.

19. J. Clyde Marquis, "The Farm Bureau's Mistake," *CG*, 7 May 1921, 15; *Hearings before the House Committee on Banking and Currency*, "Farm Organizations," 66th Congress, 3rd sess., 1921; Robert P. Howard, *James R. Howard and the Farm Bureau* (Ames: Iowa State University Press, 1983), 136ff.

20. Howard, *James R. Howard*, p. 131; William Johnson, "Charting the Federation's Course," *CG*, 24 July 1920, 15.

21. Harry R. O'Brien, "The Farmers' Woes," *Saturday Evening Post*, 22 October 1921, 21.

With the farm groups' move to Washington, then, the stage was set. On one hand, political parties were weakened by decades of reform. On the other, the farm groups had forged links from the Capital to constituencies, channels that lawmakers might use to gather information and distribute propaganda. As the wealthiest, the most widely deployed and politically the most committed of the farm groups, the Farm Bureau was the clear kingpin. But to leave it at this is to assume that a pivotal change in the relationships of legislators, lobbies, and parties followed simply and directly from the fact of the Farm Bureau's organization. Rather, before the farm lobbies could claim the hearts and minds of rural lawmakers, members of Congress had to see how they stacked up against parties in meeting electoral and policy needs. Legislators had to be convinced that they would encounter a particular complex of conditions, issues, and organizations again and again. It was this extended process of comparison and forecast that ultimately brought forth a new policy network.

Prologue: The Farm Bloc

According to many observers, the new, aggressive Farm Bureau was the impetus behind the organization of the farm bloc, an institution that bore a striking outward resemblance to a policy network. Formalized at a May 1921 meeting of nine senators in Silver's office, and chaired by Iowa senator William S. Kenyon, the Senate bloc claimed up to thirty members. Its counterpart in the House, led by Iowa's Lester J. Dickinson, was less well organized, and although some accounts put its membership at a hundred or more, the only extant rosters, including J. R. Howard's, list only twenty-eight.[22]

The bloc did little until late June 1921, when Senate leaders tried to adjourn until the House passed a tariff bill. None of the twelve measures the bloc deemed important had been acted upon, and the tariff bill would have taken precedence once the Senate reconvened. Silver, forewarned, wired local bureaus, and enough protest telegrams came in to defeat the motion. After a second aborted try at adjournment, President Harding and the Republican leadership cut a deal with the agrarians—the bloc agreed to adjourn after six pending agricultural bills were passed. The most important of these regulated the packers and the grain exchanges and extended the authority of the War Finance Corporation to make agricultural loans. The compromise got extensive coverage in the press. The farm bloc became "the most effective organized force in Congress." "Party leaders and the President himself do not venture a move without consulting it."[23]

22. Moreover, the House bloc had on its rolls only four of the twenty-one members of the Agriculture Committee (plus two future members), none of them senior. The Senate bloc, however, constituted a majority of the Senate committee. See "Howard Explains Agricultural Bloc," *American Farm Bureau Federation Weekly News Letter*, 5 January 1922, 1; "The Agricultural Bloc," *Agricultural Review*, January 1922, 11; Christensen, "Agricultural Pressure," 62; and Orville M. Kile, *The Farm Bureau through Three Decades* (Baltimore: Waverly Press, 1948), 101n.

23. John K. Barnes, "The Man Who Runs the Farm Bloc," *World's Work*, November 1922, 52; Theodore M. Knappen, "Farmers in the Saddle," *Independent*, 12 November 1921, 151.

The farm bloc's successful defiance of party leadership was a dramatic indication of what rural lawmakers and the farm groups could achieve through
joint action, and the lesson was not lost on them. For the rest of the decade,
re-creation of the farm bloc would be the farm groups' holy grail. But although the Farm Bureau was eager to tell the farm bloc story in the most
flattering terms possible—later news accounts give Silver a much more prominent role than earlier ones—farm state representatives were reluctant to push
things too far. The coalition, after all, had won only a single battle—the adjournment vote—over an opposition taken by surprise, and the passage of the
agricultural legislation was backed by GOP leadership as part of the deal.[24]

Without any evidence that the Farm Bureau could protect them, rural representatives did not want to invite retaliation from party leaders. Accordingly,
the senators and representatives involved, while keen to take credit, went to
great pains to minimize the coalition's significance. For example, Senator Arthur Capper of Kansas, described as "the one man in Congress physically able
to keep both of his ears on the ground," denied that the bloc had defied the
parties. "We simply try," the senator said, "like a big steering committee, to
get cooperation in support of measures of common interest, nobody breaking
from his political associations." Thus, the bloc took no position on the tariff,
being careful not to jeopardize its members' standing in their parties. Minnesota congressman Sydney Anderson echoed Capper's assessment. "The thing
was too loosely organized and informal for such purposes [as disrupting party
leadership]. In fact, its own members didn't consider it a definite organization
of any sort." Bloc members compared themselves to the irrigation bloc, the
ex-servicemen's bloc, and the vaunted "baby" congressmen's (freshmen) bloc.[25]

The farm bloc continued operations into the second session of the Sixty-
seventh Congress, but now under Capper's leadership—Harding had appointed Kenyon to the federal bench—it became mostly a discussion group.
It consulted with all the major farm groups, except perhaps the Farmers National Council, and over the two years of its existence it heard from speakers
ranging from Agriculture secretary Henry C. Wallace to Thomas Edison, who,
as it turns out, had his own farm plan. After its dramatic victory in 1921, the
bloc accomplished nothing more, and in the Sixty-eighth Congress no one
even attempted to reorganize it.[26]

The farm bloc, then, was the first indication that the farm groups might be
useful to agrarian legislators in pursuing their policy agendas independent of
the parties. But from the congressional standpoint, there were good reasons
lawmakers did not try to maintain their momentary freedom from the parties.
As yet, one condition for network formation, competitive advantage, was met

24. "The Farmer's Party in Congress," *Literary Digest*, 2 July 1921, 14; Alastair Montgomery, "Ferreted Facts for Farmers," *Successful Farming*, July 1921, 8.

25. Stuart O. Blythe, "Progress in Congress," *CG*, March 1926, 17; Judson C. Welliver,
"The Agricultural Crisis and the 'Bloc,'" *American Review of Reviews*, February 1922, 165;
Sydney Anderson, "The Latest Thing in Blocs," *CG*, 31 December 1921, 1; Barnes, "The
Man Who Runs the Farm Bloc," p. 59; Arthur Capper, *The Agricultural Bloc* (New York:
Harcourt Brace & Co., 1922), 117; "The Farm Bloc," *Literary Digest*, 24 December 1921, 11.

26. Shideler, *Farm Crisis*, 178–79; Capper, *Agricultural Bloc*, 146.

only ambiguously, and the second, recurrence, was not met at all. Considering these in reverse order, it was not expected by representatives that farm bloc issues would keep coming up. After the major items on the farm bloc's agenda— regulation of packers, grain exchanges, milk distributors, and so forth—had been passed, "the fighting strength of the group necessarily decreased," and only six months after its great victory, the farm bloc ran out of things to do. "Both Democratic and Republican Senators who are bloc members said today that there was at present little legislative business which seemed to require the attention of the bloc," the *New York Times* reported. "Some Republicans believe that some of the strictly 'bloc measures' already have been translated into legislation."[27]

Expectations that farm bloc issues would not recur also resulted from sanguine appraisals of the farm economy. Nearly everyone thought that the agricultural crisis that gave rise to both the agrarian agitation and the bloc, although severe, would be short-lived. In 1921 legislators had had every reason to be attentive to farmer opinion. Just after the Armistice, the bottom fell out of the grain markets. Wheat prices cascaded from a high of $2.16 a bushel in 1919 to $1.03 in 1921, and corn plunged from $1.51 to 52 cents. Over half a million people left farms in 1921, followed by another million in 1922 and 800,000 in 1923. Farm depressions, although dangerous politically, were nothing new, however. Rural discontent spurred by violent price swings and bank panics in the 1870s and late 1880s had surged and subsided quickly. Thus, the *Times* was inclined to take the bloc lightly. "It will pass with the depression from which it sprang," the editors forecast, "like the Wheel, the Brothers of Freedom, the Society of Equity, the Farmers Alliance, the Greenbackers and other shadows."[28]

Unsympathetic urban newspaper editors were not the only ones who saw the crisis as fleeting. Before 1925, the depression was widely viewed as the consequence, in Secretary Wallace's words, of "this period of world readjustment" after the war. Wallace had no doubt that "gradually farm prices will be brought into fair relation with other prices," and he and his administration rival, Commerce secretary Herbert Hoover, both predicted future shortages rather than surpluses. The worst was over by 1923, many thought. Senator Capper, for example, asserted that "the pendulum has apparently reached the limit of its swing to the losing side and is coming back," and another observer found a "phenomenal rise in agricultural prices likely."[29]

To summarize, in the early 1920s there was no hint that agricultural relief

27. McConnell, *Agrarian Democracy*, 58; "Farm Bloc Stays," *New York Times* (hereafter *NYT*), 17 February 1922, 28; "Congress and the Farmer," *Wallaces' Farmer* (hereafter *WF*), 2 September 1921, 1110.

28. "The Farm Bloc," *Literary Digest*, 10.

29. "The Farmer and His Troubles," *Current History*, November 1921, 237, 235; "Doing Something for the Farmer," *Literary Digest*, 13 October 1923, 14; David Friday, "The Recovery of Agriculture," *American Review of Reviews*, August 1923, 182; "Getting the Farmer Back on His Feet," *WF*, 14 December 1923, 1671; Herbert C. Hoover, "Some Notes on Agricultural Readjustment and the High Cost of Living," *Saturday Evening Post*, 10 April 1920, 4; Donald L. Winters, *Henry Cantwell Wallace as Secretary of Agriculture, 1921–1924* (Urbana: University of Illinois Press, 1970), 71.

presented a new problem in governing that was not likely to go away. The consensus was that the farm crisis would soon be over and with it the need for close attention to rural voices. There was, in short, no perception of a change in the environment that compelled routine consultation with the spokesmen of organized farmers. As Representative Anderson diagnosed it, "the farm bloc came into existence as an emergency means for handling some of the legislative features of this great and most unusual agricultural emergency. . . . When the cementing force of the group disappeared, the group itself dissolved."[30]

The indications that producer groups might enjoy a competitive political advantage over parties or personal networks were even more ambiguous. The 1920 election was a Republican landslide, and although resentment against wartime controls on commodity prices may have been the specific agrarian animus, the rural responses did not differ much from the rest of the country. In 1920, "a well-defined farm vote had not yet become an object of public alarm."[31]

In 1922, however, the Republicans lost most of what they had gained in 1920—seventy-six seats in the House and eight in the Senate. On the face of it, farmers had won a great victory, electing four new senators with impressive agrarian credentials—Lynn J. Frazier in North Dakota, Henrik Shipstead in Minnesota, Smith W. Brookhart in Iowa, and R. B. Howell in Nebraska. Minnesota's Magnus Johnson joined them a year later, prompting *Capper's Weekly* to opine that "Magnus Johnson, Henrik Shipstead, and Brookhart owe their elections more to the ills of the agricultural situation and their extravagant promises to redeem it than anything else."[32]

But Senator Capper's mouthpiece was almost alone in this interpretation. Shortly before the general election, the *Times,* cognizant if not omniscient, foresaw large GOP losses but made no mention of rural discontent except in Kansas, where Governor Henry J. Allen faced a tax revolt. Another reporter noted that "strenuous efforts have been made to unite the farmers in political action. Conferences have been held and propaganda distributed through every possible channel." But, he added, "the efforts have resulted in no cohesive action. . . . The present campaign and the election will see no organized revolt on the part of the producer . . . except where local conditions affect isolated candidates."[33]

Thus, the radical victories in the Midwest, while related to the agrarian unrest, seemed each to have its own theme. Minnesota senator Frank Kellogg was a sometime farm bloc associate who lost to the candidate of the new Farmer-Labor party, Henrik Shipstead. Brookhart capitalized on his prestige as a sharp-shooting National Guard colonel and renewed his attack on the railroad rate

30. Anderson, "Latest Thing," 2, 21.

31. Shideler, *Farm Crisis,* 30.

32. "Doing Something for the Farmer," *Literary Digest,* 14.

33. "Republicans Facing Fight to Hold House," *NYT,* 7 May 1922, II : 1; "Apathy of Voters Clouds Election," *NYT,* 5 November 1922, 1; Charles Moreau Harger, "Will Producers Stage a Revolt?" *Independent,* 14 October 1922, 199–200.

guarantee clause of the Esch-Cummins Act, handiwork of his rival, Senator Albert Cummins. Finally, Nonpartisan League Republican Frazier had the good fortune to run against Porter J. McCumber, a twenty-three-year veteran whose mistake was to have put his name, as Finance Committee chairman, on the 1922 Fordney-McCumber Tariff Act.[34] Advocacy of the farm group line, finally, had provided no guarantees—five of the twenty Republicans in the House farm bloc lost, the proportion no different from Republicans generally.

Rather than a victory for farmers, the 1922 elections were mainly interpreted as a victory for progressives over the Old Guard. The *Times*, for example, noted that half the Republican House losses occurred east of Ohio, signifying that the outcome was more than the result of a farm revolt. It offered Gifford Pinchot's gubernatorial victory in Pennsylvania and progressive Albert Beveridge's win over stalwart Senator Harry S. New in the Indiana Republican primary as evidence that the Old Guard was on the defensive. Legislators put things in the same terms. The *Country Gentleman* overheard one representative say to another, "It's open season for the fellow who promises most. All of us regulars are up against tough going." Replied the second, "Well, maybe so. . . . But if any son of a gun in my district thinks he can outpromise me this fall, man alive, he will have to lie some."[35]

Agrarian discontent was seen as part of a broader Progressive revival. "The farm vote," commented the southern journal *Progressive Farmer*, "was practically everywhere progressive." The "La Follette group" assumed the congressional balance of power instead of the farm bloc, and the title of best friend of the farmer passed from the farm groups' backers to the insurgents. "The farm bloc today," concluded *Country Gentleman*, "is threatened with disruption and political impotence by the very situation it created. . . . Doing something for the farmer has become too much a political asset to be left to the farm organizations." The "radical bloc" had more or less absorbed the agricultural bloc.[36]

34. Chester H. Rowell, "Why the Middle West Went Radical," *World's Work*, June 1923, 612–22; Chester H. Rowell, "The Political Cyclone in North Dakota," *World's Work*, July 1923, 265–74; Chester H. Rowell, "La Follette, Shipstead, and the Embattled Farmers," *World's Work*, August 1923, 408–20; Chester H. Rowell, "Brookhart, Howell, and 'Brother Charlie' Bryan," *World's Work*, September 1923, 478–85; "Panicky Old Guard Senators," *NYT*, 28 May 1922, VII : 4; "New Personalities in the Senate," *NYT*, 12 November 1922, IX : 1; Jerry A. Neprash, *The Brookhart Campaigns in Iowa* (New York: Columbia University Press, 1932); Reinhard H. Luthin, "Smith Wildman Brookhart of Iowa," *Agricultural History* 25 (October 1951) : 187–97.

35. "East Gave Democrats Most Gains in House," *NYT*, 15 November 1922, 2; Willard M. Kiplinger, "Future of Farm Bloc a Washington Riddle," *NYT*, 18 May 1924, VII : 20; Roy A. Roberts, "Windbags and Ostriches," *CG*, 14 October 1922, 11.

36. Clarence Poe, "The World's News," *Progressive Farmer*, Raleigh ed. (hereafter *PF*), 2 December 1922, 1011; Roy A. Roberts, "Everybody Loves the Farmer," *CG*, 6 January 1922, 13; "Washington Dazed by Big Reversal," *NYT*, 9 November 1922, 1; Kiplinger, "Future of Farm Bloc," VII : 20; Winters, *Wallace*, 90; Joan Hoff Wilson, "Herbert Hoover's Agricultural Policies, 1921–1928," in Ellis W. Hawley, *Herbert Hoover as Secretary of Commerce* (Iowa City: University of Iowa Press, 1981) : 142n.

The disinclination of rural lawmakers to reformulate the farm bloc in 1923 had a rational basis. The 1922 elections had not shown that the agricultural lobbies could protect them—the way to avoid defeat in 1922 was not to be a friend of the farmer but to be a progressive. Likewise, the farm groups had not yet come up with an issue—not even one as diffuse as farm relief—that would demand consistent congressional attention instead of mere appeasement. What the farm groups needed was an issue that farmers would mobilize around, an issue that would keep them in legislators' consciousness. That issue would be the equalization fee.

Courtship: The Early Campaign for the Equalization Fee

Before the equalization fee's advent, government fixing of agricultural prices had been an issue embraced by the radicals, while mainline farm groups and most rural lawmakers kept it at arm's length. In January 1922, for instance, the House Agriculture Committee took up two proposals for federal price-fixing. Although sponsored by participants in the farm bloc—Charles A. Christopherson, Republican from South Dakota, and James H. Sinclair, NPL-Republican from North Dakota—the bills were not farm bloc measures, and the bloc and the farm organizations were deeply split over them.[37]

The Agriculture Committee was not very interested in the schemes, although it ultimately reported the Christopherson bill. Excepting Sinclair, even the most liberal committee members—Democrat Marvin Jones of Texas and Republicans Melvin McLaughlin of Nebraska and Edward Voigt of Wisconsin—had their doubts about price-fixing. Voigt worried about the cost, Jones about the stimulus to production. McLaughlin admitted he had looked into price-fixing, but questioned where it would stop. Unlike the Senate Agriculture Committee, chaired by Nebraska senator George W. Norris and dominated by western progressives, the House committee was not naturally friendly to government intervention.[38]

Neither were the major farm groups. The Farm Bureau, the Grange, and the National Board of Farm Organizations stayed away from the House hearings, and Gray Silver limited his participation to a written brief on the fallacy of price-fixing. The lone farm group leader to come before the House committee was Benjamin C. Marsh of the Farmers National Council, which favored the Sinclair bill. But Marsh's right to speak for producers was easily dismissed. "Where do you vote?" demanded J. N. Tincher, the southwest Kansas Republican. "I voted in New York the last time," replied Marsh. Oh, said Tincher, "let us talk about that a little." Not even Sinclair came to Marsh's defense.[39]

In 1922, then, neither the farm groups nor the agrarian lawmakers were

37. "Price Fixing and the Farm Bloc," *WF*, 3 March 1922, 296.

38. *Hearings before the House Committee on Agriculture*, "Stabilizing Prices of Farm Products," 67th Congress, 2nd sess., Serial O, 1922 (hereafter *Hearings*, 1922), 133, 142–44, 25–26.

39. *Hearings*, 1922, 139; William Johnson, "Can the Government Save the Country?" *CG*, 5 May 1923, 42.

ready to try intervention in the agricultural marketplace. By 1924, the farm groups were, but, significantly, their change of heart did not rally lawmakers immediately under their banner. Representatives did not respond at once to group demands; rather, they awaited evidence that the agricultural lobbies offered electoral advantages equal to the benefits of party loyalty. In addition, lawmakers needed assurance that their dealings with the farm groups on the issue of price supports would continue into the future. These calculations were set in motion by the equalization fee, a subsidy scheme drawn up in 1921 by an Illinois farm equipment manufacturer, George N. Peek, and his lieutenant, Hugh S. Johnson. Their plan, outlined in a self-published pamphlet titled "Equality for Agriculture," set the price for the portion of a crop consumed domestically equal to a "ratio price" bearing the same relation to prices of manufactured goods as it had immediately before the war. Prices were to be propped up by dumping the "exportable surplus" abroad and export losses covered by an "equalization fee" assessed on producers.

Peek tried from the outset to interest the Farm Bureau in the plan, and the second printing of "Equality for Agriculture" bore an encomium to AFBF president Howard. Neither Howard nor his successor, Oscar Bradfute, were personally enthusiastic, but by 1924 the plan had received support from several state Farm Bureau presidents and the endorsement of the federation's executive committee.[40] In the meantime, other organizations were coming around in similar fashion. Farmers Union leaders from the Midwest like John Tromble of Kansas and Milo Reno of Iowa were enthusiastic enough to overcome the reluctance of long-time union president C. S. Barrett. Even the conservative Grange, with its distaste for political activism, moved toward market intervention in 1923, electing Louis J. Taber to replace Sherman J. Lowell as master. Seen as a compromise candidate between Grange radicals and ultra-conservatives, Taber pledged to be "conservative but progressive."[41]

The attraction of Peek's plan to the normally conservative farm groups was partly a matter of timing, partly a matter of presentation, and partly a matter of parentage. All the farm lobbies, but especially the Farm Bureau, had been decimated by the agricultural depression. "In a number of states," O'Brien reported in 1923, "the farm bureau is practically on the rocks. . . . In even the strongest Corn Belt states there have been wholesale desertions in county memberships." Federation membership plunged from 466,000 in 1921 to 363,000 in 1922, the significant gains in the East, South, and West more than offset by a huge loss—135,000 members—in its stronghold, the Midwest. The federation desperately needed an issue to excite midwestern farmers—it was about this time that it first applied the adjective *militant* to itself—but more than anything else it needed a more prosperous farm sector. After five years of chasing Muscle Shoals it was clear that the issue of cut-rate fertilizers would neither excite midwestern farmers nor improve them economically. Pressing

40. "What Is the Matter with the Export Plan?" *WF*, 11 January 1924, 47; "Farm Relief Plan at Washington," *WF*, 18 January 1924, 92; Christensen, "Agricultural Pressure," 149.

41. "National Grange Annual Meeting," *Hoard's Dairyman*, 7 December 1923, 634; "Committee to Act on Export Bill," *WF*, 7 January 1927, 6.

for government action to aid agriculture was in a very real sense a last-ditch bid for self-preservation.[42]

Of the many farm relief plans in the air, moreover, Peek's made the "fairest" demands. According to its proponents, the equalization fee averted overproduction by cutting returns to farmers whenever a greater proportion of their crop went into the export trade. The fee financed price increases without raids on the Treasury. And perhaps most important, it awarded farmers the same "American price" that tariff-protected manufacturers enjoyed.[43]

Nor could the plan's sponsors be associated with agrarian radicalism. Both Peek, a businessman, and Johnson, a former military officer, were veterans of the War Industries Board. Peek scored a victory in 1923 when Agriculture secretary Wallace, alarmed by the Coolidge administration's standpat response to the deepening farm crisis, decided to move on his own. In September Wallace presented his endorsement of the Peek plan to Coolidge's cabinet, and in November he directed USDA consultant Charles J. Brand, former head of the Packers and Stockyards Administration, to prepare a bill in consultation with Peek. Wallace's personal endorsement lent additional respectability, for as an Iowa farm editor and organizer of the Corn Belt Meat Producers Association, Wallace was highly regarded by midwestern farm group leaders.[44] Brand's bill, introduced into the House by Agriculture Committee chairman Gilbert N. Haugen, a twenty-five-year veteran from Iowa, and into the Senate by Oregon Republican Charles L. McNary—Norris had his own bill—"was not a farm organization bill. It had come from completely outside their ranks, although, from the beginning, the Farm Bureau was most closely associated with it."[45]

The House Committee was obviously impressed by the new pressure, but its members were just as clearly determined to maintain a measure of independence from the farm groups. After all, the leadership of both parties formally opposed the measure being pressed by the organizations, and the lobbies had yet to demonstrate their political muscle. The line between the ins and the outs thus was blurred at the hearings. Doubts of both admirers and detractors of the bill stressed concerns about its merits rather than its organizational support or the representativeness of its backers. A number of committee members were eager to give the farm groups and their allies a cordial reception, but few actively courted them.

Chairman Haugen, however, was one of the few, and his performance at the committee hearings is interesting both because his courtship of the farm

42. Harry R. O'Brien, "A Million Who'll Stick," *CG*, 10 March 1923, 11; Robert L. Tontz, "Membership in the General Farmer's Organizations," *Agricultural History* 38 (1964) : 143–57; John Mark Hansen, "The Political Economy of Group Membership," *American Political Science Review* 79 (March 1985) : 83–88; "Membership Paid to the American Farm Bureau Federation," mimeo, American Farm Bureau Federation, 1982, 262.

43. Winters, *Wallace*, 259–67.

44. Christensen, "Agricultural Pressure," 145; Winters, *Wallace*, 25–26, 53.

45. Fite, *George N. Peek*, 64, 100.

groups contrasted so vividly with the general reticence of his committee colleagues and because his motives seemed so transparent.

Haugen was certainly no radical. His natural caution had been reinforced by the up-and-down nature of Iowa Republican politics. He won his first nomination as a compromise candidate from a deadlocked convention. When he became one of the twenty-nine insurgents to cosponsor the revolt against Speaker Cannon, the conservatives came within 220 votes of unseating him in the next election. Haugen cut his insurgency short and backed Taft rather than Roosevelt in 1912. He was not a member of the farm bloc, and his bill to regulate the meat industry, which became the Packers and Stockyards Act, was embraced by the packers as a lesser evil than Norris's Senate bill.[46]

Furthermore, Haugen's sponsorship of the bill was not due to any close ties to Peek or to the Farm Bureau. In fact, Haugen distrusted Peek, thinking he was playing into the hands of the Democrats. A. B. Genung, a USDA staff member during Wallace's term, claimed that "McNary from the first had been going along cordially with the Peek group," but he makes no mention of Haugen. Of the Iowa delegation, a more logical choice would have been Lester J. Dickinson, "a man easily goaded" because of his scarcely concealed ambition for a Senate seat. Dickinson had chaired the House farm bloc, had close ties with the Iowa Farm Bureau, had declared for the Peek plan in 1923, and represented a cash grain district in northwest Iowa that was more fertile ground for conversions to the plan than Haugen's corn and dairy district.[47]

But Dickinson was not chairman of the committee. Haugen was, and most likely he dropped the bill into the hopper because Wallace asked him to. "There is no evidence that Haugen had any part in framing the legislation," says Fite, and "it is doubtful if [he] realized that he had attached his name to a bill that would earn him such a prominent and lasting place in the history of twentieth-century . . . farm policy." But it was hard even for a cautious man like Haugen to ignore a ground swell that stood to make him more than an obscure committee chairman. By the time the committee opened hearings, the plan had gained the endorsement both of *Wallaces' Farmer*, the most influential farm paper in Iowa, and a number of Iowa county farm bureaus.[48] What's more, the bill had the blessing of Secretary Wallace, making it something of an administration measure, even if Coolidge and Hoover were thought to be opposed. Not many legislators were in a position where aggressive advocacy carried so few risks and would redound so surely in their favor.

46. Gilbert C. Fite, "Gilbert N. Haugen," in John N. Schacht, ed., *Three Progressives from Iowa* (Iowa City: Center for the Study of the Recent History of the United States, 1980), 1–14; Benedict, *Farm Policies*, 183n.

47. A. B. Genung, *The Agricultural Depression Following World War I and Its Political Consequences* (Ithaca, N.Y.: Northeast Farm Foundation, 1954), 27; Russell Lord, *The Wallaces of Iowa* (Boston: Houghton Mifflin Co., 1947), 241; "Wheat, Corn, and Capper," *Independent*, 16 January 1926, 61; Fite, "Gilbert N. Haugen."

48. Fite, "Gilbert N. Haugen," 8; "The Export Plan," *WF*, 11 January 1924, 44; "What Is the Matter with the Export Plan?" *WF*, 47.

In this way Haugen became the cheerleader for the farm organizations backing the bill. When Farm Bureau lobbyist Gray Silver arrived, Haugen skillfully led him through the thicket:

> HAUGEN: The consoling feature about this bill is this: The price is not going to remain down at the ratio price; it is going above.
> SILVER: The ratio price is the minimum.
> HAUGEN: That is the minimum, and the price, of course, will go beyond that.
> SILVER: We trust so.
> HAUGEN: . . . The speculators and gamblers will take care of the price then, as they are taking care of it now. In order to gamble they will have to put the price above the ratio price.

Later, the gentleman from Iowa put to use the testimony of witnesses that he had disparaged only two years earlier when they appeared in favor of the Sinclair bill.

> HAUGEN: Somebody has got to pay the expense.
> SILVER: That is right.
> HAUGEN: And under the bill the farmers would take care of a part of it [through the equalization fee].
> SILVER: Yes.
> HAUGEN: The consumer would take the biggest end of it?
> SILVER: Yes.
> HAUGEN: The consumers, or the representatives of the consumers [the labor unions], say that they will take their share of it. . . . I have been in sympathy with your suggestion [to set the ratio price higher], . . . but I realize that we cannot get it, and I will be satisfied if we accomplish what we accomplish here.

Never mind, as Kentucky Democrat David Kincheloe later pointed out, that the unions had backed the Sinclair bill in 1922 and had not yet pronounced on Haugen's bill, and never mind that Haugen had not previously been a great friend of price-fixing.[49] If this was going to be Haugen's quest for national prestige, he was going to need all the help he could get, especially the help of the Farm Bureau.

Except for Haugen and South Carolina Democrat Hampton C. Fulmer, no one else on the committee worked hard to win the farm groups' favor. Proponents like Republicans Tincher and Fred S. Purnell of Indiana and Democrats Thomas L. Rubey of Missouri and Fletcher B. Swank of Oklahoma were not reluctant either to challenge the farm groups or to take into account the interests of groups that opposed farmers. Purnell, for instance, represented a chronically marginal district in western Indiana, a state with a powerful Farm Bureau whose president, William Settle, was a leader in the McNary-Haugen ranks. Nevertheless, Purnell challenged Silver, albeit cautiously, to consider an opposing point of view.

49. *Hearings before the House Committee on Agriculture,* "McNary-Haugen Export Bill," 68th Congress, 1st sess., Serial E, 1924 (hereafter *Hearings, 1924*), 395, 398, 561; *Hearings, 1922,* 78–86.

PURNELL: Will [the bill] . . . wipe out the speculation that now exists?

SILVER: It will tend to do that.

PURNELL: Do you think enough of it will be maintained to be helpful to the market?

SILVER: I am one of those who believe that the market is not maintained by speculation. Consumption is the constant support of the market. . . .

PURNELL: I have the same view, but . . . I am wondering whether or not the operation of the bill would disturb speculation and other features on the market which are generally accepted now as being helpful to it.[50]

Viewed against Haugen's performance, it is clear that although Purnell was smart enough not to cut his own throat, he was not yet willing to capitulate to the Farm Bureau's position. As in 1922, proponents were still voicing serious concerns about the effects of the bill on traditional agrarian whipping boys. Representatives Sinclair, Rubey, and Swank, favorable to the bill, joined opponents Kincheloe and Voigt in worrying about how food processors would fare under the plan. So great was the committee concern that the chairman lost his temper. "I don't understand all this worry about the packers," Haugen thundered. "I think we all agree that the packers can take care of themselves. . . . We need not lose any sleep over [them]." And Sinclair later complained that "all this discussion I have heard for the last half hour"—led by Kincheloe, Voigt, Jones, and West Virginia Democrat George Johnson, the latter two sympathetic to the bill—"has been based on a fear of what might happen to the packers and millers."[51]

But if the farm lobby was not yet "in," the treatment accorded the agricultural trades when they appeared in person was some indication that they were not "in" either. Haugen, of course, was the point man. He reminded A. P. Husband of the Millers' National Federation that a Federal Trade Commission report had alleged wartime profiteering by the millers, and he later unearthed another FTC report detailing the abuses of the meat industry. "You know something about the practices of the packers that were pointed out in that report?" he asked Norman Draper, who testified for the Institute of American Meat Packers. "We had an understanding years ago that we would simply forget about that report, . . . but you are bringing it up now. Very well; . . . but you are responsible for it." Haugen's favoritism did not escape the notice of the committee. Democrat Thomas A. Doyle, who represented Chicago's South Side, site of the Union Stockyards, finally had enough, and he came to Draper's defense. "You have been mighty agreeable about it, Mr. Chairman, but I do not think you put those same questions, in the same tone, to the proponents of the bill as you have to this gentleman." Aside from Haugen and a few others—notably Tincher, Johnson, and Fulmer—nobody was really ready to offend the processors, who, after all, were major campaign contributors.[52]

50. *Hearings*, 1924, 402, 701.
51. *Hearings*, 1924, 313, 490, 9–13, 550; *Hearings*, 1922, 82.
52. *Hearings*, 1924, 451, 470, 686–91, 156–57.

In 1924, the evidence is clear that no more than a few Agriculture Committee members were cultivating close relationships with organized agriculture. Caution rather than enthusiasm carried the day as legislators confronting something new looked for an accommodation without a long-term commitment. The farm groups' turn to price-fixing legislation had not in itself been enough to bring farm state representatives into their camp. The 1924 McNary-Haugen bill died on the House floor, and an attempt to resurrect it in the Senate failed. A 1925 version did not come to a House vote.

Commitment: The Farm Lobby Wins the Midwest

In 1926, the McNary-Haugenites came back for a third try, and the landscape was much changed. The committee was as deeply divided as before, perhaps more so. Instead of one proposal on the docket there were four: the Peek plan, the Curtis-Aswell cooperative marketing plan, the administration-backed Tincher bill, and the Grange favorite, the export debenture, backed by Jones, former Michigan Grange master John C. Ketcham, and Charles Adkins, a freshman from east-central Illinois. But by 1926, a number of representatives, most of them from the Midwest, had developed loyalties to the farm groups, and transactions with the interests assembled were markedly different from 1924. This time, even opponents of the bill—Democrats Aswell and Kincheloe joined by Republicans Franklin Fort, a freshman from urban East Orange, New Jersey, and Tincher, a strong backer of the bill in 1924—recognized that the battle was being waged on the front of organizational backing and the committee's fundamental political commitments. That is not to say controversial issues were not aired. The arguments of 1924 were reiterated and amplified, mostly by those who were as yet undecided, like Jones and six-term Republican Thomas S. Williams of southern Illinois. Now, however, a major part of the opposition strategy was to discredit the farm representatives who appeared before them.

Indeed, those hearings often had more the character of a credentials fight than a fact-gathering inquiry. Kincheloe, for instance, complained that Frank Evans, secretary of the Farm Bureau, was not able to provide him the intelligence he needed. "I want to know what the American farmers think of [the bill] and not the representatives of these organizations." Tincher, likewise, was unimpressed by the alleged unity of the Corn Belt Committee, an alliance of farm organizations, mostly Farm Bureaus and Farmers Unions, from eleven midwestern states. "You may be partially right as to the harmony that exists to-day," he told William Hirth, the committee's chairman. "But we members of this committee know that it is a joke because we have had them here before. . . . In some seasons of the year everything that the farm bureau wants the farm union is against, and in other seasons of the year the reverse. . . . I personally doubt," the gentleman from Kansas concluded, "that you are together on this."[53] The opposition doubted too that the farm lobby's demands had

---

53. *Hearings before the House Committee on Agriculture*, "Agricultural Relief," 69th Congress, 1st sess., Serial C, 1926 (hereafter *Hearings, 1926*), 372, 162, 121.

anything to do with farmer sentiment. "May I inquire if you honestly believe that one per cent of the American farmers know a continental thing about what is in your bill?" Aswell asked Charles E. Hearst, head of the Iowa Farm Bureau. The farmer, the Louisiana Democrat continued, "has to take what you say on faith, and he has lost considerably that quality of faith in the agitation of politicians. . . . I have letters from Iowa . . . saying that all this trouble in Iowa is largely caused by politicians and salaried agents that have been going around and stirring up these matters."[54]

The friends of the farm organizations came quickly to the defense. Michigander Ketcham established through his round of questions that Hearst was not a professional agitator but rather a "bona fide" cultivator of four hundred acres of the world's finest soil. When Fort challenged the right of Farm Bureau president Sam H. Thompson, an Illinois corn farmer, to speak for cattle producers, Illinois representative Adkins led Thompson through a similar biography, proving that he was an honest farmer selflessly interested in the good of agriculture and not a full-time malcontent. For good measure, Adkins helped Thompson answer a query posed by the other Illinois member, Thomas Williams, who asked why specialty crops grown in his district did not come under the provisions of the bill. Because land suitable for growing specialty crops was limited, Adkins prompted Thompson, those growers were less at the mercy of processors than corn, wheat, and cotton farmers.[55]

Moreover, the solicitude extended to the farm groups by the committee was not confined to one or two members, as it had been in 1924. With the exception of Tincher, this sentiment was shared by all the representatives from the plains. In discussing the corn provisions of the bill with David Kincheloe, for instance, Farm Bureau lobbyist Chester H. Gray ran into some trouble. Yes, he admitted, in the unlikely event that the equalization fee did not cover export losses on corn the balance would have to be paid out of the Treasury. "We have gone over that a million times," Kincheloe complained. "I understand your contention is that there is not going to be any loss; but finally, you admit if there is a loss it will come out of the Treasury." At this point, Democrat Rubey took up Gray's argument. "Suppose they make some money out of this corn deal," he asked Kincheloe, "what will they do with the profits?" "I suppose they will reimburse the Treasury," Kincheloe replied, but "I am guessing on that." "He is guessing," said Rubey, in Gray's defense. "No," Kincheloe persisted, "he did not guess at all."[56] Even if Rubey's vindication was not compelling, it at least achieved its purpose of reassuring Gray.

Further, this treatment was special to the farm lobbies, not to farmers generally. The advocates and opponents of the McNary-Haugen bill both took pleasure in shooting down the arguments of several unaffiliated farmers who had journeyed to Washington with their own panaceas. August Andresen, for example, a newly elected Republican from southeastern Minnesota, let Edwin McKnight of Medina, New York, know where he stood:

54. *Hearings*, 1926, 584–85, 161.
55. *Hearings*, 1926, 604–05, 781–84.
56. *Hearings*, 1926, 707, 825–27.

ANDRESEN: Your plan, as I take it, has received no specific endorsement from any farm organization.

McKNIGHT: No, it has not.

ANDRESEN: What chance do you think your bill has, when it has received no such endorsement from these farm organizations? Do you think we should give the farmer something that he does not advocate himself or give him something that he is not here sponsoring through his personal representatives? [57]

What mattered to the midwesterners on the committee, then, was not that the bill had the backing of some farmer, somewhere, but that it had the backing of "his personal representative."

As the decade passed the midpoint, then, congressional-group interactions had changed markedly. From a position of independence from farm groups in the early 1920s, midwestern representatives had moved to open courtship by 1926. The farm groups seem to have been as surprised as anyone by the switch. "At the beginning of their [1926] invasion of the capital the farm delegations were taken back by the unexpected manner of their reception," the *Times* reported. "They were welcomed on every hand, . . . told to get together around a table and decide just what it was they wanted." By and large, they did just that. "The bill reported by the two committees . . . was one which had been practically written by the representatives of the farmers' organizations from the wheat and corn belts and the American Cotton Growers Exchange." [58] The agricultural price support network was taking shape.

What had happened between 1924 and 1926 was a major shift in the political calculations surrounding farm policy. In 1924, it had looked as if McNary-Haugenism might be over. Grain prices had risen dramatically. Wheat jumped from 93 cents in 1923 to $1.25 the next year, and corn that had been selling for 81 cents brought $1.06. Republican vice-presidential nominee Charles G. Dawes predicted a revival of the European market and greater domestic buying power, both of which would help farmers. Democratic presidential candidate John W. Davis agreed. As Genung observed, "it was hoped and believed in Washington [in 1924] that the worst part of the actual depression was over." [59]

That optimism could make even the strongest backers of the McNary-Haugen plan a little hesitant to get too tied in with the farm groups. "I am in sympathy with some movement of this kind," Nebraska Republican Mc-Laughlin told Silver in 1924, "but I am wondering a little bit whether we are making *sufficient progress in the normal way so that we might be able to get through and be better off,* in two or three years from now, than by bolstering ourselves up in some artificial manner that may not be economical" (italics added). In keeping with these expectations, "the [1924] McNary-Haugen plan was re-

57. *Hearings,* 1926, 1227, 1349.

58. "Farmers Worried over Legislation, *NYT,* 14 March 1926, II : 1; Christensen, "Agricultural Pressure," 219.

59. Genung, *Agricultural Depression,* 36; Stuart O. Blythe, " 'Brass Tacks,' " *CG,* 11 October 1924, 6; E. V. Wilcox, "The Farmer and Democracy," *CG,* 11 October 1924, 7.

garded even by its supporters as an 'emergency measure' and therefore temporary." Senator McNary was so confident that the emergency was over that
he stated late in 1924 that he would not press his bill in the next session.[60]
Hence, 1924 only confirmed legislators' expectations that farm price support
was not an issue with which they would again have to deal.

Prices and expectations reversed themselves in 1925, however. Corn hit
bottom first, dropping 36 cents a bushel in 1925. Wheat continued to rise in
1925 only to fall back to $1.22 in 1926. A downturn following a modest up-
turn following a four-year depression was enough to make even optimists
wonder whether the farm crisis really was temporary. For many years, the
economic prophets had held out the hope that a rebuilt, prosperous Europe
would again lift American agriculture out of its doldrums. With large world
crops in 1925 and 1926 it became clear that European cash was fattening a
rebuilt European agriculture. "I do not think that [the agricultural situation]
is in the process of working itself out, of curing itself," economist E. G. Nourse
concluded at the end of 1925. "I still believe that the situation is with us and
that it is idle for American agriculture to expect a return of prosperity because of the rehabilitation of the world market on which we depended to a
considerable extent." "The easy, automatic European food market of the prewar days has gone forever," agreed Henry A. Wallace, the former secretary's
son, and Wisconsin economist B. H. Hibbard added, "we shall have surpluses
of agricultural products for many years to come."[61]

The gloom was not limited to agricultural economists. "The causes of this
[depression] are permanent," argued Iowa senator Brookhart, and "the condition itself is permanent." Consequently, said Farm Bureau president
Thompson, "farm relief is no longer considered an emergency matter."[62] The
1926 version of the Peek plan sought to establish the export corporation permanently, rather than for a few years, as the earlier bills had specified. Moreover, within a month of the burial of the 1924 equalization fee bill, farm
leaders had met in St. Paul, where they had vowed to carry on the fight with
an even more sophisticated organizational apparatus.[63]

By 1926, therefore, the expectation that midwestern legislators were going
to meet the farm organizations again on the same issue was high. That fact
did not escape the notice of committee members. Ohio Republican Charles J.
Thompson reviewed the farm bloc's many victories with Sam Thompson in
1926. "I want to say in defense of this committee," he told the Farm Bureau
chief, "that we have been trying to help the farmer. We have passed all this

60. *Hearings*, 1924, 403; Eric Englund, "The Dilemma of the Corn Belt," *World's Work*,
November 1926, 44; "Differ on Farm Bill," *NYT*, 15 November 1924, 2.

61. E. G. Nourse, "The Agricultural Outlook," *Rural America*, December 1925, 5; H. A.
Wallace, "Three Roads to Better Times," *WF*, 23 July 1926, 988; B. H. Hibbard, "What
About the Surplus?" *PF*, 3 April 1926, 438.

62. Smith W. Brookhart, "The Plight of the Farmer," *Nation*, 7 April 1926, 367; "Farmers
to Stress Relief," *NYT*, 5 December 1926, 15.

63. H. A. Wallace, "Re-forming the Battle Lines," *WF*, 18 July 1924, 985; William Hirth,
"American Council of Agriculture," *WF*, 20 June 1924, 897; Christensen, "Agricultural
Pressure," p. 151.

legislation, and yet we find that the farmer is still here, still knocking at our doors." Thompson assured him that their presence would continue: "Even if you pass this legislation I would not want to promise that we would not be back here again." In that case, the Ohioan continued, "you are always welcome to come before this committee. We like to meet around this table and thrash out these problems."[64]

The political advantages of working with farm groups were also becoming clear. The appeal of the Peek plan surprised even veteran lawmakers. Five-termer Kincheloe, for example, was baffled by how such a new idea could have such a wide following. "How can these organizations throughout the United States have any intelligent conception of the content of these bills?" he inquired of Charles Holman of the National Board of Farm Organizations. "By what method is it gotten to them?"[65] Such efficient political education was a revelation to the Committee on Agriculture in 1924.

The awareness of its potential was elevated when the farm organizations decided to play hardball. Thinking that dissension among the farm groups had hurt their chances on the floor in 1924, the Peek forces had spun out three new organizations in the next eighteen months: the American Council of Agriculture, the Corn Belt Committee, and the Committee of Twenty-two, the latter made up of businessmen sympathetic to McNary-Haugenism. The coalitions themselves were largely of symbolic importance. Both the American Council of Agriculture and the Corn Belt Committee relied heavily on their member organizations, especially the Farm Bureau. Years later, Sam Thompson recalled the Corn Belt Committee as a mixed blessing, noting that an effective lobbying effort required both an experienced Washington staff and "thorough local organization." "The Committee lacked this machinery," he both complained and boasted, "or rather, it depended on the machinery of member Farm Bureaus and other affiliated groups."[66]

The Farm Bureau became even more avidly militant than the Peek lobbies. In October 1924, the federation's *Weekly News Letter,* which was distributed to all county farm bureaus, printed the voting records of members of Congress on bills the AFBF considered important. The federation's Washington office had kept the tallies since it was opened, but to avoid charges of partisanship it had released them only when asked by Farm Bureau members. It is unlikely that their dissemination caused Corn Belt representatives immediately to tremble, but the salvo was a dramatic indication of the Federation's seriousness about this legislation. Two months later, at its annual meeting, Farm Bureau delegates endorsed the McNary-Haugen bill, ratifying the decision reached by the executive committee in January 1924.[67]

64. *Hearings,* 1926, 835–36.
65. *Hearings,* 1924, 418.
66. Sam H. Thompson, "The Battle for Equality," *Bureau Farmer,* September 1929, 8; "Corn Growers Plan Fight in Capital," *NYT,* 29 January 1926, 9.
67. "What He Saw in the Washington, D.C., Office of the A.F.B.F.," *American Farm Bureau Federation Weekly News Letter,* 9 October 1924, 1; Donald R. Murphy, "Farm Bureau Backs Export Plan," *WF,* 19 December 1924, 1633.

The Farm Bureau's next convention, in December 1925, was "the Sarajevo of the farm revolt." The keynoter was Calvin Coolidge, and the president was anything but conciliatory. He declared that the agricultural depression was over, and he condemned attempts at price-fixing. As Genung drolly put it, "it remained for Coolidge to kick over such small edifice of tolerance in the West as [Agriculture secretary William] Jardine had been able to build up." The federation's reaction was swift. The Illinois, Indiana, and Iowa delegations nominated for AFBF president Illinois Agricultural Association chief Sam Thompson, who had made an angry speech denouncing Coolidge. After three ballots, the Midwest and South put over the election of the "rough-and-ready dirt farmer," purging the conservative Oscar Bradfute, an Ohio cattle breeder invariably described as "the farmer who looks like a banker."[68]

The Farm Bureau's rebuke of President Coolidge raised quite a few eyebrows. "Among a substantial number of men here," wrote the Washington correspondent for *Wallaces' Farmer,* "the Farm Bureau has been looked upon as a 'me too' organization for the administration." No longer. The federation's actions gave enough of a jolt to rural politicians, he continued, to produce a solid front of midwestern legislators and perhaps lead to the re-creation of the farm bloc. The shock went beyond states where the bureau was well organized. "The Farm Bureau is largely a corn belt organization," the *Agricultural Review* noted. "But it has suddenly become the rallying point for numerous people in many other states who approve of the action at Chicago, but who would not otherwise affiliate or work with it. The Federation is now recognized champion and leader of the Government Export Corporation movement."[69]

At the time of the opening of the Sixty-ninth Congress in 1925, it was clear that the farm groups meant business. Whether they could back up their implicit threats was more of a question. Early in 1924, political analysts had made dire forecasts of the prospects for opponents of farm relief. "Wherever I have gone," wrote a *Country Gentleman* correspondent, "the McNary-Haugen bill has overshadowed mere candidates. . . . If it fails to pass, votes are going to be affected." Agrarian discontent augured well, insiders thought, for the presidential candidacy of Robert La Follette.[70]

Coolidge, however, won the 1924 election handily, and even scored an impressive win over La Follette and Hiram Johnson in a primary in fickle North Dakota. La Follette's Progressive candidacy fell far short of expectations, and he carried only his home state. Iowa's Smith Brookhart, the darling of agrarian radicals, won by a handful of disputed votes over conservative Democrat

68. George Fort Milton, "The Revolt of the Western Farmer," *Independent,* 22 May 1926, 597; Genung, *Agricultural Depression,* p. 38; H. A. Wallace, "Farm Bureau Votes for Export Plan," *WF,* 18 December 1925, 1665; Kile, *Farm Bureau,* 53.

69. "Farm Bloc May Reorganize in Congress," *WF,* 25 December 1925, 1696; [W. I. Drummond], "That Farm Bureau Upheaval," *Agricultural Review,* January 1926, 2.

70. Stuart O. Blythe, "Who Do the Farmers Want for President?" *CG,* 7 June 1924, 33; Elmer Davis, "Power of La Follette Group Still Doubtful," *NYT,* 24 February 1924, VIII : 10; "La Follette Hurries Back to Washington," *NYT,* 31 May 1924, 9.

Daniel Steck, whom many regular Republicans had backed openly. And although a large proportion of progressives were reelected to the House, enough new conservatives were elected to restore the control of the party regulars. The explanation of the election seemed simple enough. "A rise in the price of wheat in the summer of 1924 was enough to send millions of malcontents back to the Republican party." The Ku Klux Klan was a bigger factor than farm radicals.[71]

But 1924 was not so much a defeat as a draw. Cooperation with the farm groups had perhaps not helped a lot, but it did not seem to have hurt. One hundred twenty-nine of the 161 lawmakers who voted for the 1924 equalization fee bill returned to the House, and half of the rest, the retirees and the vanquished, were replaced by candidates with similar sympathies. West of the Mississippi River, the McNary-Haugenites lost only six representatives and two senators. Certainly these numbers do not justify the claim that "this was a mandate to the good and faithful servants of agriculture to continue their efforts," but they do indicate that a large number of House members, especially in the West, did not feel their position had hurt them. Haugen, for one, did not. Although the Agriculture Committee chairman regularly took 60 percent of the vote, in 1924 he won over 70 percent for only the second time in his career. When informed of Senator McNary's judgment that the farm crisis had passed, "Mr. Haugen declared . . . that in his campaign for re-election he had promised his support to farm relief legislation, and that he would continue to work to that end." Missouri Democrat Thomas Rubey, a cautious supporter in 1924, called upon what he had learned in the 1924 election to justify his strong advocacy of the farm groups' line in 1926. "I had a gentleman running against me in the last campaign who made that the issue. . . . I live in a district that is very close, and yet, in that campaign, after fighting it out all over the district, I received the largest majority I ever received"—in a Republican year, no less—"so I am not afraid of the McNary-Haugen bill."[72]

An equally important consequence of the 1924 election was the destruction of the La Follette Progressive party, the last third party of importance to make a real bid for the farm vote. Republican leadership retaliated for the break in party ranks, purging Senators La Follette, Brookhart, Ladd and Frazier and several Progressive representatives. Angry Iowa regulars had nearly gotten rid of Brookhart, even at the expense of losing the seat to a Democrat. The message was loud and clear: insurgency was almost as dangerous as regularity these days. In comparison, alliances with farm groups began to appear a new and less risky political alternative for dealing with an old problem. As Noyes observed, the division in the ranks of midwestern Republicanism had "left

71. "Bitter Fight Ahead on Farmers' Bill," NYT, 30 March 1924, IX : 6; "Republicans Regain Grip on Congress," NYT, 6 November 1924, 1; "The Latest Edition of the Farmers' Revolt," New Republic, 13 January 1925, 205; Harry R. O'Brien, "Why the Northwest Went for Coolidge," CG, 27 December 1924, 16; "Victories by Klan Feature Election," NYT, 6 November 1924, 1.

72. C. Reinold Noyes, "The Restoration of the Republican Party," North American Review, March 1925, 419; "Differ on Farm Bill," NYT, 2; Hearings, 1926, 1010–11.

room for much independence of action."[73] The Progressives had taken over the farm bloc in 1922; after 1924, the new farm bloc returned the favor.

Any doubts that midwesterners had about the greater advantages of cooperation with the farm groups were dispelled in 1926. Party stalwarts were in danger. "Politicians know that the issue raised in the West, namely a government subsidy to the farmers in handling the export problem, has all the earmarks of an effective campaign weapon," wrote a wire service reporter. "And the time is opportune because . . . the aspirants for Congressional nominations are looking around for an opportunity to oppose the men who hold seats in the Congress. This invariably has the effect of turning otherwise regular Republicans into insurgents."[74]

One of the earliest converts was Iowa senator Albert Cummins, facing another primary against Smith Brookhart, whom the Senate had just denied a seat. In December 1925, Cummins informed Coolidge that it would not be possible to win renomination in Iowa without backing the McNary-Haugen bill, and a few weeks later he announced that he had always been in favor of the principle of the plan, a statement damaging by the fact that he had had to make it. Cummins and Indiana senator James E. Watson, both administration regulars, suddenly became ardent McNary-Haugenites. Waston led the Senate floor fight. Cummins denounced Treasury secretary Andrew Mellon for his letter attacking the bill. Watson made it, but barely. Cummins did not, and neither did conservative Republicans L. B. Hanna in North Dakota (defeated by Nonpartisan Leaguer Gerald Nye) nor William B. McKinley in Illinois (defeated by Frank L. Smith) nor Irvine Lenroot in Wisconsin, who held his ground on the farm relief issue but lost to La Follette protégé John Blaine.[75]

The story in the House was the same. Resentment toward Coolidge administration intransigence was most extreme in Iowa, but it was pronounced in Illinois and Indiana and a factor in six other states.[76] At the end of the 1926 primary seasons, seven states were reportedly certain to send delegations pledged to the equalization fee to Congress. Kansas senator Charles Curtis wrote Coolidge that Agriculture secretary Jardine's campaign swing across the state "did the party no good," and he advised the president not to send Jardine, former president of Kansas State College, back again. Oklahoma Democrats succeeded in ousting the only member of their delegation who had voted against the farm plan. Nebraska's Melvin McLaughlin, a committee backer of the Peek bill, found himself in the fight of his life against Democrat John N. Norton, the former Nebraska Farm Bureau chief "who is preaching farm

---

73. Noyes, "Restoration," 417; Stuart O. Blythe, "When Is a Republican Not a Republican?" *CG*, 13 June 1925, 19.

74. "Mutterings of Rebellion on the Farm," *Literary Digest*, 16 January 1926, 6.

75. "Administration to Deal with Surplus," *WF*, 1 January 1926, 10; "All-Iowa Meeting Backs Export Plan," *WF*, 8 January 1926, 35; Stuart O. Blythe, "The Midwest Has a Bone to Pick," *CG*, September 1926, 12; "Senate Debates Farm Relief Bill," *WF*, 25 June 1926, 894; "Brookhart Wins Senate Nomination, Defeating Cummins," *NYT*, 8 June 1926, 1; "Iowa Primary Awakens Senate," *WF*, 18 June 1926, 872.

76. Blythe, "The Midwest Has a Bone to Pick," 12.

relief with capital F's and R's." McLaughlin lost. Even Gilbert Haugen, who ended up winning easily, was rumored to be in trouble, not because of his views, but because "he did not work half as hard as he should have to get his bill passed." "In Iowa," the *Times* concluded, "it is not a question of whether a man is for or against farm relief, but a question of how far he is willing to go."[77]

The farm organizations' strategy in these elections was remarkably subtle. If the farm groups deployed money or manpower, the practice was not extensive or unusual enough for anyone to comment on it. Rather, the organization's most potent weapon appears to have been simply voicing the leadership's displeasure or satisfaction with an incumbent lawmaker's performance, thereby encouraging or discouraging challengers. The announcement of farm leaders in 1926 that they would "campaign vigorously against congressional candidates who [did] not take a decided stand in favor of equality for agriculture" was a virtual solicitation of ambitious politicians. The prospect of a disaffected constituency brought attractive candidates out of the woodwork. As one reporter commented, "the crowd-complex is exemplified by the political movement of the agricultural population. Fluent speakers, radical utterances in farm papers, exploitation of individual losses combine to furnish fuel for the politician, who is not slow to capitalize any symptoms of unrest."[78]

Once the dust had settled after the 1926 election, then, the two conditions for the establishment of close ties with the farm groups were met. Lawmakers had learned of the advantages the farm groups offered that informal contacts and parties did not—reduced costs of political communications and greater electoral security. Likewise, lawmakers had come to expect that farm price support was an issue that was not going to die.

The two exceptions to this generalization help elaborate the basic point. The first, as I discuss later, was southerners. The second was Jasper Napoleon Tincher, the Republican from the Seventh District of Kansas. While almost every other midwesterner moved closer to the farm groups in 1926, Tincher moved away, and his reasons for moving away tell us something about why most of his colleagues moved closer. Tincher, a huge man, was bombastic and popular among House members. First elected in 1918, he became closely associated with Senator Capper because of their cosponsorship of the Grain

77. Charles Frederick Williams, "William M. Jardine and the Development of Republican Farm Policy" (Ph.D. diss., University of Oklahoma, 1970), 175; "Democrats Expect Nebraska Victory," *NYT*, 14 October 1926, 4; "Haugen in Danger of Defeat in Iowa," *NYT*, 12 October 1926, 3; "Corn Belt Revolt Stirs Republicans," *NYT*, 16 August 1926, 4; "Oklahoma," *NYT*, 3 November 1926, 4.

78. Blythe, "The Midwest Has a Bone to Pick," 128; Charles Moreau Harger, "The Political Clouds Out West," *Independent*, 1 September 1923, 82. The farm groups also helped dissuade challengers by expressing public appreciation for the efforts of their friends. See The Observer, "Taking the Temperature of Public Opinion," *Bureau Farmer*, February 1927, 7; [Chester H. Gray], "Our Washington Letter," *Bureau Farmer*, December 1927, 11; The Observer, "The 'Greatest' Annual Meeting," *Bureau Farmer*, January 1928, 4; John P. Wallace, "What Is Going On in Washington," *WF*, 22 January 1926, 112; John P. Wallace, "What Is Happening at the Nation's Capital," *WF*, 1 March 1929, 356.

Futures Act. In 1926, he decided not to run for reelection, citing the financial sacrifice of public office.[79] He changed from a champion of the McNary-Haugen plan to one of its most forceful detractors.

Tincher's explanation for the switch was that the farm relief lobby had made the bill unacceptable by deferring the equalization fee on corn and cotton to win votes, abandoning the principle that each crop pays its own way. Why this principle should suddenly outweigh the huge benefit to his southwest Kansas district, a major wheat producer, is not at first clear. On reflection, however, it becomes evident that he, like most others, was assessing his best political advantage. Tincher had built his career in the Republican party and there his prospects remained brightest. Having decided not to seek another term, he "grabbed the publicity, the prominence, and such measure of approval as there may be, for introducing [the administration's substitute bill]." The prestige and approval probably were very important, because Tincher had become something of a national party official. In 1924, he barnstormed the country debating the Republican program against Democratic congressman Alben Barkley of Kentucky. In his final term, he served as chairman of the House Republican Steering Committee, a post that gave him great influence over the House agenda. He was an important enough Republican in 1924 for the *Times* to report on his preference for Nicholas Longworth over Martin Madden for the speakership.[80] At the 1928 convention, still a prominent Kansas Republican, he had the honor of nominating Senator Curtis for president. Thus "Poley" Tincher went the opposite way because the Republican party had more to offer him than any farm group. He had come to the point in his career where he had to choose party or constituency, and he chose party.

His choice earned him the enmity of the farm lobby. Kansas Farm Bureau chief Ralph Snyder was so spirited in his attacks that Tincher threatened to organize a challenge to his KFB presidency. When *Wallaces' Farmer* reproduced a Farm Bureau map of the 1926 House vote on the bill, it made a point of identifying Tincher's district, a solitary "nay" in a sea of "ayes."[81] In the end, however, the farm groups succeeded, you might say. Tincher was replaced by Clifford R. Hope, who would become the only Republican chairman of the Agriculture Committee in the New Deal era. From beginning to end, Hope was a champion of farm price supports.

In 1926, then, the alliance of midwestern lawmakers with the farm lobby was consolidated. This institutional response, however, was not a mechanical reaction to pressure but a long, uncertain process of changing deeply embedded congressional perceptions of political interest. It had taken the longest farm depression in American history to convince agrarian lawmakers that intervention to maintain commodity prices was a recurrent issue. And it had taken electoral bludgeoning about the heads of Republican representatives to

79. *Hearings,* 1926, 1276–77.

80. "Fake Farm Relief," *WF,* 23 April 1926, 628; *Hearings,* 1926, 1273; "J. N. Tincher, Debated Barkley in 1924," *NYT,* 7 November 1951, 29; "Threaten to Bar Farm Relief at All Costs," *NYT,* 9 May 1926, 15; "Wants Longworth in Chair," *NYT,* 20 December 1924, 17.

81. *Hearings,* 1926, 1277–78; "Senate Debates Farm Relief Plan," *WF,* 4 June 1926, 820.

convince them of the farm group's competitive advantage over party. Indeed, it would seem that midwesterners moved into the farm lobby's camp only when it appeared that any other course would be suicidal.

It took so much because the parties forced the issue of commitment, as Tincher's career reminds us. Farm relief policy was not lodged in some backwater, away from the care and scrutiny of party and president. It was the major annoyance of the Harding, Coolidge, and (later) Hoover presidencies, and each administration put forth its own alternatives to head off the more radical farm lobby proposals. The farm groups triumphed because the parties lacked, not the power to contain them, but the will to channel them, a point I will develop in the conclusion. In the South, we see presently, the issue was less starkly cast.

The South Comes Aboard: Cotton and the Domestic Allotment

Up to 1926 the factors that brought midwestern legislators into alliances with the farm groups had barely touched the South. Both in the House Agriculture Committee and on the floor, rural opposition to the farm lobby was concentrated in Dixie. Of the five southern Democrats on the Agriculture Committee, only the most junior, Hampton P. Fulmer of South Carolina, had made overtures to the agricultural organizations. Texan Marvin Jones and Oklahoma Fletcher B. Swank, while sympathetic, kept their public distance, and ranking Democrats James B. Aswell of Louisiana and David H. Kincheloe of Kentucky were the equalization fee's most caustic critics.

Before 1926, southern members had no reason to get involved. The cotton and tobacco trades, unlike corn and wheat, had boomed after the war. In 1923 cotton sold at about 28 cents a pound, roughly twice as high as ever before. Likewise, tobacco held at about 20 cents, also twice the highest prewar price. Comparing the cotton market to the corn and wheat markets in 1924, the southern agricultural journal *Progressive Farmer* concluded that "while the agricultural readjustment will be somewhat slow and somewhat irregular, we cannot doubt but that it is inevitable."[82] Price stabilization was not a recurrent issue in the South; indeed, it was not much of an issue at all.

Before 1926, moreover, there was little political reason for southerners to solicit the attentions of the farm groups. Except in a few border areas, the danger posed by the Republican party was negligible. Likewise, absence of any Democratic party divisions as deep as the rift between Republican conservatives and progressives made the development of ties that could transcend such intraparty cleavages less important. This southern Democratic complacency frustrated midwesterners' attempt to forge a coalition between corn and cotton. "The corn belt, in common with the other farming sections, needs representatives who are primarily representatives of agriculture and only secondarily Republicans or Democrats," explained *Wallaces' Farmer* editor Donald R. Murphy. "The corn belt probably is better equipped this way than any other section. The South in its farming territory seems to be particularly handicapped by too many professional Democrats."[83]

82. "Better Times Ahead for Farmers," *PF*, 5 July 1924, 778.
83. Donald R. Murphy, "The Corn Belt's Next Move," *New Republic*, 28 July 1926, 275.

Finally, farm organization in the South was relatively weak. Except for fairly robust branches in Alabama and Texas, the Farm Bureau in the 1920s never had more than about seven thousand members in the South. The Farmers Union, once strongest in Dixie, had atrophied there, and its radical rhetoric had permanently alienated the large cotton planters. The Grange could muster only about six thousand members in the South during the decade. Not until the late 1930s, when the Farm Bureau moved aggressively into the region, did the national farm groups become entrenched there.[84]

In the early 1920s, the most significant farm organizations in the southern states were the state cotton cooperatives, not surprising in a region where cotton accounted for one quarter to one half of agricultural receipts. Most were organized between 1921 and 1923, with the assistance of cooperative promoter Aaron Sapiro and the state extension services. Sapiro was a charismatic attorney who had gotten his start organizing fruit and vegetable marketing cooperatives in the administration of California governor Hiram Johnson. The hallmark of the "Sapiro coops" was the "iron-clad" contract, a five-year agreement that obligated cooperative members to deliver their production to the pool. Growers were paid a cash advance equal to whatever the cooperatives could borrow against the value of the crop, with the balance paid after the pool had marketed the cotton. The cooperatives quickly flourished, and by 1924 they controlled about a quarter of the cotton crop.[85]

As political organizations, however, the cooperatives were weak, especially in comparison with midwestern Farm Bureaus. They had neither local organizations nor a Washington office—their umbrella organization, the American Cotton Growers Exchange, was based in New Orleans (the major export center). Before 1926, moreover, they had little interest in price-fixing. With a strong cotton market a program to levy a tax on cotton growers to sell cotton more cheaply abroad was not very enticing, and the Sapiro coops as a group, federated into the National Council of Farmers Cooperative Marketing Associations (NCFCMA), were implacably hostile to Peek's legislation, one provision of which would establish a government export corporation to compete with them.[86] Thus, the cotton cooperatives did not bother to respond to the early, halfhearted overtures of the Peek lobbies.

The cotton growers' lack of interest in 1926 made not a few southerners uneasy. Jones and Swank, who were from neighboring districts on the Rolling

84. Fisher, *Farmers' Union*, 16; Wilson Gee and Edward Allison Terry, *The Cotton Cooperatives in the Southeast* (New York: D. Appleton-Century Co., 1933), 38; Wiest, *Agricultural Organization*, p. 398; "Membership Paid to the American Farm Bureau Federation," 250–51.

85. Gee and Terry, *Cotton Cooperatives*, chap. 2; Grace H. Larsen and Henry E. Erdman, "Aaron Sapiro," *Mississippi Valley Historical Review* 50 (February 1962) : 242–68; William Johnson, "Cotton Cooperatives at the Crossroads," *CG*, 6 December 1924, 16. Sapiro also helped organize tobacco cooperatives. Within a year of its founding the Burley Tobacco Growers Cooperative Association had enlisted 75 percent of the burley growers. See John K. Barnes, "An Even Break for the Farmer," *World's Work*, October 1922, 612–22; Clarence Poe, "Talking about Cooperative Marketing," *PF*, 7 July 1923, 683.

86. "Federation of Co-operatives Meets," *WF*, 16 January 1925, 72; Larsen and Erdman, "Aaron Sapiro."

Plains of Texas and Oklahoma, were both caught between wheat growers who favored the Peek plan, cattle feeders who opposed it, and a major constituency of cotton producers who were undecided. Hampton Fulmer of South Carolina, actively cultivating the farm groups, was dismayed by the lackadaisical attitude of Corn Belt organizers toward cotton growers, and he pleaded for help from Frank W. Murphy, chairman of the executive committee of the American Council of Agriculture:

> FULMER: Do you not think that it would be a good idea for you people of the West to try to get in touch with the cotton people of the South . . . so that you might know more about each other's troubles, and try to work together and work out this kind of legislation in the interest of agriculture in your section and in the South?
> MURPHY: . . . Some day I hope to have the pleasure of getting down that way and getting better acquainted with your folks.
> FULMER: Our people in the South are very anxious to get in touch with your people in the West, and they cannot understand why you people, whose interests are identical to theirs, cannot get together with them and work together.[87]

The alliance of Cotton Belt and Corn Belt lobbies was first consummated when cotton prices skidded from 20 cents to 13 cents a pound in 1926. The market's slide, which had begun in 1924, piqued the cooperatives' interest in price-fixing and this was encouraged, to the displeasure of Sapiro and other leaders of the NCFCMA, by council secretary Walton Peteet. Peteet's ties to the midwestern agrarians were extensive—he had begun his career in the Texas Farm Bureau and served as head of the federation's cooperative marketing division until he was purged during its ill-fated experiment with the United States Grain Growers. Peteet and the American Cotton Growers Exchange conducted hasty negotiations with the Peek forces, winning a three-year deferral on the imposition of the equalization fee on cotton. In April 1926 the cotton cooperatives swung behind the bill.[88]

The sigh of relief among cotton district legislators was almost audible when C. L. Stealey, manager of the Oklahoma Cotton Growers Association, came before the committee to announce the alliance. Jones found the support of his cotton growers a welcome addition to the support of his wheat growers. Swank could hardly contain his excitement. "You have made as clear, logical, and intelligent a statement as was ever made before this committee," he told Stealey. Replied Stealey, to laughter, "I get a chance to vote for him, you understand." They understood. The cooperatives' about-face snapped cotton lawmakers quickly around, and when the tobacco coops signed up in 1927,

---

87. *Hearings*, 1926, 499; Irvin May, *Marvin Jones* (College Station: Texas A&M University Press, 1980), 70.

88. Benedict, *Farm Policies*, 223–24; Christensen, "Agricultural Pressure," 203–10; "Cotton Men Join with Corn Belt," *WF*, 16 April 1926, 592; "Rumpus over Farm Plan," *NYT*, 23 April 1926, 4.

David Kincheloe, theretofore a savage critic, joined Haugen as comanager of the equalization fee bill on the floor.[89]

But as important as these conversions were for the Peek lobbies—the McNary-Haugen bill finally passed the Congress in 1927—they moved southern lawmakers only to sympathy for the farm groups, far short of the political reorientation in policy-making recently consolidated among midwesterners. Southerners on the Agriculture Committee remained the most skeptical and most openly critical of the plan and its sponsors. Even though the cotton and tobacco cooperatives held ranks, thirty southern representatives nearly defected on the 1927 floor vote. Marvin Jones, to the dismay of the farm groups and the passivity of the Grange, continued to push the export debenture at the risk of jeopardizing the Peek bill. "While the export debenture plan undoubtedly had a number of things to commend it," Henry A. Wallace groused, "no friend of the farmer should have brought it in at this time." The South was still the missing element in the agricultural policy network. "The success achieved by farm leaders in getting the House and Senate to adopt a remarkable measure of farm relief last spring shows how powerful was the influence of organized Western farmers," *Progressive Farmer* commented admiringly in 1927. "It is not unlikely that the whole national program of farm legislation has been seriously crippled and delayed, if not destroyed, because of the failure of Southern farmers to stand solidly with Western farmers in organizations demanding some such relief."[90]

The conversion of the cotton and tobacco cooperatives had brought the advantages of the southern farm groups into focus for legislators. Like the Farm Bureau, the cotton associations had no history of protest and reform, as earlier southern farm groups had. They drew their membership heavily from among prosperous growers, and they left issues of race and class alone. Thus, the cotton associations offered ready-made communication and intelligence networks that did not threaten the traditional "friends-and-neighbors" conduct of Democratic politics. For Hampton P. Fulmer, the South Carolina Cotton Growers Cooperative Association centralized access to a dispersed but identifiable constituency. The same plantation growers who dominated his district, the seventh, controlled the association. Its headquarters, in Columbia, was in his district. The cotton cooperatives made the construction and maintenance of southern coalitions more efficient. Southerners had ample reason to stay in their good graces.[91]

The paucity of compelling evidence of competitive advantage and recur-

89. *Hearings*, 1926, 1080, 1074–78; "Haugen Bill Strong," *WF*, 11 February 1927, 210; H. A. Wallace, "How the Farm Bill Went Through," *WF*, 25 February 1927, 301.

90. Wallace, "How the Farm Bill Went Through," 301; "A Farmers' Organization in Every Neighborhood," *PF*, 24 September 1927, 976; *Hearings before the House Committee on Agriculture*, "Agricultural Relief," 70th Congress, 1st sess., Serial E, 1928 (hereafter *Hearings*, 1928), 23–28, 32–34, 96–98, 118–19, 190, 201–02, 222–23; "Senate Passes McNary-Haugen Bill," *WF*, 18 February 1927, 245; "More Support for Haugen Bill," *WF*, 10 February 1928, 212.

91. Robert C. McMath, *Populist Vanguard* (New York: Norton, 1975), 44–46, 124–26; Fisher, *Farmers' Union*, 55–56; Gee and Terry, *Cotton Cooperatives*, 52.

rence, however, was reflected in southerners' irresolute commitment to the farm groups. In the late 1920s, the willingness and ability of the cooperatives to continue to press the Peek plan was by no means certain. The combination of lower cotton prices and the expiration the first iron-clad contracts badly hurt the cotton cooperatives—the Alabama Farm Bureau Cotton Association lost over half its nominal membership in 1927, and the cotton growers' associations of Georgia, North Carolina, and South Carolina lost nearly 90 percent of theirs. (The tobacco coops folded as well.) To top it off, 1927 cotton prices rose back to their 1925 level.[92]

The farm lobby had no way, either, to prove its competitive advantage. As members of the minority party, southern Democrats were free from the responsibility to advance or defend a policy. They could afford to use the McNary-Haugen bill to embarrass Coolidge, Hoover, and the Republicans. With southern votes the margin of victory on the floor, the farm groups were in no position to retaliate for partisan maneuvering. Southerners in fact used the Peek lobby's dependence to extract more favorable treatment for cotton.[93]

Realization of issue recurrence and competitive advantage was not long in coming, however. In 1926 Walton Peteet had argued that intervention in cotton markets was a permanent need, as they were inherently unstable. A year later, North Carolina senator F. M. Simmons, explaining his conversion to the Peek plan, echoed Peteet, noting that "cotton surpluses are temporary, not permanent in nature." But, he continued, "the cotton industry is perennially subject to the danger of overproduction." From these forewarnings in the late 1920s the South in the early 1930s developed as deep and fatalistic a sense of permanent crisis as the Midwest. Cotton skidded to 9 cents a pound in 1930, its lowest price since 1899, and tobacco fell to 8 cents in 1931, its lowest since 1905. "In the case of cotton and tobacco," *Progressive Farmer* finally admitted in 1931, "what confronts us is not just an emergency that will pass in one year, two years, or even five years. . . . No, on the contrary, we are faced with a lasting, permanent, here-to-stay change in conditions."[94]

In 1931, likewise, the farm groups finally became politically indispensable to southern Democrats. After twelve years in the minority, the party of Jefferson assumed control of the House of Representatives, and the southern Democrats who now led the Agriculture Committee had a tough act to follow—seven years of aggressive Republican leadership on a farm plan that had proven wildly popular in agricultural regions. Of all the farm relief plans from which they might choose, the only one whose popular appeal was established was the equalization fee. But the fee was a Republican measure, and if

92. Gee and Terry, *Cotton Cooperatives*, 154; Herman Steen and Bill Stahl, "The Dark Tobacco 'Co-ops,' " *PF*, 13 March 1926, 346–47; "How Can We Save Co-operative Marketing of Tobacco?" *PF*, 6 February 1926, 152.

93. Christensen, "Agricultural Pressure," 217; B. W. Kilgore, "Farm Relief Legislation," *PF*, 15 May 1926, 596.

94. F. M. Simmons, "Cotton and the McNary-Haugen Bill," *CG*, August 1927, 12; "We Must Change Not for a Year But for a Lifetime," *PF*, 1–14 October 1931, 618; "News Farmers Want to Know," *PF*, 7 August 1926, 834.

that were not enough, European trade barriers erected in retaliation for the Smoot-Hawley Tariff Act ensured that no export dumping scheme could possibly work. Thus southern Democrats needed something new, and if they were to budge midwesterners of either party from the safety of the Peek plan, they had to offer assurances that their plan was equally safe. By obtaining the imprimatur of the farm groups, committee leaders hoped to make whatever plan they arrived at "acceptable" to midwesterners.

The endorsement of farm lobby leaders assumed great importance for southern Democrats because it was already important for midwesterners. Public endorsements gave midwestern lawmakers some measure of electoral protection. Most obviously, it provided them with a sensible excuse back home, should their actions become controversial.[95] Even more important, however, it stole some of the farm lobby's thunder. If the plan they adopted with organized backing failed or was unpopular, the organizations, not legislators, could be blamed. The farm groups could accuse cooperative lawmakers of malfeasance only at the risk of embarrassing themselves, and their political endorsements gave group leaders greater incentive to be forthright with the committee about constituent preferences.

This understanding was already in place by 1931. In 1928, the farm groups had pressed forward with a revised version of the fourth McNary-Haugen bill, which had passed Congress in the 1927 lame-duck session only to be vetoed by President Coolidge. The farm lobby's refusal to compromise on the one element of the bill certain to provoke a second veto, the equalization fee, brought the "two-edged sword" into sharp focus. "If some of us decide to follow the views of the farm organizations," Indiana Republican Fred Purnell proposed, "and [send] a bill down to the President which we know will be vetoed, and we rely upon your judgment and the farmers get no legislation, then you take the responsibility for our action." "We are not shirking that responsibility," Chester Gray affirmed. For midwesterners whose elections depended on the farm groups, endorsements carried more than a hint of coercion. "If the members of this committee . . . are seeking an alibi or defense of negative action [on the equalization fee] from the farm groups," Gray noted pointedly, "I suspect you will have to wait some time. . . . I am perfectly willing and I shall give this committee . . . a positive statement . . . as to our positive position. If a negative position is taken, that is your responsibility, and you will get no alibi from the farm groups."[96] If southern Democrats could win the farm lobby's endorsement, then, they could put the organizations' muscle to work. If they failed to win farm group approval, their program would be stymied.

Fortunately, the times were ripe for innovation. Herbert Hoover's victory in 1928 had virtually killed the equalization fee politically, and southern Democrats like Fulmer began to promote the domestic allotment plan in its stead. In contrast to the Peek plan and the export debenture, the allotment scheme envisioned no export dumping; rather, it called for direct cash payments to

95. Richard F. Fenno, Jr., *Homestyle* (Boston: Little, Brown & Co., 1978), chap. 5.
96. *Hearings*, 1928, 43, 61.

farmers for reducing acreage under cultivation, with the program funded by a tax not on producers but on processors.[97] The scheme was a marvel of political ingenuity. Because allotments were based on historical acreages in production, entry into the business would be made more difficult, and the internal commodity and regional rivalries that had been a prime constraint on the network could be contained. This feature was especially important in the Deep South, for the allotment plan would prevent the loss of even more cotton acreage to Texas, Oklahoma, and California.[98]

The farm groups sensed which way the wind was blowing. Just months after the Democrats took over the House, Hoover appointed Farm Bureau president Sam Thompson to the Farm Board, and Farm Bureau delegates appointed Vice President Edward A. O'Neal to replace him. O'Neal, the grandson of one Alabama governor and the nephew of another, was the owner of a plantation that overlooked Muscle Shoals. In 1923, after a year's stint on the executive committee, he was elected Farm Bureau vice president. Two years later, the swing of his bloc of votes made Sam Thompson president. Symbolically, that election consummated the Farm Bureau's "marriage of corn and cotton," although that alliance was more poetic than real. The Corn Belt continued to dominate the federation, but O'Neal had too many useful qualities for the Farm Bureau to pass him over in 1931—he was a southerner, a Democrat, and a cotton farmer.[99]

Under O'Neal's stewardship, the Farm Bureau moved gradually away from the Peek plan. In May 1932, it agreed to lobby alongside the Grange and the Farmers Union on behalf of almost any farm relief program, be it the equalization fee, the export debenture, or something else. As the presidential campaign swung into high gear, however, the equalization fee's prospects dimmed. Franklin D. Roosevelt's major address on farm policy, delivered in Topeka in September, strongly implied that the Democratic nominee regarded the domestic allotment as the only acceptable plan. For the Grange and the Farmers

97. Credit for its invention is given to BAE economist William J. Spillman, but it was most closely associated with John Black, the Harvard economist who endorsed it as the most promising farm relief scheme, and M. L. Wilson, the former BAE economist and professor at Montana State College who promoted it (Donald R. Murphy, "Can We Control Production?" *WF*, 16 April 1932, 219; " 'Domestic Allotment' Farm Relief," *PF*, January 1933, 3; Louis H. Cook, "Domestic Allotment," *CG*, February 1933, 10–11).

98. In 1931 and 1932, a number of southern states, led by Huey Long's Louisiana, enacted legislation mandating production cutbacks. None of the laws ever went into effect, since they stipulated that other states must first follow suit, but in 1931 acreage control received the endorsement of the editors of *Progressive Farmer*, three of whom had lent a hand in organizing the cotton cooperatives. "Today, after the failure of all other plans," they wrote, "we believe that three out of four cotton farmers would vote for the regulation of cotton acreage by law" ("The Cotton Surplus Problem," *PF*, 15–30 September 1931, 586; William D. Rowley, *M. L. Wilson and the Campaign for the Domestic Allotment* [Lincoln: University of Nebraska Press, 1970], 188; "We Must Change Not for a Year," *PF*, 618; T. Harry Williams, *Huey Long* [New York: Alfred A. Knopf, 1969], 530–33).

99. Theodore Saloutos, "Edward A. O'Neal," *Current History* 28 (June 1955) : 356–63; Kile, *Farm Bureau*, 121; Gee and Terry, *Cotton Cooperatives*, 57–62.

Union this was bad news; John A. Simpson, the union's firebrand president, loathed acreage controls, and Louis J. Taber, as befitted a Grange master, was neutral. The Farm Bureau was more amenable. For more than a year, allotment publicist M. L. Wilson, a Montana State College economist, had lobbied the state Farm Bureaus, sending out letters over the signature of Montana Farm Bureau president W. L. Stockton. Roosevelt's landslide convinced the rest. In December 1932, yielding to pragmatism, Farm Bureau leaders gave the allotment plan their private approval, and in January 1933 O'Neal made it public. "The equalization fee and the debenture . . . have not lost their attraction," Chester Gray assured Farm Bureau members, "but temporarily they have been laid aside for consideration of the farm allotment plan." [100]

By late in 1932, Democrats had a farm relief plan that had farm group endorsement. That endorsement now became a powerful lure for the Farm Bureau to dangle before southern Democrats. It restored Farm Bureau access to policy leadership that had first been gained during the early McNary-Haugen years. In 1926, the agricultural organizations "served a virtual ultimatum on [Chairman Haugen] that unless he sponsored their bill it would be offered by Representative Purnell of Indiana, thus minimizing Mr. Haugen's leadership in the contest for government assistance to agriculture." Haugen had relented. In 1932, Committee chairman Marvin Jones found himself in the same bind. Despite his grave misgivings about acreage restrictions, Jones could either sponsor the domestic allotment plan or allow the mantle of policy leadership to fall to Hampton Fulmer. Jones too relented. [101]

On the eve of the New Deal, then, the conditions that caused midwestern representatives to establish close ties with the farm groups held for southern lawmakers also. As in the Midwest, the adoption of a popular new issue by an important new group—a group represented in Washington by the Peek lobby—had not been sufficient to win southern allegiances, and the 1926 marriage of corn and cotton was one of convenience rather than necessity. Without coherent electoral competition, southern lawmakers lacked evidence that cotton-growing constituents backed up the cooperatives' requests. Without an indication that the economic troubles in southern agriculture would persist, leg-

100. Chester H. Gray, "Jobs for the Special Session," *Bureau Farmer*, April 1933, 3; Rowley, *M. L. Wilson*, 107–10, 187–88; Gilbert C. Fite, "John A. Simpson," *Mississippi Valley Historical Review* 35 (March 1949) : 563–84; Lord, *Wallaces*, 330; "News of the Farm Bureau," *Bureau Farmer*, February 1932, 8; "Farmers Not So Particular Now, Endorse 3 Brands of Relief," *Business Week*, 11 May 1932, 19; Edward A. O'Neal, "Prevent Revolution," *Bureau Farmer*, March 1933, 3; Saloutos, "Edward A. O'Neal"; Richard S. Kirkendall, *Social Scientists and Farm Politics in the Age of Roosevelt* (Ames: Iowa State University Press, 1982), chap. 2; Theodore Saloutos, *The American Farmer and the New Deal* (Ames: Iowa State University Press, 1982), chap. 3.

101. "Haugen to Sponsor Farm Bill in House," *NYT*, 20 December 1926, 2; "Relief for Farmers Demanded in House," *NYT*, 16 December 1926, 2; May, *Marvin Jones*, 95–103. Jones refused to sponsor the 1933 Agricultural Adjustment Act, however, and Fulmer received credit as its legislative author. Jones still made his support for the bill clear. See Van L. Perkins, *Crisis in Agriculture* (Berkeley and Los Angeles: University of California Press, 1969), 52–54.

islators lacked evidence that the cooperatives' demands for intervention would continue. Circumstances counseled attention, but caution.

The political imperatives of change finally arrived via a different route. The collapse of southern agriculture in the early 1930s indicated that southern demands for farm relief would certainly endure, and the Democratic takeover of the House made the support of the farm lobby politically indispensable to the southern Democrats who now led the Agriculture Committee. They needed the support of midwesterners of both parties, and midwesterners were not going anywhere without the farm lobby.

The House hearings for the 1932 agricultural adjustment bill clearly indicated that the South was finally on board. Of the eight southern committee members, two were "liberals," three were "centralists," and only one was a "conservative." Adding Jones as a moderate to liberal, that put six of the eight favorably disposed to the farm organization line. Thus, the farm organizations were not as surprised by the warm reception they got in 1932 as they had been in 1926. In fact, so certain were they of the loyalty of their committee allies that they sent only a handful of witnesses and waived most of their allotted time.[102] With a friendly committee and with President-elect Franklin D. Roosevelt pledged to support the program agreed on by "the responsible farm organizations," there was no need to get too excited.

The committee met farm group expectations. Southern Democrats could find little bad to say about the bill, which included cotton and tobacco among its four basic commodities. Hampton Fulmer was unrestrained in his enthusiasm as he led Frederick P. Lee, a Washington attorney retained by the Farm Bureau to draft the bill, through the argument:

> FULMER: It is generally understood, under the operations of the [Hoover] Farm Board, that they have tried to fix and maintain a fair price, without any control over production, and it has proven an absolute failure and a waste of money. Is it not a fact, unless you put into this legislation a mandatory cut . . . that [the farmers'] production would bring about the same thing that we have had under the Farm Board, which would mean the wasting of millions of consumers' money and therefore absolute defeat of the plan.
> LEE: That is correct, sir.
> FULMER: In other words, it would be taxing the consumer to a great extent, and if we have an overproduction it would naturally bring down the . . . price. . . . To my mind, this is one of the most important sections in the bill—that is, production control either mandatorily or by proofs furnished by the farmer.
> LEE: That is correct, sir; the reduction of acreage and the parity price are provisions that are in the interests of the consumer and of the general public as well as in the interests of the farmers.[103]

102. May, *Marvin Jones*, 100–01; *Hearings before the House Committee on Agriculture*, "Agricultural Adjustment Program," 72d Congress, 2nd sess., Serial M, 1932 (hereafter *Hearings, 1932*), 265.

103. *Hearings*, 1932, 17, 16; May, *Marvin Jones*, 102.

Chairman Jones was more interested in establishing another point. "Does this general program have the unanimous indorsement of the farm representatives?" he asked Lee. "It has the unanimous indorsement of all of the farm representatives present," the attorney replied. The endorsement was the important thing, not the technical arguments. As Jones's biographer put it, "Jones always preferred the counsel of agricultural organizations and plain dirt farmers to agricultural economists and social scientists" like Wilson.[104]

This time, criticism of the farm groups came largely from lame-duck Republicans who had been loyal allies of the farm groups. Fred Purnell of Indiana and Charles Adkins of Illinois, for example, felt betrayed and were especially eager to retaliate, even with such futile gestures as goading farm leaders. But the single midwestern Republican who remained was inclined to stay in their good graces. "In previous legislation this committee has considered that it was the purpose to make the tariff effective and that has been the yardstick used in determining the basis of the price to be sought," Kansan Clifford Hope noted. "Now, in this measure, you have departed from that theory and have taken as the yardstick the purchasing power which the commodities involved had before the war. . . . Do you think, Mr. Lee, that such a basis would be as easy to justify, assuming that we would have to justify it, as the policy of making the tariff effective?"[105] Here is the Committee on Agriculture considering an explicitly interventionist policy put forth by Democrats, and Republican Hope wants only to know if the symbolism of the new baseline is as acceptable as the symbolism of the old.

When Franklin Roosevelt took office, then, the formation of the agricultural price support network was complete. Midwesterners who had been persuaded to build close working relationships with the farm groups by Republican party strife, by a well-oiled equalization fee lobby, and by gloomy assessments of the future of prairie agriculture were joined by southerners persuaded by a promising new constituency group, by aid in building policy coalitions, and by equally gloomy assessments of the future of the Cotton Belt. In a little over a decade, farm organizations had taken a policy domain open to producers, suppliers, processors, and even consumers and made it their exclusive province.

CONCLUDING REMARKS

Competitive advantage and recurrence, we have seen, illuminate the political process by which the rise of the farm lobby and the decline of political parties brought a new style of policy interaction to agriculture. But the implications of this theory extend beyond farm price policy in the 1920s. Although policy networks may be a "characteristic form of power" in some policy domains, they obviously are neither ubiquitous nor consistently strong across domains. By focusing generally on the calculations of institutional elites choosing among

104. *Hearings*, 1932, 16; May, *Marvin Jones*, 90.
105. *Hearings*, 1932, 56, 19–20, 90–91, 101, 148–52, 204.

alternatives, the theory allows us to predict not only the presence of policy networks but also their absence. Policy networks, the theory asserts, should not exist where interest groups do not enjoy competitive advantage or where groups, issues, and circumstances do not recur.

One need not range far to uncover examples of the failure of competitive advantage. In the late 1930s, for example, several organizations representing small business owners set up shop in Washington. None of them, however, had the membership, money, or commitment to garner much attention. In fact, all were little more than zealots with post office boxes. Consequently, "nothing approximating a subsystem of activity is possible" in small-business lobby interactions with Congress. "Instead of a subsystem, a pattern of inter-action between the small business groups and the committees has developed which might best be described as a 'struggle for legitimacy.' " The Senate and House Small Business Committees, locked into a battle for turf with Banking and Currency, finally abandoned the small-business lobby altogether. "Find-ing no advantage in using [the National Small Business Men's Association], the Senate Committee turned to trade associations" like the National Associa-tion of Retail Druggists.[106] Small-business lobbies never had the kind of con-stituency backing needed to supply competitive advantage.

Failures of policy networks to coalesce also stem from absence of recur-rence. Despite their remarkable success, for instance, the environmental lob-bies seem not to have established links with Congress in the style of agricul-ture. "The normal congressional response," Price reports, "has been a certain wariness of becoming identified as a pro-environmental 'extremist.' " Among the reasons why, one is important here: the ecology agenda is distinctly tran-sitory. Environmentalism rode into Congress in 1970 on a wave of public euphoria climaxed by Earth Day, but its momentum has proven very difficult to sustain. In 1970, 53 percent of Gallup's respondents identified "pollution" as the nation's most important problem. By 1974, however, ecological con-cerns had been eclipsed by two new issues that were substantially antagonistic to it, inflation and energy, and business opponents of environmental regula-tion enjoyed a resurgence. Thus, once the initial wave of public enthusiasm was spent, the environmental lobbies were hard pressed to demonstrate a durable claim to the special attention of legislators. The future of environ-mental politics has never been as predictable as the future of agricultural pol-itics, and lawmakers accordingly have had less incentive to rely heavily on the environmental groups for their counsel. No one wants to get caught on the downside of the "issue-attention cycle."[107]

106. L. Harmon Zeigler, *The Politics of Small Business* (Washington: Public Affairs Press, 1961), 84, 85, 79.

107. David E. Price, "Policy Making in Congressional Committees: The Impact of 'Envi-ronmental' Factors," *American Political Science Review* 72 (June 1978) : 564; Anthony Downs, "Up and Down with Ecology: The Issue-Attention Cycle," *Public Interest* 28 (Summer 1972) : 38–50; Mary Etta Cook and Roger H. Davidson, "Deferral Politics: Congressional Decision Making on Environmental Issues in the 1980s," in Helen M. Ingram and R. Ken-neth Godwin, eds., *Public Policy and the Natural Environment* (Greenwich, Conn.: JAI Press,

Finally, policy networks will not be significant in areas where parties and interest groups do not compete. "The subjects of labor, education, and poverty," Fenno notes, "pose issues over which Democrats and Republicans have tended to divide and which have often been the major points of domestic disagreement in Presidential and congressional campaigns. . . . Put conversely, the executive branch, clientele groups, and House members have been especially quick to use party resources to fight their battles in nationally controversial policy areas." Where party cleavages reflect interest group cleavages, then, competitive advantage is not an issue—interest group politics and party politics converge.[108] Lawmakers can do no better by following interest group cues rather than party cues because the dictates are the same.

The rarity of party-pressure group convergence serves to underscore a fundamental point about the relationship of party politics to interest group politics: pressure politics reflects the failure of parties to absorb and channel conflict. When parties emphasize interest cleavages, as in disputes between business and labor, lobbies march in lockstep with parties. As Schattschneider pointed out, they have nowhere else to go.[109] When parties fail or refuse to emphasize cleavages, however, the battle for loyalties commences. The tenacity with which both parties opposed McNary-Haugenism forced rural lawmakers and the farm groups to test their strength and thereby opened Pandora's box.

The inability of parties to absorb conflict, moreover, is an inherent failing. Parties must decide what issues are important, and first choices preclude countless later choices. Republicans in the 1920s, for instance, could not embrace the farm groups without endangering the positions of northeastern party leaders. The first rule of party leadership is protect the ground already secured, maintain a strong battle front, resist any breaks in the line. Political parties are not naturally inclusive. On the contrary, they are naturally exclusive.

Encouraging political parties, then, will not be enough to combat the biases and inefficiencies of pressure politics. Party cleavages simply cannot mirror all important cleavages, and those conflicts that parties fail to channel will be fought elsewhere. The fashion of our time has been to identify close relationships between representatives and interest groups as the problem and stronger parties as the solution. The experience of agriculture in the 1920s should give us pause. Change in the politics of lobby and legislator ultimately will come from within the Congress, not from without.

1985), 47–76; Charles O. Jones, *Clean Air* (Pittsburgh: University of Pittsburgh Press, 1975), 56; Daniel R. Grant, "Carrots, Sticks, and Consensus," in Leslie R. Roos, ed., *The Politics of Ecosuicide* (New York: Holt, Rinehart & Winston, 1971), 101; J. Clarence Davies III and Barbara S. Davies, *The Politics of Pollution*, 2nd ed. (Indianapolis: Bobbs-Merrill Co., 1975); Ripley and Franklin, *Congress*, 125–31.

108. Richard F. Fenno, Jr., *Congressmen in Committees* (Boston: Little, Brown & Co., 1973), 31–32.

109. Schattschneider, *Semi-sovereign People*, chap. 3.

LOUIS GALAMBOS
Johns Hopkins University

"Choosing Sides": Comment

In the past century the American political system has changed in dramatic ways. A new national state has been created, and a substantial part of the nation's goods and services has been entrusted to its care. New administrative agencies allocate most of those resources, working in tandem with a multitude of private and other public organizations. Complex webs of fiscal interaction tie state and local governments—themselves greatly enlarged—to the nation state. All these public bodies are surrounded by and closely allied with formidable interest groups, with political action committees, with business corporations and foundations, and with various professional organizations. Swirling about this great governmental mass in recent years are the consultants, lawyers, and technicians who slip in and out of the public sector as administrations change or their careers dictate; these policy professionals, wherever they land, make use of their special knowledge and contacts in particular areas of public activity.

Although we have barely begun to understand how this new state was actually created or how it functions, two features of the modern brand of polity have attracted considerable attention in recent years. One is the declining role of the political parties. In the late nineteenth century they were dominant institutions that garnered allegiance from voters who participated enthusiastically and regularly in the party rituals and elections of the day. That is no more the case, and considerable scholarly attention has been directed at describing and explaining this transition. Another feature of the modern system that has aroused substantial academic comment is the so-called iron triangles—I prefer to call them "triocracies"—that have emerged as agencies, legislators, and interest groups have formed lasting, mutually beneficial alliances. These compacts have proven to be highly durable and controversial elements in our political system. They are frequently condemned for their inflexibility in defense of programs that appear to have been rendered obsolete by a changing environment.

Indeed, both the triocracies, or triangles, and the changes in the parties are more often lamented than fully understood, and there rests the great value of John Mark Hansen's study of the emergence of the agricultural policy network in the interwar era. Hansen relates these two phenomena in a model that is novel and intriguing. It is novel because it approaches interest group politics not from the side of the groups seeking or defending particular policies but from the viewpoint of the politicians who either give or deny the groups what they want. Hansen's model is novel, too, in that it sets minimal conditions for such an alliance or working arrangement—his policy net-work—to develop. What are needed, Hansen demonstrates, are assurances that interest group demands will recur and that the groups will serve the politician's intelligence and reelection needs better than the parties (the chief alternative) will. This theory and history of the agrarian network are intriguing because they link party decline and triocratic government, providing at least partial explanations of the relationships between two of the most significant transformations in American democracy in the past hundred years. They are intriguing, too, because they employ a rational actor model of the sort that has long characterized economic theory.

The model will probably satisfy more political scientists than political historians for fairly obvious reasons. The actors—in this case, politicians—are assumed to be maximizing creatures concerned above all with reelection. That is why they calculate so carefully the relative advantages of obtaining information from and working closely with the regular party structure or with the interest groups. The party—itself actually complex patterns of personal relations, expectations, and obligations—offers the politician-actor access to funds, to organized support, and to information about constituency attitudes. But the interest groups can provide all these as well, and they have the advantage of being able to offer highly specific, well-targeted information and goals. Functionally specialized, the groups are seldom interested in a broad range of policies, and Hansen traces in his history the progressive narrowing of the agricultural lobby's focus as price and production controls became the central issue of farm politics in the twenties and thirties.

The actor's choice—party or interest group—is a crucial element in the model. Although I find no reason to question Hansen's emphasis on the idea that the policy issues must appear to be of a recurring nature before a network will form, I am far less convinced that politicians are usually forced to make a clean choice between the two alternatives. The essence of astute political behavior is the avoidance of such damaging choices; compromise is what one would normally expect, especially where a legislator's state party is concerned. Price and production controls in farm commodities did, of course, provoke two vetoes by a Republican president, and as Hansen establishes, the national party was opposed to the farm groups over this issue. But I find no specific evidence in his article that particular legislators broke with their state organizations as a result of their votes on the McNary-Haugen bills. I would be surprised if they did.

If they made a choice, then, it was to lean one way or another on one specific issue, and that in turn suggests that the choices were matters of degree and were scalar, not binary. In microeconomic models actors make choices between mutually exclusive goods or services: if you buy a car, you cannot use the same money to buy a house. But legislators in their personal political careers seldom face that sort of choice, particularly if they can avoid it. Successful legislators, we should assume, are successful in part because they arrange reality so that they finesse such harsh choices. I for one see no reason why Hansen's model cannot be adapted to allow for accommodations and

compromises. Over time they would cumulate and in effect eventually constitute the sort of "choice" he has in mind. The model in its scalar form would
not be as neat as the one Hansen offers. But it would probably be truer to the
kinds of political behavior the author is analyzing.

Hansen is well aware of the gradual manner in which legislator–interest
group relations shift over the years. He remarks that in legislative hearings
they "move from contentiousness to attentiveness to solicitousness." Indeed,
this sort of scalar process, rather than a sudden shift from the party to the
interest group, seems to me to have been the essence of the legislative process
in the 1920s. In 1921 the farm bloc negotiated a settlement with the national
party leaders in order to gain for the farmers what they had usually wanted
in the past: public authority to change the economic performance of those
other parties (the packers, the grain exchanges, the sources of credit) with
whom farmers did business. One year later Congress passed the Capper-Vol-
stead Act, which gave the burgeoning farm cooperatives relief from the antitrust laws; Hansen neglects this measure, but it was an important milestone in
a movement that had already garnered substantial state support for farm
marketing organizations. In this phase of the agrarian movement, farmers
and their legislators focused at last on their own markets and their own behavior—a trend that climaxed, as Hansen establishes, with the McNary-Haugen bills and the New Deal's controls. If one puts the cooperative experiments
back into the history, the picture that emerges is more consistent, I believe,
with a scalar than a binary model. When the cooperatives failed, farm groups
as well as their legislators simply took one more step toward tight coercive
controls. A scalar or incremental model helps us analyze the sequence that led
to the decision, as well as the crucial final step itself (the one on which Hansen's model focuses attention).

The rational actor model raises other questions as well, but they are of less
concern to me. Certainly the legislator-actors were more complex than Hansen's theory allows them to be. Ideology might on occasion have influenced
their choices. Tradition too could have shaped behavior, especially where the
choices made (for controls) involved rejecting values (competition and indi-
vidualism, for example) sanctioned by long experience in political economy.
But what the model takes away in complexity, it gives back in the form of
improved analysis. Without Hansen's theory, we are left with some very poor
alternative explanations.

Three alternatives come to mind. One stems from progressive or liberal
historiography, which explains legislative behavior of this sort by reference to
altruism, to ideology, and to participation in a reform movement. The liberal
approach forces one to distinguish between the McNary-Haugen bill (a good
measure prompted by the people) and the efforts of oil producers to bring
their markets under control in the 1930s (a bad measure prompted, these
historians would have it, by the so-called interests of capital). Hansen's theory
forces no such choice: like the Keynesian theory, Hansen's model is value-
free in terms of outcomes. Using his approach, we can, for instance, compare
to good effect the efforts of farm and business groups to influence legislators,
and we should be able to achieve a better understanding—from the legisla-

tor's perspective—of why some groups succeeded and others failed to replace the parties as a source of information. Using the progressive synthesis, we were not even likely to ask these questions, let alone develop convincing answers.

A second form of explanation is generated by radical historiography, which stresses the extent to which legislators naturally aligned themselves with well-heeled interests, especially those of business and of the groups that associated themselves with business. Once organized agriculture stopped bashing big business—as the groups Hansen studies generally did in the early 1920s—and joined the corporate-liberal combine, farmers could expect an appropriate payoff. McNary-Haugen was part of that payoff, as was the agrarian legislation of the 1930s. In this construct, legislators made class-oriented decisions as they opted for the affluent middle-class, property-owning agrarians and decided to ignore the agricultural underclass of sharecroppers and farm laborers. This approach unfortunately leaves out the political parties for the most part. Hansen's model gives them a significant role in the political history, a role they clearly deserve. Moreover, his analysis enables us to explain why legislators shifted their positions, something the radical history has difficulty treating in nonconspiratorial terms. Hansen makes the legislators important decision makers, not merely products of their pressure group environment.

Finally, there is the so-called revisionist historiography, which stresses the complexity of decision making and in effect leaves us where we were before we tried to formulate an explanation. Revisionists have broken down the simple lineups that characterized the progressive view of politics and developed some interesting hypotheses—Richard Hofstadter's concept of "status anxiety," for example—about the motivation of political actors. But revisionists have not developed a general explanation of party decline, nor have they related that phenomenon, as Hansen does, to the rise of interest groups. His model explains why legislators shifted their orientations and thus altered in decisive ways the American political process.

On this playing field, against these three opponents, Hansen is a clear winner. His approach can explain better than any of the three alternatives the timing of network formation and the development of the relevant legislation. His mode of analysis is neutral in regard to the specific content of the legislation, the time period involved, and the precise nature of the legislative or interest group actors. It will be as useful in analyzing the post–World War II military-industrial-university complex as it is in treating the agrarian networks of the 1920s. In that sense his model is more powerful than any of the historical explanations I have mentioned.

With some slight adjustments Hansen's theory should also be useful in explaining more contemporary phenomena than the agricultural networks of the twenties and thirties. In the period since World War II, the organizational environment in Washington, D.C., has become very dense. The number of interest groups has expanded, as have the number of congressional staff members. The choices legislators make have become correspondingly intricate, as they balance one group against another. Hansen's model can handle that sort of complexity since the legislator's decision is the same in every case;

he or she is deciding between two alternative sources of information and they could be two interest groups just as easily as they could be a party and a pressure group. Convinced as I am that the networks Hansen is analyzing are some of the most important institutions in our modern administrative state, I am intrigued by these possibilities for an extension of Hansen's path-breaking work.

"Choosing Sides" also suggests to me that political scientists are in the future going to be doing much more historical institutional research, and that political historians are going to have to rethink much that they have written on the years between 1900 and World War II. What was happening in agriculture was also happening in organized labor, in business, and in the professions. Legislators in the states and the U.S. Congress were being approached by more and more such pressure groups. We have learned a great deal about the groups and their needs. But the legislators, as such, have been left out of our political history, in part because historians have lacked the analytical categories they needed in order to generalize about legislative behavior in network formation. With that type of tool now in hand, scholars will be able to retill the familiar fields of the Progressive Era and the 1920s. Even the New Deal calls for some reappraisal along these lines.

We need to ask, for instance, to what extent the clustering of legislation in the reform eras was a product of the two conditions Hansen sets forth. This is not the sort of question historians have been asking of their sources, nor have many political scientists been doing the type of research called for by this line of reasoning. On the basis of work done in recent years on the twenties, we do know that at that time numerous interest groups became closely aligned with the government in much the same way that the farm organizations did. This was true of cotton textile manufacturers, oil producers, lumber interests, and numerous other groups. In many cases the goals they sought were not realized until the 1930s, when the Great Depression provided a justification for legislative innovation. It also helped satisfy Hansen's two conditions for a transition from party to interest group politics. This line of analysis promises to improve our understanding of these two important decades—one frequently associated with conservative and the other with liberal politics—and of their close interrelationships in terms of institutional and political processes of change. By opening up subjects such as these, Hansen's work promises to have a significant impact on both the theory and the history of U.S. political behavior in the twentieth century.

JOHN MARK HANSEN

Reply to Professor Galambos

Thinking about how to make sense of political history is a difficult task, and Professor Galambos has identified many of the important issues that make it that. I would like to address the most central.

Our major difference is over the theoretical and descriptive utility of constructing for legislators a choice between political parties and interest groups. As a description of the real options lawmakers face, the binary choice I pose is, I concede, *usually* inaccurate. In many instances representatives can satisfy both parties and lobbies, especially, as Professor Galambos suggests, by exploiting the differences between the national and state party organizations. But this strategy also has its limits. Although many midwestern party elites were sympathetic to McNary-Haugenism, for example, an equally significant faction was opposed: witness the 1924 senatorial contest in Iowa, where Republican regulars bolted to the candidate of "rum, rebellion, and Romanism," Democrat Daniel Steck, rather than be implicated in the heresies of Smith Brookhart. Because of their treachery (or Brookhart's?), Steck became Iowa's first Democratic senator since before the Civil War. In Iowa and elsewhere, the demands of parties and pressure groups are not always reconcilable.

If ever parties and interest groups disagree, moreover, it makes little theoretical difference whether the empirical choices of legislators are scalar or binary. Members of Congress can take the advice of parties or groups in whatever mix they like, but those who lean too far in the wrong direction will not be back for another term. Even legislators who balance party and group demands are choosing one informant over the other because that last scalar increment may be the difference between winning and losing. Whether they leaned a little too far or a lot too far, the electoral outcomes are the same. Thus, the theoretical problem is identical whether the empirical options are binary or scalar. Members of Congress choose advisers *as if* they are choosing one or the other.[1]

Finally, the costs of starting from descriptively correct assumptions are greater than they may appear. Posing scalar rather than binary choices obviously complicates theory building, but the sacrifice of analytical power is only part of the story. The more significant danger is that the problem itself might be lost. The binary construction forces legislators to do theoretically what they do empirically: choose sides. If lawmakers could always reconcile the wants of pressure groups and parties, they would never in any nontrivial sense act contrary to the wishes of either. Policy networks are important, however, only because the demands of lobbying groups are met *at the expense of* the interests of national leaders, political parties, and the greater good. What really matters, then, is that lawmakers favor interest groups over political parties. Asking why they do so is the point at which the analysis should begin.

1. David R. Mayhew, *Congress: The Electoral Connection* (New Haven: Yale University Press, 1974), 13–17; Milton Friedman, "The Methodology of Positive Economics," in *Essays in Positive Economics* (Chicago: University of Chicago Press, 1953), 3–43; and Armen A. Alchian, "Uncertainty, Evolution, and Economic Theory," *Journal of Political Economy* 58 (June 1950) : 211–21.

TERRY M. MOE
Stanford University

Interests, Institutions, and Positive Theory: The Politics of the NLRB

The claim that institutions "matter" is a subject of lively debate in the study of politics today. It is also something of a nonissue that is not really being debated at all. The reason it can be both at once is that the claim is loaded with theoretical baggage. If it is taken to mean that the actions of politicians or bureaucrats are in fundamental respects autonomous of social interests, the statement can easily prove controversial. If it is taken to mean that institutional context shapes the decisions of political actors, or that the relation between social interests and political outcomes varies with the institutional setting, then there is not much to debate; for there has long been a virtual consensus among students of politics that institutions do matter in these general respects.[1]

All theories of political outcomes are unavoidably about social interests and political institutions. Controversy productively centers not around whether one or the other matters, but around precisely how they matter and what their relative explanatory powers are. Pluralists give explanatory emphasis to social interests, but in no sense do they ignore the integral role of institutions.[2] Proponents of the "new institutionalism" give greater explanatory weight to institutions, but social interests still have important roles to play in their theories.[3] Stereotypes aside, the basic goal of all concerned is to move toward

1. For an overview of these issues and the surrounding literature, see Stephen D. Krasner, "Approaches to the State: Alternative Conceptions and Historical Dynamics," *Comparative Politics* (January 1984) : 223–46; Theda Skocpol, "Bringing the State Back In: Strategies of Analysis in Current Research," in Peter B. Evans, Dietrich Rueschemeyer, and Theda Skocpol, *Bringing the State Back In* (Cambridge: Cambridge University Press, 1985); and James G. March and Johan P. Olsen, "The New Institutionalism: Organizational Factors in Political Life," *American Political Science Review* 78 (September 1984) : 734–49.

2. Among other classic pluralist works, see David B. Truman, *The Governmental Process: Political Interests and Public Opinion*, 2nd ed. (New York: Knopf, 1971); and Robert Dahl, *Who Governs? Democracy and Power in an American City* (New Haven: Yale University Press, 1961).

3. March and Olsen, "The New Institutionalism."

theories that demonstrate how social interests and political institutions jointly determine political outcomes. The disagreement is over how this can best be accomplished and what it is likely to yield.

These same themes have oriented recent developments in positive political theory, particularly those concerned with explaining government regulation of the economy. The best known economic theories—sometimes (now inappropriately) called capture theories—are societally driven. Economic interests are taken as fundamental, and theoretical attention centers on the logic by which these interests are translated into political influence and public policy. The institutions that actually accomplish this translation—legislatures, executives, agencies, interest organizations—are included implicitly: they are "functions" that map interests onto outcomes. No attempt is made to model them or understand how they work. What these theories provide is essentially a pluralist, balance-of-power explanation of the division of political spoils, anchored in rational choice assumptions that link individual interests to political action.[4]

The debate is joined by recent work in the positive theory of institutions. Social interests are part of their explanations, too, because politicians and bureaucrats are motivated to please voters and interest groups. But attention is generally directed to how actors within political institutions make decisions, both individually and collectively, and how structure shapes the associated political outcomes. Concern may rest with the stabilizing impact of legislative rules and procedures on policy decisions, for example, or the extent to which legislative committees can control regulatory agencies. These theories look inside the economists' institutional black box—but their orientation does not lead them to ask the kinds of questions a societally driven theory would want to have answered. At present different purposes are at work.[5]

As in the larger literature, it seems fair to say that the overriding purposes of the two sides are basically the same: to understand, as simply and clearly as possible, how all these components fit together in generating public policy. In effect, the economic and institutional theories are starting points for moving toward this goal, with the choice of starting point determined by some prior notion of what is most important. The economists believe that, although dif-

4. George J. Stigler, "The Theory of Economic Regulation," *Bell Journal of Economics and Management Science* 2 (Spring 1971) : 3–21, and "Free Riders and Collective Action: An Appendix to Theories of Economic Regulation," *Bell Journal of Economics and Management Science* (Autumn 1974) : 359–65; Sam Peltzman, "Toward a More General Theory of Regulation," *Journal of Law and Economics* 19 (1976) : 211–40; Gary Becker, "A Theory of Competition among Pressure Groups for Political Influence," *Quarterly Journal of Economics* 98 (1983) : 371–400, and "Public Policies, Pressure Groups, and Deadweight Costs," *Journal of Public Economics* 28 (1985) : 329–47.

5. For a thoughtful perspective on the positive theory of institutions, see Kenneth Shepsle, "Institutional Equilibrium and Equilibrium Institutions," in Herbert F. Weisberg, ed., *Political Science: The Science of Politics* (New York: Agathon Press, 1986). For a comparison of the economic theory of politics and the positive theory of institutions, see Thomas Romer and Howard Rosenthal, "Modern Political Economy and the Study of Regulation" (Paper presented at the NSF/CMU Conference on Regulation, Airlie, Va., September 12–14, 1985).

ferent institutions provide different translations of interests into policy, the essence of an explanation is that equilibrium regulatory outcomes reflect the underlying balance of economic interests; we should build our models accordingly. Institutionalists argue that the omitted translation processes are in fact the keys to an understanding of politics; they want to focus on models of elite decision making and political structure.

There is good reason to think that, in the long run, both approaches will move toward more comprehensive models that offer balanced, well-integrated perspectives on interests, institutions, and policy. But in the short run, what positive political theory has to offer are two opposing perspectives on the explanation of politics, both of them highly selective and in their early stages of development. Important as both may be for theoretical progress, at this point they can be misleading about what to expect in politics, what to look for in studying it, and how to explain what is observed.

My purpose in this article is to suggest more concretely why this is so and to illustrate the need—even in the short run—for positive theories whose orientations toward politics are distinctly different from those now popular. As a vehicle for making these theoretical points, I explore the regulatory politics of one agency, the National Labor Relations Board (NLRB), over the last half century. The analysis is broadly concerned with a whole range of topics that traditionally find their way into detailed historical accounts. These include the ways in which economic interests are aggregated and brought to bear in politics, the roles and relative influence of the president and Congress, the rise of bureaucratic professionalism, the emergence of informal routines for resolving conflict, and the pervasive consequences of the American Constitution for political action and influence. But my approach here is neither detailed nor, in a methodological sense, historical. What I want to do is construct an argument—one that abstracts from most of the details, offers an interpretation of the broad sweep of events, and is very much in keeping with the rational choice tradition.[6]

The article is divided into two parts. The first is concerned with developing this argument about the NLRB. Here I attempt to impose a certain logical structure on the historical development of the NLRB's regulatory politics and suggest how an inherently complex set of considerations might be integrated into a reasonably simple and systematic explanation. This explanation reflects the operation of strong reciprocal relationships among social interests, political institutions, and public policy, and it holds that the logic by which these are bound up with one another is the key to NLRB politics. In the second part of the article, I return to the economic theory of politics and the positive theory of institutions. After outlining their general perspectives on interests,

---

6. The argument I present here is based in part upon the available literature and in part on interviews I have conducted with present and former participants in NLRB politics—people who have variously occupied positions in the agency, the White House, the House and Senate Labor committees, the Department of Labor, the major business and labor groups, and law firms. Collectively, their experiences with the board span the entire period, from the 1930s and 1940s to the present.

institutions, and policy, I bring the analysis of the NLRB to bear in assessing their explanations and arguing the need for reorientation.[7]

THE INSTITUTIONAL POLITICS OF THE NLRB

An Introduction to the Puzzle

In his classic article on congressional oversight, Seymour Scher offers a vivid account of an independent regulatory agency in serious political trouble.[8] The time was the early 1950s, shortly after the Republicans had taken control of the presidency and both houses of Congress. The agency was the National Labor Relations Board. Its troubles hardly seem surprising. Widely regarded as a zealously prounion agency whose decisions undermined the economic well-being and managerial autonomy of business, the NLRB found that its political opponents were now in the driver's seat. Business groups activated their congressional allies on the labor committees, who in turn, launched furious attacks on the NLRB. Such niceties as administrative due process and agency independence, which members of Congress were quick to embrace in principle, were consistently violated in the struggle for political control. The NLRB, in turn, was overwhelmed by political turbulence.

Scher's account would seem to square well with recent efforts to understand regulatory agencies with reference to the pattern of costs and benefits their decisions impose on constitutents.[9] In the NLRB's case, the impact of agency decisions is concentrated in the opposing, well-organized constituencies of business and labor. This type of environment is noted for producing conflict and turbulence—initially as one side resists regulatory legislation backed by the other, and later as the two well-armed camps and their political allies struggle to gain advantage in policy and administration. The early history of the NLRB bears this out beautifully. The Wagner Act of 1935 creating the agency, the Taft-Hartley Act of 1947 reforming the agency's structure and mandate, and congressional oversight of administration—all provoked political turmoil.

Yet the rest of the NLRB's history does not conform at all to Scher's account. The turning point, in fact, is the very same period that Scher writes about in documenting the agency's political misfortunes in Congress. Although not apparent at the time, this ultimately proved to be a watershed in NLRB history, ushering in an extended period of peace and stability that, until very recently, was largely unbroken by the political turmoil that had earlier seemed a permanent part of its political life.

The explanation that seems to account best for these developments is insti-

---

7. This article is an early, abbreviated version of a book I am now in the process of writing. The argument I outline here—or a close relative of it—will be developed and documented in greater detail in the book.

8. Seymour Scher, "Congressional Committee Members as Independent Agency Overseers," *American Political Science Review* 54 (1986) : 911–20.

9. See especially James Q. Wilson, *The Politics of Regulation* (New York: Basic Books, 1980). Wilson has been most responsible for popularizing this environmental typology, which has found its way into both the economic theory of politics and the positive theory of institutions.

tutional. It centers on the NLRB, but it derives more generally from an analysis of the institutional system in which the agency is anchored and the ways in which the major components of that system fit together in jointly determining what we see as NLRB politics and behavior. The emergence of peace and stability is not fundamentally due to the way costs and benefits are distributed, nor is it due to the power of particular politicians or legislative committees. The puzzle is to try to figure out what the relevant system looks like, not to try to isolate prime movers or fundamental causes.[10]

The Constitution, Legislative Stalemate, and Agency Politics

Let me begin with a familiar institutional feature of American politics: the constitutional system of separation of powers and its tendency to promote legislative stalemate. Groups seeking positive governmental action need to put together multiple majorities. They need to win many times over in various political areas. But groups seeking to block legislation need win only once. Policy initiatives that stimulate opposition by an intense minority, as major initiatives tend to do, are therefore almost always destined to fail.

Politicians know this and are discouraged from pouring their efforts into such initiatives. Not only are the probabilities of success low and the direct costs of political battle high; the opportunity costs are staggering. Politicians have full agendas. They lack time, resources, and staff to do everything they might want to do. Moreover, they know they can achieve nothing alone, so they trade votes and variously invest their resources in hopes of accumulating political capital. A major legislative initiative tends to crowd everything else off the agenda, soaking up time and resources and threatening to deplete political resources as chits are called in to secure an unlikely victory. These costs are ordinarily prohibitive.

The same applies to interest organizations. Even allegedly powerful business and labor groups have political operations that are not very well financed, staffed, and organized. They have to be careful about how they choose to spend their resources. The more general the group's interests, the fuller and more diverse the agenda, the larger the number of politicians it must cultivate and be able to count as allies, and the more it is absolutely necessary to worry about priorities and opportunity costs. A strong interest in a new area of legislation does not mean the group will take action even if the probability of success is reasonably good. A serious effort to gain legislative victory may well torpedo everything else the group is interested in attaining.

Most of the time, politicians and interest groups will forgo almost all the major initiatives they would like to see enacted. Suppose, however, that conditions seem just right for success on a particular initiative, a political attack is

10. I should say at the outset that, although a truly well-balanced treatment of NLRB politics would take systematic account of the courts, I will not attempt to do so here. The courts place important constraints on what agency decision makers can do and provide important points of access for business and labor in their attempts to shape NLRB policy. But the central themes of the following analysis would not be altered in any fundamental way were the courts dealt with explicitly.

launched, and the issue is actually won. Should that happen, the new policy becomes the new status quo; and by virtue of constitutional impediments to change, it becomes virtually impossible for opponents to overturn. Indeed, because these obstacles are so severe, the opponents will quickly find it in their own self-interest to stop trying—until the day, perhaps in the distant future, when conditions are again just right.

When an agency's environment contains strong and opposing interests, as the NLRB's does, these institutional forces shape its political life. Although conflict of interest and struggle for advantage are built into the relationship between the two sides, intense legislative battles are not. They may periodically go to war on those rare occasions when one side or the other thinks it will benefit from battle. And, even more rarely, the policy status quo—the agency's mandate—may change. But the normal state of affairs is likely to be a cold war in which neither side is willing to initiate full-scale legislative hostilities. Peace, in other words, is normal in the arena of substantive legislative politics. During times of peace, the groups may well continue to struggle for advantage, but they will struggle in other arenas—focusing, for instance, on presidential appointments or the budget. In these and other ways, the constitutional system combines with the NLRB's interest group environment to impose a certain structure on agency politics.

Legislative Conflict

Since the organization and conduct of collective bargaining came to be considered potential targets of governmental intervention, the legislative stars have lined up perfectly only twice: once for labor in 1935 when it achieved victory in the Wagner Act and once for business in 1947 when it pushed through the Taft-Hartley Act. For the last forty years, business and labor have either tried unsuccessfully to gain legislative advantage or, more often, have simply accepted the prevailing status quo in this area and pursued other, more promising items on their crowded political agendas.

The Wagner Act emerged out of the confluence of a number of circumstances, among them the depression and the shattering of confidence in markets, a sustained wave of strikes that threatened even more serious economic instabilities, the election of a huge Democratic majority to Congress in 1934, and the breakdown of the National Industrial Recovery Act (NIRA). Management interests, led by the National Association of Manufacturers (NAM) and the Chamber of Commerce, fought the legislation fiercely. Labor supported it, but unionization of the work force was in its early stages, and organized labor was not a potent political force that could dominate business in a head-to-head political fight. Labor did not even have President Roosevelt on its side until after the NIRA collapsed. Labor won, but only because it benefited from circumstances largely beyond its control.[11]

---

11. On the politics surrounding the creation and early years of the NLRB, see James A. Gross, *The Making of the National Labor Relations Board* (Albany: State University of New York Press, 1974); Irving Berstein, *The New Deal Collective Bargaining Policy* (Berkeley: University of California Press, 1950), and *Turbulent Years* (Boston: Houghton Mifflin, 1970); Arthur M.

The Wagner Act provided a legal framework conducive to unionization and stable labor-management relations. Workers were to select exclusive union representatives in free elections, and management was legally obliged to recognize and bargain with certified unions. The election and collective bargaining processes were protected, moreover, by the stipulation that certain behaviors on the part of management—for example, firing a worker for union activity—were illegal "unfair labor practices." A new independent agency, the National Labor Relations Board, was created to oversee the conduct of elections and to handle unfair labor practice charges. Business immediately went on the attack against the new agency, moving through the courts, Congress, and the presidency to challenge virtually everything the NLRB tried to do. The AFL, often in alliance with business and congressional conservatives, launched attacks of its own—claiming that the NLRB was zealously favoring the CIO and concepts of industrial unionism.

After the war, the political stars lined up for the second time. Postwar unemployment and inflation led to a wave of serious strikes in 1945–46, and unions came to be widely viewed as disruptive, greedy, and undeserving. Even moderate politicians found it electorally popular to call for labor law reform. The NLRB had made it back on the agenda. Republicans, campaigning on the slogan "Had enough?" swept to victory in both houses of Congress in 1946, and under the leadership of Senator Robert Taft of Ohio, the new chair of the Senate Labor Committee, they immediately set about the task of devising a new labor law. By late summer, the House and Senate had passed the new legislation by large majorities, overturning a veto by President Harry Truman.[12]

Although there had been strong sentiment for truly radical action—for example, eliminating the NLRB and relying on regulation by the courts and/or the states—the legislation able to command a veto-proof majority was relatively moderate. The basic framework of the Wagner Act was maintained. There still existed an NLRB whose functions were to oversee representation elections and process unfair labor practice charges. The new mandate was, however, better balanced between the interests of labor and business. Among other things, Section 8B outlined certain actions by unions—secondary boycotts, for instance—that would henceforth be regarded as unfair labor practices, and Section 14B outlawed the closed shop and gave the states the authority to pass right-to-work laws. The act also reformed the NLRB's internal structure. Most important, it made the agency's general counsel independent of the board and a presidential appointee with a fixed term of office. This

Schlesinger, Jr., *The Politics of Upheaval* (Boston: Houghton Mifflin, 1960); Christopher L. Tomlins, *The State and the Unions: Labor Relations, Law, and the Organized Labor Movement in America, 1880–1960* (Cambridge: Cambridge University Press, 1985); Peter H. Irons, *The New Deal Lawyers* (Princeton: Princeton University Press, 1982).

12. On the politics leading up to Taft-Hartley, see especially James A. Gross, *The Reshaping of the National Labor Relations Board* (Albany: State University of New York Press, 1981).

meant that the board would no longer be able to control the initiation of cases or the legal arguments NLRB lawyers used in prosecuting them.[13]

The Taft-Hartley Act hardly settled matters. Labor was outraged at its loss and made the reversal of Taft-Hartley its number one priority. By no coincidence, President Truman made it a central campaign issue in the 1948 election. That he was able to do so advantageously testifies to how brief business's window of opportunity had been. Through Truman and congressional liberals, labor attacked the new law in general and heaped particular criticism on the new general counsel and his "unworkable" relationship to the board. Business defended the general counsel but launched attacks of its own against the basic Wagner Act framework and an agency that, in its view, was still populated from top to bottom with prounion zealots. A special committee was set up in Congress to monitor the NLRB's compliance with Taft-Hartley, and agency officials were endlessly dragged before it to justify their decisions.[14]

The conflict was still raging when Dwight Eisenhower assumed office. The two sides were basically in stalemate. Despite all the fighting, there had been no meaningful statutory change since Taft-Hartley, for neither side could command the overwhelming support needed to bring it about. The year 1953, however, seemed to offer business its big chance. For the first time since 1932, Republicans controlled the presidency and both houses of Congress. Robert Taft was Senate majority leader. Everything seemed to be right—but there was a problem: factional disagreement on what exactly should be done. One faction wanted to eliminate the NLRB entirely and opt for regulation by the federal district courts and the states. The other favored separating the board and the general counsel, turning the former into a labor court and relying on presidential appointments to control it. The radical faction consisted of small business and its allies in the House Labor Committee and in the Commerce Department. The more moderate faction was led by big business and its supporters in the White House, on the Senate Labor Committee, and in Commerce. Their battle was complicated by a third force: Secretary of Labor Martin Durkin, formerly with the AFL, who claimed that Eisenhower had promised him reforms favorable to labor.

Legislative stalemate led by default to a minimalist administrative approach: keep the NLRB and try to change its policies through appointments. Staunch opponents of unionization saw this as an admission of defeat, but there was little more they could do. No legislation was enacted. Business's golden opportunity was suddenly gone.

13. For an overview of the provisions of the Wagner and Taft-Hartley acts, as well as other aspects of the board's mandate, see Frank W. McCulloch and Tim Bornstein, *The National Labor Relations Board* (New York: Praeger Press, 1974).

14. Perhaps the most exhaustive account of the NLRB's tumultuous politics in the Truman and early Eisenhower years is provided by Seymour Scher, "The National Labor Relations Board and Congress: A Study of Legislative Control of Regulatory Activity" (Ph.D. diss., University of Chicago, 1956). I draw on his account here and in the remaining paragraphs of this section.

The Transformation of the NLRB

The political world of labor-management relations was nevertheless about to undergo a transformation. Peace would replace conflict. Political action would shift its focus from Congress to the presidency. And a new politics of labor-management relations would become institutionalized, bolstered by the emergence of widely shared expectations about the procedures and criteria by which important decisions were to be made.

At the heart of this transformation was legislative stalemate, brought about by an underlying shift in the balance of power. Organized labor had grown substantially in size, strength, and organizational coherence since the early years of conflict. The very existence and operation of the NLRB had been responsible for much of this growth—by the mid-1950s there were some five times as many union members as there had been in 1934, one year before the Wagner Act went into effect. The political battles with business, particularly the stinging loss in 1947, had also triggered important changes: they convinced AFL and CIO leaders to abandon any lingering adherence to Samuel Gompers's voluntarism, to develop an organizational capacity for continuous, effective political action, and to find means for resolving their internecine struggles for jurisdiction and power. By the mid-1950s the AFL and CIO had merged, their Committee on Political Education (COPE) was a major political force in American elections, and the unions had grown into a formidable political opponent of business.[15]

This promoted peace. Business and labor finally had to face the fact that neither could alter the labor laws or the NLRB in any significant way through legislation. Both sides had wasted scarce political resources fighting battles that had proved unwinnable; in the process, they had forgone other items on their increasingly crowded agendas. Stalemate encouraged a reordering of priorities, and the groups were less disposed to petition their political allies in Congress for action. As legislation paled as a viable strategy, Congress became a less attractive arena for seeking political advantage. The groups took their struggles elsewhere.[16]

15. See J. David Greenstone, *Labor in American Politics* (New York: Knopf, 1969); Sumner H. Slichter, "Are We Becoming a 'Laboristic' State?" *New York Times Magazine*, May 16, 1948 : 11ff.; Sumner H. Slichter, James J. Healy, and E. Robert Livernash, *The Impact of Collective Bargaining on Management* (Washington: Brookings Institution, 1960); David Brody, *Workers in Industrial America: Essays on the Twentieth Century Struggle* (New York: Oxford University Press, 1980).

16. As I point out later, there are two exceptions (prior to the full-scale battles of the late 1970s): the politics of Landrum-Griffin and the unions' attempt to repeal 14(B) in 1965. But these were not of great consequence for the structure of NLRB politics. I should also note that the shift away from Congress included the appropriations committees, which I do not discuss in this article. The NLRB is a reactive agency, processing cases as they come in, and its budget goes to process the caseload. There is substantial agreement among the NLRB, the OMB (previously BOB), and the appropriations committees about the tight linkage of budget and administrative effectiveness; and, although the standard belief is that business benefits

From the 1950s to the present day, labor and business have been sufficiently equal in political power to guarantee legislative deadlock. The slow, steady decline in unionization over the last three decades—which, in the view of many, produced a corresponding decline in labor's political clout—has not broken the stalemate; labor is still powerful enough to veto any significant labor-management legislation not to its liking. As long as its power is above this threshold, secular declines or fluctuations will leave the stalemate unaffected.[17]

But politics has gone on even in this world of legislative deadlock. The two sides have continued to press for advantage wherever they can, particularly in the appointments process, and the constellation of forces surrounding their struggle has largely defined the reality of NLRB politics. This brings us to a second fundamental transformation—really a set of related transformations—also with roots in the 1950s: there have been important historical changes in the types of actors and interests involved and in their institutional setting. Perhaps the most important of these has concerned big business.

Although the leaders of big business, often through their control of the NAM and the Chamber of Commerce, had historically led the fight against unionization, many began to adopt a more accommodationist view in the decades following Wagner and Taft-Hartley. Again, the NLRB played a key role in bringing this about. Owing to the board's administration of the act, big business found itself increasingly unionized over time, and for many of the largest companies union-management relations became a normal, expected part of doing business. With unions now a fact of everday life, "enlightened" corporate management searched for ways to make the best of the situation, and they organized accordingly. Over time, regularized relations with unions became incorporated into the very structure of business, institutionalizing accommodation.[18]

---

from delay, whereas labor is hurt, business has not (with rare exceptions) made systematic efforts to pressure for reduced budgets. Most participants, even within business, seem to favor an efficient NLRB. Moreover, the aspects of agency performance they most want to influence, the board's final decisions, are unrelated to the budget anyway. Thus, it is not surprising that the NLRB's budget has been all but depoliticized. In effect, it is determined by a technical formula relating money to expected caseload.

17. On the unions' organizational decline, see, for example, Seymour Martin Lipset, ed., *Unions in Transition* (San Francisco: Institute for Contemporary Studies, 1986); Richard B. Freeman and James L. Medoff, *What Do Unions Do?* (New York: Basic Books, 1984).

18. On the transformation of labor relations within big business, see Thomas A. Kochan and Peter Capelli, "The Transformation of the Industrial Relations and Personnel Function," in Paul Osterman, ed., *Internal Labor Markets* (Cambridge: MIT Press, 1984); Clinton S. Golden and Virginia D. Parker, *Causes of Industrial Peace under Collective Bargaining* (New York: Harper, 1955); George Strauss, "Industrial Relations: Time of Change," *Industrial Relations* 23 (Winter 1984) : 1–15; D. Quinn Mills, "Management Performance," in Jack Steiber, Robert B. McKersie, and D. Quinn Mills, eds., *U.S. Industrial Relations 1950–1980: A Critical Assessment* (Madison, Wisc.: Industrial Relations Research Association, 1981); Audrey Freeman, *Managing Labor Relations* (New York: The Conference Board, 1978).

Economically, this meant that tough bargaining and vigilant protection of managerial prerogatives would be combined with organizational mechanisms to promote harmony, cooperation, stability, and smooth working relations with the union. Politically, it counseled moderation. A corporation and its union often have interests in common (combating foreign competition, for example) and are natural allies on some political issues. Because they need one another and because each has formidable means of retaliating against the other, they have reason to accommodate each other when their political interests are in conflict.

Radical reform of the labor laws, or even a radical reconstitution of the NLRB through appointments, is not an obvious priority goal for big business anyway. The board is of greatest economic consequence for nonunion employers and the unions that seek to organize them. Board decisions about the organizing process—for example, about employer free speech in election campaigns, about the appropriate bargaining unit, or about when elections may be overturned—cut to the core of union activity. Organizing is what the unions are all about. This assures that the board will be a priority with labor. Similarly, for nonunion employers NLRB decisions can mean economic upheaval and constitute serious threats to traditional entrepreneurial notions of control; they, too, feel intensely about the board and its politics. But big businesses that are thoroughly unionized—U.S. Steel, GM, the large defense contractors—find the board less relevant to their economic well-being. Legal issues bearing on representation campaigns and certification are usually not of much consequence, nor, in fact, are many of the laws governing unfair labor practices, since regularized relations with unions and more sophisticated managerial approaches have made it rare for the large corporations to engage in these sorts of actions. Thus, although certain issues in labor law remain quite important to them—for example, whether decisions to subcontract or shut down operations are mandatory issues for bargaining, or whether the board must defer to arbitration—the NLRB will not ordinarily be accorded anything like the priority it received in the early years when bloody battles over the initial organization of major industries were being fought. After the union organizing successes, labor relations increasingly became a settled matter, a matter for labor relations professionals, and the corporations concentrated their political efforts on taxes, inflation, environmental protection, consumer protection, and other issues of greater economic interest.

This does not mean that the major corporations suddenly became "prounion" or dropped all interest in labor law reform. They remained concerned about the power of labor unions and their continuing threat to managerial control of business, and they actively promoted—through the appointments process and legal action in the courts—a more management-oriented interpretation of labor law. But they no longer dedicated themselves to destroying the NLRB or the basic framework of the NLRA. For the most part, they now accepted both and contented themselves with chipping away at the margins. The extremists in the business sector, doubtless the overwhelming majority if each businessman counted equally, thus found themselves with an accommodationist top leadership. Big business was no longer the united vanguard of antiunionism. This was a substantial force for moderation in the NLRB's political environment.[19]

Thus, the creation of the NLRB set in motion forces that ultimately transformed the agency's interest group system and the structure of its politics. Business and labor were now sufficiently well balanced to ensure that under most conditions legislative battles would produce stalemate. NLRB politics would shift to other arenas. Both sectors were now more coherently governed and less threatened by volatility. Business had become dominated by moderates who favored stability and continuity in the prevailing labor relations framework. The stage was set for a new era of peace.

The Politics of Appointments

Since the early 1950s, the politics of the NLRB have centered around presidential appointments to the agency. The transformation of the labor-management environment produced this shift in the group struggle and, at the same time, provided a new context that would condition how the struggle over appointments is played out. The group context only conditions appointments, however; it does not determine them. The economic actors in the labor-management community must channel their influence through the formal apparatus of government, whose actors have interests of their own to pursue and resources with which to do so. Viewed over time, this channeling of influence turns out to be highly structured and routinized. The two sides struggle over appointments, but time after time their struggle proceeds according to entrenched expectations about how the game should be played and what it should yield: expectations that derive, to a large extent, from the de facto imposition of order by politicians.[20]

The Appointments Process as a Repeated Game. It is useful to think of the appointments process as a repeated game. Each appointment is a decision that business and labor want to win, but they both know that fights are costly and that there will be many other appointments to follow—and possibly many other fights. This in itself tends to impose structure on their joint behavior in two basic respects. First, assuming they do not discount the future too heavily, they have certain incentives to go along with cooperative means of resolving their underlying conflicts of interest; rather than paying all the costs of fighting each decision as though it were a one-time affair, they can settle on some

19. A nice illustration of the political cleavage between big-business moderates and small-business extremists can be found in Scher, "The National Labor Relations Board and Congress." See also Sar A. Levitan and Martha R. Cooper, *Business Lobbies* (Baltimore: Johns Hopkins University Press, 1984); and Mark Green and Andrew Buchsbaum, *The Corporate Lobbies: Political Profiles of the Business Roundtable and the Chamber of Commerce* (Washington, D.C.: Public Citizen, 1980).

20. The analysis of appointments is based largely on interviews with participants. In almost every case individuals requested confidentiality—in part because the labor relations community is fairly small and tightly knit, and they do not want to go on record as having said anything disparaging or controversial about their acquaintances. At this stage, at least, I am accordingly not in a position to indicate through citations who said what.

rules for peaceful division of the spoils in the long run. Second, they have time and opportunity within the sequence of appointments decisions to move incrementally toward a set of rules that implicitly recognizes the powers and interests of both sides, and from which neither—given the likelihood of retaliation by the opponent and the collapse of beneficial cooperation—has an incentive to defect.[21]

In fact, NLRB politics are strongly influenced by these incentives for rule-governed cooperation between business and labor. It is clear that many leading activists on both sides do think in these terms. They are concerned about the long run; they know that any short-term gouging of the other side will lead to retaliation and thus to instabilities and costly political battles that it is in everyone's interests to avoid; and they willingly conform to what is sometimes referred to as the "traditional" way the appointments game is played.

But this is only part of the appointments story—for the two sectors are really in no position to pull off this kind of cooperative arrangement. Both sectors are heterogeneous, and neither has a coherent leadership group that can aggregate interests and act for the sector as a whole—there are various leading figures on both sides. Aside from representing somewhat different interests, these leaders can and do have different discount factors. Some think in the long run and implicitly buy into the logic outlined above, whereas some are explicitly concerned with getting every political advantage they can in the short run—they are more than willing to fight if they think they can win, regardless of threats of future retaliation by the other side.

The repeated game scenario is complex because the two sectors themselves are complex. Whether cooperation and rule-governed behavior could ever take root in such a setting is questionable. And this is not the real setting of appointments politics anyway—the real setting is more complicated still, for the president and the Senate make all the formal decisions, and any arrangements must somehow be compatible with their incentives as well. Interestingly, however, it turns out that these complications have the effect of substantially simplifying the appointments game for everyone.

The President and NLRB Appointments. We can think of U.S. presidents as being motivated by two basic concerns, elections and governance. The first has to do with gaining office and holding it. The second has to do with what he accomplishes while in office, and thus how he will be regarded once he has left the scene. The electoral incentive is strong during the first term, but, although there are still promises to be kept, it declines during the second. The governance incentive is strong throughout, dominating during the second term. History has affected the relative importance of these incentives as well. Since Roosevelt, presidents have increasingly been held responsible by the public for promoting legislative programs, for managing the bureaucracy, and for producing economic prosperity. This has magnified the political im-

21. On the logic of cooperation among self-interested actors, see Robert Axelrod, *The Evolution of Cooperation* (New York: Basic Books, 1984).

portance of governing in the president's calculus and has been a driving force behind the development of the institutional presidency.[22]

The obvious conclusion to be drawn from this is that Republican and Democratic presidents should normally act differently on NLRB appointments. And in fact they do. Take the situation typically faced by Republican presidents. They have strong incentives to reward their core electoral supporters, business, with appointees to their liking. But their electoral coalition is heterogeneous; the Teamsters and some of the building trades unions must also be listened to, and they will press for appointees more sympathetic to labor.[23] In addition, Republican presidents know that, given all the impediments arising from separation of powers, even a heterogeneous electoral coalition cannot alone guarantee successful governance. They know, in particular, that they will be far better able to pass their legislative programs and smoothly manage the bureaucracy if prime movers in the labor movement, particularly the AFL-CIO, can somehow be co-opted or at least persuaded not to engage in active disruption. Labor knows this, too, and its leaders ask for favors in return. This gives labor a basis for playing a role in NLRB appointment decisions (and many other decisions as well). Republican presidents, then, have incentives to consult with labor on appointments and to accommodate their interests—by picking nominees who are only moderately probusiness, for instance, or, in the sequential stream of appointments decisions, by balancing off several probusiness nominees with one or two who may even be viewed as prolabor. Democratic presidents, of course, do just the reverse.

The leaders of business and labor, experienced as they are in politics, are well aware of how the president's incentives are structured and how he will tend to approach appointments decisions. They know they have bases of influence, and they are reasonably shrewd in determining what they can and cannot get. When a Republican president first assumes office, business groups expect to be favored in NLRB (and other) appointments. But they also know their relationship with the president is one of mutual advantage: he needs them for electoral and governance reasons, just as they need him if they are to get what they want from government. Because they also know they will be dealing with "their" president on many issues, they seek a harmonious and productive relationship, and they are not going to endanger that by making hard-line demands. When a Democrat controls the presidency, labor becomes the in group—but, again, realizes it cannot expect the president to ignore business and accepts a secondary business influence over appointments.

It is of key importance here that the president, business, and labor all see any given NLRB appointment as but a small part of the grand political game. A president who must deal with Suez or Vietnam or the oil crisis or any num-

22. See Terry M. Moe, "The Politicized Presidency," in John E. Chubb and Paul E. Peterson, *The New Direction in American Politics* (Washington, D.C.: Brookings Institution, 1985).

23. Perhaps the most striking example of labor's electoral influence on a Republican president came in 1972 when Nixon, courting Teamster support, acceded to their demand that he reappoint the liberal John Fanning.

ber of other issues of national and international significance can hardly invest much capital in a single board appointment. Business and labor, too, have many irons in the political fire and certainly cannot afford to devote much time or attention to a single appointment. Although heterogeneity and disorganization may make it difficult for the two sides to arrive at a cooperative solution, they will ordinarily be happy to acquiesce—or at least be unwilling to spend valuable resources in opposition—if someone could just impose and enforce a decision they could live with. This is what the president does.

Thus the basic structure of NLRB appointments is very simple. The president's incentive is to accommodate the interests of both sides, giving greater weight to the interests of the in group, and to arrive at solutions that divert neither attention nor resources from all the other things the White House must do. This means, above all: keep the peace. The leaders of business and labor, aware of their inherent conflict of interest, aware of the president's incentives, and eager to embrace acceptable solutions that allow them to get onto more important matters, have found this pattern of asymmetric weighting agreeable. They may not always be overjoyed with the appointments presidents make—but they do not expect to be, and the structure ensures that they almost never want to go battle over them.

The Senate and NLRB Appointments. Because the Senate must confirm presidential appointees, the Senate Labor Committee's jurisdiction over the board gives it a formal basis for influence. In principle, this can be used by senators on the committee and their allies in business or labor to bring about appointments more to their liking than the president would otherwise be willing to make. To maximize their impact, senators might participate actively in the earliest stages of the appointments process—in the generation, screening, and evaluation of names—thereby precluding presidential control of the committee's agenda.

But although the Senate Labor Committee is not inconsequential for board appointments, this scenario vastly overstates its actual role. To understand why, we must begin by recognizing that the Senate's role in appointments—all appointments, not just for the NLRB—has long been governed by an entrenched normative structure of its own. These rules of the appointments game reflect a modus vivendi that has evolved over many decades, implicitly resolving much of the potential conflict between the president and the Senate and among the senators themselves regarding who will control appointments.[24] Except on special appointments (to the courts, for example), the primary rule is deference to the president: he has a right to build his own administration as he sees fit and thus to have his appointees confirmed as long as

___

24. Note that the repeated-game logic of cooperation applies to the historical emergence of these norms, just as it does to the relationship between business and labor in their struggle for influence. See Axelrod, *The Evolution of Cooperation,* for discussion of its widespread applicability to politics. The literature on appointments per se, however, is not oriented by this or any other theory. The most comprehensive overview can be found in G. Calvin Mackenzie, *The Politics of Presidential Appointments* (New York: Free Press, 1981).

they are not clearly unqualified. What, then, counts as "unqualified" and therefore as a legitimate reason for voting against confirmation? Here, the basic rule is that there must be a "smoking gun" of some sort—a serious character flaw, criminal conduct, demonstrable bias, or obvious inability to carry out the duties of the job. A candidate's ideology is not a legitimate basis for voting no.[25]

For these reasons—and because senators, like presidents, must save their efforts for the bigger fish they have to fry—senators of all ideological stripes are strongly disposed to vote affirmatively on virtually every presidential nominee. Ideology (backed by group complaints) may prompt some senators to look high and low for the smoking gun that would give them a legitimate excuse for voting no. But, if the White House and the groups have done their jobs, there will not be anything to find. What about the early stages of the process, then? Do senators get involved early in order to influence the slate of candidates under active consideration? Again, they have better things to do. Except in special circumstances, as when a senator wants to push his own staffer for an appointment, senators play little or no role in appointments until the decision has effectively been made in the White House. At this point they are informed and the candidate will meet with interested members as a courtesy; but there is typically very little drama about the outcome.

Business and labor understand how senators' incentives are structured. This prompts them to focus their energies on the early, presidential stages of the process and to expect that the important decisions will be taken there. It also makes them very cautious about launching a confirmation fight; although senators want to please their group allies, they have strong incentives not to join the fray, and they will exact a heavy price should they finally agree to go along—a price that may rule out asking them for support on many other legislative issues. This can turn into a real fiasco if the candidate is in fact defeated and the president responds by nominating someone worse—a prospect the out group greatly fears. Thus, the normal group reaction to a presidential nominee who is quite liberal or conservative is to do nothing beyond making symbolic statements of public protest.

Perhaps the most graphic illustration of the Senate Labor Committee's role comes from Nixon-Ford years, when these Republican presidents were faced with a liberal committee led by Democratic chair Harrison Williams and ranking minority member Jacob Javits, both friends of organized labor. Despite their positions of influence, neither Williams nor Javits played a role of any consequence. More to the point, they did not really try. Although their staffers were sufficiently well connected to know of any significant developments in the appointments process, they and their senators were not actively consulted or involved. Their participation was almost entirely limited to the formalities of confirmation. Javits did try to promote two candidates for differ-

25. Since Watergate, senators have been somewhat more likely to scrutinize presidential appointees in general. But the extent of this is exaggerated by media accounts of a few spectacular cases. If there has been any breakdown in the norm of deference to the president, it has been of only marginal importance.

ent positions on the board, but he did not try terribly hard, and both candidates were firmly rebuffed by the Nixon White House. The word was that Javits's support for a candidate was the kiss of death.

The Appointments Process. The appointments process never ends. Both sides know that at least one of the five board members slots will come open each year and that a general counsel will have to be appointed at least once every four years. So the people from each sector whose job it is to handle such things are constantly keeping their eyes open for attractive candidates, and appointment possibilities are frequent topics for ad hoc discussion among well positioned members of the labor-management community.

Things begin to crank up several months before an actual vacancy occurs. On the business side, the formal spokesmen are the Chamber of Commerce, the National Association of Manufacturers, and (since 1973) the Business Roundtable. Key staffers and leading members from the labor committees of these organizations, along with other activists who are essentially free-lancers, have over the years developed extensive networks of contacts throughout the national community. With each prospective opening they turn to these networks to generate names, to provide thorough background information on potential candidates, to document their ideological predispositions and views on labor issues, and to work toward a short list of candidates (sometimes an explicit ranking) that represents a reasonable consensus among the major participants. This last function is not always easy, due to the heterogeneity of the business sector. The clearest divergence is between unionized big business and nonunionized small business, the latter led most vociferously by the textile industry. In the end, business speaks with more than one voice. The major associations may submit somewhat different lists, delegations of respected management attorneys may go to the White House themselves in support of certain candidates, and CEOs from major companies may act on their own behalf.

The labor side is somewhat more structured. The AFL-CIO is at the center of political activity generally, and its position on candidates carries far more weight than that of any individual union. Decision making on appointments, moreover, is centralized in the federation's leadership. In practice, usually one or two officials will be responsible for these duties, and, although they consult with union presidents and labor lawyers informally, they are in a position to determine who the federation's candidate will be. This is the single most important piece of information the president can have from the labor side. It is not, however, all that counts. Unions outside the federation are also politically important, and they will have their own routines for arriving at lists of favored candidates; the Teamsters do it, for example, by working toward a consensus among the lawyers—some within the union, some in private firms—representing them around the country. And even within the AFL-CIO, constituent unions may sometimes have their own favored candidates and let their views be known to their contacts in government.

The two centers of presidential activity are the White House and the Department of Labor. In the White House one or more people, usually in the personnel apparatus, are responsible for labor appointments. They may not be especially well informed about labor-management relations, but they are acutely aware of the president's interests and intentions, and they are responsible for gathering all relevant information about an appointment and seeing to it that a formal decision is made and sent to the Senate. The Department of Labor's involvement in these matters is generally handled by a small number of high-ranking officials, themselves presidential appointees, who are well connected in the labor-management community and thoroughly knowledgeable. The department is involved in appointments activity from the very earliest stages, in part because its job is to maintain liaison with labor and business, and in part because its officials are so deeply anchored in the labor-management community that they are automatically drawn into the process anyway. They are in touch with the White House and can communicate any information about how the administration is leaning and what criteria it wants to stress.

Under a Republican administration, the business activists are the initiators. They are responsible for coming up with "good" candidates who represent some measure of management consensus and whose appointment will be compatible with the president's objectives and incentives. Business's search is therefore designed to include information about labor's views and is guided by information about current presidential concerns—his preference for a woman or a black, for instance. The constraints imposed by the presidential machinery tend to force a measure of coherence on the various actors in the sector. They are encouraged to look for the same types of candidates and they know consensus candidates will be favored by the president, so in the end there is often substantial overlap in the candidates they agree to support.

Labor's representatives, meanwhile, are not active participants in the Republican process. Any names they might generate would be suspect. They are consulted on an ad hoc basis by both business and government insiders, and they may be influential in determining which of the candidates acceptable to business ultimately gets chosen. In some sense they have a veto over particularly obnoxious candidates—but they must be, and are, very selective in using it. They cannot cry wolf too often without violating expectations about their proper role; and anyone they successfully veto will be replaced by another candidate whose place on the priority list they cannot control. This uncertainty prompts the out group to accept the vast majority of candidates that business and the administration have a political interest in putting forth. A standard saying among all of them is, "the devil you know is better than the devil you don't."

Under a Democratic administration, labor is the initiator responsible for coming up with good candidates, and business is the out group that largely reacts to developments as they occur. The AFL-CIO is at the center, and the Department of Labor and the White House pay special attention to what it wants. This, plus the usual White House pressures for conformity and guidelines for candidate's suitability, tend to discourage much of the heterogeneity in labor's support of candidates. The AFL-CIO, the Teamsters, and other active unions and individuals will usually be in substantial agreement.

Whatever the partisanship of the administration, the early stages of the process are almost entirely in the hands of the groups. The relevant officials in the Department of Labor may be interested at this point and provide guidance or assistance, and some senators may also get interested, especially if they have a candidate to push, But almost all of this is routine—a few phone calls and letters. The White House, meanwhile, is typically not interested at all. Its personnel people are doing their best to handle the crush of appointments that must be made to positions throughout government, and they cannot be bothered too early.

White House involvement tends to proceed in two steps. First, staffers send out signals of presidential concerns and criteria, and they initiate or at least open themselves up to meaningful communications with the Department of Labor and the groups (particularly the in group). This kind of interaction, which may go on for some time, structures the search process that the others are carrying out. As the formal deadline approaches, everyone's attention begins to center around a small number of candidates, all of whom are somewhere in the realm of acceptability, and intense jockeying among these candidates' supporters goes into the home stretch. It is at this second stage of its involvement that the White House begins to assume control of the process.

Each of the candidates under serious consideration carries with him two sets of baggage, one that bears directly on job performance and one that does not. The first includes ideological predispositions, professional qualifications, leadership capacity, and acceptability to business and labor. The second includes all kinds of extraneous considerations of broader political relevance to the president. What is the candidate's gender, race, and ethnicity? Which sponsors will be pleased or offended and what can they be expected to do about it? Can the appointment of this candidate be used to purchase support of politicians who play pivotal roles on other matters, such as pending legislation, of greater importance to the president?

Primarily because of this second set of considerations, the White House treats the choice among contenders as a delicate matter. It is highly secretive, playing its cards close to the vest and often delaying a decision until the last possible minute. As costs and benefits are being weighed internally, rumors begin to spread about who is likely to get the job—giving rise to reactions among the various participants that provide the White House additional information on which to base its calculations. It is common to hear or read reports that a given candidate has a lock on the appointment, only to find soon thereafter that someone else has gotten it.

Thus, given its limited resources and attention span, the White House does its best to wring political advantage out of each NLRB appointment. The traditional screening process, carried out by the groups in conjunction with the Department of Labor, guarantees a short list of acceptable candidates. The president cannot go far wrong by appointing any of them. But each has political value beyond his basic acceptability, and the relative values of candidates may rise and fall almost daily with developments in the larger political context. The president's final choice may therefore turn on what appear to be immediate, idiosyncratic considerations. In fact, this is but the last, highly constrained step in a process that gives full play to the much more fundamental concerns of the labor-management community.

Once the president has made a decision, the name is transmitted to the Senate Labor Committee. At this stage, there are rarely any surprises. The interactive nature of the process ensures that, if there is some problem—such as a long-standing personal antagonism between a candidate and the senator from his state or a "smoking gun" of some kind—the White House becomes aware of it before announcing the nomination. Accordingly, the White House expects that any qualified individual it nominates will be confirmed. Everyone else expects the same.

Institutionalization.   Over the years, the politics of NLRB appointments have become institutionalized. Participants speak of the "traditional" way in which appointments are made. They know their own roles, they know everyone else's roles, and a new vacancy on the board prompts them to do what they have "always" done—evoking what is roughly a programmed response by the system, with all roles meshing well with one another.

Different participants adhere to these patterns for different reasons. Some are oriented by something like a repeated-game logic of cooperation. They view asymmetric weighting, the criteria employed in assessing candidates, and other components of the traditional process as reflections of an implicit agreement between business and labor—one that protects their mutual interests in the stability and continuity of labor law while providing mutually acceptable rules for the resolution of their inherent conflicts of interest. Others think in the short term and are eager to take advantage of the other side with extremist appointments. But they find that the president has strong incentives to make moderate appointments and that they cannot successfully pressure senators to do anything about it. To have any influence at all, they know they have to play by certain rules: they recommend candidates the president is likely to take seriously, they participate in ways that lend credibility to their recommendations, and they make demands and exert pressure only when politicians are likely to be receptive.

The traditional structure of appointments accommodates both types of players. On the one hand, it looks very much like the kind of rules business and labor might agree upon if they had the capacity for coherent action and took a long-run view of their relationship. On the other hand, it describes the ways noncooperative participants would behave in the face of political realities that seriously constrain what they can achieve and how they can most profitably go about it. The politicians are the keys to all this. They bring order to the group struggle. Their locations in the larger institutional system determine how their own incentives are structured, and this in turn imposes structure on what the various leaders of business and labor—whether they favor cooperation or conflict—must do to influence political outcomes.

Once a structure like this becomes entrenched, whatever the complexities of motivation and context that give rise to it, it generates expectations that tend toward self-perpetuation. Everyone knows that this is the way things are done. Everyone knows that certain criteria have regularly been followed by both sides. There are strong expectations that all this will continue; participants plan for it, organize for it, build their political arguments around it. In speeches before Congress, before business and labor groups, before meetings of the American Bar Association labor law section, and other public forums, the various group leaders and politicians find themselves publicly committed to behaving in certain ways and consistent with certain criteria. Before long, expectations that once may simply have described existing patterns of behavior come to take on normative value. This reinforces the tendency of all participants to play by the traditional rules.

Political Control and Professional Autonomy

The organization and performance of the NLRB have been deeply influenced by this institutionalized politics of appointments. Most obviously, its policies have been systematically responsive to changes in presidential administration. Scholarly research is virtually unanimous in this conclusion: the NLRB has moved into a probusiness direction under Republican presidents and in a prolabor direction under Democratic presidents, and this movement seems to be due almost entirely to the types of people that have been appointed.[26] The participants themselves are quick to agree; experienced actors in and around the agency, and in both camps, point to presidential appointments as *the* political determinant of NLRB performance.

This has the look of strong presidential control of the agency—and in some sense, that is just what it is. Liberal presidents get liberal boards and conservative presidents get conservative boards, just as we would expect if presidents were effectively controlling bureaucratic outcomes. But for reasons the foregoing analysis suggests, the observed congruence between presidential partisanship and NLRB performance does not imply what we normally think of as "control," at least on the president's part.

An illustration from the Eisenhower years is particularly telling. At the time, the NLRB was a live issue. Conservatives in and out of government could not agree on what to do about the agency, but they did agree that things had to change, and that after so many years out in the cold they finally had an opportunity to turn things around. How did Eisenhower use this appointment power? Having the luxury of two vacant positions to fill almost immediately, he chose Guy Farmer, a moderate conservative, and Philip Rodgers, an aide to Senator Taft and among the most conservative members ever to sit on the board. Rodgers wanted to be chair. Eisenhower chose the moderate Farmer instead, much to the displeasure of Taft and the more antiunion elements of

26. See Terry M. Moe, "Control and Feedback in Economic Regulation: The Case of the NLRB," *American Political Science Review* 79 (1985) : 1094–1116; McCulloch and Bornstein, *The National Labor Relations Board;* Charles D. Delorme, R. C. Hill, and Norman J. Wood, "The Determinants of Voting by the National Labor Relations Board on Unfair Labor Practice Cases: 1955–1975," *Public Choice* 37 (1981) : 207–18; William N. Cooke and Frederick H. Gautschi III, "Political Bias in NLRB Unfair Labor Practice Decisions," *Industrial and Labor Relations Review* 35 (1982) : 539–49; Kenneth McGuiness, *The New Frontier NLRB* (Washington, D.C.: Labor Policy Association, 1963).

the Republican coalition. That, moreover, was the end of the president's involvement with the NLRB's new leader. Neither before nor after the appointment did anyone from the administration try to direct Farmer's behavior or shape his views about the agency and its mandate. There was no presidential attempt to devise plans, discuss policy, exchange views, or play on team loyalties. He was strictly on his own.[27]

That was just fine with the new chair. As a well-known and respected attorney within the labor-management community—one who, in fact, had earlier served as a trial examiner and as associate general counsel with the NLRB— Farmer had his own ideas about how the agency should be reformed. Most important, there were some prounion legal principles—regarding, for instance, constraints on employer free speech during representation campaigns—that he thought should be overturned in favor of interpretations that, in his view, were more balanced and fair. He was first and foremost a labor relations attorney, however, not an ideologue or a politician, and his approach to policy-making was highly structured—and insulated from political interference—by the standards and norms of his professional community. Decisions would be made on a case-by-case basis, using the same adjudicatory process the NLRB had always used, and changes in the law would occur as the board responded to whatever cases came through the pipeline. Each board member would arrive at his own decisions, based on his professional judgment and the assistance of his legal staff. The members of the new conservative majority, the new team in charge of the NLRB, would not meet to discuss cases or strategy. Nor would they have a larger game plan for the agency that they openly discussed with one another. Nor, in fact, would Farmer actively try to coordinate their actions.[28]

This illustrates two general points about the NLRB that have held true throughout its subsequent history. First, the president and his administration have confined their active involvement to the appointment stage and have made no additional effort to control the performance of the agency. Second, the appointees have been professionally oriented, and the agency's decisions have been made under conditions that place great emphasis on individual autonomy and professional judgment.

The Nature of Presidential Control. Many NLRB officials view the administration with some bewilderment. They do not know exactly how they were appointed or why. Often they have never met the people who in all probability played

27. Because of its specificity, I should point out that this material is based on interviews with Farmer, Stanley Strauss (legal counsel to Philip Rodgers), and other familiar with the Eisenhower board. The same basic story is told by a long line of participants about subsequent boards.

28. His professionalism did not rule out all strategic behavior, of course. In order to ensure greater control over policy, for instance, Farmer temporarily did away with decision making by three-member panels and required that all cases be heard by the full board. Similarly, he deferred some controversial cases until, with Eisenhower's appointment of Beeson in 1954, he had a new majority. But strategy was not allowed to violate the sanctity of decisions on individual cases.

key roles in their "success." Prior to their appointment, they may have had a conversation with someone in the White House, but it probably consisted of little more than pleasantries, and almost certainly had nothing to do with the substance of labor law or plans for the agency's future. After taking their positions at the NLRB, there would be no contact with the administration of any consequence.

Although this might seem a bit odd on the surface, we must remember that presidents are not fundamentally concerned with controlling the NLRB or indeed any given agency. They want to make their electoral coalition partners happy or more numerous, and they want to enhance their capacity to govern. In a context of legislative stalemate, interest groups have turned their attention to appointments and the president has responded in a manner consistent with his underlying ends, extending a primary role in candidate selection to his coalition partners and a secondary role to the out group. The question is: do interest groups also hold the president responsible for how the NLRB actually performs? If so, then he would presumably have incentives to extend his involvement with the NLRB beyond appointments. If not, then his political job would be over once the appointments were made, and he would normally not care about controlling the agency.

Since the early years of turmoil, it appears that interest groups have not demanded active presidential control of the agency. The most obvious reason is that the NLRB is an independent, adjudicatory agency surrounded by strong norms that constrain the president's proper role—another way of saying that Congress, the press, and members of the labor-management community will act to penalize any serious transgressions. Groups cannot realistically expect the president to control the agency, and they do not make such demands.

Yet independence really means that the president cannot fire the agency's top officials or intervene directly in agency policy-making. It does not prevent his administration from making its policy views and expectations well known to these officials, nor from appointing the kinds of people who can be trusted to follow the administration's lead. Interest groups could demand this kind of presidential control and thus a more active involvement than simple appointment. But they do not do this either.

The reason is that the groups do not really want the president to intervene. They want to control the NLRB themselves. The president is an outsider, after all, when it comes to the labor-management community. He is not one of them. He is a politician who responds to pressures and concerns that could easily cause trouble, and whom they may not be able to control should he become actively involved on a continuing basis in NLRB affairs. He is useful to them—and they, of course, are useful to him—but even as coalition partners they do not and never will have identical interests.

From this standpoint, the traditional appointments process is a wonderfully appropriate arrangement. Business and labor groups identify, screen, and essentially select candidates according to their own criteria. The president's authority and political incentives are important underpinnings of the rules governing how this process is structured, and he makes the final choice. But, within the rules, the groups are in charge of the agenda—and the people ultimately appointed are more theirs than his. The very rationale of the appointments process, therefore, is inconsistent with true presidential control of NLRB performance. The people he appoints are not intended to be his to control.

Professionalism. What kinds of people do business and labor look for? The established pattern, rationally based on the realities of power politics, is that the groups largely restrict themselves to moderates acceptable (asymmetrically) to both sides. Many leaders, moreover, would not stack the board with partisan extremists even if they could; this would throw labor law into chaos and cause tremendous uncertainty on both sides, particularly given the likelihood of retaliation by the other side later on. Although all participants would not go along with this cooperationist approach to the ideology question, it is generally recognized that the two sides have a common interest in ensuring that labor law is in the hands of experienced, knowledgeable people who understand the issues and, whatever their ideologies, make intelligent decisions that can be clearly and realistically applied to labor-management relations.

Each board member must be in a position to control his legal staff, give them direction, and, if his ideology is to be effective in technical decision making, take the lead. The job, moreover, will make him a public figure; he will have to make speeches, attend professional conferences and meetings, and participate in other contexts where he will be called upon to defend his legal positions and try to win others in the community over to his side. The professional demands upon the board's general counsel, who is in sole charge of the investigation-and-prosecution side of the agency and rivals the chair in prominence and public exposure, are doubtless still greater than those on an ordinary board member. For both positions, business and labor seek candidates who, they hope, will be strong and influential with their colleagues, their subordinates, and the labor-management community more generally.

By and large, they are looking for the same type of person. An experienced attorney who is well known, widely respected, and firmly anchored in the labor-management community obviously fits the bill nicely. The only real conflict of interest is that each side also wants people who are known to be partial to its own interests. But this is not a practical problem because the political system has a way of resolving the conflict peacefully—the traditional structure by which groups and presidents jointly determine appointments to the board. Thus, business tends to search for respected professionals who are moderately conservative, and labor for responsible professionals who are moderately liberal.

Professionals are difficult to control, but their behavior is fairly easy to predict. And that, of course, is at the heart of all this. A professional, if given total autonomy and insulated from external pressures, can be counted upon to behave in a manner characteristic of his type. That is what true professionalism is all about. This very predictability ensures business and labor that their mutual interests in stability, clarity, and expertise will be protected. The professional's ideology will inevitably influence his judgment of the merits of cases, but this too is predictable and part of the game. It is the vehicle by means of which the group struggle is translated into a measure of group control over NLRB policy.

The Professional—and Politically Responsive—NLRB. Two historical forces have contributed greatly to the professionalization of the NLRB. The first, as we have seen, derived from the logic of board politics and had its greatest influence on the agency's leadership structure. During the early years of legislative conflict, the groups and their political allies were struggling for control in an all-out battle in which everything about the agency and its mission was up for grabs. There was no widely shared understanding that the agency ought to be insulated from politics and run by professionals, no uniform group demands that politicians make appointive and legislative choices accordingly. The groups sought any kind of intervention or influence they could get. Nothing was securely buffered from politics. But as legislative stalemate set in and the appointments process for resolving the group struggle became institutionalized, new rules of the political game shifted the configuration of environmental forces on the NLRB. Under this new regime, both sides recognized and pursued their shared interest in professional NLRB leadership.[29]

The second historical force shaped the agency from the bottom up. When the NLRB first began regulating labor-management relations, employers and unions found themselves in need of legal counsel. But there really was no such thing as "labor law" until the board and the courts created it, and there was no labor bar within the legal profession to handle the new demand. During the 1940s and 1950s, law schools adapted their curricula, practitioners began specializing in labor law, and the supply of attorneys rose to meet the regulation-induced demand. The NLRB quickly became a stepping-stone to a successful legal career; employers and law firms put a premium on young lawyers with knowledge of the board and experience in handling labor cases, and a brief stint at the NLRB became an obvious way to build a career.

This fundamentally changed the agency inside and out. In the early years, the board tended to attract people (as field examiners, for example) who believed in its mission of promoting unionization, often were not professionally oriented, and intended to make careers of government service. With the rising market demand for NLRB-trained labor lawyers, the board found itself attracting young attorneys who took a professional, legalistic view of the agency's mission and looked to the external labor bar for norms, standards, status, and future employment opportunities. Its lower-level employees were increasingly professionals, not members of the movement. Externally, the NLRB was increasingly surrounded by a large labor bar of its own creation—a great many of whose members had spent their years of apprenticeship at the board and, through that experience, developed an abiding respect for the NLRB as an institution and for the legal framework it administers.

29. For accounts of NLRB personnel problems (at all levels) during the early years—along with the political problems they caused—see Gross, *The Reshaping of the National Labor Relations Board,* and Scher, "The National Labor Relations Board and Congress."

In an important sense, the NLRB's professionalism is self-enforcing. The agency is thoroughly colonized by professionals who are proud of their organization and openly sensitive to any hint of attempted political influence by outsiders. It is watched from the outside by other professionals in the labor bar who feel the same way and who provide an important reference group for those on the inside. Officials of the NLRB, indeed attorneys at all levels, gain status and respect from their fellow professionals in the bar; should they want to move out into private practice—or into the Department of Labor or one of the congressional labor committee staffs—their careers would depend upon what these people think of them.

It would not be an easy matter, then, for a politician or interest group to try to influence NLRB officials. The officials themselves would tend to resist and perhaps even threaten to expose the incident. Even if certain officials were vulnerable, too many others inside and outside the agency are watching for any evidence of such behavior, and it is likely to be discovered and penalized. There is, moreover, insulation by competition as well as profession; labor is constantly on the watch for illegitimate influence attempts by business, and business is doing the same for labor. One would like nothing better than to catch the other in the act.

With rare exceptions, all attempts at influence are indirect. The major interest groups see to it that NLRB officials receive copies of their publications, which often contain position statements on labor issues. They also invite officials to give speeches at their conventions, to participate in seminars, and to encourage in other ways the kind of interaction that communicates the groups' views without any suggestion of influence. Board officials are presumably not immune to these sorts of signals—they were, after all, chosen in part because of their symphetic stance toward one side or the other. But they are under no pressure and are offered no obvious inducements to comply, and their basic orientation is clearly to rely on their own professional judgment.

They get very little attention from politicians. The president, far from trying to influence them, does not even bother to send them strong signals of his policy preferences. Nor do congressman. Members of Congress do sometimes try to influence the general counsel's appointment of personnel in the regions, usually because unions in their districts have urged them to do so. But these are normally rebuffed on professional grounds. In fact, it is the NLRB's consistency in doing so that keeps the number of such patronage demands to a minimum, and agency officials are acutely conscious of that.

The professional NLRB is not the same agency it was thirty or forty years ago. The politics of appointments have ensured a measure of systematic political control by politicians and interest groups. But the vehicle of control, professionalism, has taken root in the agency as well as its environment, transforming both. In general, this is a welcome development to business and labor, for professionalism helps safeguard their shared interests while it minimizes the likelihood that their underlying conflicts of interest will devolve into mutually destructive behavior. Yet, should the day come when one or more of the main actors wants to play the game differently, they will find that professionalism has become an institutional force to be reckoned with, a force with its own interests and resources that can fight to resist changes in the status quo.

Threats to Equilibrium

Throughout this period, the economy was reasonably prosperous, stable, and insulated from foreign threats. Particularly in established oligopolistic industries, business could afford to accommodate the interests of its unions with rather substantial concessions, since the costs would ultimately be passed on to consumers without seriously threatening growth or profits. Neither side was driven by painful economic adversities to pursue risky, high-stakes political strategies.

With their political powers in rough balance, they had few opportunities for winning major legislative victories anyway. Business won marginal changes in the NLRB through the Landrum-Griffin bill in 1958, but this victory was a fortunate by-product of widely publicized scandals in union governance that had little directly to do with the NLRB.[30] Business essentially capitalized on a motherhood issue not of its own making and of broad interest to politicians and citizens of both parties. In 1965, the unions tried to capitalize on the Democratic landslide to achieve repeal of Taft-Hartley's section 14(B). But President Johnson had a far-ranging social agenda to pass, 14(B) was assigned lower priority by his administration, and, by the time its turn came, congressional liberals could not muster the necessary support. The repeal was killed in the Senate by filibuster.[31]

Neither of these battles destroyed the emerging understanding about how NLRB politics were to be conducted, but they clearly could have. In general, environmental changes constantly threaten to undermine the NLRB's political equilibrium. Inflation, unemployment, and other economic problems affect the economic relationship between labor and management, with implications for their political goals and strategies—implications that may lead even cooperation-oriented leaders to abandon informal rules and opt for political conflict and confrontation. Changing political opportunities may also lead to the outbreak of hostilities, particularly in their effects on the strategies of leaders already disposed to seek short-term advantage. Were an election to hand control of the presidency and an overwhelming majority of Congress to the same party, the in group could decide that the time was right for a major battle. A third kind of change, however, is more threatening still: a change in the way politicians accommodate the interests of business and labor. The traditional system is largely held together not by the naturally cooperative efforts of business and labor but by the imposition of structure by politicians. If for some reason the groups were faced with politicians of a different type—politicians who insisted on imposing a different kind of structure—this could destroy the rules of the game and fundamentally reorient NLRB politics.

Beginning in the mid-1970s, the NLRB's equilibrium was threatened by each

30. For an account of the politics surrounding Landrum-Griffin, see Alan K. McAdams, *Power and Politics in Labor Legislation* (New York: Columbia University Press, 1964).

31. See, for example, Joseph Goulden, *Meany* (New York: Atheneum, 1972).

of these sources of instability. One series of disruptions, stimulated by hard economic times and changes in political opportunities, saw labor attempt to break the legislative stalemate to achieve common situs picketing and labor law reform.[32] Other, potentially far more serious disruptions followed because of the election of Ronald Reagan—who, in dealing with business and labor, refused to play by the traditional rules. How did the structure of NLRB politics weather these storms?

Legislative Conflict, Appointments Conflict. After years of peaceful coexistence, political and economic conditions during the mid-1970s promoted the outbreak of hostilities in the politics of labor relations. Unemployment, inflation, declining membership, and weakening leverage in collective bargaining and organizing led the unions to place greater value and urgency on labor law reform. And their political opportunities for victory looked quite good. For the common situs bill in 1975: the Democrats had just won an enormous congressional majority in the landslide of 1974, and although a Republican was president, Secretary of Labor John Dunlop was a supporter of the bill and had succeeded (he claimed) in getting the president to agree to sign it. For labor law reform in 1977–78: the Democrats still had control of Congress and had just gained control of the presidency; organized labor thought it had all the necessary bases covered.[33]

I will not recount the political battles that ensured. Suffice it to say that, after some three years of intense and costly conflict, business and labor fought to a draw. Common situs picketing lost in 1975 when President Ford reneged on his apparent promise and vetoed the bill. It lost again in 1977 when it failed to pass the House. General labor law reform went down to defeat by filibuster in 1978 after passing the House and mustering majority support in the Senate. The results were typically American: organized labor had plenty of resources and overwhelming political support, but everything was not just right and business was able in each instance to find a way to block. By the time the dust had cleared, neither side needed to be reminded about the reality of legislative stalemate.

These battles did not change the law, but they did change the political relationships between business and labor in two important respects. First, the spirit of accommodation had clearly given way to mistrust, hostility, and recrimination. Business had been forced to defend itself and along the way had seen its darkest suspicions about labor validated and reinforced. Labor was

---

32. The battle over common situs picketing was concerned with whether individual unions should have the legal right to picket an entire construction site; in practice, this would often allow them to shut down work by subcontractors and members of other unions working at the same site, enhancing their economic power in collective bargaining with employers. Labor law reform was concerned more generally with union-supported modifications of the Taft-Hartley Act intended to reduce delays and increase the penalties for employer violations of the law.

33. For accounts of these turbulent years, see, for example, Levitan and Cooper, *Business Lobbies;* Green and Buchsbaum, *The Corporate Lobbies.*

bitter about losing and complained loudly about business's unfair and unde-mocratic tactics. Its leaders searched for ways to retaliate and make up for lost ground.

Second, in the process of defending themselves, the various elements of the business sector emerged with a substantially enhanced capacity for wielding political power. Among other things, they had learned how to put together ad hoc committees to agree on goals and tactics and to raise and coordinate resources; they also learned how to stimulate grass-roots campaigns directed at critical members of Congress. From this point on, the politics of business and labor would never be quite the same, for—just as it had in Taft-Hartley—the interest group system had been transformed as a result of the political battle. This was an unintended consequence of labor's mistaken belief that it could win a major legislative victory.

It appears that both these effects of battle—the poisoning of the atmos-phere and the shift in the balance of power—had destabilizing consequences for the traditional structure of NLRB politics. This showed up in three highly unusual appointments conflicts that erupted during the waning years of the Carter administration.[34]

The first involved the nomination of William Lubbers as general counsel in 1979–80. Lubbers had long been on the staff of board chair John Fanning, and both were well known as liberal Democrats highly sympathetic to the unions. The proposal that Lubbers move over to the sensitive job of general counsel, which is supposed to be formally independent of the board and its chair, incensed business—as did the rumor that Fanning and Lubbers were dedicated to enacting, through administrative means, some portion of the labor law reform package just defeated in Congress. Working behind the scenes in traditional ways, business activists let it be known that Lubbers was flatly unacceptable. But they also gave their endorsement to several alternative can-didates proposed by important elements within labor. Two of these candi-dates were actually union lawyers—by historical standards, this was an un-precedented compromise by business. In effect, they were saying "anyone but Lubbers."

The AFL-CIO refused to back off. Its leaders were hungry for a victory and eager to retaliate against business. They were also upset with President Carter, whose lukewarm support of labor law reform had, in their view, helped cause its defeat. The Lubbers matter became a symbol of his commitment to labor, and they insisted that he prove himself by sticking with the appointment. The result was a nomination that, in the past, labor would never have pushed, the president would never have endorsed, and business would never had been forced to fight.

Business responded by unleashing its newfound political strength. Senators of both parties were bombarded by mail, phone calls, and personal contacts

34. The following is based on interviews with John Fanning, Betty Murphy, Donald Zim-merman, John Truesdale, Robert Thompson (Chamber of Commerce), Randy Hale (Na-tional Association of Manufacturers), Douglas Soutar (appointments activist for business), Lawrence Gold and Thomas Donohue (AFL-CIO), Robert Baptiste (Teamster lawyer), and many others.

from thousands of business constituents. They found a vanguard in the newly arrived conservative senators, particularly Orrin Hatch. Everyone realized that this was not to be a norm-governed appointment, for the Lubbers fight was a direct spillover from labor reform.

Meanwhile, board member Betty Murphy's term was set to expire in December of 1979, and her reappointment got caught up in the Lubbers controversy. Although Murphy, a Republican, was regarded as acceptable to both sides and a natural for reappointment, an attempt was made behind the scenes to get business to accept a deal: Murphy would be reappointed if opposition to Lubbers were dropped. Business refused to bite; by traditional standards, the suggestion was outrageous. As the Carter White House gave themselves maneuvering room by letting the reappointment drift, Murphy took the bull by the horns and announced she would not seek another term.

Murphy's troubles prompted aspiring candidates to begin campaigning for her job. By the time she dropped out, Donald Zimmerman, minority counsel on the Senate Labor Committee, had positioned himself for the nomination. As a liberal who was well known and liked and who had worked hard in support of labor law reform, Zimmerman was just the type of candidate that labor and Democratic presidents traditionally settled upon to fill Republican slots on the board. He was still more attractive because he was being vigorously promoted by Javits, who had announced plans (which he later changed) to retire. As the out group, business normally would not have opposed a candidate like Zimmerman, and the nomination would have gone through smoothly. But these were not normal times—and, to compound matters, the Carter White House made a tactical error of great consequence: they decided not to announce the Zimmerman appointment until after the Lubbers matter had been settled.

After a bitter fight that stretched out for months, Lubbers was finally confirmed in late spring of 1980. Business leaders, furious that labor had forced an unacceptable nominee down their throats, vowed to defeat Zimmerman— with whom they already had a score to settle because of his earlier support of labor law reform. The delay also meant that Zimmerman would be considered in the middle of an election year; if business could put his confirmation off, a Republican president might be able to fill the slot. So the two sides again battled it out in the Senate.

While the conflict raged, member John Truesdale's term was set to run out in August. A moderately liberal Democrat, Truesdale was highly regarded and well liked by both sides. He wanted reappointment, labor and the Carter White House wanted to reappoint him, and business allowed in private that under normal circumstances he would be entirely acceptable. But, in their view, Truesdale's reappointment was unavoidably connected to everything else—and they went all-out to deny him the slot.

In these final battles, business won one and lost one. Zimmerman was ultimately confirmed after three cloture votes. Truesdale's confirmation was successfully held up until after his term expired. He was later given a recess appointment by Carter but then was quickly replaced by Reagan.

All of this happened within just a year and a half. During that short span, a traditional appointments structure that had governed board politics for over two decades fell victim to the fallout of legislative conflict. Labor's defeats in common situs picketing and labor law reform led them to seek victories elsewhere, to make hard-line demands on President Carter, and to retaliate against their opponents. Business, flush with legislative victory and organized for action, was not about to be pushed around; should labor attempt it, the business community was determined not only to defend itself but to retaliate in kind. The destabilizing effects of legislative conflict showed up in a series of appointments battles that, by traditional rules, would never have occurred. Lubbers would not have been nominated, in deference to the serious concerns of business. Zimmerman and Truesdale would both have been confirmed without incident. In fact, had it not been for the chain reaction among events, Murphy would likely have been reappointed and Zimmerman would never have been considered, much less fought over.

These threats to the NLRB's political equilibrium illustrate an important point: although the structure imposed by the president has traditionally been a fundamental constraint on business and labor, producing moderate appointments and regularized politics, this structure can be overwhelmed when the economic combatants elevate the NLRB to top priority. When groups find it is no longer in their interests to play by the rules—which is more likely when economic times are bad or political opportunities are just right—they can abandon them and strike out on their own. This reminds us once again that the president does not have the power to impose a structure unilaterally. A structure is only stable and consequential if all the relevant actors are willing to live within it.

The Reagan Presidency. Disruptions of this magnitude tend to be unusual and temporary. The heat of politics—and with it, the incentives for hostile, recriminatory behavior on both sides—can be expected to die down with the passage of time. Even during the worst of it, moreover, there is little evidence that the board's professionalism and insulation from political influence were qualified in any serious way. There was good reason to believe that, with legislative conflict receding into the past and clearly ruled out for the near future, business and labor would slowly settle down to their traditional routines, and the board itself would remain protected from instability and uncertainty.

But then something happened that neither side anticipated: the election of 1980 left labor-management relations under the jurisdiction of a new kind of politician—one with his own policy agenda, and whose approach to the NLRB was not simply a response to pressure from business and labor. These politicians happened to be conservatives led by Ronald Reagan and Orrin Hatch, but they would have been just as disruptive to traditional routines had they been liberals. Their position on the ideological scale was beside the point. The problem was that they were not fundamentally concerned with accommodating the interests of business and labor. They were playing by different rules.[35]

35. The following is based largely on interviews and news accounts. For general treatments of Reagan's appointments strategy, see National Academy of Public Administration, *Recruiting Presidential Appointees* (Washington, D.C.: National Academy of Public Administrations, 1985); and Richard Nathan, *The Administrative Presidency* (New York: Wiley, 1983).

When Reagan was elected president, the groups reacted much as they always had the changes in presidential partisanship. Business was the lucky in group, and it went about the task of candidate recruitment and assessment for a full range of governmental jobs, including those dealing with labor-management relations. Labor, as befits the out group, was not actively involved but expected to be consulted in some fashion. Very quickly, however, there were danger signs that a different brand of appointments politics was afoot. When Reagan announced that his secretary of labor was to be Raymond Donovan, business and labor were stunned. Nobody had any idea who he was. Normally, Republican presidents had consulted closely with both sectors in making this appointment, coming up with men of stature who commanded respect all around—people like James Mitchell, George Shultz, and John Dunlop.[36] But Reagan had not gone this route. Worse, he had chosen someone who was an outsider to the labor-management community and not even minimally connected to important components of it. Donovan did not know the issues, the programs, or the people. He had simply been a loyal and extraordinarily successful fund-raiser in the Reagan electoral campaign—apparently his only qualification for the job.

Reagan was immediately in a position to fill two vacancies on the board. Business went through its traditional motions, tapping its network of activists and aggregating their views to come up with acceptable names—which were submitted directly to the White House, since the administration paid no attention to Donovan on these matters. It turned out, however, that it was paying no attention to business or labor either. Names came in, but they never came out again. The White House personnel operation was, in the words of one business leader, a "black hole."

It soon became apparent that Reagan's appointees would reflect his own and Senator Hatch's brand of conservatism, and that they would be generated without the help of traditional networks. Pendleton James, the White House personnel director, had his own network of Reagan supporters to perform the recruiting functions.[37] The criteria for judging candidates gave heavy emphasis to ideology and involvement in the Reagan campaign. Professionalism was a distinctly secondary consideration. Apparently no serious effort was made to locate experienced, well-respected members of the labor bar who also happened to be conservative. Appointees could be young, inexperienced, little known, even disrespected and feared.

Labor went on the attack right away by challenging Reagan's nominee for chair, John Van de Water, in 1981. Although the unions were not entirely unmotivated by a desire to retaliate for past wrongs, their opposition here had a firm basis in tradition. Van de Water lacked the usual qualifications for the job, and in fact would never have passed muster in business's own recruitment and evaluation process. He was a management consultant from southern California whose business involved, among other things, advising employers on how to avoid unionization. He was not a practicing labor relations

36. See, for example, *Congressional Quarterly*, August 28, 1982, 2113–14.
37. See National Academy of Public Administration, *Recruiting Presidential Appointees*.

attorney and was hardly known to members of the labor-management community. The smoking gun was easy enough to uncover: labor would portray him as biased, a "union-buster." This tag was only compounded by his lack of experience and professional reputation.[38]

Business, initially disappointed and surprised by the nomination, rallied to his defense in order to support the president and deny labor a highly symbolic political victory. Hatch, now chair of the Senate Labor Committee, had a nominal majority but could not guarantee the support of liberal Republicans, with whom labor had much influence. In the early fighting, labor succeeded in delaying Van de Water's confirmation; but Reagan responded by granting him a recess appointment. For the next year and a half Van de Water would sit as NLRB chair while labor and business fought over whether he would be confirmed to serve out the remainder of the five-year term.

Labor won the battle but lost the war. They ultimately defeated Van de Water's candidacy, and he resigned in December of 1982. The problem for labor, however, was that Reagan controlled the appointments agenda. Van de Water was gone, but the identity of the next nominee was up to the president. As the Reagan White House and everyone else knew at the time, labor had used up a great many of its outstanding chits in fighting Van de Water. Its Senate supporters were weary of spending their time and energy fighting board appointments and were eager to get onto other, more important things—of which there were plenty in the early years of Reagan's assault on the establishment.

The Reagan White House now played its trump card: it nominated Donald Dotson to fill the position of chair. Dotson was staunchly antiunion, a crusader for the Reagan cause, and a protégé of Jesse Helms. Although he had a background in labor law and corporate experience in the conduct of labor relations, he was not the type that business itself would have recommended for the job. He was too extreme and uncompromising—and, as insiders well knew, he had an abrasive personality that promoted administrative conflict, bad feelings, and instability. He spelled trouble, and business leaders were not looking for trouble. They were, as always, looking for responsible professionals who would strictly adhere to traditional standards in moving the board toward a more conservative posture. But the Reagan White House was interested in destroying established traditions, not in following them, and they turned a deaf ear to business's suggestions for filling the slot. They also were unperturbed by direct reports from business that Dotson had "problems" that counseled against his being appointed. Fully aware of what they were doing, the White House went ahead with it.

A key factor was that Dotson, an ideologue and loyalist, was eminently confirmable even in these turbulent times. Earlier, he had routinely been confirmed to the less sensitive job of assistant secretary of labor for labor-management relations by these very same senators; thus they would find it difficult to do an about-face and brand him wholly unsuitable now. The White House's calculation was correct. The unions, fearing they faced the devil incarnate,

38. See, for example, *Business Week,* July 6, 1981, 27–28.

had little left with which to fight the nomination. After a brief delay, it sailed through on a voice vote.

Dotson's missionary zeal and abrasive personality have combined to wreak havoc on business-as-usual at the NLRB. He and his new colleagues—conservatives who, like Dotson, were products of the conservative network and confirmed without incident—immediately set about transforming the board's interpretation of the act.[39] One business publication put it this way: "In only 150 days the new majority has reversed at least eight major precedents. By some estimates, it has already recast nearly 40% of the decisions made since the mid-1970s the conservatives found objectionable. The AFL-CIO says the current board is ruling in favor of unions only about one-third as often as the boards that preceded it since 1970. And Dotson says that he and two other Reagan appointees, Robert P. Hunter and Patricia Diaz Dennis, will continue to reverse existing precedents."[40]

From the moment he became chair, Dotson aggressively sought to extend his control and disrupt agency routines. Decision making was purposely slowed down to the point where the board's processing of cases nearly ground to a halt. He battled the general counsel in an attempt to ensure that the latter's powers were used in conformity with the agency's newly dominant philosophy. The board began turning down the general counsel's recommendations for injunctions and internal appointments. Dotson even hired an official from the National Right to Work Committee—hardly a popular group within the labor-management community (or the NLRB)—to review the general counsel's legal briefs before cases were argued in the courts.

Labor and the Democrats were apoplectic. As one union leader put it, "It's like a bad dream, a case of the fox in the chicken coop."[41] Many business leaders were also upset, however, because this was precisely the kind of thing they had tried to avoid over the years. Their widespread discontent did stimulate a political backlash. Lengthy hearings were conducted in the House to investigate Dotson's conflict with the general counsel, the backlog of cases, and other indicators of disarray at the agency. Various members of the business community and prominent management attorneys, careful to keep their opposition out of the public eye, petitioned the White House directly—as did Jackie Presser of the Teamsters, only to have his efforts to strike a deal (Teamster support of Reagan's reelection in return for Dotson's departure) turn up in the newspapers.

But little has happened to meet these requests. At this writing, Dotson remains with the agency, pursuing his mission. The White House may be listening more seriously to business in its appointments decisions, and its recent nominees for the board and general counsel have been somewhat more moderate and professionally oriented.[42] But the traditional routines are still not

39. See, for example, Penn Kemble, "The New Antiunion Crusade: How Reagan's NLRB Is Subverting Industrial Democracy," *New Republic*, September 1983, 18–20.

40. *Business Week*, June 11, 1984, 122.

41. *Congressional Quarterly*, December 29, 1984, 3168.

42. See, for example, *Business Week*, March 25, 1985, 34.

the foundation of the recruitment process; they must compete with the White House's own network, and the agenda is controlled from the center. In the meantime, Reagan and Hatch have remade the board in their own image, and they give no indication of changing course.

At a news conference in 1983, when these developments were midstream, the AFL-CIO's Lane Kirkland clearly anticipated their profound implications for the structure of labor-management politics: "For the first time, appointments to the NLRB have been of a character that represents the perversion of the Board into an instrument of antiunion employers. And I think that serves notice that all the old rules are off."[43]

Political Routine and the Ideological Politician. It is indeed a case of the fox in the chicken coop. The fox, however, is not Donald Dotson. It is instead a new kind of politician: one who has his own agenda and programmatic concerns that do not arise simply from interest group pressure; one who is not automatically responsive to established interests because they have a stake in the status quo he is out to change; and one who does not respect the traditional rules they have worked out among themselves to apportion and wield governmental power, because he wants to turn governmental power toward his own ends.

Reagan, Hatch, and politicians like them may not be around for long in the key positions of authority. On the other hand, we may be in the midst of a trend toward more ideologically polarized politics, and events we now regard as departures from tradition may signal the norms of tomorrow. It is difficult to tell. The general point, however, is that politicians have their own bases of institutional power—and there is no guarantee that they will use their power to accommodate the organized interests. In the area of labor relations, this kind of direct linkage between economic groups and their political allies seemed to hold quite well for several decades. And because it did, the traditional structure of NLRB politics proved compatible with the incentives of all concerned, determining how government would work in "their" policy area. But with the dawning of the Reagan era this was no longer possible, because critical politicians refused to go along with the deal. They insisted on using their institutional power in ways the established groups had never demanded and did not support.

The intervention of politicians does not have to involve radical change or disruption. Today's NLRB is in turmoil largely because of Donald Dotson. Had almost any highly regarded attorney in the labor relations community been appointed chair, however conservative the appointee, most of this could have been avoided. The agency's structures and process would have been left intact, cases would have been processed as efficiently as before, and there would probably have been no internal struggles for power. The agency simply would have been taken over by conservatives, and they would have proceeded to make new law through adjudication—just as the Eisenhower board did.

The Dotson experience, however, is typical of the dangers the traditional

43. Quoted in Kemble, "The New Antiunion Crusade," 20.

system automatically avoids. Ideology aside, a "responsible professional" would not behave in so disruptive a manner. He would respect the same criteria and procedures that others in the labor relations community do and conduct himself accordingly. An appointments process oriented around professionalism protects the organizational integrity of the agency. At the same time, it allows for a measure of political responsiveness, since professionals may have their own ideological leanings. There is no reason why Reagan-Hatch politicians cannot find ideological professionals to suit their ends. But in this instance, because they studiously avoided reliance on established groups, and because they placed less value on organizational integrity and stability than on ideology, they happened to hit on just the wrong person for the job. Under the old system this would never have happened.

The Future of NLRB Politics

The traditional structure of NLRB politics faces an uncertain future. Most of the economic and organizational forces that promoted instability during the last decade have continued. Even were wild cards like Dotson not part of the picture, the traditional structure threatens to be eroded or simply torn asunder by these forces for change. At least as problematic, moreover, is the experience of destabilization itself—for unexpected outcomes during the last decade of turmoil seem to have suggested at least to some participants, in business especially, that a return to the traditional structure may not in fact be in their best interests. Destabilization is a learning experience that can easily promote further destabilization and ultimately perhaps a new and different equilibrium.

Inflation in the 1980s is not what it was in the late 1970s, and unemployment has dropped from its peak in the early Reagan years. But foreign competition, deregulation, the decline of heavy manufacturing, the rise of service industries, the penetration of nonunion firms into highly unionized sectors (construction, for example)—all have continued to put substantial pressure on established businesses to cut costs, innovate, and break from comfortable organizational routines. Many businesses that found it advantageous to accommodate unions in the past are being driven to more confrontational postures. Subcontracting, "double-breasting," expansion into nonunion regions of the country, active resistance of union organizing efforts in new or nonunion plants, insistence on bargaining concessions—these and other confrontational measures are becoming commonplace as business fights economic adversity.[44]

Measured as a proportion of the total work force, unions have been losing membership steadily since their peak in 1954 or so, and economic adversity appears to have exacerbated their organizational woes. This decline did not find a simple reflection in NLRB politics. The traditional structure, like structures generally, was not sensitive to marginal changes in group resources. It

44. See, for example, Freeman and Medoff, *What Do Unions Do?;* Strauss, "Industrial Relations: Time of Change"; Leo Troy, "The Rise and Fall of American Trade Unions: The Labor Movement from FDR to RR," in Lipset, *Unions in Transition.*

guaranteed that labor would be in the driver's seat when the Democrats were in power—and, even during the Carter years, business would gladly have accepted labor's normal lock on appointments and control of the board had labor not abrogated the "agreement." The organizational decline of unions is important, rather, for its potential threshold effects. Should the trend continue, unionized big business will eventually come to believe that unions are not inevitable after all, that it is not an organizational imperative to accommodate unions and "organize around" them—and this could prompt them to reject established routines for conflict resolution. Thus, although a great many changes in the relative powers of business and labor may be consistent with the traditional structure, there comes a point at which one party's weakness will undermine the peace by prompting the other party to go for victory through conflict.

This confluence of trends—economic adversity in combination with the organizational decline of unions—is a double danger to the traditional structure. But it is aggravated considerably by the actual experience of institutional instability during the last decade, which taught the actors, especially within business, some important lessons. Despite hard economic times and real incentives to reduce labor costs, business was not politically aggressive. Its leaders still wanted to play the game of labor-management politics according to the traditional rules. But two destabilizing developments beyond their control served to open their eyes. First, labor initiated legislative conflict and, in defending itself, business put together a political juggernaut whose power and effectiveness far exceeded its own expectations. It would approach future battles with new, bolder assessments of the probability of victory. Second, Reagan imposed on the NLRB a brand of radical antiunionism that business leaders did not demand and, in fact, had long resisted. But, especially in an environment of economic adversity and union decline, some business leaders began to realize over time that the reality of an antiunion NLRB was not to be feared at all—that it proved quite consistent with their own, more confrontational approaches to unions. They were, in effect, dragged kicking and screaming into the brave new world of political antiunionism by presidential leadership, and some saw that what was clearly impossible in earlier decades was now quite possible indeed.

While most of the threats for political change nowadays come from the AFL-CIO, the unions are caught in a defensive scramble. They need a significant political victory to stop their downward slide. They talk about scrapping the traditional structure, but they would be far better off if it could be reconstituted and stabilized. It is business that is the real agent of change, even though its leaders have often been too cautious to pursue it. Economic, organizational, and political changes have begun to open their eyes, and they may be in the process of viewing their interests and available strategies in a very different light. If this continues, it could sound the death knell for traditional NLRB politics.

Finally, there is still another important factor working in the same direction: ideological politics, or something resembling it, may become more intense in the coming years. The primary reason is not that ideologues per se are likely to be more prevalent in American politics, although this is possible, but rather because, as political power shifts to the South and West, even accommodationist politicians may be far less responsive to unions and unionized big businesses, and thus less willing to allow the established groups to control labor-management regulation through mutually agreeable rules. Like Reagan, these politicians may approach the NLRB more as outsiders with their own agendas, leaving the agency and its environment vulnerable to disruption and conflict.

All these factors tend to undermine the traditional structure of NLRB politics, to promote economic conflict between business and labor, and to encourage both sides to expand the scope of political conflict by carrying their fight to Congress and the White House in search of redress, including major legislative reforms. Even in the face of all this, however, it is important to remember that there are strong forces for stability at work, too. The traditional structure has been deeply entrenched for many years; it is a subtle and pervasive part of the modus operandi and institutional memories of actors on both sides; and it describes the way major actors think NLRB politics ought to be conducted. These ideas and expectations do not give way easily. Second, the NLRB's professionalism and its firm anchoring in the labor relations community are not going to fade away easily either. They have become institutionalized over a long period of time, insulating the agency from much of the turbulence surrounding it and protecting its integrity as an organization. They contribute a core of stability and an inherent capacity for regeneration that even a turbulent political environment will find difficult to dislodge.

THEORETICAL DISCUSSION

The politics of the NLRB can be divided into three periods. The first was one of legislative conflict, in which business and labor battled over the very legitimacy of the agency and its mandate. The second was one of peace and routine, as legislative stalemate shifted the political struggle to appointments, a set of implicit rules emerged for resolving conflict, and the agency became both highly professional and systematically responsive to changes in presidential partisanship. The third period was one of threats to established political and professional routines, as legislative conflict erupted once again and a new player—the ideological politician—insisted on departing from traditional practices.

I have tried to construct an argument that imposes a certain order and logic on the NLRB's politics. This argument, its discursive mode of presentation notwithstanding, has something in common with both the economic theory of politics and the positive theory of institutions. It is anchored in the self-interested behaviors of politicians, bureaucrats, interest groups, and voters. It attempts to explain how politics operates to translate economic interests into public policy. It is concerned with how political equilibria are established and disrupted.

For reasons I will outline below, however, the argument also suggests that much of what is interesting and important about NLRB politics is not easily accounted for by these prominent, "opposing" theories in the literature—at least as they now stand. This conclusion may seem to follow all too readily from the license I have been allowed in purely verbal argument. Free of the constraints of simplicity and formal rigor, I have been able to drag in all kinds of things that most theoretical exercises would ignore. But there is more to it than this. The most important questions raised here are questions of general orientation, not of detail or comprehensiveness. In what follows I want to suggest why this is so and what its consequences are for our efforts to understand politics. I will begin with a brief overview that summarizes the central features of each theory. I will then put the NLRB analysis to use in assessing these features and arguing the need for reorientation.

The Economic Theory of Politics

Although some of the most influential works in the modern study of politics have been written by economists, the line of thinking nowadays referred to as "the" economic theory of politics is only distantly related to most of these and does not always share their perspectives on politics.[45] The economic theory derives from the distinctive ideas and traditions of the Chicago school and traces its lineage to George Stigler's 1971 article, "The Theory of Economic Regulation."

Stigler's early statement is perhaps best known for the argument that regulatory agencies do the bidding of the regulated interests—not simply because they get captured, as political scientists had long argued, but because they were designed from the beginning to be the servants of business. Behind his capture thesis was a more ambitious purpose: to construct the analytical foundations for a general economic theory of governmental action. The core notion is that all actors in and out of government behave rationally in their own self-interest, and thus attempt to use government—and one another—to achieve their own ends. The theoretical task is to put the tools of neoclassical economics to use in explaining how interests translate into governmental outcomes.

Stigler and his Chicago colleagues have definite views, of course, on how this translation comes about and how it should be modeled, and these views have shaped the contours of the economic theory as it has developed over the years. Among its basic features:

1. *Economic interests:* While the methodology is individualistic, the focus is on groups of individuals who have interests in common. Politics is a struggle among economic groups for control of government.
2. *Mobilization of resources:* Interests do not automatically give rise to the effective mobilization of resources. Their connection is understood with reference to the "logic of collective action," first outlined by Mancur Olson, from which it follows that there is a mobilization bias in favor of small

45. See, for example, Anthony Downs, *An Economic Theory of Politics* (New York: Harper & Row, 1957), and *Inside Bureaucracy* (Boston: Little, Brown & Co., 1966); James M. Buchanan and Gordon Tullock, *The Calculus of Consent* (Ann Arbor: University of Michigan Press, 1962); William Niskanen, *Bureaucracy and Representative Government* (Chicago: Aldine-Atherton, 1971).

groups, particularly those having one or more members with sizable individual stakes in political outcomes.[46] It is but a short step to the conclusion that concentrated business interests have overwhelming advantages over more diffuse groups (especially consumers) in mobilizing for regulatory politics and getting what they want.

3. *Control of politicians by economic interests:* The electoral self-interest of politicians (and parties) leads them to act as conduits for group interests. Their political choices are functions of group pressure.[47]

4. *Control of bureaucrats by politicians:* Bureaucrats are not motivated directly by elections, but they are controlled (via appointments, budgets, and the like) by electorally driven politicians. This chain of control from groups to politicians to bureaucrats ensures that policy will reflect the underlying balance of power among the various interests. It also suggests that there is little to be gained from modeling politicians, bureaucrats, and their complicated surrounding institutions, since they simply operate to provide a smooth, faithful translation of interests into policy.

5. *Modeling strategy:* These are models of comparative statics, as is common in neoclassical microeconomics. Concern rests with identifying equilibria, examining their properties, and exploring the changes in equilibria that result from changes in exogenous factors. Here, the equilibria describe governmental allocations of costs and benefits among the groups and the stable field of pressures on which these allocations are based. Taken as givens are individual and group interests, their resources, and the rules (proxies for institutions) by which interests and resources are politically translated.

The theory has developed in roughly the following way. Stigler's original emphasis was on the type of regulatory environment commonly associated with traditional economic regulation: the proposed costs of regulation (which may turn to benefits under capture) are concentrated on certain sectors of business, while the proposed benefits (which may turn to costs) are diffused throughout the consuming public. His conclusion was that business dominates the regulatory agencies by political design. Both the approach and the substantive implications of his model were soon generalized by his colleagues.

Sam Peltzman provided the first reasonably comprehensive mathematical expression of the theory, showing in the process that Stigler had overstated the dominance of the concentrated group: electorally motivated "regulators" (a proxy for all mediating institutions) will favor concentrated interests, but they will not ignore the interests of the diffuse group entirely. Even unorganized consumers have some weight in the institutional translation because, if nothing else, many of them vote. Owing to Peltzman's efforts, the economic theory of capture came to be understood as a more general theory of balance of power among contending groups. Within this broader framework, virtual

---

46. Mancur Olson, *The Logic of Collective Action: Public Goods and the Theory of Groups,* 2nd ed. (Cambridge: Harvard University Press, 1971).

47. See Sam Peltzman, "Constituency Interest and Congressional Voting," *Journal of Law and Economics* 27 (1984) : 181–210

dominance by one group could be seen as a special, though perhaps empirically common, analytical case promoted by concentrated-diffuse environments. Other patterns of interests and resources would imply different balances and thus different policy outcomes.[48]

Gary Becker formalized these ideas in a still more general model. The stylized institutional intermediaries—Peltzman's "regulator" and Stigler's "party"—were gone, replaced by an institutional black box transforming economic inputs into political outputs according to assumed mathematical rules. The stylized conflict between two opposing groups was replaced by a competitive system composed of multiple groups with variable interests and resources. The result was very much in keeping with Becker's announced intention: to build an economic model of political pluralism.[49]

The work of Stigler, Peltzman, and Becker has had a pervasive influence on how economists and some political scientists seek to explain and study politics. There is now a growing body of theoretical work that attempts to expand on their ideas, as well as a growing body of empirical work that attempts to explain actual political outcomes with reference to the underlying economic interests and pressures. In all of this, political institutions are virtually ignored.[50]

What exactly justifies this inattention to institutions? One reason, certainly the most obvious one, is the presumed chain of control: groups control politicians and politicians control bureaucrats, so the groups get what they want. This tends to be the rationale the Chicago school writers themselves give in their written work. But this is really just symptomatic, for the Chicago school has a broader tradition of denying the importance of institutions.

An integral part of this tradition is Coase's theorem, which asserts that, in the absence of transactions costs, rational individuals will enter into the exchanges necessary to reach socially efficient results.[51] And they will do this regardless of their institutional context. In terms of social efficiency, then, institutions "do not matter," and it would be a mistake to ascribe them fundamental theoretical roles.[52]

Another familiar theme is that institutions are endogenous in the long run.

48. Peltzman, "Toward a More General Theory of Regulation."

49. Becker, "A Theory of Competition among Pressure Groups for Political Influence."

50. For a review and critique of this literature, see Roger Noll, "Economic Perspectives on the Politics of Regulation," in Richard Schmalensee and Robert Willig, eds., *Handbook of Industrial Organization* (Amsterdam: Elsevier, forthcoming). See also Martha Derthick and Paul J. Quirk, *The Politics of Deregulation* (Washington, D.C.: Brookings Institution, 1985); James Q. Wilson, *The Politics of Regulation.*

51. Ronald Coase, "The Problem of Social Cost," *Journal of Law and Economics* (1960) : 1–44.

52. Coase's theorem, along with its assumption of zero transactions costs, has direct implications—never thoroughly addressed by writers in this tradition, to my knowledge—for the economic theory's perspective on political control and other aspects of institutional politics. It is also inconsistent with Olson's logic of mobilization. These issues will be considered later. For one account (somewhat different from mine) of how transactions costs figure into the economic theory, see Noll, "Economic Perspectives on the Politics of Regulation."

Because different institutions may give rise to different socially efficient outcomes, groups will prefer those institutional arrangements under which they do best and will act to impose them. Thus, only economic interests and resources are truly fundamental. Institutions are largely epiphenomenal. As a modeling convenience, they are taken as fixed or exogenous in the economic theory of politics—but it is a mistake to think, in contemplating the consequences of shifts in institutions, that they can in practice take on a full range of values. In equilibrium, they too will mirror the economic balance of power.

These themes are not explicitly woven into the economic theory of politics. There is, to my knowledge, no sustained, written argument in the Stigler-Peltzman-Becker tradition that systematically sets out a general justification for virtually ignoring political institutions. More than anything else, perhaps, it is a theoretical perspective on politics that fits comfortably within the Chicago school's worldview. To the extent that this is so, detailed attention to institutions—and eventual convergence with the positive theory of political institutions—may be a long time in coming.

The Positive Theory of Institutions

It would be natural to surmise that the positive theory of political institutions (hereafter PTI) arose in reaction to this institution-free theory of politics, but it did not. It is anchored in social choice theory, a vastly larger body of literature that, in building upon the pioneering work of Kenneth Arrow, has traditionally been concerned with the implications of voting rules and, in particular, with the instabilities and paradoxes of majority rule.[53]

PTI began to emerge out of a recognition that these concerns were missing something quite essential about politics: its pervasive stability. Congress, for instance, makes decisions by majority rule, but its highly structured decision making hardly resembles what social choice theory would lead us to expect. Why so much stability in a political world that relies on inherently unstable methods of voting? Their answer is that institutional rules eliminate much of the instability by systematically constraining the alternatives available to decision makers. PTI is an effort to provide a theoretical foundation for understanding why and how this occurs and with what consequences for collective choice.[54]

All of this ultimately has to do with who wins and who loses in politics. Different rules promote different outcomes that favor different actors—and the actors are well aware of this. An abstract concern for the relationship between rules and outcomes, then, quickly leads to issues of strategic behav-

---

53. Kenneth J. Arrow, *Social Change and Individual Values*, rev. ed. (New York: Wiley & Sons, 1963).

54. See Kenneth A. Shepsle, "Institutional Arrangements and Equilibrium in Multidimensional Voting Models," *American Journal of Political Science* 23 (1979) : 27–60; Shepsle, "Institutional Equilibrium and Equilibrium Institutions"; William H. Riker, "Implications from the Disequilibrium of Majority Rule for the Study of Institutions," *American Political Science Review* 74 (1980) : 432–47; Kenneth A. Shepsle and Barry R. Weingast, "Structure-Induced Equilibrium and Legislative Choice," *Public Choice* 37 (1981) : 503–19.

ior: self-interested actors will put existing rules to use in engineering outcomes to their own advantage, and they will press for the adoption of still
more favorable rules. An explanation of policy derives from the interconnec-
tion of rules and strategy.

The substantive focus of much of this work has been on Congress, commonly the agenda powers inherent in legislative rules—for example, those
defining the jurisdictions and prerogatives of committees and their chairs.
The general picture is one in which congressional policy is largely dependent
on such rules. They determine not only how decisions are to be made but also
who will have power in shaping them. Whether any given set of interests is
reflected in policy depends in large measure on the institutional location of
its supporters.[55]

Having established a firm foundation for the study of Congress, PTI has
slowly extended outward to incorporate other institutions. While aspects of
the presidency and the courts have been touched upon and doubtless will
receive more extensive treatment in the future,[56] almost all the theoretical
extensions to date have had something to do with the bureaucracy and, not
surprisingly, congressional-bureaucratic relations. A major component of this
work addresses issues of political control. To what extent and by what means
is Congress able to control the bureaucracy? How effective is congressional
oversight? A closely related component has to do with legislative delegation
of power to the bureaucracy. When will Congress delegate and when will it
choose to make policy itself? What kind of bureaucracy will Congress choose
to create?[57]

55. In addition to the above cited works, see, for example, Arthur T. Denzau and Robert
J. Mackay, "Gatekeeping and Monopoly Power of Committees: An Analysis of Sincere and
Sophisticated Behavior," *American Journal of Political Science* 27 (December 1985) : 1117–34;
Barry R. Weingast and William J. Marshall, "The Industrial Organization of Congress,"
Working Papers in Economics (Stanford: Hoover Institution, 1986).

56. See, for example, Randall L. Calvert, Mathew D. McCubbins, and Barry R. Weingast,
"Political Control and Agency Discretion: The Fallacy of Execution" (Paper presented at the
annual meeting of the American Political Science Association, August 1986); Thomas H.
Hammond, Jeffrey S. Hill, and Gary J. Miller, "Presidents, Congress, and the 'Congressional
Control of Administration' Hypothesis" (Paper presented at the annual meeting of the
American Political Science Association, August, 1986); Robert J. Mackay and Carolyn L.
Weaver, "The Power to Veto," Working Papers in Political Science (Stanford: Hoover Insti-
tution, 1986).

57. See, for example, Barry R. Weingast and Mark J. Moran, "Bureaucratic Discretion or
Congressional Control? Regulatory Policymaking by the Federal Trade Commission," *Journal of Political Economy* 91 (1983) : 765–800; Barry R. Weingast, "The Congressional-Bureaucratic System: A Principal-Agent Perspective with Applications to the SEC," *Public Choice*
44 (1984) : 147–92; Richard Barke and William Riker, "A Political Theory of Regulation
with Some Observations on Railway Abandonments," *Public Choice* 39 (1982) : 73–106; Mathew D. McCubbins and Thomas Schwartz, "Congressional Oversight Overlooked: Police
Patrols versus Fire Alarms," *American Journal of Political Science* 28 (1984) : 165–79; Mathew
D. McCubbins, "The Legislative Design of Regulatory Structure," *American Journal of Political Science* 29 (1985) : 721–48; Morris P. Fiorina, "Legislative Choice of Regulatory Forms:
Legal Process or Administrative Process?" *Public Choice* 39 (1982) : 33–66.

This work looks inside the economists' black box and traces the congressional and bureaucratic linkages by which interests are translated into public policy. In doing so, it has begun to draw upon a rapidly developing body of theoretical work within economics that focuses on issues of organization, hierarchy, and control.[58] At the heart of this "new economics of organization" is the notion that institutional arrangements are responses to the collective action problems that arise precisely because transactions costs in political exchanges tend to be appreciable—that is to say, precisely because transactions costs are far more onerous and consequential than the Chicago school is willing to recognize.[59] New analytical tools, among them principal-agent models of control and game-theoretic models of cooperation, are beginning to be employed in PTI's attempts to understand how political actors jointly structure their behavior—how they create institutions.[60]

Although work along these lines is in its infancy, it is clear that the institutions thus created can serve as systematic constraints on individual and collective choice to the extent that they are—whether by design or evolution—"higher order" decisions very difficult to overturn in the normal course of decision making. The structure of existing rules, then, should tend to be relatively insensitive to ebbs and flows in the preferences of political actors, and the rules can easily live on when the original supportive basis for them has evaporated or turned to opposition. Thus, the rules that structure the translation of economic interests may in fundamental respects be quite out of sync with them.[61]

Obviously, there is a lot going on here, making the literature as a whole difficult to summarize in any neat fashion. Certain basic claims and orienta-

58. For an overview with applications to politics, see Terry M. Moe, "The New Economics of Organization," *American Journal of Political Science* 28 (1984) : 739–77. See also Oliver Williamson, *Economic Institutions of Capitalism* (New York: Free Press, 1985); Weingast and Marshall, "The Industrial Organization of Congress."

59. There is an interesting irony at work here: the new economics of organization traces its roots to a seminal article by Coase, in which he argued that organizations arise because of—and therefore are explained by—attempts by rational actors to minimize transactions costs. See Ronald Coase, "The Nature of the Firm," *Economica* 4 (1937) : 386–405. Thus, the economic theory of politics and the positive theory of institutions are both grounded in classic articles by Coase—but they are different articles that proceed from diametrically opposed assumptions. His "Nature of the Firm" assumes transactions costs are substantial and uses this to explain the emergence of organizations. "The Problem of Social Cost" argues that, in a world of zero transactions costs, individuals can overcome collective action problems through market exchange. There is nothing inconsistent about the two arguments per se. The economic theory tends to adopt a "negligible transactions costs" view of the world, whereas PTI and the new economics of organization tend to embrace a "high transactions costs" view—with very different consequences, obviously, for their explanations of politics.

60. See Axelrod, *The Evolution of Cooperation;* Shepsle, "Institutional Equilibrium and Equilibrium Institutions"; McCubbins, "The Legislative Design of Regulatory Structures"; Calvert, "The Role of Reputation and Legislative Leadership" (Mimeo, Washington University, St. Louis, 1986).

61. For a discussion of some of the issues surrounding institutional "inertia," see Shepsle, "Institutional Equilibrium and Equilibrium Institutions."

tions to politics are nonetheless broadly characteristic of the positive theory of institutions as it has developed thus far, and a brief outline of some of these will be helpful in drawing contrasts with the economic theory.

1. *Economic interests:* Constituency interests, even when left implicit, are fundamental and taken as fixed. They are modeled with reference to individual voters rather than interest groups. PTI is driven by the politics of voters within electoral districts, whereas the economic theory is driven by pressure group politics.

2. *Mobilization of resources:* PTI directs little formal attention to the link between interests and the mobilization of political resources, and, as yet, the logic of collective action does not play the central role here that it does in the economic theory. The strength of interests within districts tends to be taken as given.

3. *Control of politicians by economic interests:* As in the economic theory, politicians are assumed to be electorally motivated and thus conduits for constituency interests.[62] How these interests find reflection in policy, however, depends on how they are distributed across districts, where their supporting politicians are located in the institutional system, and what the system's rules look like. Moreover, simple institutional changes—for example, changes in committee jurisdictions or composition—can cause dramatic shifts in policy. Although politicians are "controlled" by constituents, then, there is no simple or smooth match between constituency interests and public policy. In the absence of knowledge about institutions, we have little basis for expecting any particular relationship between them.

4. *Control of bureaucrats by politicians:* To date, much of PTI's work on bureaucracy tends to emphasize congressional control, which dovetails nicely with the economists' claims. But this emphasis is more a reflection of PTI's current Congress-centered view of the political world than anything else. The fact is that PTI's analytical foundations intrinsically point in the opposite direction: Congress should tend to exercise little control over the bureaucracy. The nature of the electoral incentive, for instance, implies that

---

62. Two points should be made here. First, the all-or-nothing nature of majoritarian elections (an institutional property) and candidate strategies (which are institutionally conditioned) imply that virtually identical constituencies might elect politicians with very different support coalitions; even though both politicians might subsequently act as conduits, very different constituency interests would get reflected in their political choices. See Morris P. Fiorina, *Representatives, Roll Calls, and Their Constituents* (Lexington, Mass.: D. C. Heath, 1974). Second, because transactions costs are so high, constituents cannot achieve a high degree of control over politicians. Were politicians motivated to pursue their own policy preferences (were they ideological, for instance), they would have some flexibility to do so even in the presence of electoral constraints. PTI typically assumes, however, that politicians care only about reelection and that their policy preferences are entirely induced, so these sorts of control issues are rarely explored. For early attempts to do so, see James B. Kau and Paul H. Rubin, "Self-Interest, Ideology, and Logrolling in Congressional Voting," *Journal of Law and Economics* 22 (1979) : 365–85; Joseph Kalt and Mark Zupan, "Capture and Ideology in the Economic Theory of Politics," *American Economic Review* 74 (1984) : 279–300.

members of Congress will normally place low priority on directly controlling administrative agencies, that they will tend to avoid serious oversight
activities, and that they will tend to tolerate agency discretion within wide
ranges of behavior. The principal-agent model suggests, moreover, that
even when legislators do have incentives to control agencies toward specific ends, they are likely to meet with some measure of failure, owing to
the conflicts of interest, information asymmetries, and opportunities for
bureaucratic "shirking"—that is, owing to the enormous transactions costs—
that inevitably characterize the control relationship.[63]

5. *Modeling strategy:* Like the economic theory, PTI is largely an exercise in
comparative statics concerned with identifying equilibria and understanding what happens in response to exogenous changes. In the typical analysis, constituency is left implicit, politicians have fixed (constituency-in-
duced) policy preferences, the basic institutions (such as agenda-setting
rules) are assumed given, and attention then centers on the equilibrium
outcomes that derive from self-interested behavior under the specified institutional conditions. Questions might then be asked about how exogenous changes—for example, in preferences, in committee composition, in
agenda rules—affect equilibrium policy outcomes and what they imply about
the powers of various participants. Although there is a real concern for
understanding how institutions emerge, and thus for treating them as endogenous to the theory, most of the actual analysis treats them (usually for
reasons of modeling convenience) as exogenous determinants of behavior.

A Case for Theoretical Reorientation

In what follows, I will regard these theories as basic orientations toward the
study of politics. They tell us, in general terms, what is likely to be important
in politics, and thus what to look for and how to explain what we find. They
structure our thinking and guide our research. The question I want to address is not whether they are right or wrong in any strict sense, but how well
they seem to capture the essence of what is going on. The politics of the NLRB
provides a useful substantive foundation for this kind of assessment because
it is clearly and unavoidably a product of the dynamic interplay among economic interests, political institutions, and public policy. How helpful are these
prominent theories in making sense of all this?

Economic Interests. The economic theory of politics and the positive theory of
institutions offer very different accounts of how, why, and with what consequences economic interests are translated into public policy. Both, however,
take economic (or, more broadly, social) interests as the foundation and driving force of politics. Politicians spring into action, policies are proposed and
fought over, bureaucrats are subjected to political control, and all the rest,

---

63. For a general discussion of these issues, see Terry M. Moe, "Congressional Control of
the Bureaucracy: An Assessment of the Positive Theory of 'Congressional Dominance',"
Legislative Studies Quarterly 12 (1987): forthcoming; McCubbins and Schwartz, "Congressional Oversight Overlooked."

because economic interests seek gain or protection from government. The nature of these interests shapes the nature of politics.

There is clearly much truth to this. The problem is that it distracts attention from the reciprocal connection between interests and politics. Just as economic interests shape politics, politics also shapes economic interests—and, in so doing, participates in transforming the very forces that determine the future nature of politics itself. If the dynamics of mutual causation produce an equilibrium, it will be one in which interests and politics are rendered compatible through an iterated process of mutual adjustment. Both are transformed.

In the case of NLRB politics, a nice illustration is the clearly endogenous change in the interests of big business. During most of the first half of this century, big business was violently opposed to the rise of labor unions and led the political attack against them. But its perceived interests in labor-management politics underwent a major transformation beginning in the 1930s. This transformation was to a large extent a function of politics. The passage of the National Labor Relations Act, the creation of the NLRB, and the subsequent administration of the act put the force of the government behind the fledgling labor movement and systematically promoted the success, growth, and strength of trade union organizations. When the dust began to settle during the 1950s, the big business community as a whole was highly unionized; small businesses, as before, were not. This was to drive a political wedge between them.

Big business underwent an organizational transformation in the process. Unions were in some sense an alien force, but, by organizing employees "inside" business, they prompted a vast array of internal organizational responses. New structures emerged for dealing with matters ranging from major policy decisions to personnel functions to shop-floor operations. People with distinctively new backgrounds and orientations were recruited or drawn into these structures. Personnel and labor relations, in particular, were increasingly staffed by professionals in such fields as industrial relations, industrial psychology, and labor law whose view of unions was more "enlightened" and accommodating than that of their predecessors.

In pervasive ways, unionization became institutionalized in the organization of business—which had not simply "learned to live" with unions, but had organized around them. Although, as before, conflict might promise to lower costs somewhat, it now also threatened to promote far-ranging uncertainties, instabilities, and disruptions for the organization in its pursuit of economic gain. Harmonious relations with unions became good, safe business. This was reinforced by three basic features of the new political economy. First, unionized businesses that were organized for accommodation and harmony were also unlikely to be violators of the labor laws. Second, although all businesses feared the growing power of labor in general, unionized businesses knew that their individual interests were enhanced when their competitors became unionized too. And third, businesses and their unions often had common economic and political interests and thus had much to gain from working together.

A skeptic might claim that business's fundamental interests in profits and managerial autonomy remained unchanged, and that this more moderate political orientation toward labor was simply a strategic adjustment to an altered environment. But this interpretation misses the point. In both the economic theory of politics and the positive theory of institutions, "interests" tend to be understood not in terms of an individual's goals (like profit maximization) but in terms of what those goals imply for positions on policy in a given context. Interests flow from goals, they are more proximate to policy, and they are inevitably context-dependent. In the case of the NLRB or any other agency, the relevant economic interests of business are those that reflect the gains and losses associated with various political alternatives. Thus, although big business doubtless remained driven by profits and managerial autonomy throughout this entire period, its interests in the politics of labor-management relations—including, specifically, the net benefits associated with political attacks on labor—changed dramatically and, as a result, so did its policy positions and political behavior.

The result was a substantial moderation in big business's interests on issues of labor-management relations, which had the associated effects of blunting the business community's political attack on labor and leaving the mass of small businesses without the kind of aggressive antilabor leadership they desired. This was a major force for change in politics—but it was a force arising from transformations that were triggered years earlier by politics itself.

Although it is a bit too early to tell, it appears that the political turbulence of the late 1970s and early 1980s may be promoting yet another transformation—back toward antiunionism. Bad economic times and the weakening of union organization have clearly contributed to this, giving management greater incentives to challenge their unions. But this was not enough to stimulate a reverse transformation, for business's accommodationist past was now institutionalized in its own structure, policies, and personnel practices. Politically, big business continued to play much more moderate roles than a simple economic analysis would lead us to expect. The political battles initiated by labor during the Carter years, however, along with Reagan's unwanted and feared radicalization of the NLRB, forced business to confront a less stable, more conflictual world of labor-management relations—and the experience may well be changing some business leaders' views of where their best interests lie. If such a reverse transformation is in fact underway, politics will have played a key part in bringing it about.

In general, then, the relationship between business interests and politics has clearly been a reciprocal one, a relationship of mutual dependence. The same sort of argument could obviously be made for labor. To suggest that politics arises from the "underlying" economic interests, then, is to mischaracterize the causal process. We might just as meaningfully say that economic interests arise from the "underlying" politics.

The Mobilization of Resources. The extent to which economic interests find their reflection in public policy is crucially dependent on the political resources that can be mobilized on their behalf. The positive theory of institutions has little to say about mobilization, since it has focused to this point on voters, elections, and the formal apparatus of government. The economic theory of politics, on the other hand, has a great deal to say about how resources are mobilized. In fact, the theory is essentially an elaboration of Olson's logic of collective action. It is a theory of politics built around a theory of mobilization.

Olson's contribution to the study of collective action is justifiably regarded as pathbreaking, but the economic theory asks far too much of it. Olson's analysis is about individuals. It asserts that, because common interests entail collective goods, the free-rider incentive inhibits individuals from contributing. In the aggregate, this inhibition operates differentially: small, concentrated interests are more likely to overcome free-rider problems than large, diffuse groups are. For the economists, this logic explains the translation of economic interests into political pressures. Although it is clear that interest organizations are institutional intermediaries in this process of mobilization, and in fact that they are the central political actors in bringing pressure to bear on politicians, there is no need to take them into account explicitly. This would only complicate what is already a powerful explanation.

There is a curious logical problem associated with the Chicago school's reliance on Olson's theory of mobilization. Traditionally, they have relied on Coase's theorem in downplaying the importance of institutions and arguing that voluntary exchange promotes social efficiency. The thrust of this theorem is that, in a world without transactions costs, people will be able to overcome collective action problems in jointly arriving at efficient outcomes. But this is just another way of saying that, in a world without transactions costs, Olson's theory does not hold. Olson's well-known assertions about free-rider incentives and biases in the mobilization of group resources are valid only when transactions costs are in fact significant. Thus, the two theories about collective action are derived from opposing premises, and their conclusions cannot be simultaneously embraced. To the extent that transactions costs become important, whether empirically or by assumption, Coase's theorem and its benign perspective on mobilization and social efficiency must increasingly give way to Olson's logic and its pessimistic implications. To the extent that transactions costs decrease in significance, Olson gives way to Coase. The economic theory, however, has developed without any explicit recognition of the logical tension between the two theories. It appears to base its arguments on both. Ultimately, of course, this ambiguity will have to be eliminated in some fashion, and what the economic theory has to say about politics could change substantially as a result.[64] In what follows, I will simply ignore the inconsis-

64. Acknowledging the significance of transactions costs, for example, would do more than simply justify the theoretical role now accorded Olson's logic of mobilization. It would also lead to the conclusion that political control is often highly problematic—which directly undermines the economic theory's presumed chain of control from groups to politicians to bureaucrats, as well as its claim that public policy can be explained without any attempt to model these links in the chain. By acknowledging the importance of transactions costs, the economists would presumably be led to the kind of theoretical perspective now being developed within the positive theory of institutions.

tency and consider some of the other problems involved in the economic theory's attempt to put Olson's logic to use in understanding politics.

One of the most glaring of these is that, in the real world of politics, we are never dealing with a state of nature in which interests simply "give rise" to organizations to represent them. The political world is already organized. In most political contexts, the relevant question is not whether the affected interests will get organized, but what the existing organizations will decide to do—what positions they will take, how they will allocate their resources, what strategies they will follow.

In the NLRB's case, the most important economic interests are those expressed by the organized interest groups that structure the business and labor sectors; the Chamber of Commerce, the NAM, the Business Roundtable, the AFL-CIO (and its major unions), and the Teamsters. These organizations have existed for years, and they are established players in NLRB politics. They routinely speak for—and are expected by politicians, bureaucrats, and other groups to speak for—the interests of business and labor. They know the agency and the issues surrounding it, they know the other players and their institutions, and they have the staff and resources on hand to take action should it be needed. When an issue arises regarding the NLRB, they will be the major actors who determine which economic interests get represented and how.

These established organizations are institutions in their own right. In a very consequential sense, they have interests of their own—most obviously, in growth, survival, security. Consider the trade unions. Because the organizational well-being of unions has long been shaped by the national regulatory framework and the NLRB's administration of its provisions, unions have incentives to take political action on their own behalf, not simply on behalf of the "underlying" worker interests. Trade union interests and worker interests are not the same. Perhaps the most salient illustration is the long, bitter fight between the AFL and the CIO. This was primarily a conflict between fundamental organizational interests, a conflict anchored in the AFL's traditional organization around craft principles and in its leaders' unwillingness to make the major organizational adjustments and accommodations necessary to promote the unionization of whole industries. With the rise of the CIO, the two institutions fought head-to-head in jurisdictional battles over workers and in political battles over labor law and the NLRB. They also had very different political allies, the AFL often siding with Republicans, southern conservatives, and employers' organizations against the CIO and its liberal Democratic supporters. This conflict shaped the economics and politics of labor-management relations—and of the nation as a whole—for some two decades. Yet it arose largely from interests that the economic theory entirely dismisses: the interests of the mobilizers.

What we need is theory that can explain the behavior of these key organizational actors, a theory that views them as something more than simple vehicles for the promotion of "underlying" interests." Ironically, an extension of Olson's logic to issues of organizational behavior—an extension the economic theory does not make—ought to lead to this same conclusion. Consider what his analysis has to say about workers. In an economic state of nature, workers suffer from collective action problems in the extreme and cannot hope to achieve organization if common interests are the only motivation. Organization requires selective inducements; Olson emphasizes, in particular, legal coercion (via union security agreements), social pressure, and violence. Note, however, that these bases for union membership have nothing to do with politics or collective goods generally. Indeed, even if members thoroughly disapproved of the political positions and activities of union leaders, they would have no rational incentive to leave the organization, by Olson's logic, for they are tied in by selective inducements and would continue to contribute regardless. If we take Olson's theory of mobilization seriously, therefore, we are driven to a conclusion that stands the economic theory of politics on its head: there is no necessary connection between organizational politics and the underlying economic interests. Organizational leaders should have substantial autonomy in deciding which interests to "represent," in allocating political resources, and in pursuing their own, institutional interests.[65]

Whether we begin with an economic state of nature or bow to the obvious fact that the political world is already organized, then, it appears that mobilization, pressure, and their relation to the underlying interests can be explained only by means of an institutional theory. This theory must focus on issues of organization, attempt to account for the political choices of organizational leaders, and inquire into the various institutional mechanisms (such as democratic control structures) by which member interests may in practice constrain what leaders do. It must also attempt to place interest organizations in their larger institutional context. The fundamental structure of NLRB politics, for instance, is largely a reflection of the regularized relationships that have developed over the years among a fairly small number of these organizational actors. How the Chamber of Commerce, the NAM, the AFL-CIO, and the Teamsters have allocated their political resources and exerted pressure in NLRB politics has been a function of their adaptive adjustments to one another, their acceptance of presidential "rules" for conflict avoidance, and the serious constraints on legislative adventurism imposed by the separation of powers. To an appreciable extent, their mobilization activities are environmentally explained—we understand them not simply by understanding the organizations themselves, but by understanding the institutional makeup and structure of the environment in which they operate.

It is not enough, moreover, to recognize that their political choices are shaped by environment. The organizations themselves—like the economic interests they purportedly represent—stand in reciprocal relation to politics. They are agents of influence that bring pressure to bear on politicians, but they also can be transformed by the political outcomes they help to bring about. The National Labor Relations Act and the NLRB, most obviously, dramatically boosted the growth and success of union organizations, contributed mightily to the industrial unions' challenge to craft dominance, and, in general, transformed the institutional structure of the labor movement. Labor's defeat in Taft-Hartley prompted a massive increase in the resources they chose to devote to

65. For an attempt to extend Olson's logic to issues of organization, see Terry M. Moe, *The Organization of Interests* (Chicago: University of Chicago Press, 1980).

politics and a drive toward organizational coordination and unity. This, in turn, led to a permanent shift in the interest group system. Similarly, labor's furious drive to achieve common situs picketing and labor law reform in the late 1970s had the unintended side effect of significantly enhancing the capacity of business groups for mobilizing political resources. This shift, too, has lived on.

The economic theory of politics directs us to look past all this. Its problem is not that it fails to model the rich complexity of interest group politics; rather, it simply fails to provide any valid link between interests and political pressure. All the important theoretical issues turn out to be institutional.

Control of Politicians by Economic Interests. In both the economic and positive theories, there is a standard technology for modeling politicians: assume they are motivated by reelection and that they adopt policy positions as means to this end. Voters and groups have policy positions, but politicians do not. Their policy positions are "induced." This technology seems to have worked well so far, both as a modeling convenience and as a basis for explaining political behavior. But it can be pushed only so far. As formal models move beyond distributive politics and purely legislative arenas to include other types of policies and participants, and as the study of institutions sheds new light on questions of political control and autonomy, it becomes less clear that politicians can reliably be viewed as conduits for constituency and group pressure.

In the case of the NLRB, an obvious illustration derives from the role of President Reagan in bucking the traditional structure of NLRB politics. Recall that this structure emerged over the years in no small part because earlier presidents, taking an accommodationist approach to business and labor, had implicitly imposed a framework that took the interests of both systematically into account and because this framework proved acceptable (not coincidentally) to the groups. Regularity and order reigned instead of continual conflict. When Reagan took office, he was expected to play by the traditional rules, and the "demands" coming into the White House from business, labor, and their political supporters were shaped accordingly. But he did not respond like his accommodationist predecessors. In a sense, he did not respond at all. The result was an extended period of turmoil.

This is one of the most interesting and important periods in the modern history of the NLRB. Yet the politicians-as-conduits notion not only fails to anticipate this kind of outcome; it encourages an after-the-fact explanation that is wholly incorrect: that Reagan must have done what he did in response to the demands of organized business.[66] The reality is that even the more conservative insiders in the business lobby were shocked by Reagan's approach. The more fitting explanation is that Reagan had his own agenda that transcended the particularistic demands of interest groups. His was, in effect,

66. An alternative is that Reagan was indeed responding to business pressure, but to the antiunion, small-business elements of his support coalition. Interviews with participants strongly suggest otherwise. The Reagan administration was taking the initiative on these matters, not responding to pressure.

an ideological agenda. And, with respect to the NLRB and its traditional structure of politics, Reagan acted autonomously of group interests and pressures in carrying the agenda out.

In a world of electoral politics and rational actors, there should be nothing anomalous about this sort of behavior. Politicians, like the rest of us, do have their own policy preferences, and although the electoral system gives them incentives to suppress these preferences in favor of those of their constituents, they are not invariably kept out of office for failing to do so. It is probably true that purely accommodationist politicians are, on the average, more likely to survive repeated elections. But an "unresponsive" politician's ideology may happen to fit his constituency reasonably well in the short term; and, even if it does not, there is enough ignorance and uncertainty in voting—and enough besides policy that matters to voters (like casework or simple name recognition)—to suggest that even rigidly ideological politicians will maintain a presence in politics. They may even turn up as president of the United States or chair of the Senate Labor Committee.

Much the same thing can be said through the logical apparatus of the positive theory of institutions. Application of principal-agent models of hierarchic control implies that elections and other means of voter (or group) oversight are imperfect mechanisms of control—and thus that politicians, should they wish, will have a measure of flexibility to pursue their own policy objectives. To some degree, they can behave ideologically, autonomous of constituent interests, and get away with it. There is no logical basis, then, for thinking that rational politicians must toe the line and act as simple conduits. Those who adopt a more autonomous posture may be acting quite rationally, too— and their behavior, different from that of accommodationist politicians, may be crucial to an explanation of events.[67]

There is, finally, a different sense in which the politicians-as-conduits notion can prove highly misleading, and this can be so even if politicians are pure accommodationists. Consider the case of senators in the politics of NLRB appointments. Senators were sufficiently eager to satisfy their business and labor allies in these contests, but they were not free to do the groups' bidding. There were various reasons for this, but the most interesting, theoretically, has to do with the normative structure of the appointments process: promotion of group interests would in many cases—particularly those involving opposition to presidential candidates—involve a violation of historical norms outlining how senators expect one another to behave, as well as how the president expects them to behave, in the politics of appointments.

These norms, like those of senatorial courtesy, reciprocity, and many others that structure politics, seem to have a firm anchoring in rational self-interest.[68] They appear, more specifically, to help resolve collective action prob-

---

67. See Kalt and Zupan, "Capture and Ideology in the Economic Theory of Politics."

68. On these issues generally, see Axelrod, *The Evolution of Cooperation,* and Weingast, "A Rational Choice Perspective on Congressional Norms," *American Journal of Political Science* 23 (1979) : 245–62.

lems, both among the senators themselves and between the Senate and the president. In the absence of some set of rules, the appointments process (and policy-making generally) could easily degenerate into chaotic conflicts, leaving everyone worse off. The irony is that the norms, which derive their rationale from the electoral self-interest of individual politicians, operate to make politicians unwilling to respond to their constituents on many issues. They want to be responsive, but they "can't."

This in turn has the effect of structuring the behavior of the groups. As sophisticated participants in the sequential stream of political decision making, the groups "play by the rules" in pressuring their political allies. They do not pressure politicians to be responsive, and do not expect them to be, when such behaviors would conflict with the larger normative structure that constrains the politicians' pursuit of self-interest. In part, they do so because the politicians would resist anyway. But they also do so because they are long-term participants in policy-making, and they want harmonious, beneficial relationships in the months and years ahead. Thus, the AFL-CIO and the Teamsters surely wanted to defeat many of the Republican appointees to the NLRB, and their allies in the Senate would like to have gone along. But the senators were constrained by appointments norms to support "qualified" nominees regardless of ideology, and they generally "could not" vote in opposition. The labor groups understood this and typically did not pressure the senators to oppose conservative appointments.

Even when politicians are solely motivated by their electoral self-interest, then, their behavior may easily seem mysterious if not placed in its larger institutional context. Politicians do not simply balance or otherwise respond to interest group pressures. Nor, in fact, do groups even bring pressure when it seems they have objective interests at stake. The key is that electoral self-interest gives rise over time to institutions—like the normative structure surrounding appointments—and these institutions, which are themselves resistant to group pressure in the short term, serve to constrain how both the politicians and the groups pursue their own ends. As a result, the politics of electoral self-interest looks very different than a simple pressure model would suggest. Politicians are not conduits for the pressures immediately being brought to bear. To the extent they can usefully be regarded as conduits at all, they are conduits for the vast historical field of constituency pressures—from their districts and the districts of others, going back into the distant past—that gave rise to the rules constraining their current behavior.

The Control of Bureaucrats by Politicians. The economic theory of politics has little to say about political control of the bureaucracy beyond the claim that control is unproblematic. The positive theory of institutions is increasingly turning its attention to this issue, and the long-term prospects are bright. At this stage, however, what it has to tell us is not always very helpful. The problem is that its general orientation to the study of control is often inappropriate.

In the first place, the PTI literature tends to view Congress as the center of the political universe, and its orientation to the study of control is structured accordingly: congressional committees are the preeminent political taskmasters, seeking—with substantial success—to constrain bureaucratic behavior toward legislative ends. This approach threatens to miss what is most interesting and essential about bureaucratic politics and political control.

Early in the NLRB's political history, legislative stalemate caused an institutional shift in the group struggle that, by past standards, virtually cut Congress out of the picture. Throughout the following decades, agency politics was structured around presidential appointments. The president was the pivotal actor, not the Congress. The House Labor Committee was left to debate legislation that, with rare exceptions, would never get to the floor. The Senate Labor Committee was an integral participant, but not because of legislation or oversight; it was important because of its role in the appointments process—and, even here, its influence was severely constrained by, among other things, historical norms governing its "advice and consent."

This is not to say that Congress was unimportant to NLRB politics. Although infrequent, legislative battles were major events in the NLRB's political history, and Senators Wagner, Taft, and Hatch, among others, played roles of great consequence. The point is simply that we are most likely to gain a balanced perspective on bureaucratic politics if we think more broadly about the institutional system as a whole rather than about a "central" institution that presumably gives orientation to all the rest. The importance of Congress for any given agency depends on developments within the larger system, not on powers that are somehow intrinsic to Congress itself.

PTI's analytical foundations also tend to encourage a rather selective view of what political control is all about. Its analyses are beginning to follow the lead of recent work in the economics of organization by understanding control in principal-agent terms—with, for example, a committee as principal and the bureau as agent. This imposes a distinctive perspective on the fundamentals of the control problem: one actor tries to pursue his own interests through the actions of a second, whom he intentionally tries to control by structuring incentives, monitoring performance, and issuing criteria and directives.

This is a promising approach to the clarification and analysis of abstract issues of control and, with proper use, will doubtless contribute to our understanding of political control relationships. But its application is not so straightforward. Note, in particular, how misleading it would be in the NLRB case. The NLRB is highly responsive to presidential partisanship—it is more pro-union during Democratic years, more probusiness during Republican years—and the mechanism for bringing these systematic policy changes about is clearly presidential appointments. Yet, prior to Reagan at least, presidents were not motivated to control the NLRB and made no effort to structure incentives, monitor, or issue guidelines. Presidents "controlled" the agency without trying or caring. We might say that the real principals were business and labor, for they did monitor the NLRB and implicitly structure the incentives of its bureaucrats by determining the types of individuals (professionals with known ideologies) appointed to the board. But what the groups did and how much influence they had cannot be understood apart from the informal rules structuring the appointments process—rules they did not choose alone, that emerged from their inherent competition and conflict of interest, that allowed for participation by others, and that forced them to act largely through the president. As they found out when Reagan assumed office, moreover, the president is not simply an agent of group control: he can use his powers to change the rules and to strip the groups of most of their capacity to structure the incentives of NLRB officials.

No one controls the NLRB, yet it is clearly under control. It is controlled by its surrounding institutional structure, and most immediately by the structure of presidential appointments politics. Within this framework various actors from the White House, the Department of Labor, business, the unions, and the Senate routinely play their expected roles, generating regular shifts in NLRB performance with presidential partisanship. The key to understanding political control, therefore, rests with an explanation of this distinctive structure of NLRB politics—where it comes from, how the various participants fit into it, and how it constrains NLRB policy. Principal-agent models—and, more generally, perspectives on control that rivet attention on the conscious, intentional efforts of one actor to control another—tend to misconstrue the essence of the problem. In politics, control is often indirect, unintentional, and systemic.[69]

The spillover effects of PTI's characteristic approach to control can be substantial, extending well beyond the usual questions of who has influence over whom. To take a noteworthy example: it encourages us to think of professionalism and political control as opposing explanations of bureaucratic behavior.[70] Professionals are oriented by goals, standards of conduct, and career opportunities that derive from their professional community, giving them strong reasons for resisting interference and direction by political outsiders; and their specialized information and expertise give them formidable resources for resisting with some measure of success. Thus, professionalism is a foundation for bureaucratic autonomy. The more autonomous a bureau is,

---

69. There have been some promising moves in this direction within PTI, but they still get back to notions of direct control. McCubbins, for instance, argues that agencies are largely controlled by virtue of the structural—programmatic, organizational, procedural—constraints imposed by Congress. Once these are in place, Congress "controls" the agency without intense monitoring and all the rest. His assumption, however, is that legislators design these structural constraints for optimal control—this is their purpose. Thus, it is ultimately grounded in a model of conscious, intentional control. See McCubbins, "The Legislative Design of Regulatory Structure." Much the same can be said of McCubbins and Schwartz, who argue that legislators have little incentive to engage in continuous oversight for control purposes ("police patrol" oversight), that their incentive instead is to intervene in response to constituency "fire alarms." When these bells go off, however, they wield their various rewards and sanctions to whip bureaucrats back into line. Again, bureaucrats are held in check by direct efforts to control their behavior. See McCubbins and Schwartz, "Congressional Oversight Overlooked."

70. See especially Weingast and Moran, "Bureaucratic Discretion or Legislative Control?"

the less it is controlled by politicians, and vice versa. By this account, the relationship between autonomy and control is zero-sum.[71]

As we have seen in the NLRB's case, however, professionalism and political control are more usefully understood as integral parts of the same institutional system. Professionalism is valued by business and labor because it protects their mutual interests in stability, clarity, and expert judgment. They also value it as a vehicle for the orderly exercise of political control: the choice of professionals with known ideologies—the choice of types—guarantees the groups a measure of control over the agency without the necessity of exercising any direct influence. Thus, the NLRB is highly autonomous, run by professionals according to their own best judgment without interference from politicians or groups. At the same time, it is firmly under political control and very sensitive to the shifting political winds.

That professionalism and political control might mesh in this way should not be too surprising. For any agency, they must emerge as integral components of the same system of relationships. To the extent that relationships among rational actors tend to move toward equilibria compatible with the incentives of all participants, it seems likely that professionalism and political control may often fit together rather productively—or in ways, at least, that current notions tend to overlook. Here, professionalism is not an opposing force that militates against control. It is the very vehicle that makes systematic political control possible.

Modeling Politics. The theme running through all this is that an explanation of NLRB politics is rooted in the dynamics of the institutional system. All the major components—interests, mobilization, institutions, policy—are endogenous and mutually dependent. Although contributors to the economic theory of politics and the positive theory of institutions would probably agree that this is generally true in politics, they purposely choose not to model politics in this way. Their models are exercises in comparative statics. Most of the basic features of politics are taken as exogenous; reciprocal relationships of mutual dependence are ignored; and no serious attention is directed to system dynamics. The system is not really treated as a system.

Given the current state of technology, this is a perfectly legitimate modeling strategy. In practice, however, it proves to be much more than a strategy. The fact is that the models become intellectual forces in their own right and operate to structure the study and explanation of politics. As they do so, they channel attention and serious inquiry away from the dynamics of the institutional system. Reciprocal causality, adaptive adjustment, and other systemic considerations are given low priority. They are not seen as essential.

In the NLRB's case, however, they clearly are essential. Without simply summarizing ground that has already been covered, perhaps the best way to

71. This general perspective on professionalism and political control is widely accepted in political science and is not confined to PTI. See, for example, James Q. Wilson, *The Politics of Regulation,* and Francis E. Rourke, *Bureaucracy, Politics, and Public Policy,* 3rd ed. (Boston: Little, Brown & Co., 1984).

reemphasize the point is to consider three broad areas of theoretical significance: the agency and its environment, informal institutions, and political change.

1. *The agency and its environment:* From the standpoint of current models, NLRB behavior is a response to the environmental influences of politicians and economic groups. It is a product of its environment. Yet attention to the political history of the agency suggests that this is just part of the story. For the environment was fundamentally transformed by the NLRB.

The NLRB began life in a turbulent environment composed of little more than two hostile camps. As the board set about its task of regulating labor-management relations, however, society began to adapt and develop in direct response. Unions became much stronger, economically and politically; big business took a more moderate approach to labor-management politics and would no longer serve as the militant vanguard of antiunionism; legislative battles over the NLRA died down, and politics became routinized around presidential appointments. The regulation-induced demand for legal counsel stimulated the rise of the labor bar, and the board's role in their apprenticeship served to instill in them a respect for the institution and its statute; they would serve as important guardians of the agency's professionalism and integrity. As a by-product of its normal regulatory activities, then, the NLRB set in motion social forces that, despite the underlying conflict of interest between business and labor, produced an environment far more peaceful, regularized, and supportive of the agency than anyone might have imagined forty years ago.

Any attempt to explain the NLRB's own behavior, therefore, must reckon with the strong mutual dependence between agency and environment. For all the obvious reasons, the NLRB was indeed a product of its environment. But the environment was also very much a product of the NLRB.

2. *Informed institutions:* Institutions do not always take the form of statutes, written contracts, formal organizations, or constitutions. Congressional decision making is structured by universalistic norms.[72] The budgetary process is structured by traditional roles and entrenched expectations.[73] And the list could easily be extended. Routines, norms, and other aspects of regularized or "cooperative" behavior are clearly central to all of politics. They are informal but highly consequential political institutions.

The basic structure of NLRB politics is not called for by law or statute. It arises from the self-interested behavior of actors who are mutually dependent, whose interests are often in conflict, whose resources are scarce, and whose environments are enormously complicated. Matters that might otherwise provoke costly battles—again and again—are settled by structure. In the NLRB's case, the appointments process did not become routinized through mutual agreement, although there are participants on both sides who do think in those terms. It became routinized largely because of the way appointments

72. See Weingast, "A Rational Choice Perspective on Congressional Norms."
73. See Aaron Wildavsky, *The Politics of the Budgetary Process,* 3rd ed. (Boston: Little, Brown & Co., 1979).

are embedded in the dynamics of the institutional system. The president, by virtue of his institutional location, has the authority to make appointments and, prior to Reagan, the incentives to accommodate group interests in particular ways. He essentially imposes a structure they can live with. Senators are crucial to this structure, in contrast, because their institutional locations and the associated informal rules lead them to resist interfering, which in turn prompts business and labor not to end run the presidential structure to fight their battles in the Senate. The structure as a whole works and becomes entrenched because it is consistent with the incentives of all the major participants.

Theories of comparative statics, however much they express an interest in the full range of political institutions, have the effect of encouraging us to overlook and deemphasize these informal aspects of political structure. Their focus is on those structural features that can conveniently be taken as fixed: the formal powers of committee chairs, legislative procedures, rules defining committee jurisdictions. Informal rules and norms, although recently the focus of much attention in game theory, are for now a bit difficult to incorporate into the more conventional models of institutions.[74] Because they are informal, they are nowhere written down, so it is unclear what they actually are or require; they generally emerge over time through the adaptive adjustments of many participants, and thus they have a dynamic character that seems to distinguish them from formal rules; and they are "enforced" by the voluntary actions of participants rather than by legal or administrative policing actions, which again introduces a dynamism not often associated with rules. In the absence of an institutional theory that fully recognizes these dynamics, we are guided by models that highlight the more fixed and formal aspects of political structure—whether or not these are central or even of much relevance to an explanation.

3. *Political change:* The economic theory of politics sees change in terms of marginal adjustments: a small change in an exogenous factor—interests or resources, say—produces a marginally different equilibrium outcome. The positive theory of institutions argues that political institutions do not work that way. They stabilize politics by ensuring that whole ranges of underlying fluctuations do not upset the prevailing equilibrium. When change does occur—because of a strong liberal replacing a strong conservative as committee chair or because of the passage of a new statute—it tends to take the form of a discontinuous jump to a new equilibrium rather than a smooth marginal adjustment. The system moves by fits and starts.[75]

The NLRB analysis is broadly consistent with PTI's perspective on political change, but its attention to system dynamics points to some important elaborations. First, the NLRB has a nested structural pattern that generates different types of change. Some changes take the form of dramatic shifts in politics and policy resulting from shifts in the general legal structure, as happened with

---

74. For a discussion of their relevance to PTI and its further development, see Shepsle, "Institutional Equilibrium and Equilibrium Institutions."

75. See Romer and Rosenthal, "Modern Political Economy and the Study of Regulation."

the Wagner and Taft-Hartley acts. This structure has been essentially fixed since 1948. Yet nested within it is a further structuring of politics around presidential appointments—and, by virtue of this structure, change regularly occurs every time there is a change in presidential partisanship. This cyclical change, although in some sense discontinuous, is quite smooth compared to the kind of change entailed by alteration in the general legal structure. It is, moreover, responsible for virtually all the change in NLRB politics that has occurred over the last forty years. What we find is regular systematic change within a broader framework of stability.

Second, these structures are differentially sensitive to pressures for change. The general structural framework has remained fixed throughout the decades despite clear fluctuations in group strengths, economic interests, and general economic conditions. The structure of appointments politics is also insensitive to these forces, but not to the same degree. It is an informal structure that rests in part on a recognition among major participants that following the rules is in their own best interests. When economic times are especially bad or political opportunities for gain especially good, certain participants may find it advantageous to break with tradition; and when they do, the fabric of "cooperation"—the structure—can come apart. The same thing can happen when a maverick politician, new on the scene, decides not to play by the old rules or listen to the established players. The appointments structure is more vulnerable to these sorts of things than the broader formal structure is. It is also well suited to reflect changes in the interests, intensity, and resources of the established groups, since they are continually bringing their weights to bear—in a structured way—on presidential decision makers, and their weights can vary as their electoral importance and roles in governance vary. Thus, the appointments structure does respond to economic and political forces—but, in responding, it orders and regularizes the way they are expressed.

Third, part of the reason for the emergence of the informal appointments process is the very resistance of the broader formal structure to change. In some sense, the informal is an adaptive response to the formal. Separation of powers and rough equalization of group strengths produced legislative stalemate: the inability to seek change through formal structure. This shifted the focus of politics away from the legislature toward presidential appointments, around which there developed an informal structure that was responsive to the groups in a way the formal structure could not be. Interestingly, this reflects the kind of dynamics that writers in the economic theory of politics sometimes refer to when they claim that institutions do not matter much—for what we observe is that, when groups and politicians find their choices uncomfortably constrained by structure, they search for other ways to get what they want. In doing so, they create informal institutions that "supplement" formal institutions and promote a degree of flexibility and system responsiveness that goes beyond what the positive theory of institutions would lead us to expect. What the economic theory ignores—and PTI implicitly recognizes—is that the original constraints are not eliminated in the process, and that the search for better arrangements leads to new institutions that are inherently resistant to change themselves.

CONCLUSION

In reflecting on these theories, a brief digression on the disciplines of economics and political science is instructive. The economic theory of politics plays a role in political science that is, in an important sense, analogous to the role played by the neoclassical theory of the firm within economics. The neoclassical theory of the firm is not really about firms at all, but rather about how various economic inputs (labor, capital, land) find their expression in aggregate economic outcomes (the equilibrium prices and supplies of economic goods). The firm is nothing more than a production function, a black box that effectuates this translation. The economic theory of politics adopts the same basic methodology in explaining the connection between economic interests and public policy: the political institutions that bring about the translation are, again, a black box. In both cases the presumption is that an adequate explanation of outcomes can be achieved without modeling the translation process itself.

Within economics, there were dissenters from the theory of the firm who felt that outcomes could not be explained adequately without attention to organization, or simply that the firm was an important subject of explanation in its own right.[76] But for years their attempts to model firms as organizations attracted little support or attention from mainstream economists. The emergence of the new economics of organization over the last decade has dramatically turned matters around. Suddenly, organization is a legitimate and important theoretical topic, and new models of rational behavior are being put to use in exploring issues of structure, hierarchy, and control. Arguments that economists ought to be concerned with filling in the black box are no longer dismissed out of hand.

In political science, it is the positive theory of institutions that plays this role of filling in the black box. The difference is that neither the economic theory of politics nor its black box methodology was ever dominant in political science to begin with. PTI arose out of a different body of theory altogether, in reaction to social choice issues of voting and instability. Nonetheless, its contributors have proceeded to develop an institutional theory that links social interests to political outcomes in a way that overlaps substantially—and increasingly—with the new economics of organization. In both disciplines, the general form and content of institutional theory are essentially the same, and they are becoming more alike as time goes on. What we are witnessing is the early formulation of a truly general, rational-choice theory of social institutions, one that knows no disciplinary boundaries.

To the extent that such a theory can be constructed, it will eventually supplant any black-box theory that claims to link social inputs to social outputs. But, again, we live in the short run, and for now these two approaches to theory are competitors. The economic theory of politics and the positive theory of institutions both offer frameworks for the explanation of public pol-

76. Most notably, Richard M. Cyert and James G. March, *A Behavioral Theory of the Firm* Englewood Cliffs, N.J.: Prentice-Hall, 1963).

icy—and, as we have seen, these frameworks currently have very different implications for the way we study and think about politics.

Most generally, they give rise to perspectives that mirror basic features of the much more broadly based debate within political science between pluralist and institutionalist explanations. More specifically, they entail perspectives on the mobilization of group pressure, political leadership, political control of bureaucracy, professionalism and autonomy, agency-environment relationships, the emergence of informal structures, the nature of political change, and a host of other issues that go to make up our understanding of how the political system works. Because these theories are still developing, what they entail is not set in concrete—new evidence, arguments, and theoretical insights can and doubtless will prompt them to move in new directions that seem conducive to better explanation. This is what progress is all about.

The purpose of this article has been to clarify what these theories have to say and to argue the need for reorientation. The NLRB analysis was the vehicle for all this. As an attempt to impose logical order on the political history of an important economic regulatory agency, this article has tried to bring into focus the central concerns of both theories—how economic interests, via institutional translation, find their reflection in public policy—and to provide a substantive basis for assessing their approaches to politics.

The economic theory does not come off especially well. In the first place, its logic is often unclear and on important points is inconsistent—for example, regarding the relationship between Coase's theorem and Olson's logic of collective action (the former is premised on the insignificance of transactions costs, the latter is premised on the opposite), and the implications of Olson's theory for the autonomy of interest groups leaders (which severs the logical connection between interests and their "representation" by groups). It appears that the economic theory simply lacks a coherent logical foundation and literally needs to be reformulated. In the second place, it has little to say about most of the interesting aspects of politics, and what it does have to say is often misleading.

The positive theory of institutions is on much firmer logical and empirical footing. Although some of its early emphasis on congressional control is inconsistent with its logical foundations in the new economics of organization, this line of work points toward the construction of a powerful theory—not simply of institutions per se, but of the system of connections linking interests, institutions, and outcomes. Empirically, it has more to say about various aspects of politics than the economic theory does, and what it says is more often insightful and on target.

Even in the short term, then, there are strong reasons why PTI's general orientation to politics is preferable to the economic theory's. The analysis of the NLRB, however, underlines the need for reorientation. Most generally, PTI's current approach to politics is itself misleading in certain respects. Problems tend to arise because it is not sufficiently concerned with institutional dynamics—with mutual dependence, adaptive adjustment, process, feedback, and other aspects of systemic behavior. Modeling convenience may be persuasive argument for treating economic interests, group resources, institutions, and many other components of politics as fixed, but we now run the risk of allowing these models to structure our thinking about politics in ways that can be inappropriate.

Thus, while it may not be surprising, on reflection, to find that the NLRB played a truly major role in transforming its own environment, or that its politics was largely explained by informal rather than formal structures, or that it was controlled by the system as a whole rather than by direct intervention by interested actors, these are precisely the sorts of phenomena that PTI currently leads us to overlook. Rather than pointing to the essentials of NLRB politics, it tends to rivet attention on Congress, the agenda powers of congressional committees, committee control of bureaucracy, and other familiar theoretical topics that, in the NLRB's case, are peripheral to an explanation. A systemic perspective would not only direct attention to questions of dynamics; it would resist the tendency to assume that any particular institution is the prime mover. The central problem is to figure out how the various pieces fit together to form a coherent whole. To this point, PTI has been far more concerned with the pieces themselves.

It is of more than passing relevance here that the larger literature on political institutions, much of it historical and almost all of it qualitative in nature, has generally not viewed PTI as a promising theoretical foundation. The reason, it seems fair to suggest, is not simply that the theory's rational choice models are too sophisticated to be easily understood or incorporated into the study of institutions. It is, rather, that contributors to this literature tend to think more broadly and comprehensively about their subject matter. Implicitly, they think in terms of systems and their dynamics—about history, about process, about how the various components of the institutional system fit together. Whether their theoretical notions are correct or very promising is another matter. What is important is that PTI's general orientation to institutional questions is seen as too narrow, and too narrowly technical, to shed light on issues these writers regard as fundamental. There is no debate between the two bodies of literature. They just proceed in parallel, largely ignoring one another.[77]

This is most unfortunate, because PTI has vast potential as a theoretical foundation for the study of institutions generally. This is already becoming clear in international relations, in which the theory of repeated games, transactions costs economics, and other components of the new economics of organization have recently attracted much attention.[78] Interestingly, it has made less headway on the domestic side. One of the major topics of debate in the institutionalist literature, for instance, surrounds the "autonomy" of state actors;[79] but there is little recognition at this point that the positive theory of

77. See March and Olsen, "The New Institutionalism," for a review.

78. See, for example, Robert Keohane, *After Hegemony* (Princeton: Princeton University Press, 1984); R. Harrison Wagner, "The Theory of Games and the Problem of International Cooperation," *American Political Science Review* 77 (1983) : 330–46.

79. See, for example, Eric Nordlinger, *On the Autonomy of the Democratic State* (Cambridge: Harvard University Press, 1981).

institutions speaks directly to this issue and provides a coherent, potentially very powerful basis for explanation. Much the same can be said for the more familiar, less controversial aspects of domestic politics—the routines of the budgetary process, the norms of congressional behavior, and other patterns that regularize a good portion of political behavior. These, too, are natural subjects for explanation within the theory.

A call for reorientation, therefore, has implications that extend well beyond our efforts to understand bureaucratic politics. Just as attention to institutional dynamics is necessary if PTI is to realize its potential in explaining the politics of agencies like the NLRB, so the same kind of reorientation would enhance its value—and, more practically, demonstrate its relevance—to the study of institutions generally across all areas of political science.

NOTES AND EXCHANGES

JOHN BRIGHAM
University of Massachusetts, Amherst

Right, Rage, and Remedy:
Forms of Law in Political
Discourse

When political activists talk about strategy and when they address each other, legal forms are an integral part of their language. Some movements, like alternative dispute resolution, build on a general critique of the legal process. Others, like gay rights, seek to fulfill legal promises or, as in the feminist antipornography campaign, they present broadsides against the law's oppression. These ideas about law are not bound in standard law books; but they give meaning to social relations, and they must be understood as significant parts of the legal order. To attend to them is to illuminate a part of law's social reality and, more specifically, to see how law informs social action. Such ideas and the relations they create are law *in* society.

LAW IN SOCIETY

Law is conventionally understood as rules made by government or commands from the sovereign. This is a positivist view, and approaches the constitutions, statutes, and official holdings as "the law." Consequently, the offices and institutions of the state determine what is legal. For example, the Supreme Court's 1973 decision on abortion *Roe* v. *Wade,* is "the law" on abortion in America. According to this tradition about what law is, people outside the institutions and offices of the "legal system" receive rather than generate law. They may advocate change and apply pressure on the law, but their advocacy is not itself understood as part of the law. The prolife movement, for instance, advocates a change in the Supreme Court's decision on abortion through either a new decision or a constitutional amendment. Movement politics in this framework, even when it has potentially great legal significance, remains something other

I gratefully acknowledge comments on earlier drafts by Stuart Scheingold, Isaac Balbus, Phyllis Farley Rippey, Sally Merry, Austin Sarat, and Christine Harrington.

than law. When a bishop proposes that "abortion is murder," Americans will tend to understand him to be preaching rather than articulating a valid legal claim.

Because those who study the law and its impact work from this picture of law disembodied from society, their insight into the law's effects or the social reality of law is limited. Even social scientists who study law *and* society together have maintained the distinction between social reality and the law.[1] They contend only that reality differs from the *ideal* of law governed by texts and judicial orders. In dividing society from governing institutions, positive legal theory misses the way social action depends upon law. To account for law as it exists in the practices of those who deal with it, we must move from "law *and* society" to the perspective of "law *in* society."[2]

More specifically, the perspective I wish to sketch here treats the law as part of society. In one sense, I mean to suggest how commands and rules structure the claims of political movements and how movements are dependent to some extent on available law. The more complete formulation, however, is one that moves beyond the view of law in society as a mere recipient of social forces to a definition of how groups know the law and what they make of it. The crucial point is that rules made by government infuse and inform the movements themselves by becoming an essential part of their thought, their identity, and their social boundaries. Thus, we shall be concerned in this note with antipornography feminists as they struggled with the legally sanctioned availability of pornography, with gay activists as they came to know their movement in terms of a constitutional right to equal treatment, and with the dispute resolution alternatives movement as it depends for its very existence on its lawyerly conception of "the law." This perspective on law in society allows us to examine movement discourse for what it tells us about rules and commands as they permeate social consciousness and structure social action, rather than simply exist as edicts.

Beyond Law as Symbol

My approach to law is associated with recent scholarship that studies symbols. Rooted in the legal realism of the 1930s, a law in society perspective was nurtured in the symbolic politics studies of Joseph Gusfield and Murray Edelman. More recently, scholars have moved from recognition that symbols are important to another level of inquiry. Stuart Scheingold and Isaac Balbus writing in the mid-1970s, represented this shift in the approach to the study of law in society. They called attention to the political role of legal rights and brought the symbolic to the level of the concrete institutional. The impact of symbols, according to Scheingold, was that they "condition perceptions, establish role expectations, provide standards of legitimacy, and account for the institu-

---

1. Stewart Macaulay, "Non-Contractual Relations in Business: A Preliminary Study," *American Sociological Review* 28 (1963) : 55.

2. See in particular the work of the Amherst Seminar in Legal Process and Legal Ideology in *The Legal Studies Forum* 9 (1985); David Nelken, "Beyond the Study of 'Law and Society'?" (Unpublished manuscript, 1986).

tional patterns of American politics."[3] Writing about groups and rights and focusing on rights strategies as they were adapted in collective action, Scheingold heralded greater attention to the symbolic dimension of law as a political resource. Still, the actual effect of legal ideas remained open to question because of their contingent or derivative status. In this regard, Balbus's work on legality was particularly challenging because it elaborated law in terms of market commodities, thus joining American scholarship to a materialist position flourishing for some time in Europe.[4]

Gusfield himself has since pushed further beyond the positivist view of law. While remaining attentive to the social force of law and legal process, his recent writing calls into question the common distinction between what legal scholars call "the judicial process," which includes "the style and logic of appellate court decisions," and what the sociologist refers to—the acts of police, attorneys, and courts.[5] He has investigated the authority of legal process, especially as it presents itself ritualistically, in order to take a look at all aspects of "state law." The "stuff" that "law students study," legislation and appellate court decisions, is for Gusfield an illusionary referent for law because it portrays an order that is "certain, consistent, and powerful."[6] He has observed that the ritual and drama of the legal process has a marked effect on the social reality of law.

The foundation for this latter observation has been located in the relationship between the conceptual life of the community and the conceptual parameters of case law, statutes, and treatise literature. In a recent discussion justifying attention to what he calls "mandarin materials," Robert Gordon discusses the traditional "stuff" of the law school curriculum as "an exceptionally refined and concentrated version of legal consciousness."[7] Legal scholars have long been confident that the tools and categories familiar to lawyers stand behind many of the ways ordinary people think about the world. Gordon describes the materials of elite legal thinking as illuminating "the vernacular, the common forms of legal discourse," and he points to research that found the basic elements of formal legal rules of property and contract internalized by laypeople and routinely applied on contexts remote from officials and courts.[8] According to Gordon, "field-level studies would reveal a lot of trickle-

3. Stuart Scheingold, *The Politics of Rights* (New Haven: Yale University Press, 1974), xi. See also Murray Edelman, *The Symbolic Uses of Politics* (Urbana: University of Illinois Press, 1967).

4. Isaac Balbus, *The Dialectics of Legal Repression* (New York: Russell Sage, 1973); "Commodity Form and Legal Form: An Essay on the 'Relative Autonomy' of the Law," *Law and Society Review* 11 (1977) : 571; Zenon Bankowski and Geoff Mungham, *Images of Law* (London: Routledge & Kegan Paul, 1976); Bernard Edelman, *Ownership of the Image: Elements for a Marxist Theory of Law* (London: Routledge & Kegan Paul, 1979).

5. Joseph Gusfield, *The Culture of Public Problems: Drinking-Driving and the Symbolic Order* (Chicago: University of Chicago Press, 1981), 141.

6. Ibid., 143.

7. Robert Gordon, "Critical Legal Histories," *Stanford Law Review* 36 (1984) : 127.

8. William Simon, "Legality, Bureaucracy and Class in the Welfare State," *Yale Law Journal* 92 (1983) : 1198–1269; R. Wiesberg, "Deregulating Death," *1983 Supreme Court Review*, 303.

down effects—a lot of mandarin ideology reproduced in somewhat vulgarized forms."[9]

Current work affirms the relevance of this line of inquiry and also reveals the continuing tendency of its proponents to come at the subject from divergent positions, doctrines, and practices. Owen Fiss, for example, has recently discussed law in society in terms of the "rich and generous body of decisions on free speech" produced by the Supreme Court. Drawing on the work of Harry Kalven, he describes this as a "Free Speech Tradition."[10] The result, according to Fiss (and Kalven), is that "free speech is now part of our general culture, and . . . the decisions of the Court implanted that principle in our culture, nurtured it, and gave it much of its present shape."[11] Backing up this claim is new ethnographic work on these traditions "in society." Anthropologist Sally Merry has focused on legal ideology among working-class disputants who use the courts, finding that "experienced plaintiffs come to see rights as an opportunity, a basis for action, rather than a guarantee of protection."[12]

In political science, the closet analog to this sort of work has been impact analysis, and here too a new spirit is challenging the assumptions on which the field was originally constructed. Charles Johnson and Bradley Canon have enhanced our picture of messages from the courts by calling attention to their reception by different audiences. Similarly, Thomas Dalton has given philosophical sophistication to our idea of what messages mean in his study of how different communities relate to criminal justice policy.[13] Elsewhere, I have discussed the ideological impact of judicial decisions by looking at a decision's influence on the substantive discourse of politics and the channels of political action of which it is a part.[14] Yet to take account of the nature and significance of research that is being done in other fields, the positivist baggage of law as orders, which is still maintained by the impact framework, needs to be jettisoned. The *constitutive* character of legal practices alludes to something more than the reception of law words from on high.

The Constitutive Character of Legal Practice

Movements are constituted in legal terms when they see the world in those terms and organize themselves accordingly. All the movements discussed below are in this sense constituted, at least in part, by law. Legal forms are evident in the language, purposes, and strategies of movement activity as practices. When activists speak to one another their *language* contains practices of,

9. Gordon, "Critical Legal Histories," 121.

10. Owen Fiss, "Free Speech and Social Structure" (Unpublished manuscript, 1985).

11. Ibid., p. 1.

12. Sally Merry, "Concepts of Law and Justice among Working-Class Americans: Ideology as Culture," *Legal Studies Forum* 9 (1985) : 59–71, at p. 67.

13. Charles Johnson and Brad Canon, *Judicial Policies: Implementation and Impact* (Washington, D.C.: CQ Press, 1984); Thomas Dalton, *The State Politics of Judicial and Congressional Reform* (Westport, Conn.: Greenwood Press, 1985).

14. John Brigham, "Judicial Impact upon Social Practices," *Legal Studies Forum* 9 (1985) : 47–58. See also *Civil Liberties and American Democracy* (Washington, D.C.: CQ Press, 1984).

about, or in opposition to the legal system. For example, the feminists who met at Seneca Falls in the mid-nineteenth century to start the women's rights struggle spoke of "a sense of right," and they rallied to the cry "Equality of Rights."[15] When political activists articulate their *purposes,* their discourse is further situated relative to law. Gay rights activists of the 1970s addressed claims to city councils for new ordinances to protect them from discrimination, and in the 1980s they sought to extend legal protections for AIDS victims by establishing that the disease cannot be transmitted by "casual contact."[16] Finally, when activists develop *strategies,* they reveal a politically significant view of the legal system. The strategies followed by the civil rights movement—marches and sit-ins—were not always legal but they were generally orchestrated to affect law in the long run.

My argument is that although much of society's law is evident in the opinions of judges, the social reality of law is also evident in the shared practices of movement activists. We can further say of these practices that they are constitutive to the extent that they help define certain basic social relations such as who is in, who is out, and even how we identify certain interactions as political movements. What I hope to do in this research note is to briefly suggest this constitutive dimension of law by pointing to its manifestations in the formative language of these very different political movements.

MOVEMENT PRACTICES

Law infuses American social life and appears in its political language. Here, three forms of law in society will be discussed. I have called them "right," "rage," and "remedy." These three categories are not exhaustive, but they capture a broad range of significant political action and legal signification. Movement discourse—a stump speech, a keynote address, or a letter to the editor—may draw on ideas about law so settled and so distinctive that in themselves they define a given movement's "practices." These practices are constituted by, and in turn constitute, different and identifiable interpretive communities. Political language links legal form to the practices of these interpretive communities, and the practices can be seen in talk about purposes, in the style of discussion, and in political strategies.

Right and the Bathhouse Controversy

"Right," as a manifestation of law in society, means reliance on governmentally promulgated rules backed by threats. This is the most familiar legal form. It is grounded in the Declaration of Independence and appears today in the women's movement, the civil rights movement, and the gay rights movement. The particular practice identified with this form is instrumental. The law is

15. Elizabeth C. Stanton, "Declaration of Sentiments," *The First Convention ever Called to Discuss the Civil and Political Rights of Women* (Seneca Falls, N.Y., 1848). See also Eleanor Flexner, *Century of Struggle: The Woman's Rights Movement in the United States* (Cambridge, Mass.: Harvard University Press, 1975).

16. Gay Health Clinic, "Safe Sex," San Francisco, 1983.

used as a tool, a source of opportunities that one might not otherwise be able to employ. Rights are assertions that the state will eventually support one's position. They claim a given, but rights are contentious. They press and delineate disharmony while holding that they are grounded in the authoritative structure assured at least in principle by the state.

Rights related to sexual preference became associated with protections against discrimination in the late 1960s and, shortly afterward, with issues of privacy. Until the Supreme Court decision in *Bowers* v. *Hardwick* in 1986,[17] there was more political action than judicial decision in this area. Gay rights statutes were passed in a number of American cities, and in many of these they were subsequently repealed. This, briefly, was the background against which the AIDS epidemic emerged from 1981 until 1985 when the bathhouse closings began to surface as a political issue.

The AIDS virus had been isolated in 1981, and by 1983 enough had been publicized about the disease to stimulate a panic reaction. As reported by the San Francisco AIDS Foundation, people began calling about shared toothbrushes and gay waiters in restaurants; San Francisco bus drivers passing through gay neighborhoods wore surgical masks. As the initial terror subsided and the ongoing challenge of the crisis became apparent, the rights issues came to the fore. There was growing concern about the bathhouses, which public health officials in San Francisco had described as "sex establishments" where men engaged in "high-volume, high-frequency sex."[18] The bathhouses quickly became symbols of tolerance for a community concerned about repression. While some gay activists described bathhouse owners as capitalists trying to make themselves out as civil libertarians, civil liberties lawyers often spoke in defense of the baths in abstract terms without defending the social behavior they fostered.

Other positions on the issue ranged from advocates of voluntary closure, the position held by the Harvey Milk Lesbian and Gay Democratic Club in San Francisco a year earlier, to those who believed that mandatory closure was inevitable. Doug Scott, president of the San Diego Democratic Club, addressing closings in that city, argued for voluntary measures as a move that would be good for public relations and might stem the threat of more extreme action that could affect all gay men. This was a response to the perception of fear among the public and health professionals. In Scott's words, "If we aren't seen as cooperating and are seen as little children saying 'no, don't take this away,' they'll feel perfectly justified in whatever actions they take. They'll go further than the baths."[19]

Richard Cruz and the Baths. As the controversy raged through the winter of 1985–86 in San Diego, Richard Cruz responded to Scott and developed the

17. A constitutional challenge to Georgia's law against sodomy, this Supreme Court decision was grounded in the privacy doctrines developed in the late 1960s. Justice White distinguished gay rights from those of married persons, holding the latter to be more expansive (85–140 [1986]).

18. Katie Leishman, "How San Francisco Coped," *Atlantic,* October 1985.

19. Russell Lewis, "The San Diego Bathhouse Controversy," *Sappho Speaks* (1986).

civil libertarian position: "The issue surrounding bathhouse closure is not one of finding whipping boys on whom to vent our anger and frustrations before heterosexuals do. . . . It is whether we as gays and lesbians will co-conspire with the forces of reaction that would rob us of our fifth amendment constitutional right to due process in the protection of our life, liberty and property."[20] In a manner emblematic of past struggles, he claimed a new legal definition, one discovered in the midst of a crisis through the clarification of already recognized values. This assertion of right came as a response to a perceived threat from the straight community. Public reaction to the spread of AIDS and moves to close gay bathhouses was the specific threat, but in general, the sense of medical crisis paralleled a perceived political and perhaps cultural shift in the United States to the right. The public relations response was thus dubbed a co-conspiracy "with the forces of reaction that would rob us of our fifth amendment constitutional right to due process."[21]

Cruz's assertion was of a vested right and a tradition of honoring that right, albeit a recently discovered one. Although the earlier rights movements had relied more on equal protection than on due process, property, privacy, and assembly rights, the demand here as there was for protection in the law. On the other hand, the language used was fearful, without the confidence in a better future seen in other rights struggles. Cruz wrote: "The baths in the 1960s brought together under one roof these myriad forms of sexuality in a safe gay haven. . . . Close down the baths and our brothers are back on the streets as outlaws." And he continued: "Most of the heterosexual majority hates us. . . . We are fatally deluded if we think that by punishing our 'perverts' and 'tainted merchants' we will be miraculously spared."[22]

In the end, the rights claim was more like a stance, a political position, than an appeal to reason. It was directed within a movement context, not to the outside and the unconverted. Lawyers are involved, of course, but the discourse itself is not deferential to lawyers. It is not mediated by professional position and the institutional claims about courts and papers. The discourse, the practice, in this struggle is about rights.

Rights provide us with a paradigm from which to consider the presence of legal form in political discourse, which is itself not legal in the positive sense—that is, not a command of the sovereign. Its substance often comes from past conflicts, and its form is linked to the adversarial structure of Anglo-American law. Rights are a political resource because, as Scheingold observed, they contain beliefs about how things should be done. What he called "the myth of rights" is a potent belief system to which one can appeal for redress. The significance of rights, then, lies less in the political power behind them and much more in their congruence with beliefs about social justice or right conduct.[23] As a movement practice, rights is particularly appropriate for a group under siege, one that had flourished under one legal climate and can appeal

20. Richard Cruz, "Letter to the Editor," *The Gayzette* (San Diego, Calif.), 1986.
21. Ibid., 1.
22. Ibid., 2.
23. Scheingold, *Politics of Rights*, 83.

to and clarify accepted legal protections as both the climate and the material environment threaten to degenerate.

Rage about Pornography and the First Amendment

"Rage," as an ideological form evident in the movement against violent pornography, focuses on the same instruments of government appealed to by gay activists—the courts, the judges, and the doctrines of law, but it identifies them with oppression rather than protection. The discourse of rage reveals a struggle *against* the law and an avowed intention to transform it. The relationship perceived between law and rights translates into social resistance to legal subversion. This form of political discourse relies on intense emotion and disquietude.

The literature on social movements from Seymour Martin Lipset to Michael Walzer, classifies advocacy of fundamental change as ideologically extreme rather than emotionally intense.[24] In the case of movement practice, however, we can situate politics by its intensity. This is clearly the best way to see the feminist outrage about pornography. Radical feminists argued that in a male-dominant society sexuality involves danger and that dominant-subordinate power relationships in sex as it is normally practiced perpetuate violence against women. The movement in the early stages went so far as to identify the instruments of law with terrorism.

In movements like the opposition to abortion, a law, specifically the 1973 Supreme Court decision in *Roe* v. *Wade,* can be the focus of the rage and change in the law can be a strategy. It is also possible, however, that no particular law will become the focus, while law in general or a body of law will be the subject of political unrest. In this sense the movement plays off and situates itself against the dominant conception of what the law authorizes. The feminist opposition to pornography is a case in point. The practices that constitute it are a reflection, a mirror image, of a broad rights claim, in this case, the right to free expression.

We should note, as background, that this movement has been predominately middle class and rooted in left liberal feminism. Women Against Pornography (WAP) has been influenced by the same counterideological critique that was posed against left males in the late 1960s by movement women (we won't make the coffee; we won't take the minutes) and that was influential at the onset of the women's movement. The movement was also closely tied to university and professional settings with many of its major events situated in institutions like the NYU law school in the seventies and Barnard College at the end of the period, in 1982. The feminist case has subsequently been caught up in debates over what is pornographic, over free expression, and over the nature of legislation as a form of politics. Thus, the link between state law and ideology has changed over time. Rage, of the sort that equated state law and terrorism, dominated the feminist case against pornography at the end of the 1970s, before the movement became involved with enacting local ordinances.

24. See Egon Bittner, "Radicalism and the Organization of Radical Movements," *American Sociological Review* 28 (1963) : 928–40.

To capture the antipornography movement at its inception, I will focus on a 1978 address by Andrea Dworkin.

The commentary by Women Against Pornography in the late 1970s saw the law on the side of the pornographers and proposed that law had in fact fostered the wide range of pornographic material then available. All the while the movement skirted the edge of censorship and was continually confronted by civil libertarian arguments for free expression. The shift in tactics to passing legislation began to appear in 1983. After an unsuccessful try in Minneapolis, feminists succeeded in getting an ordinance passed that attacked pornography in Indianapolis.[25] The major aspects of the Indiana ordinance are its "findings" that "pornography is a discriminatory practice based on sex which denies women equal opportunities in society," and its definition of pornography as "the graphic sexually explicit subordination of women, whether in pictures or in words." As Joel Grossman has argued, such "ordinances attempt[ed] to bypass th[e] morass of inscrutable constitutional doctrine by defining pornography as a form of sex discrimination."[26]

Andrea Dworkin, New York City, 1978. In the fall of 1978, a diverse collection of feminist radicals and law students gathered at New York University to discuss the emerging issue of "violent pornography."[27] Andrea Dworkin's speech, "Pornography: The New Terrorism," reveals the key ideological practices at work. As she put the case: "The oppressor, the one who perpetrates the wrongs for his own pleasure or profit, is the master inventor of justification. He is the magician who, out of thin air, fabricates wondrous, imposing, seemingly irrefutable intellectual reasons which explain why one group must be degraded at the hands of another."[28] Of particular significance here is the focus on harm or danger to women. Recently, legal traditions operating at the level of belief rather than authority have called attention to links between pornography and violence. In the context of the feminist case, the attempt to demonstrate that pornography causes violence is reminiscent of the "clear and present danger" test in First Amendment discourse. The idea that there are exceptions to the constitutional right of free speech when there is a possibility of physical harm is so characteristic of the First Amendment tradition that the movement discourse would, at first glance, appear to be derivative.

It is, however, characteristic of the feminist case against pornography and the discourse of rage generally that it turns against the subtle formulations of constitutional law. Law is seen as epiphenomenal, a product of patriarchy, and a rationalization: "when pornographers are challenged by women," the legal establishment punishes the women "all the while ritualistically claiming

25. *American Booksellers Association* v. *Hudnut*, 598 F. Supp. 1316 (1984).

26. Joel Grossman, "The First Amendment and the New Anti-Pornography Statutes," *News for Teachers of Political Science* 45 (1985) : 16.

27. "Colloquium, Violent Pornography: Degradation of Women Versus Right of Free Speech," *New York University Review of Law and Social Change* 8 (1978–79).

28. Andrea Dworkin, "Pornography: The New Terrorism," *New York University Review of Law and Social Change* 8 (1978–79) : 215–19.

to be the guardians of 'free speech.' "[29] In an important sense, of course, this defiance of the explicit free speech tradition shows the pervasive influence of constitutional doctrine on feminist practice for it contains a tacit recognition of the hegemony of a free expression ideology in the broader political culture. In fact, the controversy over the charged relationship between protected speech and pornography was far more powerful ideologically than anything that might be found in actual legislation or judicial opinion. What feminists raged against was a mythical First Amendment with the emphasis on pure tolerance commonly placed there.

It is, then, this popular ideology of free expression rather than formal constitutional law on free expression that has influenced the politics of the feminist case. While the formal constitutional law depends on distinctions, movement practice depended on blurring them. While the doctrine sets standards for determining what is obscene, the idealized popular position permits no qualitative evaluation of speech. The result is an ideological practice insensitive to the adaptability and subtle evaluations possible in state law and different in its impact from state law. Thus whereas Richard Cruz invoked hallowed rights and sought to clarify their applicability, the consciousness raising and mobilization of the antipornography campaign supported—in fact, these strategies may have dictated—the refusal to clarify and define and the denial that law had the doctrinal flexibility to cope with the situation. The fabric of offense was seen as all of a piece whether it be sexuality in an advertisement for diapers or the brutality of hard-core pornography. According to Dworkin: "The violence is always accompanied by cultural assault—propaganda disguised as principle or knowledge. . . . In this propaganda, the victim is targeted. This propaganda is the glove that covers the fist in any reign of terror."[30]

This movement, constituted by its opposition to free speech, could not have existed as it did without notions of law derived from the First Amendment. From the forum at NYU's law school in the late 1970s where a new movement against pornography was articulated to the most recent debates in the left and feminist press, the tension between expression and censorship has been intense.[31] In a politics constituted in this way certain consequences are foreordained, like who will join on what side (and who will already be there). We might have expected feminists and pornographers to be on the same side, sharing an abhorrence of the Victorian moralists. But, this debate over the First Amendment displaced an alignment that might have been expected on purely cultural grounds.

Remedy and Family Mediation

Out of the attacks on formalism in the early part of this century and the concern for efficiency expressed by legal reformers like Roscoe Pound in his

29. Ibid., 218.
30. Ibid., 216.
31. Carole S. Vance, *Pleasure and Danger: Exploring Female Sexuality* (Boston: Routledge & Kegan Paul, 1984); Ann Ferguson, "The Sex Debate in the Women's Movement: A Socialist-Feminist View" (Paper supplied by the author, 1984).

1906 speech, "Popular Dissatisfaction with the Administration of Justice,"[32] has arisen a movement for informalism, conflict resolution, mediation, or alternative dispute resolution. The movement is based on a distinctive remedial form, called "remedy" here.[33] The remedial form of law in society puts forth the settlement of conflict as an overriding concern. The movement ideology is remedial owing to its commitment to reaching a resolution, often referred to as "getting to yes," which is an article of faith in the movement. It is an alternative form of conflict management. It follows and is an extension of the progressive revolt against formal processes in the courts.

Law in this form is paradoxically grounded in a negative assessment of law by lawyers. This is because ostensibly the remedial form is opposed to the legal process as it is formally constituted, but in practice it depends on the form epitomized by courts and lawyers as a foil. It is thus close to the state apparatus even while it eschews the state's procedures. It seeks to institutionalize the absence of both rage and right, considering them obstacles to reaching an amicable settlement. This form appears in a variety of settings from plea-bargaining to family mediation and the debates generated take pride in their orientation to procedural rather than substantive issues.

Pound's 1906 speech condemned "the sporting theory of justice" where he said lawyers tend to seek private advantage instead of searching for truth and justice. A subsequent conference based on that speech, the Pound Conference in 1976, assembled the characteristic mix of judges, lawyers, and law school academics who have carried forward the ideology of remedy. Chief Justice Burger opened this conference with a call for reform in the direction of alternative dispute resolution (ADR). "It is time to explore," he said, ". . . new ways to deal with such family problems as marriage, child custody and adoptions" outside what he called "the formality and potentially traumatic atmosphere of courts."[34] Some speakers at the conference were critical. Simon Rifkind and Laura Nader decried the absence of talk of rights and charged that the conference sought to close access to the courts. But the former chief justice had anticipated their concerns. In responding, he expressed desire for "the speediest and the least expensive means of meeting the legitimate needs of the people in resolving disputes," and he linked informal mechanisms with court congestion.[35] Court costs and delays were cornerstones of the ideology of alternatives.

Robert Mnookin and Lewis Kornhauser, law professors who were early supporters of the alternatives movement in family situations, described the

32. Roscoe Pound, "The Causes of Popular Dissatisfaction with the Administration of Justice," *American Bar Association Reports* 29 (1906) : 395.

33. Mediation and conflict resolution, along with delegalization, disputes processing, and alternative dispute processing have enough in common to constitute an ideology. See Christine Harrington, *Shadow Justice* (Westport, Conn.: Greenwood Press, 1985); "Socio-Legal Concepts in Mediation Ideology," *Legal Studies Forum* 9 (1985) : 33–39.

34. Warren E. Burger, "Agenda for 200 A.D." (Keynote address at the Pound Conference, 1976), 34. See also Leo A. Levin and Russell R. Wheeler, "The Pound Conference: Perspectives on Justice in the Future," in *Proceedings of the National Conference on the Causes of Popular Dissatisfaction with the Administration of Justice* (St. Paul: West Publishing Co., 1979).

35. Ibid., 32.

ideology of remedy in the area of domestic relations as "an alternative way of thinking about the role of law at the time of divorce."[36] The alternative would be a new perspective. Rather than viewing law as "imposing order from above," they saw mediation "as providing a framework within which divorcing couples can themselves determine their post dissolution rights and responsibilities." The ideological foundation for moving from courts to informal appendages was the belief in mediation as leading to a form of "private ordering," or what Lon Fuller called the law that parties bring into existence by agreement.[37] As media activity, such as the motion picture *Kramer v. Kramer,* broadened public support, the community of interested professionals turned to building institutions to provide remedial alternatives.

Frank E. A. Sander, ABA Conference, 1982. During the Pound conference, Frank E. A. Sander, a law professor at Harvard University, had discussed "Varieties of Dispute Processing."[38] This presentation in 1976 paved the way for his keynote address at the First ABA Conference on Alternative Means of Family Dispute Resolution in June of 1982. The conference took place in Washington, D.C., was funded by a special committee set up by the bar association and various foundations, and received support and programmatic assistance from newly established groups like the National Institute for Dispute Resolution, funded by the Ford and Hewlett foundations. The second address by Sander, chair of the American Bar Association's Special Committee on Dispute Resolution, is a good example of the discourse of remedy. It epitomizes a focus on remedial action as it is structured by a view of the legal system: "I am surprised at how often even litigators say to me in disgust, 'There must be a better way to resolve some of these cases.' . . . A skilled mediator may be able to inject the needed element of constructive problem solving that makes the difference between a fruitless donnybrook and a civilized divorce."[39]

Sander's discussion is infused with a practice familiar largely to lawyers and those who are around courts or those who define themselves in terms of lawyers and courts. It is not that the law is the only place we find disputes or that disputes inevitably lead to legal issues, but rather that disputing is a term of art for a particular movement. Disputes are the social reality, the paradigm on which this form of law is based. As it is used by Sander, the disputes paradigm is a practice for the movement. From a phenomenon in social life, disputes, the movement has built a structure of understanding that transforms these social episodes into a highly organized aspect of political culture.

In his speech Sander paid homage to Fuller, but he played down the issues of court congestion that the chief justice had introduced as the basis for his

36. Robert H. Mnookin and Lewis Kornhauser, "Bargaining in the Shadow of the Law: The Case of Divorce," *Yale Law Journal* 88 (1979) : 950.

37. Lon Fuller, "Mediation—Its Forms and Functions," *Southern California Law Review* 44 (1968) : 353.

38. Frank E. A. Sander, "Varieties of Dispute Processing," in *Proceedings of the National Conference on the Causes of Popular Dissatisfaction with the Administration of Justice.*

39. Frank E. A. Sander, "Family Mediation: Problems and Prospects" (Keynote address at the First ABA Conference on Alternative Means of Family Dispute Resolution, June 1982).

interest in alternatives to court. The "problem" addressed by the movement was elaborated with reference to anthropological research and community relations. Sander presented "reports from the field" in the form of commentary from "litigators" and looked to the skills of the intermediary for opening a path away from the "donnybrook" and toward "civlization." The family was conceptualized in terms of characteristics to which remedial processes are addressed, such as intensity of feeling and the continuity of relationships. The inevitability of disputes in this setting demanded, for Sander, an institutional response.

Consequently, a characteristic of this speech was its heavily procedural and institutional focus. Although it dealt with conflict in the family, the real passion and interest came in discussions of the various forms for channeling that conflict rather than the substance of the conflict itself.[40] In this sense, the contrast with rights and rage is apparent. On the other hand, the closely linked networks of professionals pursuing shared goals establishes that the remedial ideology is, in fact, carried by a political movement. The authority for this discussion came from within the legal community. The speaker was a Harvard professor, his bibliography was overwhelmingly from law reviews or about law, and the authorities from whom he drew his material were either in law or part of the growing paraprofessional community in dispute resolution. Shared practices identified law as a problem. The dispute resolution alternative was tied to this problem as part of a political strategy with significant consequences for how power is wielded in America.

CONCLUSION

I began by linking this inquiry with related social research. There are other linkages that, in conclusion, might make clear some of its broader applications. In "Ideology and Ideological State Apparatuses," Louis Althusser described how different parts of what he called "the social formation" perpetuate submission to the ruling ideology, or "domination of the ruling class 'in words,' " and in the acceptance of the words as social practices. "The existence is material."[41] This research note suggests the material consequences of law's authority, the discourse that calls people together in time and place and provides the focus for their political activity.

The present inquiry has skirted questions of class conflict in favor of a less determined picture of groups. It has, however, offered a perspective on groups different from the "demographic" approach (farmers, women, and so on) that is a part of the pluralist perspective. Here, representative descriptions give way to observations about political discourse as an ideological frame. We have looked at groups conceptually in the way they articulate demands and constitute their own identity. This, it is hoped, will lead to a deeper understanding of such political factors as group strategy while at the same time giving depth to our picture of law.

"Law" beyond official discourse, texts, or obviously legal trappings is hid-

---

40. Ibid., 355.
41. Louis Althusser, *Lenin and Philosophy* (New York: Monthly Review, 1971), 166.

den. Law constituted at the level of belief and practice rather than canon or rule is often taken for granted, becoming one of society's givens. As Joseph Gusfield put it in his study of drunk driving, "The definition of the problem, which participants in the process took for granted, was to me problematic."[42] By illuminating that which gets buried among the givens, I have tried to indicate how legal form in the practices of distinct communities—gays appealing to constitutional rights, feminists outraged about legal protection for pornography, and mediators offering the bar a new technique for settlement— makes these groups what they are. By further developing this mode of analysis, we may better understand what it means to be a movement and to act politically in a legal order.

42. Gusfield, *Culture of Public Problems*, 6.

KAREN ORREN
University of California, Los Angeles

Organized Labor and the
Invention of Modern Liberalism
in the United States

There is perhaps no political topic that has been given such relentlessly comparative treatment as the American labor movement. It is rare to read any comprehensive political or historical study of organized labor that is not cast, implicitly or explicitly, against the greater class consciousness of European counterparts. The explanations advanced for the uniqueness or the lack of vigor in the American strain—abundance of land, immigration, early suffrage, a revolutionary heritage of "republicanism"—constitute most of what exists in the way of theories about American labor politics.[1]

At the very least, comparisons such as these risk highlighting contrasts at the expense of common and arguably more fundamental tendencies. But there are other problems as well. In the first place, seen against the background of European labor parties, American trade unionism and its historical relationship to government appear in negative and sentimental tones: a compromised political destiny for the workers and a legacy of repression and broken promises to haunt the legitimacy of the liberal state.[2] The contemporary dis-

---

1. A representative selection of recent books on labor stressing these themes would include Mike Davis, *Prisoners of the American Dream* (London: New Left Books, 1986), and Gwendolyn Mink, *Old Labor and New Immigrants in American Political Development* (Ithaca: Cornell University Press, 1986), on immigration; Alan Dawley, *Class and Community, The Industrial Revolution in Lynn* (Cambridge, Mass.: Harvard University Press, 1976), on suffrage; and Sean Wilentz, *Chants Democratic* (New York: Oxford University Press, 1984), on republicanism. A useful review of explanations for American labor exceptionalism is in Eric Foner, "Why Is There No Socialism in the United States?" *History Workshop Journal*, Spring 1984, 57–80.

2. In addition to the books cited above, see Christopher L. Tomlins, *The State and the Unions* (Cambridge: Cambridge University Press, 1985), and David Montgomery, *Workers' Control in America* (Cambridge: Cambridge University Press, 1979). In the current period the specter of labor disorder has increasingly faded. However, it continues to figure in analyses of government stability. For example, on the accord between labor and the business

cipline of political science offers little to fill out the picture. Labor is not a good example of "interest group liberalism" and is at best a minor participant in studies of politics that take as their starting point the market functions performed by business corporations.[3] The result has been to leave the nation's largest organized group in analytic limbo, suspended between domestic models it does not fit and comparative themes that stress its most negligible aspects.

Second, whole conceptions of American political development and of American liberalism itself have been inspired by the relative weakness of radical politics among U.S. workers and of socialist ideologies advanced in their name. Again, these are not based on a study of trade unionism or working-class politics as such, but locate the peculiarities of the American case in other factors.[4] If prefigured images of failure are set aside, however, the labor movement's connections to the development of American liberalism can be specified, in the actual events. Proceeding from there, with liberalism understood as the product of conflict and change rather than as an all-consuming process, these broader conceptions of American political development—and also the comparative questions concerning who is an exception to what—might be usefully reexamined.

The following research note proposes this alternative formulation. Although it is only an outline, among the ideas it is intended to challenge are the following: that the historical project of organized labor in American political development has been the confrontation with industrial capitalism; that the significance of trade unionism—the strike, collective bargaining, and so on—is primarily as a strategy or weapon in that confrontation; and that the labor movement has played only a minor role in shaping American political

---

corporation at the foundation of the contemporary liberal regime, see Samuel Bowles and Herbert Gintis, "The Crisis of Liberal Democratic Capitalism: The Case of the United States," *Politics and Society* 11, no. 1 (1982) : 51–93.

3. Theodore J. Lowi describes how the unions' "clientele agency," the Department of Labor, steadily lost jurisdiction over labor-related matters in *The End of Liberalism* (New York: W. W. Norton, 1967), 118–22. Charles E. Lindblom ascribes an unprivileged, "inferior" position to labor unions in polyarchies except in special circumstances approximating a general strike in *Politics and Markets* (New York: Basic Books, 1977), 175–76, 198–99. For an opposing view, see Karen Orren, "Union Politics and Postwar Liberalism in the United States, 1946–1979," *Studies in American Political Development* 1 (1986) : 215–52.

4. Louis Hartz, *The Liberal Tradition in America* (New York: Harcourt Brace, 1955); see also Seymour Martin Lipset, *The First New Nation* (New York: Basic Books, 1963). Samuel Huntington analyzes political change in terms of conflicts arising from the recurrent gap through history between the American creed consisting of political ideas and principles and political reality, and in that sense he departs from the consensus interpretation of Hartz. However, he *premises* his argument on the distinctive absence in the United States of working-class radicalism, explained in the usual terms: "This was a result of the prior achievement of universal white male suffrage, the general openness of political institutions, the continuing opportunities for vertical and horizontal mobility, the ethnic diversity and geographic dispersion of the working class, and the preexisting prevalence of the liberal-democratic norms of the American Creed" (*American Politics: The Promise of Disharmony* [Cambridge, Mass.: Harvard University Press, 1981], 19–20). Labor is given no further attention in Huntington's account.

culture and institutions. I argue that the emergence of the labor movement marked the final stage in the destruction of the ancient feudal ordering of personal relations; that besides being a method to improve working conditions, trade unionism was an expression of the new system being raised; and that organized labor played a critical role in defining the procedures of contemporary liberalism. The title word *invention* is (with due regard for its recent overuse) meant to emphasize the creative, formative dimension of American labor's history. I might have chosen *constitution,* in order to convey the new and stable configuration of political authority and representation that was brought into being as a consequence.

I.

To say that the historical project of organized labor has been different from the confrontation with industrial capitalism, and that trade unionism has been something other than a strategy, is not to deny the economic context of labor organizing or that strikes and boycotts have been, among other things, potent social weapons. But neither taking these elements at face value nor viewing them against their formal opposites (for example, precapitalist work life, electoral strategies) will elucidate their political meaning. Avoiding settled categories, the route I propose starts with the particular issues contested, then moves on to the broader structures at stake, and finally to organizational tactics and their significance.

The analysis may begin with the early decades of the twentieth century, one of the most vivid and intensively studied periods of industrial conflict. For scholars who emphasize the role of capitalist organization in labor developments, these years represent a turning point in the crisis that began in the 1870s. The dominant interpretation is that the forces of the state, through a national Supreme Court solicitous of the interests of capital, contrived to thwart working-class demands, demands made both directly on industrialists by union activity and through state legislation.[5] But upon close inspection, this position is not satisfying. From the standpoint of political development, it has nothing much to add. Although it no doubt captures important features of the status quo, the problem of exactly how, for example, the unions threatened or were compatible with the existing constitutional order cannot be understood with reference to either the violence of the struggle or the jurisprudential ingenuity of labor's opponents.

More important, the model of labor politics derived from capitalist-state resistance does not explain the data very well. It is silent on the important issues the Court decided in labor's favor. It ignores the fact that the laws in dispute at the federal level had been passed in numerous states dominated by

5. See, for example, Robert G. McCloskey, *The American Supreme Court* (Chicago: University of Chicago Press, 1960), chap. 5 and pp. 150–60; Arthur Selwyn Miller, *The Supreme Court and American Capitalism* (New York: Free Press, 1968), 55–62; Mink, *Old Labor,* 185–86, 237ff; Arnold M. Paul, *Conservative Crisis and the Rule of Law* (Gloucester, Mass.: Peter Smith, 1976), chaps. 6 and 7; Tomlins, *The State and the Unions,* chap. 3.

both major political parties. It overlooks the circumstance of accord, rather than of conflict, that usually prevailed between the decisions of the Supreme Court and those of state judges who, unlike their federal brethren, had to stand for reelection. Even if doubts on all these scores are suspended, however, a careful reading of the Court's opinions reveals the extent to which they fail to conform to what is usually thought to be the quintessential legal tenet—the central cultural metaphor—of the period. This, of course, is freedom of contract, what one leading scholar has called "the holy of holies for the knights errant of laissez faire."[6] Instead there appear intimations of a legal structure supporting quite a different way of ordering social relations, a structure antedating industrialization and as far removed from the precepts of Thomas Jefferson and Horace Greeley as of Stephen Field.

This deeper structure may be indicated by pointing to three of the Court's most important adverse decisions on the subject of labor organizing—*Adair* v. *United States* (1908), *Coppage* v. *Kansas* (1914), and *Hitchman Coal & Coke Co.* v. *Mitchell* (1918).[7] It will be recalled that in *Adair* and *Coppage*, the Supreme Court decided it was a deprivation of due process of law for the U.S. Congress and the state of Kansas, respectively, to make it a crime for employers to require of new or continuing employees that they agree not to be members of a labor union. *Hitchman* upheld a federal court injunction restraining officers of the striking United Mine Workers from attempting to organize a mine that had made nonmembership in the union a condition of employment. In each case, the decisions were based expressly on the liberty constitutionally guaranteed employers and employees to secure and provide services on terms freely chosen; in each case, the specific property right of the employee in his or her own labor, including the right to join a labor union, was affirmed. Hypocrisies or even absurdities in the Court's treatment of these matters need not detain us. What is striking, however, is the reliance, in reaching the results, on doctrines, uncontradicted in the dissenting opinions, that are in a different spirit from the pure vapors of contract theory.

According to the principles of contract theory, for example, parties *voluntarily* assume their legal obligations upon entering their agreement, and their intentions form the basis for any actions or disputes later on. But in each of these decisions the Court explicitly presumes, without evidence or serious inquiry into pertinent facts, that all the workmen in question were employed "at will." "At will" meant that either party could terminate the employment and the expectation of future employment for any reason and without prior notice. In the law of master and servant, employment at will was an alternative principle to employment for a specified term. The American courts had recently settled on the rule that employment would be considered at will unless otherwise provided by contract, rather than by a determination based on the payment period or customs of a given trade, as was the rule in England.[8] Both rules, however, were *prescriptive*, not voluntary.

6. McCloskey, *American Supreme Court*, 153.

7. 208 U.S. 161; 236 U.S. 1; 243 U.S. 229.

8. Sanford M. Jacoby, "The Duration of Indefinite Employment Contracts in the United States and England: An Historical Analysis," *Comparative Labor Law* 5, no. 1 (Winter 1982),

Another characteristic of contract theory is abstraction, without a priori references to concrete circumstances that might arise between the parties. But in these cases, the Court ascribes a *definite content*, a code of proper employee behavior (and one that is also not based on inquiry into the intentions of the parties). In *Hitchman*, for example, employees had not become members of the defendant union before the strike began, but had indicated by their signatures a willingness to join when and if the list being compiled reached a certain number of names. The Court thought it "highly significant" that this list was kept secret; the opinion noted the fact that the organizers addressed the men in a foreign tongue; and it said that every worker "acted a lie" upon signing, in violation of the goodwill the company should expect from its employees. Similarly, in *Coppage*, the Court disassociated itself from the view that the employer had no right "to dominate the life [or] interfere with the liberties of employees in matters that do not lessen or deteriorate the service," and averred how in "an ordinary contract of employment, the worker must serve his employer and him only, so long as the relations shall continue."[9]

A final discrepancy with nineteenth-century contract theory concerns the novel use at this time of the conspiracy doctrine. Although the use of the conspiracy doctrine has often been noted by scholars in the field, less attention has been paid to the underlying legal principle causing the association of worker-confederates to be unlawful. The opinion in *Hitchman* states it succinctly: "The right of action for persuading an employee to leave his employer is universally recognized." Justice Pitney insisted that this right "rests upon fundamental principles of general application, not upon the English statute of laborers." In fact, as will be explained below, the law of enticement had only recently been generalized, under the rubric of interference by third parties, to cover all types of contracts, but it still remained part of the law of master and servant. It would have been a new idea to businessmen, on the other hand, that they might not persuade customers away from their competitors. The Court conceded as much:

> Defendants' acts cannot be justified by any analogy to competition in trade. They are not competitors of plaintiff; and if they were, their conduct exceeds the bounds of fair trade. Certainly, if a competing trader should endeavor to draw customers from his rival, not by offering better or cheaper goods, employing more competent salesmen, or displaying more attractive advertisements, but by persuading the rival's clerks to desert him under circumstances rendering it difficult or embarrassing for him to fill their places, any court of equity would grant an injunction to restrain this as unfair competition.[10]

In other words, even among business competitors, relations with employees are afforded special legal protection. Although some American judges like Pitney were reluctant to say so, this protection, like the other discrepancies

---

85–128. On the inconsistency between the at will rule and contract doctrine, see Jay M. Feinman, "The Development of the Employment at Will Rule," *American Journal of Legal History* 20 (1976) : 118–35.

9. 245 U.S. 225, 229, 239, 255; 236 U.S. 1, 19, 13.

10. 245 U.S. 229, 252, 259.

with contract theory noted above, had their basis in the sinews of Anglo-American law.

II.

The only full-length study to emphasize the question of feudalism in American political development denies that it existed. As if to confirm his own assertion that American political thought is absorbed in the idea of the middle class, Hartz pronounces the United States born liberal, free of Old World feudalism, apparently without considering that feudalism had extended its reach beyond the aristocracy and the bourgeoisie. Preoccupied by the absence of European-style radicalism, and succumbing to the Whiggish slogans he exposes, Hartz ignores the ancient forms enclosing the daily life of the working classes, the cracking of which would be the most urgent problem of nineteenth-century politics in the United States as well as in Europe.[11]

It is true that wages were not established by governments as they occasionally had been in colonial and revolutionary years, that what was left of indentured labor had been made unconstitutional by the Thirteenth Amendment, and that, by the late 1800s, an employer could not administer corporal punishment to his employees unless they were apprentices or seamen. But in their essentials, the relations between masters and servants had been fixed in law, both by statutes and common law, for several centuries. In the Supreme Court cases discussed above, for example, the legal prescription of employment duration dates from the Tudor period; laws against enticement are found in the Statutes of Labourers, beginning in the reign of Edward III, and their origin can be traced to the regulations of the medieval guilds.[12]

Here we might touch on some of the main features of this extensive but straightforward system of legally regulated subjugation as it existed toward the end—not the beginning—of the nineteenth century.[13] There were two

11. Hartz, *Liberal Tradition*. As already suggested in n. 4 above, the absence of feudal institutions is accepted without further analysis in studies that otherwise understand political change in U.S. history very differently from Hartz. For another recent example, see Samuel Bowles and Herbert Gintis, *Democracy and Capitalism* (New York: Basic Books, 1986), 30–31. The term *feudalism* as used in this note refers to the relation of lord and man, reproduced up and down the political hierarchy, which was the characteristic organizing principle of medieval society in England (and elsewhere in Western Europe). See Marc Bloch, *Feudal Society*, vol. 1 (Chicago: University of Chicago Press, 1961). The specific relation of master and servant appeared in English law in the fourteenth century. Prior to that, laborers were regulated by the highly uniform customs of manors, boroughs, and guilds.

12. Sources consulted on the English background of American law include William Holdsworth, *A History of English Law*, vols. 2–4 (London: Methuen, 1936), and Frederick Pollock and Frederic William Maitland, *The History of English Law*, 2 vols. (Cambridge: Cambridge University Press, 1968). On the legal status of employees in prerevolutionary America, see Richard B. Morris, *Government and Labor in Early America* (New York: Octagon Books, 1965), chap. 9.

13. Unless otherwise indicated, the legal account in this section is based on H. G. Wood, *A Treatise on the Law of Master and Servant* (Albany, N.Y.: John D. Parsons, 1877).

guiding principles: one, laborers were free in the sense that they could dispose of their labor of their own volition and have their contracts with their employers enforced in the public courts; and two, labor was transformed by acts of obedience into services, over which their employers acquired a proprietary right. Both of these may be seen at the point of entry into the contract. By definition, the laborer who is free and therefore permitted to enter in the relation must be sui juris, that is, not dependent upon the will or control of another. Any such disability would also interfere with the premise of obedience to his or her future employer; otherwise, the contract could not be enforced. This requirement excluded lunatics, idiots, married women, unemancipated infants, enlistees in the armed forces, and all persons with "any other engagement incompatible with that he was about to enter." [14] It is instructive that business corporations, in the 1870s allowed by the law to hire and discharge workers through their agents like any other individual, had until recently before then not been permitted to enter or terminate employment contracts except in writing and under the seal of the company. The previous rule reflected the *personal* nature of the relation intended, and also the corporation manager's deficiency in the autonomy required to enter into a labor agreement.

Regarding conditions of work, the weight of tradition was felt most heavily in the matter of working hours. Today, the hours issue in bread-and-butter unionism is often viewed as secondary to the wage question. But the portion of each day the employee must, according to law, obey his or her employer explains the recurrent political prominence of the ten-hour campaign; and it makes working people's arguments, that only the shorter day would allow them to become educated and active citizens, seem less rhetorical than they might appear. Here is one of the influential treatises of the period on the topic of the working day:

> By the statute of 5 Eliz., Chap. 4, it was provided that "if a servant works by the day or by the week, they must continue working from five in the morning till after seven at night, from the middle of March to the middle of September, and all the rest of the year from twilight to twilight, only from March to September as aforesaid. They are to be allowed two hours for breakfast, dinner and drinking, and from the middle of May to the middle of August an half hour more for sleeping, and all the rest of the year an hour and a half for breakfast and dinner, and for the absence of every hour, *the master may defalk . . . the wages,*" and in some respects, particularly so far as relates to the time of working and the length of time permitted for the taking of meals, the provisions of this statute have generally become part of the custom of laborers in this country.

As for whether an employee might recover wages if asked by an employer to work on a Sunday, precedents and authorities cited included, among others, practices prior to the year 500, Edward the Confessor, *The Mirror of Justices,* and Lord Coke: "Thus it will be seen that, except in those states where pro-

14. Ibid., 7, and chap. 1, passim.

hibited by statute, a contract made to labor upon the Sabbath in any lawful employment, or indeed any contract, is as valid as though made upon any other day." [15]

Enforcement of the labor contract was available to both parties as a matter of right, but this mechanism was made far more onerous for the employee. Employers had recourse to the self-executing remedy of discharge, whereas workers who quit or suffered some wrong under their contract had to rely on the legal process for any wages due them. Employees who were dismissed, for example, could recover wages for work already completed, but only upon a showing by unequivocal evidence that they had not been guilty of insubordination. Further, such proof was made difficult by the law's willingness to recognize any legitimate reason given by the employer for the discharge, even if this reason was different from that given at the time of discharge, or had not even then been known. If an employee hired for a specific term quit without legal cause, he or she normally could not recover wages already accrued.

Although the remedy of specific performance against a worker who unlawfully terminated a contract is sometimes cited as the hallmark of feudal labor relations, in America it appears not to have been available even in colonial times except when a specific job contracted for—such as constructing a building or digging a road—was left uncompleted.[16] A more common disposition was imprisonment, by which the employer claimed property rights over the employee's body until such time as other property could be produced to pay the remaining debt, determined in the form of damages by a court. Imprisonment for debt stemmed from a statute promulgated in 1285 during the reign of Edward I and had been incorporated into the laws of the American states. As the latter were gradually repealed, owing in large part to the efforts of the workingmen's parties of the 1830s, analogous actions were substituted to the same end. One resort, for example, was to the claim of the employee's criminal intent to defraud; and in many states mere nonperformance of labor services was prima facie evidence of fraudulent intent.

The proprietary interest of the employer in the employee's labor is shown no less unambiguously in the rights enforceable against third parties. Two actions of the common law protected the employer against the loss of workers' services. The first was *per quod servitium amisit* ("by which he lost his services"), allowing employers to recover against anyone who through a wrongful act caused injuries to any of their employees to the extent that the latter could not perform their duties. This writ predates the Statutes of Labourers by at least a century to the time of Bracton. The action could not be taken if the worker was actually killed, reflecting the fact that it was the labor that had been contracted for and owned by the employer, not the laborer himself or herself. The employer assumed legal responsibility for acts employees undertook in the course of performing their duties that caused injuries to an outside

---

15. Ibid., 174, 180.

16. This is consistent with the cases in Morris, *Government and Labor*, 221–23. On specific performance as a feudal institution, see, for example, Philip Selznick, *Law, Society and Industrial Justice* (New Brunswick, N.J.: Transaction Books, 1969), 127–28.

person, much as if those injuries had been caused by the employer's machine or animal. This was the case whether the acts in question had been authorized or were necessary to the job, and without regard for the intention, negligence, or malice of the employee. Second, as already suggested above, the employer was protected against the enticement of his or her worker, by any means, away from the employer's service. The writ of enticement applied to contracts at will, as well as for a specified term or piece of work, and to anticipated as well as existing labor contracts. As indicated, it also applied to the crime of conspiracy—a confederation to commit the unlawful act of enticement. Again, the servant's intentions were considered irrelevant. Whereas in ordinary torts, the "intervening will" rule broke any causal connection between the breach of a promise and a third party's interference, the laborer, once having entered the employment contract, was treated in law as lacking free will.

III.

Given the system described, it hardly needs explaining how profound a shock, psychologically, must have registered from a labor strike. A strike was a collective act over the partitions erected to keep the worker under the employer's personal sway. It was an act of defiance against the primary rule of obedience. Above all, the labor strike must have had the force of its own strategic fitness: objective and tactic linked in a single action, of a type blunted for us by the routines of Taft-Hartley, but known in the freedom rides and sit-ins of the civil rights movement. The employees' message was that they were unwilling to continue working under the conditions set down by the master; their tactic, to stop work.

The progress of organized labor may be understood, perhaps not too artificially, as a series of prolonged advances against a succession of peripheries encircling the employment relation and fortified by the courts. The inner periphery was the wall of the workplace itself, containing the master and the worker. Once over that, labor encountered a jagged boundary, separating those inside into irregular units according to industry and craft. Beyond lay the terrain occupied by employers against whom strikes were impractical, and their suppliers and customers. Occasionally the unions would attempt an attack from the rear through legislation. But with certain exceptions, such as the laws against imprisonment for debt, these were unsuccessful; the statutes in the 1840s shortening the workday, for example, could not be enforced. This perspective differs, then, both from one that would date modern trade union development from the period of intense industrialization during and after the Civil War rather than from the start of the nineteenth century, and from one that would see an important theoretical difference between trade unionism and "political" action rather than recognize them as alternate means to the same inevitably political end.[17]

17. The post–Civil War periodization is standard throughout a broad range of labor movement studies. See, for example, John R. Commons, David J. Saposs, Helen L. Sumner, E. B. Mittelman, H. E. Hoagland, John B. Andrews, and Selig Perlman, *History of Labour in*

For the most part, to secure their early objectives, unions relied on the strike, which was both the battering ram and the regimental flag of each advance. This double aspect of the strike was vital to the labor movement's achievement. Had the strike been simply a weapon, it could have been managed because it usually caused a response that provoked violence, justifying state intervention. A refusal to work under the old conditions, on the other hand, stymied the courts. At the employer's demand, judges could enjoin the violence, let the workers starve, imprison their leaders, assess exorbitant damages. But they could not lawfully order the men back under the old workplace regime, at least not without throwing over the Constitution. Thus, in the bitter strike against the Northern Pacific Railroad in 1893 that left passengers and equipment stranded, the circuit court reviewed a lower court injunction that, among other things, had ordered workers to return to their jobs. Retaining the sections of the writ that forbade destruction or taking possession of railroad property or otherwise interfering with operations, Justice Harlan struck out a clause restraining employees from "combining and conspiring to quit, . . . with or without notice, as to cripple the property or prevent or hinder the operation of said railroad." Harlan raised the question of whether an equity court could prevent such quitting:

> An affirmative answer to this question is not, we think, justified by any authority to which our attention has been called or of which we are aware. It would be an invasion of one's natural liberty to compel [an individual] to work for or to remain in the personal service of another. One who is placed under such constraint is in a condition of involuntary servitude—a condition which the supreme law of the land declares shall not exist within the United States, or in any place subject to their jurisdiction.[18]

The recognition of this principle, however, was not immediate. During the early phases of labor organizing, courts ruled strikes per se illegal. The first case for which there is a court record was a successful prosecution in Philadelphia in 1806 by forty-six master cordwainers against their employees for conspiring to strike in order to raise their wages. Since I suggest that the course of unionism should be viewed continuously, as the successive overcoming of ancient barriers, it is worth citing in some detail the judge's charge to

---

the United States, vol. 2 (New York: Macmillan, 1936); Jeremy Brecher, *Strike!* (San Francisco: Straight Arrow Press, 1972); and David M. Gordon, Richard Edwards, and Michael Reich, *Segmented Work, Divided Workers* (Cambridge: Cambridge University Press, 1982). The American brand of "pure and simple" or business unionism, as opposed to European-style labor politics, was given its clearest exposition in Selig Perlman, *A Theory of the Labor Movement* (New York: Macmillan, 1928). In recent years, labor historians, influenced by the work of E. P. Thompson, Herbert G. Gutman, and others, have undertaken a more comprehensively social approach to working-class life. See David Brody, "The Old Labor History and the New," *Labor History* 20 (Winter 1979) : 111–26. However, the distinction between trade unionism and political action remains deeply embedded.

18. *Arthur v. Oakes,* 63 Fed. 310 (1894), 317–18.

the jury. Arguments were made then that would become familiar over the next century.

The first argument concerned the detrimental effects of collective, as opposed to individual, action. The position corresponds to the law of conspiracy by which an act ordinarily legal becomes illegal when undertaken by persons jointly. Here the judge discovered an operational reason for finding employees' organizations criminal:

> One man determines not to work under a certain price and it may be individually the opinion of all; in such a case it would be lawful for each to refuse to do so, for each stands alone, either may extract from his determination when he pleases. In the turn-out last fall, if each member of the body had stood alone, fettered by no promises to the rest, many of them might have changed their opinion as to the prices of wages and gone to work; but it had been given you in evidence, that they were bound down by their agreement, and pledged by mutual engagements, to persist in it, however contrary to their own judgment.[19]

Second, the justification offered for actually suppressing such combinations was indicative of what had been a recent practice of government setting wages to match the cost of commodities.[20] The judge denounced "artificial regulation . . . dependent on the will of a few who are interested":

> Is the rule of law bottomed on such principles, as to permit or protect such conduct? Consider it on the footing of the general commerce of the city. Is there any man who can calculate (if this be tolerated) at what price he may safely contract to deliver articles for which he may receive orders, if he is to be regulated by the journeymen in an arbitrary jump from one price to another? . . . It is impossible that any man can carry on commerce in this way.[21]

The mercantilist theme, which identified the worker's isolated and subordinate state with the welfare of the community, was prominent during this period. It had an ancestor in the fourteenth century, when the labor shortage and disarray following on the Black Death prompted regulations in the Statutes of Labourers. In *People* v. *Fisher* (1835), which was an important case because it was the first to apply an American statute, the New York champerty law, against strikers, the court held that collective quitting was "productive of derangement and confusion, which certainly must be considered injurious to trade."[22] After unions had moved beyond the first periphery, this idea was not successfully argued again until the next era of state regulation, under the Sherman Act.

Third, and finally, the judge in the Philadelphia cordwainers' case invoked

---

19. *Commonwealth* v. *Pullis* (1806); in John R. Commons, ed., *A Documentary History of American Industrial Society*, 10 vols. (Cleveland: Arthur H. Clark, 1910), 3 : 234.

20. Morris, *Government and Labor*, chaps. 1, 2.

21. Commons, *Documentary History*, 3 : 228–29.

22. 14 Wend. 10 (Sup. Ct., N.Y. 1835), 19–20.

the massive structure of past decisions, and presaged what would continue to be the most resistant legal defense against the unions' attack a century later. Pointing out that the by-laws of the cordwainers' association were not "the laws of Pennsylvania," he reminded the jury that even

> the acts of the legislature form but a small part of that code from which the citizen is to learn his duties, or the magistrate his power and rule of action. These temporary emanations of a body, the component members of which are subject to perpetual change, apply to the political exigencies of the day.
>
> It is in the volumes of the common law we are to seek for information in the far greater number, as well as the most important causes that come before our tribunals. That invaluable code has ascertained and defined with a critical precision and a consistency that no fluctuations in the political body could or can attain not only the civil rights of property, but the nature of all crimes from treason to trespass. . . . Those who know, know that it regulates with a sound discretion most of our concerns in civil and social life.[23]

The labor movement may be said to have broken through the first wall with the decision of *Commonwealth* v. *Hunt* in 1842. In a case arising from a strike against shoe and boot shops employing nonunion members, Judge Lemuel Shaw found no criminal action per se in employees' combinations because people are "free to work for whom they please, or not to work, if they prefer" and thus "to collectively exercise their acknowledged rights in such a manner as to best serve their own interests."[24] Shaw was a leader of the Whig party of Massachusetts, which was at that time vigorously competing for labor votes. His decision also reflected the economic ideology of the era. He posed the example of a village baker, impoverished by his neighbors' opening a rival bakery after he had refused, although making a good profit, to lower the price of bread. Shaw saw the neighbors' object as "laudable":

> We think, therefore, that associations may be entered into, the object of which is to adopt measures that may have a tendency to impoverish another, that is, to diminish his gains and profits, and yet so far from being criminal or unlaw-ful, the object may be highly meritorious and public spirited. The legality of such an association will therefore depend upon the means to be used for its accomplishment.[25]

Following *Commonwealth* v. *Hunt,* then, the main test of whether a strike was lawful was determined by whether the purpose of the action was lawful; and the courts proceeded over the next several decades to develop a rough com-mon law on this subject. The purpose of the strike was usually considered lawful if it was to secure higher wages or shorter hours, provide more work for union members, prevent unequal distribution of labor during slack times, or other similar measures to improve working conditions. Strengthening a local union or trade unionism in general or deliberately injuring a plaintiff's

23. Commons, *Documentary History,* 3 : 231–32.
24. 4 Metcalf 111 (Mass. 1842), 130.
25. Ibid., 134.

business was considered unlawful by a majority of courts. If a strike had a lawful purpose, it still should not be accomplished by unlawful means, which included force, fraud, coercion, slander, or violence.[26] Such tests clearly left a great deal to judges' discretion, but they also enabled a degree of legal calculation and better strategic planning by labor organizers.

Another important development during the pre–Civil War period was the removal by the courts of any doubts as to whether the law of enticement still covered employees now working in factories, who were no longer housed and fed by the employer and, most important, whose employment contracts were usually at will. The question arose in the English tort case of *Lumley* v. *Gye* (1853), which concerned the luring away of an opera singer by a theater owner from a competitor who had previously engaged her services. There had been a contract for employment, but it did not fit into the hierarchical mold of master-servant relations. *Lumley* v. *Gye* discovered that the enticement action was based not only in the Statutes of Labourers, but also in such common law actions as trespass and assumpsit, which protect the interests of contracting parties.[27] This clarification, and the contractual frame in which it was accomplished, had the advantage of permitting judges to avoid unfashionable language about masters and servants while holding employees securely under the protections against enticement. It would find ready service against labor's next wave of actions in the 1870s and 1880s. But as we shall see, it also proved to be an instance of judicial overreaching, for it eventually both led to doctrinal disarray and handed the unions a new legal argument with strong ideological appeal.

After the legalization of unions and of the strike action itself for a range of industrial purposes, there remained what is called in the parlance of contract "all the world." This realm included employers against whom it was impractical for the unions to organize directly and those against whom strikes had been unsuccessful. The boycotts that had been tried—preventing employees and customers from entering the premises and blocking delivery of supplies—had caused violence and were enjoined on that ground by the courts. Accordingly, the unions now deployed a new kind of strike, the so-called peaceable labor boycott, whereby union members refused to work on any material purchased from or supplied to the company targeted for organizing. (Actually, this was one of two kinds of peaceable boycotts. The other was refusing to patronize retail customers of the company and circulating information that the company was "unfair to labor.") In the peaceable boycott, the injury to the targeted company was clear. But no workers had been enticed away; there was no violence or intimidation that would constitute illegal means under the laws against conspiracy; and the targeted company had no contractual relations with the striking employees. The legal problem presented was

26. Relevant cases on purposes may be found in Charles E. Carpenter, "Interference with Contract Relations," *Harvard Law Review* 41 (1927–28) : 728–63, espec. 760–61. On means, see John M. Wigmore, "The Boycott and Kindred Practices as Ground for Damages," *American Law Review* 21 (July-August 1887) : 509–32.

27. 2 El. & Bl. 216, 118 Eng. Rep. 749 (Q.B. 1853).

whether the company·had been injured criminally, or even wrongfully, by the union.

In the sequence of legal problems and their solutions, which then caused a new round of problems, the old system was unraveling. Courts initially gave a variety of answers to the dilemma of the peaceable labor boycott, but the idea that took hold was that of borrowing the contractual terminology used for enticement in *Lumley* v. *Gye* and extending it to contractual relations in general. All contracts could then be protected from outside interference, including interference by labor unions. This step was taken in *Temperton* v. *Russell* (1893), where a union was sued for threatening a supplier with a strike, in order to get him to stop selling to another supplier who had defied a strike threat intended to cut off another employer, with whom the union sought to strengthen its bargaining position. The union was held liable for intentionally procuring the breach of property rights in the contracts.[28] But now the problem was how this breach of property rights through "enticing" away suppliers and customers was different from what people in business do everyday. The new solution was to recognize a privilege for third parties to interfere in contract relations based on the right of competition. The new problem: unions asked that they too be considered competitors, freely competing in trade.

This nettlesome issue was joined in the Massachusetts Supreme Court case of *Vegelahn* v. *Guntner* (1896), a suit against two upholsterer unions and their agents for maintaining a two-man patrol to keep customers, deliveries, and employees from entering the premises of a furniture company the unions were striking. The court agreed with the company that the patrol constituted illegal intimidation and rejected the unions' claim that their attempt to secure better wages was justified as competition. "A combination to do injurious acts expressly directed to another, by way of intimidation or constraint, of persons employed or seeking to be employed by him is outside of allowable competition and is unlawful."[29]

Massachusetts State Justice Holmes criticized this reasoning in dissent. He invoked *Commonwealth* v. *Hunt* and the doctrine there, according to his reading, "that competition is worth more to society than it costs."

> I have seen the suggestion that the conflict between employers and employed is not competition. But I venture to assume that none of my brethren would rely on that suggestion. If the policy on which our law is founded is too narrowly expressed in the term free competition, we may substitute free struggle for life. Certainly the policy is not limited to struggles between persons of the same class competing for the same end. It applies to all conflicts of temporal interest. . . .
>
> If it be true that workingmen may combine with a view, among other things, to getting as much as they can for their labor, just as capital may combine with a view to getting the greatest possible return, it must be true that when combined they have the same liberty that combined capital has to support

28. 1 Q.B. 715.
29. 167 Mass. 92, 99.

their interest by argument, persuasion, and the bestowal or refusal of those advantages which they otherwise lawfully control.[30]

Judges continued to enjoin peaceable labor boycotts according to a variety of theories; they almost never condoned them. But they no longer seemed to know exactly the reason. They said it was because the ultimate purpose of improving working conditions was remote, whereas the immediate purpose, the threat of economic injury, constituted unlawful coercion; or because with the peaceable boycott unions used unlawful means of moral intimidation; or because the boycott's restraint of trade was in violation of the Sherman Act; or that strikes and boycotts were illegal if based on "malicious intent."[31] This was a scramble, with no longer any clear line of doctrine to absolve the courts from the charge of applying the law in an arbitrary and biased way.

IV.

Some of the leaders of the early American labor movement seem to have understood their historical task similarly to what has been argued here, as the culminating phase in a social reconstruction extending over several centuries. Stephen Simpson, for instance, Jacksonian turned Whig and a founder of the Workingmen's party, wrote that it was time the "inconsistencies and discrepancies between theoretical constitutions and feudal laws and customs be discovered, exposed, and resisted."[32] But the intentions of such leaders were largely irrelevant, as were the intentions of the leaders of the religious reformation in the sixteenth century, which was, in this interpretation, one of the labor movement's important predecessors. Certainly religious reformers did not intend to change constitutional history by their arguments over communion tables and priestly collars. Labor leaders, as they pursued strategies of strikes and boycotts, were unconcerned that they were, in the process, enlarging the frame and inventing the forms of collective action fundamental to contemporary American liberalism. The achievement was theirs nonetheless.

A consideration of the idea of labor's centrality in American political development must include, along with an elaboration of the dismantling sketched above, two other large sections of analysis. One must be the legislative dimension of modern liberalism, the new patterns of collective pressure and representation successfully asserted by the labor movement and instituted as part of the broader political culture. The other must be the administrative dimension—the creation of private and state agencies and rules for the mobilization and stabilization of industrial forces, including but not restricted to labor. This was made necessary by labor's disruptions of the old order of social re-

---

30. Ibid., 106–07.

31. See "The Right of a Trade Union to Enforce a Boycott," *Michigan Law Review* 7 (1908–09) : 499–502; and "Tortious Interference with Contractual Relations in the Transformation of Property, Contract, and Tort," *Harvard Law Review* 93 (1980) : 1510–39, 1533 ff.

32. Stephen Simpson, "Political Economy and the Workers," in Joseph L. Blau, *Social Theories of Jacksonian Democracy* (Indianapolis: Bobbs-Merrill, 1954), 138 and passim.

lations and was undertaken by groups other than the labor movement itself. In the space remaining, I will briefly suggest some contents of the first section.

The claim that labor *enlarged the frame* of collective action derives from labor's extension of group pressures to the private economy. Group organization and petition to public agencies were well-established practices—according to such observers as de Tocqueville, definitive—of early nineteenth-century American politics. But an intricate system of law protected private business affairs from outside interference. If there is a single principle that characterizes the labor movement's gradual transformation of this system, it might be the principle of "contract breaking." John R. Commons wrote of the "liberty to violate contracts" in connection with his argument that the conceit of contract did not adequately describe the continually renewing relations between employer and employee.[33] As we have seen, however, the worker was bound by a contract, even if not by an idealized voluntary one; and the progress of trade unionism has been the forcible breaking of contracts in an ever-widening circle of associations. It is likewise a fair description of subsequent social movements that each has entailed the breaking of or interference in private contracts. No doubt there are exceptions, but the idea would encompass, at least in significant respects, prohibition, civil rights, the consumer movement, environmentalism, the women's movement, and, to pick an up-to-date example, corporate disengagement from South Africa.

The primary purpose, however, is not to locate origins or authorship in the labor movement. It is to clarify how trade union activity, directed toward immediate and nonpolitical industrial objectives, destroyed long established political boundaries and created new ways of behaving politically. Legally speaking, this meant the redefinition of elements in the law of torts. Torts concerns the inducing of wrongful acts or occasioning of harms: how the law draws the line between, for example, "inducing" and "intimidating" versus "advising" and "facilitating" a breach of contract; how it allocates property rights, privileges of competition, and the rights that society members not directly involved in a dispute have, for example, against coercion; what it considers as evidence of "malicious intent"; and so forth. All of these had hemmed in the field of lawful group pressure. Here the specific *forms* or tactics of trade unionism take on their immense political importance. For it was through the insistence on the legality of these forms—not on higher wages and shorter hours—that the labor movement accomplished this redefinition.

The steps by which unions performed this formative role against decades of opposition can be suggested in connection with picketing, an action that has had broader political applications than the labor strike. Today, picketing is such a common tactic of political activists that its legitimacy is taken for granted. Yet picketing was held by the courts to be per se illegal, as intimidation and interference with commerce, for a longer time than were both strikes and simple boycotts. "There is and can be no such thing as chaste vulgarity, or peaceful mobbing or lawful lynching. When men want to converse or per-

33. John R. Commons, *Legal Foundations of Capitalism* (Madison: University of Wisconsin Press, 1968), 302–03.

suade, they do not organize a picket line." Even after the passage of the National Labor Relations Act (NRLA) in 1935, as many courts took this position as there were courts that allowed picketing as a lawful activity.[34]

Picketing against private parties became an available method of group pressure only after labor unions successfully challenged its proscription, first, in connection with a lawful strike. This occurred in *Senn* v. *Tile Layers Protective Association* (1937), when the Supreme Court recognized picketing as a federal question, ruled that a Wisconsin law sanctioning picketing during a strike did not violate the employer's property rights under the Fourteenth Amendment, and stated in dicta that "the union might, without special statutory authorization by a State, make known the facts of a labor dispute, for freedom of speech is guaranteed by the Federal Constitution." *Thornhill* v. *Alabama* (1940) followed this lead and supported picketing on free speech grounds against an injunction based on a state loitering law.[35] After *Thornhill*, employers still had their rights to carry on business without illegal interference; now, however, interference by picketing, when connected with a strike, was no longer tortious but privileged, based on the competing right of free speech.

The second necessary step was the establishment of picketing as privileged interference when it was not connected with a strike. That was the decision in *American Federation of Labor* v. *Swing* (1941), stated in imagery similar to our own: "A state cannot exclude working men from peacefully exercising the right of free communication by drawing the circle of economic competition between employers and workers so small as to contain only an employer and those directly employed by him."[36] Although consumers, environmentalists, and others today are still subject to injunctions and other restraints related to the purposes and manner of their picketing, the burden of justification has been shifted to the other side. (Since 1938, civil rights picketing against racial discrimination has been under the protection of the Norris LaGuardia Act as a "labor dispute.")

An interesting contrast to picketing is the unavailability of the boycott to nonunion groups, partly as a result of the unions having secured the legality of this action by legislation, instead of through industrial confrontation and litigation. Boycotts are per se illegal under the Sherman Act, except for certain immunities established by statute or by the judiciary. The Sherman Act, which according to its legislative history did not intend to impose liabilities except on business groups, was interpreted broadly by the Supreme Court in the *Danbury Hatters* case (1908) to embrace nonbusiness groups and, in particular, labor unions.[37] Subsequently, labor succeeded in procuring its own protection by statute in the Clayton Act (1914), leaving boycotts by other groups out in the cold. Boycotts have been nevertheless widely used; by civil rights groups to protest discrimination; Jewish groups to retaliate against Mexico

34. "Picketing and Free Speech," *Harvard Law Review* 56 (1942) : 180–218. The quotation is from *Atchison, T. & S.F. Ry.* v. *Gee,* 139 F. 582 (S.D. Iowa 1905), 584.

35. 301 U.S. 468 (1937), 478; 310 U.S. 88.

36. 312 U.S. 321 (1941), 326.

37. *Lawlor* v. *Loewe,* 235 U.S. 522.

for an offensive United Nations vote; environmentalists against Japanese products for that nation's killing of whales; academic, professional, and feminist groups in favor of the Equal Rights Amendment; the religious right against television networks; Catholic bishops to prevent the selling of an English translation of the *Liturgia Horum*. But often such actions, as with the last three instances named, have had to answer suits for damages and injunctions.[38]

We might mention one more field opened up by the labor movement to the contest of private groups. This is the courts of equity, through the vehicle of a suit for injunctive relief. In *United Mine Workers* v. *Colorado Coal Co.* (1922) it was held that trade unions, although unincorporated, could be sued in the federal courts.[39] At first, the decision was regarded by union leaders as one of the greatest setbacks organized labor had ever received. Within a few months, however, the New York Cloakmakers came up with the argument that if unions could be sued they should also be allowed to sue, and succeeded in obtaining an injunction against their employers' trade association for breach of contract.[40] Up to that time, equity courts, as the legally designated protector of property rights, had offered recourse only to business interests and governments. When the cord between equity and property, which had been especially strong in the American courts, was severed, the way was prepared for the expansion of equitable protection of numerous other rights and interests that is so prominent a feature of the contemporary political landscape.

The law of collective action continues to evolve. For example, whereas certain labor boycotts have been curtailed by the 1947 and 1959 amendments to the NRLA, the Supreme Court more recently overturned an injunction against a boycott of white Mississippi merchants by civil rights groups seeking to desegregate local public facilities, and found a new free speech right for consumers to engage in refusals to patronize. This decision prompted legal scholars to speculate about possible reverberations back onto labor's own rights to boycott.[41] To the general reader such a development is not likely to seem of particular consequence. This impression would itself confirm the depth and permanence of what has been changed overall.

V.

Assuming the validity of the research outlined, is there anything in it that bears on the study political institutions more generally? Two points emerge.

38. See Ronald E. Kennedy, "Political Boycotts, the Sherman Act, and the First Amendment: An Accommodation of Competing Interests," *Southern California Law Review* 55 (1982) : 983–1030.

39. 259 U.S. 344.

40. See Alpheus T. Mason, "Organized Labor as Party Plaintiff in Injunction Cases," *Columbia Law Review* 30 (1930) : 466–87. The cloakmakers decision is *Schlesinger* v. *Quinto*, 192 N.Y. Supp. 564 (Sup. Ct. 1922).

41. See, for example, Michael C. Harper, "The Consumer's Emerging Right to Boycott: *NAACP v. Claiborne Hardware* and Its Implications for American Labor Law," *Yale Law Journal*, 93, no. 3 (January 1984) : 409–54. The case in question is *NAACP* v. *Claiborne Hardware*, 102 S. Ct. 3409 (1982).

First, the idea that contemporary liberal politics is an invention, so to speak, of the labor movement is a reminder that institutionalist, pluralist, and other approaches to studying politics are not approaches only, but may also refer to changing features in the empirical universe under study. Without underestimating the importance of public and private structures in, for example, contemporary labor politics, it is also correct to observe that employment relations were more hierarchically structured by formal institutions in the nineteenth century than in the twentieth; at least the earlier system of regulation did not contemplate the possibility of legitimate collective action upon which industrial policy is predicated today.

The tendency to lose sight of this changing reality through an engagement with analytic theories may be illustrated by an example drawn from Alan Dawley's influential study of the industrial revolution in Lynn, Massachusetts. Dawley's analytic foundation, as he calls it, is the concept of social class. As one of the new breed of social historians he believes that if "it is to be effective, class analysis must provide an accurate explanatory framework for subduing the chaos of individual experience and making it intelligible as the social experience of groups of people over time."[42] Speaking of early nineteenth-century community integration, he says:

> Given household organization, no group of townspeople could consolidate instruments of power to be used against other social groups. As long as the household was the basic unit of production, class ties among journeymen were indistinct. As long as propertied artisans sold commodities and performed manual labor in a day's work, the class position of the artisan was ill-defined. And as long as the scale of production and the size of the individual firm remained small, the power of capital in the hands of the shopkeeper was held in check.[43]

Dawley's account of the conscious experience of groups and individuals may be accurate. However, by overemphasizing the absence of concerted action on the part of community elites against laborers, he minimizes the importance of the legal institutions of the time. This imbalance causes a distorted view of the instruments and distribution of power in Lynn. Conversely, an analytic stress by political scientists that "institutions matter," without attention to the degree and character of social voluntarism complementing institutions at different periods of development, may obscure the deepest commitments of political regimes, and of their complexity.[44]

---

42. Dawley, *Class and Community*, 4.
43. Ibid., 24.
44. An important study of American state building, and a major contribution to the contemporary institutionalist literature on political development, is Stephen Skowronek, *Building a New American State* (Cambridge: Cambridge University Press, 1982). Skowronek's historical analysis—of how institutions such as parties and courts acted with other interests to obstruct the development of a vigorous and coherent system of national administration—is addressed to the "problem" (in an evaluative sense) of American state building, both historically and today. The view that the weakness and fragmentation of the American state ought

A second, related point concerns the value of more carefully distinguishing among the elements in often holistic ideas of state-society relations for given historical periods. In the labor literature, an excellent (if controversial) example is set by William M. Reddy in his study of the textile trade in nineteenth-century France. Reddy argues that the "idea of the market" permeated both the dominant culture and government institutions prior to the implementation of actual mechanisms of supply and demand in industry, particularly in the wage sector.[45] The labor case likewise suggests the problem of imposing overly unified models of state development—the United States was governed by a Madisonian-liberal state in the early nineteenth century, a "state of courts and parties" in the mid-nineteenth century, an interest–group liberal state in the mid-twentieth century—without regard to the discrete connections to society within them, and how these may separately change and coexist. For example, in the enforcement of the legal system that regulated labor relations in the early nineteenth century, there was full coordination, and arguably no important political distinction, between law courts and employers. In other important respects, however, state and property interests were differentiated, and the American state to that extent was a liberal state. There is, indeed, evidence this differential development worked to labor's advantage. During the Revolution, indentured servants were released from their bonds against their master's will upon being impressed into the militia; in 1840, labor unions secured the ten-hour day on federal works as a means of pressuring private industry to reduce hours.

These observations bring this note full circle. The account of American political development sketched above differs from Hartz's and others' in that theirs do not consider the persistence into the nineteenth century of the feudal institutions that have been described. From this perspective also, a fundamentally "radical" character may be attributed to the American labor movement. Finally, a more refined view of the transition to liberalism, in the United States and elsewhere—one that sees the dismantling of the old order in stages—should provide new avenues of inquiry into the comparative questions with which Hartz began. I suggest as a point of departure the query, why has pure and simple unionism been so weak among European workers?

---

to be considered a problem is, at least in part, expressed from a vantage point outside the analysis itself. An interesting companion reading to Skowronek is Barry Karl, *The Uneasy State* (Chicago: University of Chicago Press, 1983). Karl sees a rough public ideology in favor of associationalism, and not institutional stalemate, behind the same historical resistance to government centralization and reform.

45. William M. Reddy, *The Rise of Market Culture* (Cambridge: Cambridge University Press, 1984).

LETTERS TO THE EDITORS

To the editors:

Samuel Kernell's article "The Early Nationalization of Political News in America," in *Studies in American Political Development: An Annual* (1986), 1 : 255–78, raises issues that are at once interesting and puzzling. He measures the number and length of all political articles in leading Cleveland newspapers through the middle decades of the nineteenth century in order to ask about the amount of newspaper attention paid to local, state, and national political issues. He observes that local issues were predominant only very early in the nineteenth century and that they declined quickly over time. Kernell concludes that politics nationalized far earlier than historians like Robert Wiebe had ever thought. Wiebe's "island communities" were gone by 1845. It is a clever piece of research of substantial significance.

When the statistics the argument rests on are examined, however, the research raises substantively difficult problems. The methodological issue: why use that slippery statistic of percent? Percent tells us the nature of the mix of political news, the total political news summing to 100 percent. But why not report straight column inches? Is not the question the actual *amount* of news?

Prompted by these thoughts, I have used Kernell's data, which he represents in figure 1, p. 262, to estimate the actual column inches of political news available to readers by topic. My estimates are presented in the table below. (These estimates are, from my crude interpolation of the graphs, reminders to us of how graphs make the work of future researchers more difficult. Data reported in graphs lose precision—precision the original researcher went to a great deal of effort to obtain.)

Political News Level	Column Inches, By Year									
	1820	1830	1835	1840	1845	1850	1855	1860	1870	1876
National	70	245	444	550	680	6,437	1,142	3,485	2,200	2,600
State	128	120	256	173	838	1,815	713	938	200	300
Local	122	125	170	400	170	660	457	1,348	458	820

As if to confirm the rule "everything is harder than you think it is," the raw numbers make Kernell's originally tidy and convincing analysis begin to slip away, with no easy counteranalysis waiting in the wings. Judging from actual amount of news, one could claim that on the average, interest in local politics grew substantially from 1820 until the end of the study period, 1876. So did national news. Even state news, which seemed about to disappear when viewed in the form of graphed percents, grew. It tripled in actual amount between 1820 and 1876.

Because there is so much variation from the 1820s to the 1870s in the actual amount of news, and because the question I have asked is, "How much did various kinds of political news grow?" I have converted the data to natural logs and plotted the result (fig. 1). Such conversion graphs the relative growth and allows some discussion of change. Again, all forms of political news grew. This graph focuses our attention on the questions of order and change in magnitude. Kernell's original percentaging did this also, but now it is possible to observe the sequencing. In

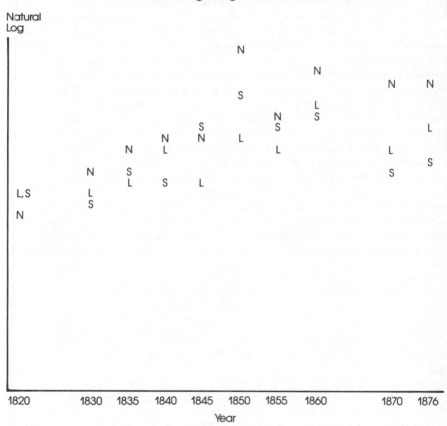

Figure 1.
Plot of Column Inches of Political Reportage;
Natural Logs, Origin Set at Zero

Note: N: national political news; S: state political news; L: local political news. Graph points have been calculated from data reported in text.

1820, state and local news were equal, national at the bottom—the only time national news *was* at the bottom. In my opinion, this first decade should really be thrown out, for Cleveland was a self-promoting frontier community of 150 souls. I would interpret this news ordering as that of a newspaper more in the business of selling Cleveland to potential settlers and investors than in reporting news to local folk. By 1830, the community was more securely established, national news was in ascendence, and with the exception of one year, it stayed that way. Although state and local political news both grew over the period as a whole, they alternated in being the least reported, with local news staying ahead of state news for the last three time periods sampled, when both declined absolutely.

So where do these measures lead us? Overall, political news grew for all levels of government, but national news grew more. Interest in local politics did not diminish; it grew absolutely and also in relation to state political news. Were the data series to be extended further, say to 1920, we might predict a diminution in local political news, although this may not have happened until after the New Deal and World War II. And since the city is Cleveland, local political news must have been highly topical again in the 1970s. Clearly, we can say that the tidy and comprehensible picture presented in the original article does not hold.

One can only speculate on what further data might reveal. What, for instance, would a plot of column inches per electoral office tell us? In 1830 Cleveland had about one thousand people, by 1876 over 100,000: in all probability the amount of news per local office declined considerably. But Kernell makes clear that this is more than news about elections, so the correct measure may remain the simplest: total space devoted to news, unmanipulated by any other variable.

Two further possibilities remain. First, does writing news about a subject mean necessarily that it is important? Nineteenth-century newspapers borrowed copy heavily from one another, and national news copy was more appropriate for publication in Cleveland than was political news about other localities like Albany or New York City. The wire services today help out local newspapers with copy, and again, local political news does not bear much repeating outside of its own context. If today we counted the column inches devoted by all newspapers to varying kinds of political news, and counted only original words—that is, did not multiple-count the wire service copy—local political reportage would unquestionably outdistance all other forms. This is the case simply because each local news item is unique and not reprinted elsewhere. In other words, more original reportage is written about local news today than is written about national news. By this measure, local political news could be claimed to dominate our print media.

A second possibility is to conclude from the recalculated data that interest in local politics had begun a bumpy decline, dropping from 1860 to 1876 and perhaps beyond. That is a plausible if not well-established scenario. Let us for the sake of argument accept it, measuring the two swallows of 1870 and 1876 as a summer. We know that political participation levels were probably lower for local elections than for national ones, mirroring the news levels. We also know that overall participation rates have been declining for the past century. Why not interpret the newspaper interest and electoral participation rates in local politics as an index of local political progressiveness, forecasting the trajectory of national events? In this view, "low" would mean "advanced." Therefore, "low" could be interpreted as voters registering their satisfaction with successfully institutionalized decisions rather than as apathy or disinterest.

To sum up, I doubt that the three levels of news should be treated as a mix, the parts of which equal one whole, a whole that by virtue of percentaging stays constant over time. However, the article raises a new set of exciting questions and research possibilities concerning the nature of local, state, and national governments. I hope to see more evidence brought to these problems, for local government's very pervasiveness and multiplicity have kept it too long from our conceptualization of the American state.

Eric Monkkonen
University of California, Los Angeles

Samuel Kernell replies:

The trends in news coverage at each level of government, with which Professor Monkkonen takes exception, were designed to measure the degree to which political news shifted up the federalism ladder, and its timing, during the middle decades of the nineteenth century. I remain convinced they do so better than the alternative measure he has proposed. No matter how one breaks down the trend data, the results are the same: during the half century under study, Cleveland's newspapers turned increasingly to national institutions and politicians for their news. They did so to such an extent that by the 1870s, roughly four times as many articles were published by these dailies on national public affairs as on local events. This remains to my mind the critical evidence that one must consider in rethinking the state of public life in America as it entered an era of breakneck modernization.

Professor Monkkonen seeks to restore a place for local politics in America's political development. However much national news may have increased, he argues, local news was also claiming ever greater space in Cleveland's papers. Spurning those "slippery" percentages, Monkkonen prefers logarithmic transformations of the number of articles at each level of government. Such data are not required to recognize that the volume of stories at each level increased over the time period.[1] The log values shown in his figure merely muddle the issue by concealing the far greater growth in national news.

How should one interpret the increasing volume of local stories? Monkkonen suggests they reflect the larger scale of local government as Cleveland grew from a hamlet into an urban transportation center. It is a reasonable argument, but the evidence available from reworking my data is simply insufficient to test it. Even

---

1. Log values are perhaps best used descriptively to flesh out common patterns across variables whose values differ or change dramatically. In a more recent examination of the Cleveland data, Professor Gary C. Jacobson and I employ log values in this way. See "Congress and the Presidency as News in the Nineteenth Century," *Journal of Politics* (1987), forthcoming.

left in their natural state, the raw totals are too slippery to read much from them. The trends could simply be a function of the size of the newspapers. As circulation and advertising grew with population, newspapers became larger. Excluding advertising and announcements, the *Annals of Cleveland,* for example, lists 8,940 news entries for 1876 compared to only 391 entries for 1835. Probably, more of every type of news was being reported.

In order to assess the real growth in local coverage, one must control for this inflation. We need, consequently, to return to percentages—in this instance, news at each level of government as a percentage of all news. Fortunately, the *Annals* is formatted in such a way as to allow us to obtain reasonably accurate estimates of the relative growth of political coverage without having to code all articles. Each entry in the *Annals* is numbered, and the index groups them into general subject categories. Table 1 lists the total number of news entries (again, excluding advertising and announcements) and the percentage included under the heading of "Politics and Government."[2] Using the proportion of local and national news reported in Figure 1a of the original article, I have estimated in Table 1 the relative

Table 1. Distribution of Local and National Politics in Relation to All News

| | Total News Entries[a] | Share "Politics and Government"[a] | Estimated Share of All News | | | |
| | | | Local | | National | |
	N	%	N	%	N	%
1820	187	29	12	6	28	15
1830	393	45	27	7	97	25
1835	391	52	24	6	99	25
1840	1,422	41	235	17	267	19
1845	1,219	28	34	3	206	17
1850	2,731	45	87	3	865	32
1855	3,105	37	207	7	668	22
1860	2,238	46	154	7	657	29
1870	2,986	40	107	4	1,012	34
1876	8,940	60	652	7	3,969	44

[a] These figures derive from a count of entry numbers listed by general topics in the index of each *Annals of Cleveland.* Even these "total" figures exclude advertisements (which varied dramatically from one year to the next) and brief, miscellaneous announcements, including birth and death notices.

2. For several reasons, the number of political articles measured in this way is significantly larger than those reported in Figure 1a of the original article. First, the definition of political news is more inclusive than the one we used. Any news involving a government agency tended to be included under this rubric in the index. Second, because the synopses were so brief as to make coding unreliable, we excluded from analysis all entries of one column inch or less. Frequently, these consisted of announcements and brief anecdotes to fill in the interstices of articles. I failed to note this in the appendix; for a fuller discussion of the meth-

share of all news entries that dealt with local and national politics. The figures reveal an extraordinary stability in the volume of local political coverage. The year, 1840, remains an outlier and probably reflects the exceptional political circumstances of that year, which are discussed in the article. For the rest of the era, no more than 7 percent of the news concerns local politics.

The story for national political reporting is different. Although controlling for the overall increase in news dampens the upward trend in national news somewhat, the relative level and increasing share of national political news remains impressive.

None of these findings should lessen our enthusiasm for Professor Monkkonen's thesis that the profusion of local political units during this era contributed profoundly to the character of America's political development. Indeed, until the appearance of the progressive presidents early in the next century, rampant particularism, rooted in localism, dominated political discourse in Washington and the nation.

Brookings Institution

---

odology employed here, see Kernell and Jacobson (1987). Third, I drew samples for the 1870s, where here the entire population of articles is included.